FOCKE WULF JET FIGHTERS

FOCKE WULF JET FIGHTERS

JUSTO MIRANDA

FONTHILL

Fonthill Media Language Policy

Fonthill Media publishes in the international English language market. One language edition is published worldwide. As there are minor differences in spelling and presentation, especially with regard to American English and British English, a policy is necessary to define which form of English to use. The Fonthill Policy is to use the form of English native to the author. Justo Miranda was born and educated in Spain; therefore, British English has been adopted in this publication.

Fonthill Media Limited
Fonthill Media LLC
www.fonthillmedia.com
office@fonthillmedia.com

First published in the United Kingdom and the United States of America 2018

British Library Cataloguing in Publication Data:
A catalogue record for this book is available from the British Library

ISBN 978-1-78155-664-1

Typeset in 10pt on 13pt Sabon
Printed and bound in England

Contents

Introduction

In the summer of 1936, the Messerschmitt Bf 109 won the fighter contest for the re-equipment of the *Jagdflieger*. That meant that the firm had priority in receiving the most advanced in-line engines: the Jumo 210 and the Daimler-Benz DB 600, DB 601, DB 603, and DB 605.

In these circumstances, the biggest success of the Focke-Wulf *Flugzeugbau* was the choice of the BMW 801 radial engine for the Fw 190 fighter, thus avoiding having to compete against Messerschmitt for the in-line engines.

During the Second World War, Kurt Tank thoroughly researched the possibility of using all available, including those in the design phase, engines for their fighters. In August 1941, he considered replacing the engines of future versions of Fw 190 with the new BMW 801 D-2, BMW 801 E, and BMW 801 F radial engines. Between April 1942 and February 1944, the prototype Fw 190 V19 was used to test nine engines: BMW 801 J, BMW P.8028, DB 603, DB 609, DB 614, DB 623 A, Jumo 213 A-1, Jumo 213 A-2, and Jumo 213 S. He also considered the installation of the Jumo 222 A in the V19 and of the Jumo 222 E in the Focke-Wulf Ta 154, but a detailed study revealed that the power and weight of these engines, originally designed to propel bombers, outweighed the structural strength of the airplanes.

Projected in 1939 as a 2,000-hp scaled-up version of the BMW 801, the BMW 802 was too heavy for its installation in the Fw 190 fighter. In June 1941, the Bad Eilsen *Projektabteilung*, main designer team of Focke-Wulf firm, created a 125 per cent homothetic version, with 13-m wingspan and 5,400-kg maximum weight, which was suitably adapted to the new engine.

That same year, the monster BMW 803 A was developed, designed to propel the long-range bomber Focke-Wulf Fw 238 and the gigantic flying boat Blohm & Voss P 200. It did not seem possible to use such a heavy engine in a fighter, but Bad Eilsen solved the problem by designing a twin-boom airplane that allowed its installation in pusher configuration.

The new Argus As 413 engine with 4,000 hp was expected to be available in the spring of 1945 and the Focke-Wulf design team created two rear swept wing projects that could be used: the high-altitude interceptor P.0310.025-1006 and the heavy night fighter P.0310.251-23.

Other aircraft manufacturers were forced to consider using rockets and ramjets to propel their fighter projects. Kurt Tank preferred to explore the possibilities of other models of turbojets produced by the German industry, which were too large or too small to be used by the Messerschmitt Me 262 or Arado Ar 234. At the beginning of 1945 an enlarged variant of the Focke-Wulf Ta 183 was designed in Bad Eilsen that could use the gigantic turbojet BMW 018 originally created for the *Strahlbomber II* bomber.

Plans were also made to use the small turbojet HeS 8 as a turbo-supercharger of the high-altitude fighter Focke-Wulf Fw 190 A-10. Details of the HeS 011 turbojet were released in 1943, and mass production was scheduled to begin in March 1945 at Munich, Bad Aibling, Rosenheim, Kochendorf, and Waltersdorf.

The new engine was easier to build than the complicated axial-flow types 003 and 004 and the aeronautics industry expected that its relative abundance would allow its use by other manufacturers less favoured by the *Oberkommando der Luftwaffe* (OKL).

In November 1944, the Me 262 W.Nr. 130015 was fitted with various experimental intake ducts in front of its port side turbojet, to measure thrust losses. Trials showed that the 3-m duct reduced thrust by some 135 kp. The HeS 011 generated less thrust than the turbojets developed by the British and this circumstance forced the designers of fighters to use air ducts and tail pipes of the shortest possible length to avoid undue friction losses. The simplest aerodynamic solution used in the Messerschmitt Me 262, Heinkel He 280, and Gloster Meteor was to install two turbojets in nacelles located on the wings.

If the turbojet was installed on the back of the fuselage, during the rotation at take-off, the air intake was badly located in the aerodynamic shadow zone generated by the nose and cockpit hood, receiving insufficient air flow and risking loss of thrust at a critical moment. If it was installed in ventral position, there was a danger that foreign matter would be sucked into the compressor and the air intake would suffer insufficient air flow during retraction of the nose undercarriage leg. The possibility that, during an emergency belly landing, the turbojet might explode because of the impact was also considered.

The wind tunnel tests showed that the wing nacelles of the Me 262 produced compressibility buffeting during high speed dives because of the turbulence generated between the nacelle and the undersurface of the wing. It was also verified that the nacelles increased the frontal area of the airplane, decreasing the maximum speed. It was preferable, if not simple, to install the turbojet inside the fuselage. The designers of Bad Eilsen tried to do that with the Focke-Wulf 1-TL *Jäger Projekt III*, but their lack of experience in the design of air intakes resulted in an excess of drag, with turbulences generated between the air-scoops and the upper wing surface.

In *Projekt IV*, they refined the design by adopting a twin boom configuration, with the air intakes placed in front of the wing roots. However, this time, it turned out that the drag was generated in the air ducts, designed in an 'S' shape, and in the joining area between the tail plane and the two tailfins. The loss of speed was considered excessive. The optimal configuration for a jet fighter was discovered independently by the designers of Blohm & Voss, Messerschmitt, and Focke-Wulf. It consisted of a circular nose air intake, an air-duct completely straight and as short as possible, and rear swept wings. This formula made the Blohm & Voss P.211 the winner of the *Volksjäger* contest, while the Focke-Wulf Ta 183 won that of the *Jägernotprogramm*.

During the Cold War, the Messerschmitt P.1101 was used by the Americans to experiment with different configurations of variable geometry and influenced the F-86 Sabre swept wing design. The Ta 183 influenced the design of the Soviet fighters MiG-15, La-15, and Yak-30, the Swedish Saab J 29, the Argentine IAe 33, and the British experimental RAE transonic aircraft.

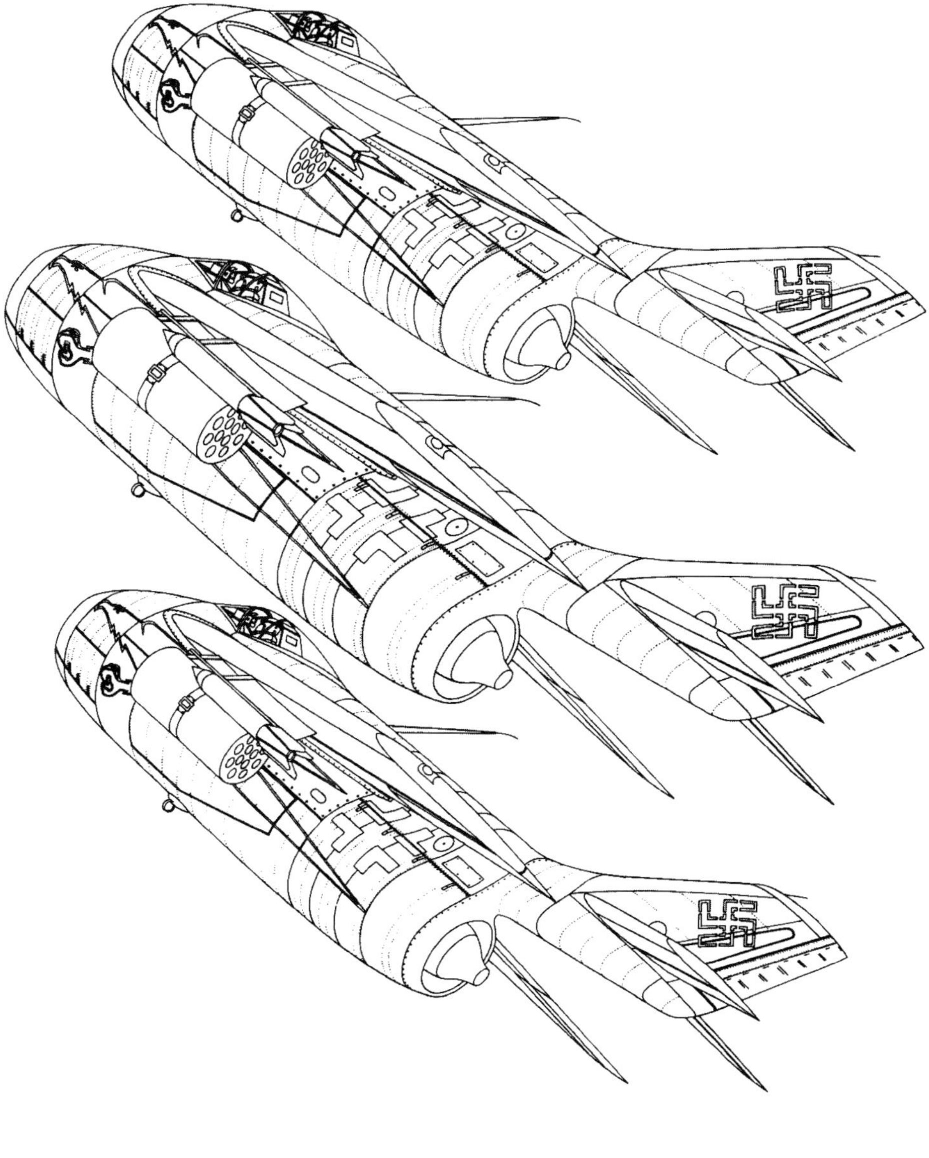

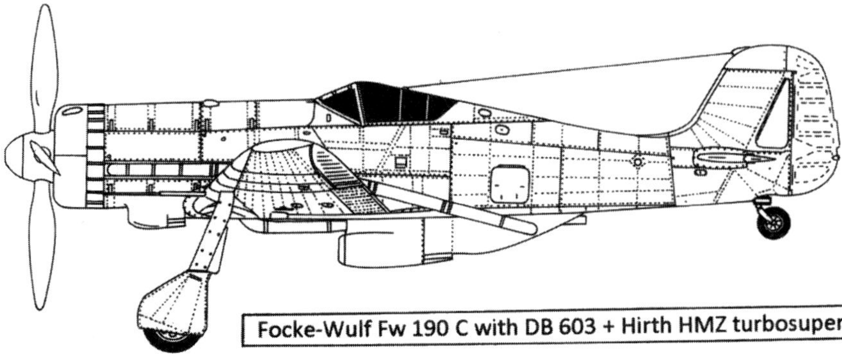

Focke-Wulf Fw 190 C with DB 603 + Hirth HMZ turbosupercharger

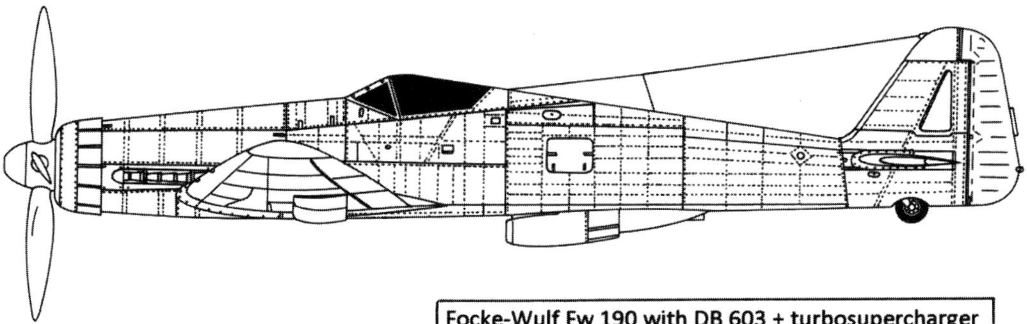

Focke-Wulf Fw 190 with DB 603 + turbosupercharger

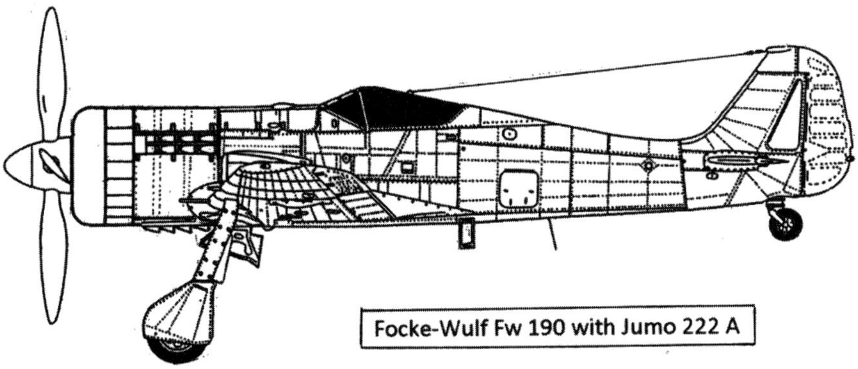

Focke-Wulf Fw 190 with Jumo 222 A

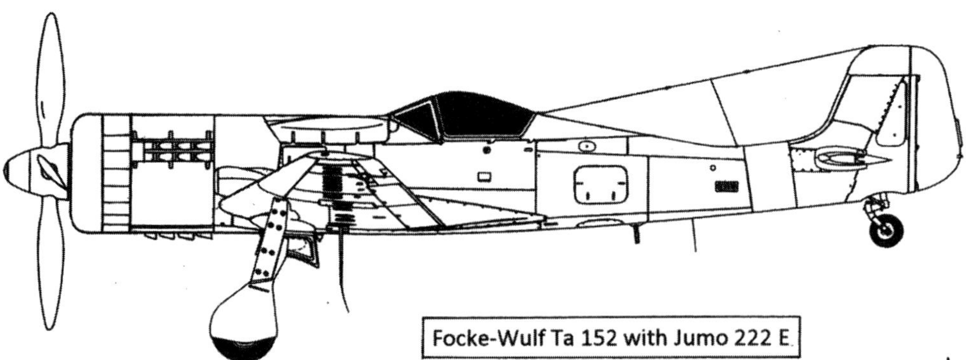

Focke-Wulf Ta 152 with Jumo 222 E

2m.

MIRANDA

Focke Wulf Fw 190 V19 with DB 609

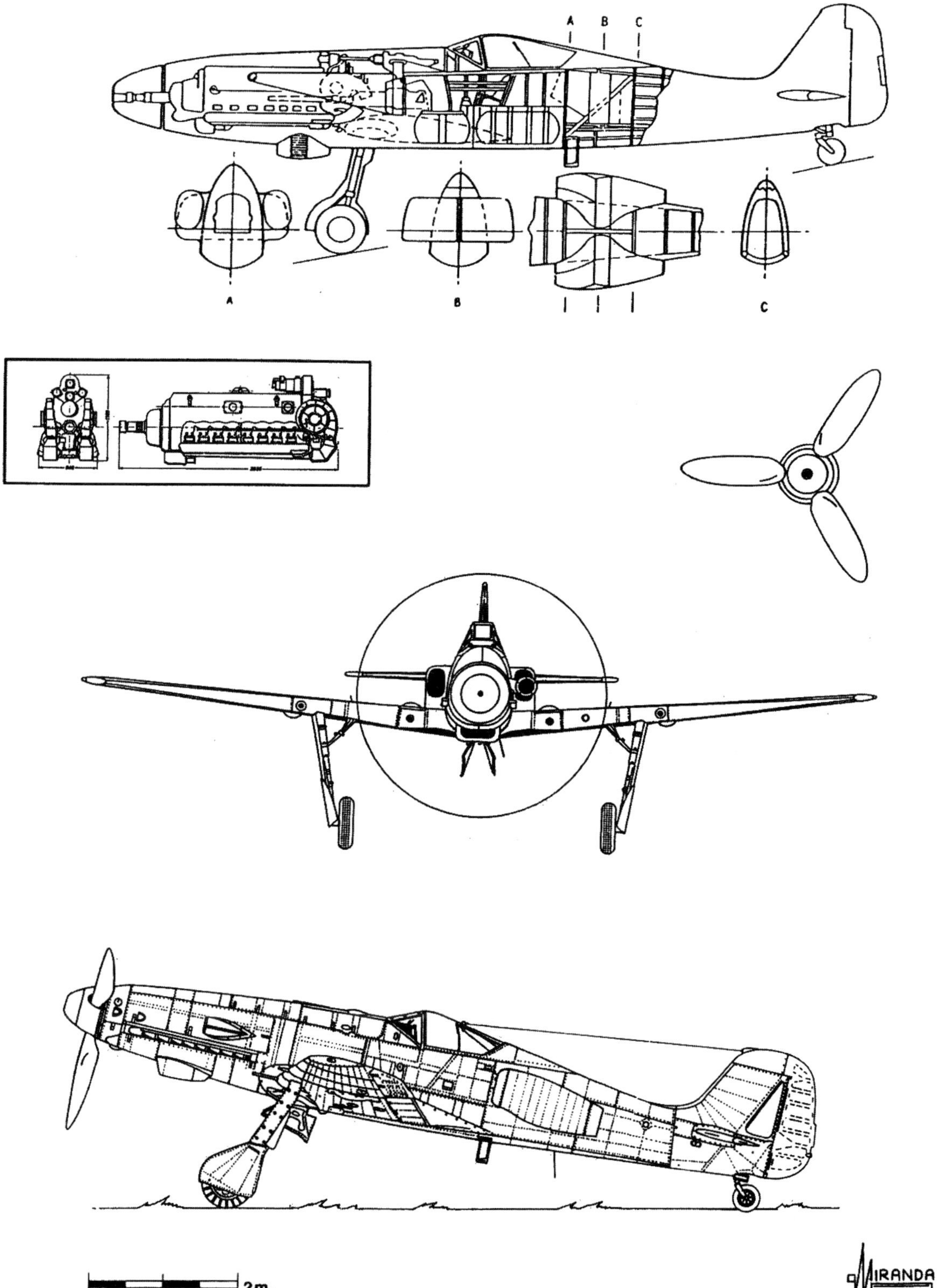

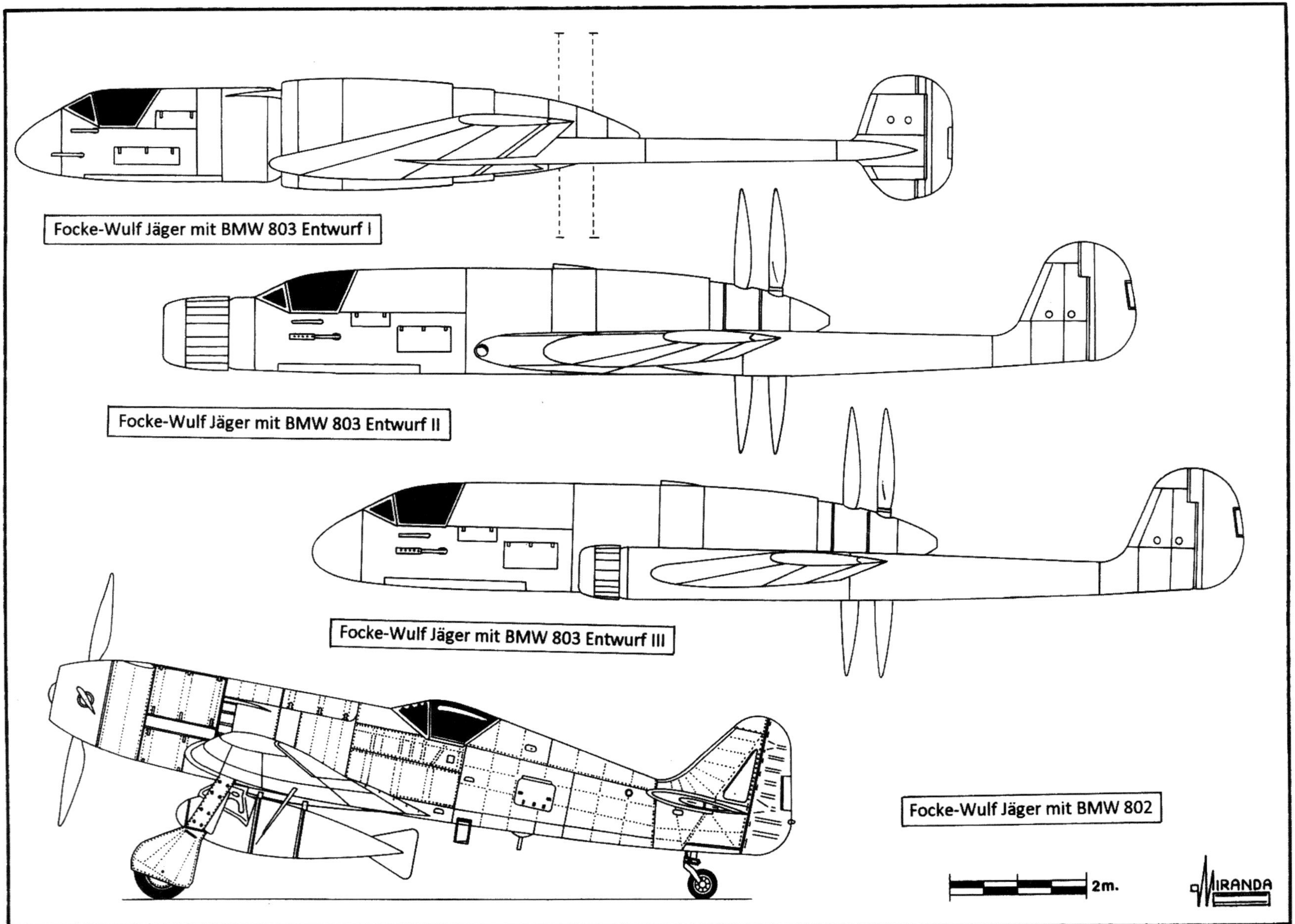

Focke-Wulf Jäger mit BMW 803 Entwurf I

Focke-Wulf Jäger mit BMW 803 Entwurf II

Focke-Wulf Jäger mit BMW 803 Entwurf III

Focke-Wulf Jäger mit BMW 802

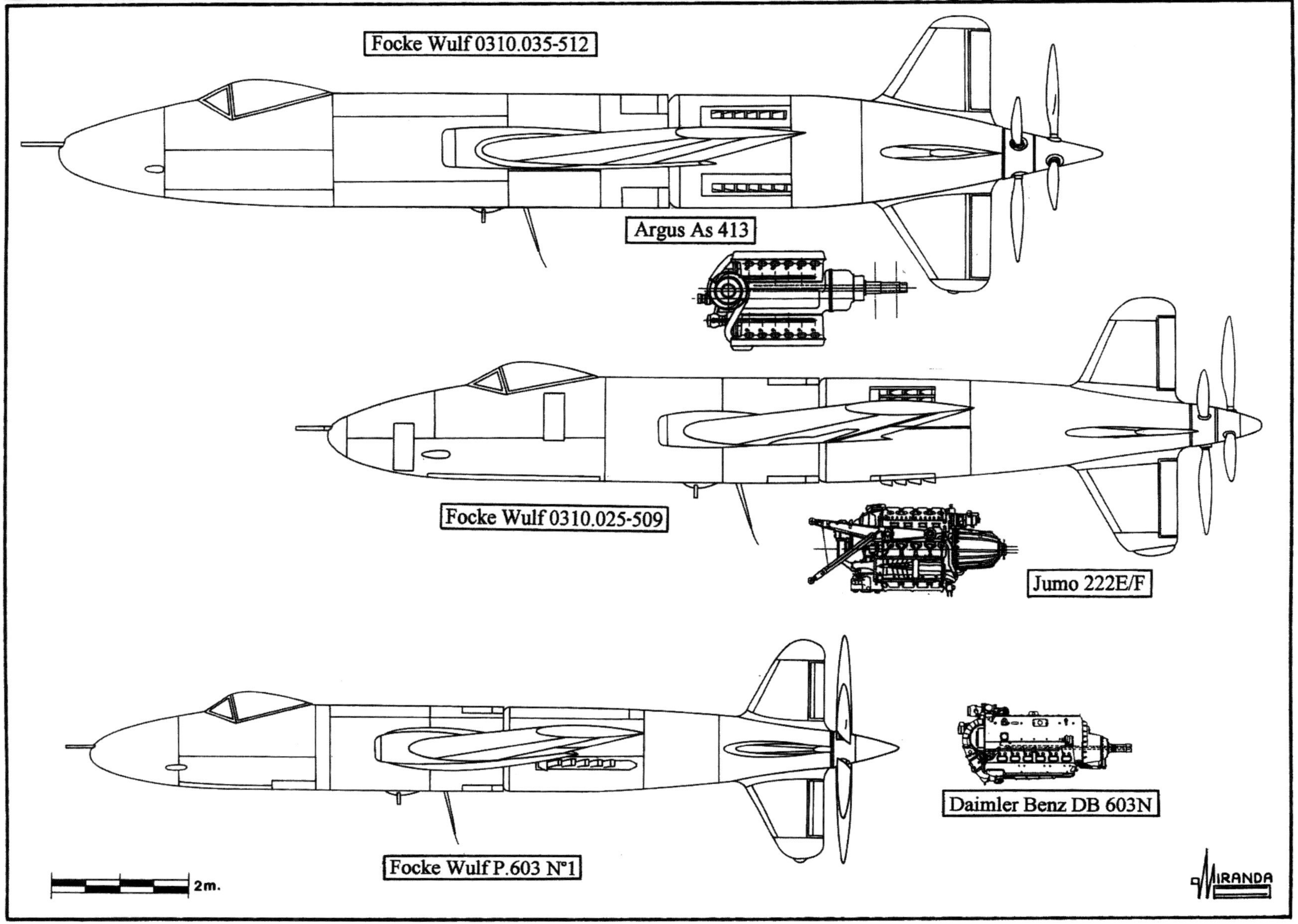
Focke Wulf 0310.035-512
Argus As 413
Focke Wulf 0310.025-509
Jumo 222E/F
Focke Wulf P.603 N°1
Daimler Benz DB 603N
2m.
MIRANDA

1

Focke-Wulf Fw 190 A-10 *Höhenjäger*

The Fw 190 fighter's inadequate performance at high altitude was a constant source of concern for the *Technisches Amt* (Luftwaffe Technical Office). Officially, the BMW 801 radial engine was supposed to produce its full power at 7,000 m but it actually had difficulties above 6,000 m.

Three units of the Fw 190A-3/U7 (works numbers 137528, 137530, and 137531) were built in September 1942. They were intended as light high-altitude fighters with a BMW 801 D-2, two superchargers and a ceiling of 11,900 m, a widened 12.5-m wingspan, two MG 151/15 machine guns, two air intakes, and external *Kiemenklappen* cooling flaps. The operational tests performed by the *Stab II. Jagdkorps* between July 1943 and May 1944 were unsatisfactory and no additional units were built. The Fw 190 V45 (works number 7347) and V47 (works number 530115) prototypes had a 12.3-m wingspan and were also built to test their manoeuvrability at high altitude.

On 20 May 1942, some *Reichsluftfahrtministerium* (RLM) officials met with Messerschmitt and Focke-Wulf representatives in Augsburg, to set forth their requirement for a special high-altitude fighter capable of intercepting high-flying bombers on a combat ceiling above that of the Me 262. The answer from Messerschmitt was the Me 155B project, powered by the DB 628 engine, which shared a high degree of component commonality with the standard Bf 109G. On 3 January 1944, the project was transferred to Blohm & Voss as BV 155A. This firm built up to four prototypes until the beginning of 1945. On the other hand, Focke-Wulf initiated three projects known as *Höhenjäger-1* (high-altitude fighter), *Höhenjäger-2*, and *Höhenjäger-3* (Ta 152H).

Höhenjäger-1

In 1943, four airplanes of the Fw 190 A-1 type (works numbers 0046, 0047, 0048, and 0049) were modified to be transformed into the 'B' series prototypes. This conversion consisted of the installation of a pressure cabin and one BMW 801 D-2 engine with GM-1 power boost injection system. The 0046 had a new wing with a span of 10.24 m.

Flying tests were performed between January and August 1943 in Hannover-Langenhagen and Rechlin.

The problems encountered with the canopy pressurisation system had not been overcome and the B-0 series were then abandoned at the end of 1943 in favour of the projected 'C' series.

Höhenjäger-2

The Fw 190C was never mass produced, with only twelve prototypes ever built. The initial tests made with the Fw 190 V13, equipped with a DB 603 A and a 10.5-m wingspan, showed excellent performance over 10,000 m, although the turbo-supercharger intended for the 'C' series was not yet fitted at this stage.

The Fw 190 V18/U2 prototype, fitted with a new 12.30-m wingspan, four-bladed propeller, and one of the first Hirth 9-2281 turbochargers, was flight tested on 19 November 1944. The shortage of raw materials in Germany meant it was not possible to produce a suitably heat-resistant alloy before the war ended. Therefore, although the turbo-superchargers themselves worked well, the pipes of exhaust gases were unable to withstand the high temperatures. In October 1944, it was impossible to increase the life of turbo-superchargers to more than twenty hours. Only when the Jumo 213 engine was made available was it feasible to build fighters with ceilings of 11,000 m.

The Fw 190 C, derived from the Fw 190 V18/U2 prototype (with 12.3-m wingspan, a length of 9.5 m, a wing area of 20.3 sq. m, and a HMZ turbosupercharger), would have reached mass production stage had the Focke-Wulf engineers have solved the issue of the heat-resistant alloy of the engine exhaust pipes on time. Instead, the *Höhenjäger-3* programme gained priority, culminating with the construction of the excellent Ta 152 H in 1945.

Focke-Wulf Fw 190 H

This is the denomination frequently given in specialised literature to refer to the Fw 190 A-10, a high-altitude interceptor project based on the Fw 190 A-3/U7, with pressurised cockpit and a wingspan of 12.3 m.

To solve the issue of the turbo-superchargers, Kurt Tank's team studied the possibility of using a HeS 8 turbojet suspended under the fuselage belly to feed the radial engine with pressurised air. The air from the nineteen-blade centrifugal compressor passed through a vertical duct installed within the hollow pod that was connected to the air intake of the BMW 801 D-2. The exhaust gases from the piston engine were sent to another duct descending to the secondary air mixer of the turbojet to be injected in the radial-inflow turbine. Both engines used 96-octane gasoline of the C3 type.

The OKL did not consider the HeS 8 the right choice for mass manufacturing. Given its thrust of just 600 kp, only thirty prototypes were built. The Fw 190 H would have had a wing area of 20.30 sq. m, a maximum weight of 4,000 kg, 65 kg of armour, and 524 litres of fuel, besides two MG 151/20 cannon in the wing roots, with 250 rounds each.

Fw 190 *mit Strahlrohr* (Ramjet)

Based on the data published by the end of 1943 on the tests performed with the Sänger ramjets in the *Deutsches Forschungsinstitut für Segelflug* (DFS), the firm decided to build its own design of *Strahlrohr.* The programme was conducted under the leadership of Dr.-Ing. Otto E. Pabst in the Focke-Wulf gas dynamics department at Kirkhorsten. The first designs of the new engine, dated spring 1944, represented a much shorter type of ramjet than the Sänger and had a length to diameter ratio of 2 to 1.

The first prototype, as described in Report No. 09045 by mid-August, had a diameter of 237 mm and fifty-nine injectors of the Fang-Diffuseur type. It was tested in the *Luftfahrtforschungsanstalt* (LFA) Brunswick, using hydrogen as fuel. From September, hydrogen was replaced by propane in some tests but, after the bombardment of the *Leunawerke* factories, the propane was replaced with vaporised petrol in the operational versions. For this reason, it was necessary to design a compact heat exchanger to vaporise and superheat the fuel.

The thrust produced by this type of ramjets depended on an absolute aerodynamic perfection of both the external surface and the internal air duct, in the design of which intervened Dr.-Ing. Theodor Zobel of the LFA Völkenrode and Dr.-Ing. Küchemann of the *Aerodynamische Versuchsanstalt* (AVA), Göttingen.

Flight tests were expected to be carried out using a Fw 190 A-10 with BMW 801 F-1 piston engine and two Pabst ramjets (with fifty injectors, 960-mm diameter, 1,920-mm length, and 1,150-kp estimated thrust) installed in the wingtips. According to the data of the project of 23 April 1944, the airplane would have an overall wingspan of 12 m.

The construction of the first two prototypes of 960 mm was more difficult than expected, due to the high internal pressures and the deformation of the outer surface caused by the heat. Not a single unit had been finished at the end of the war in Europe.

Fw 190 A-10 Höhenjäger

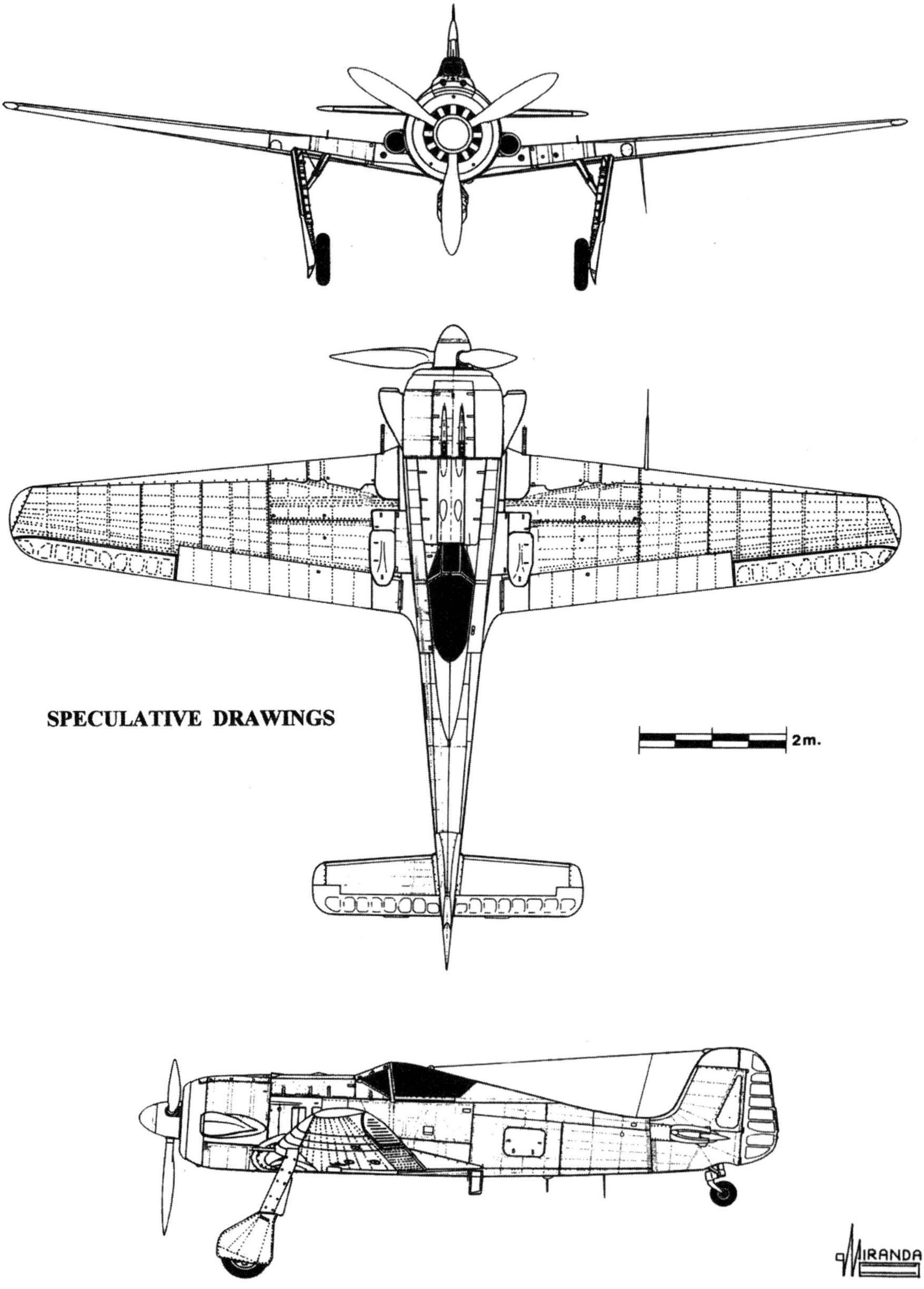

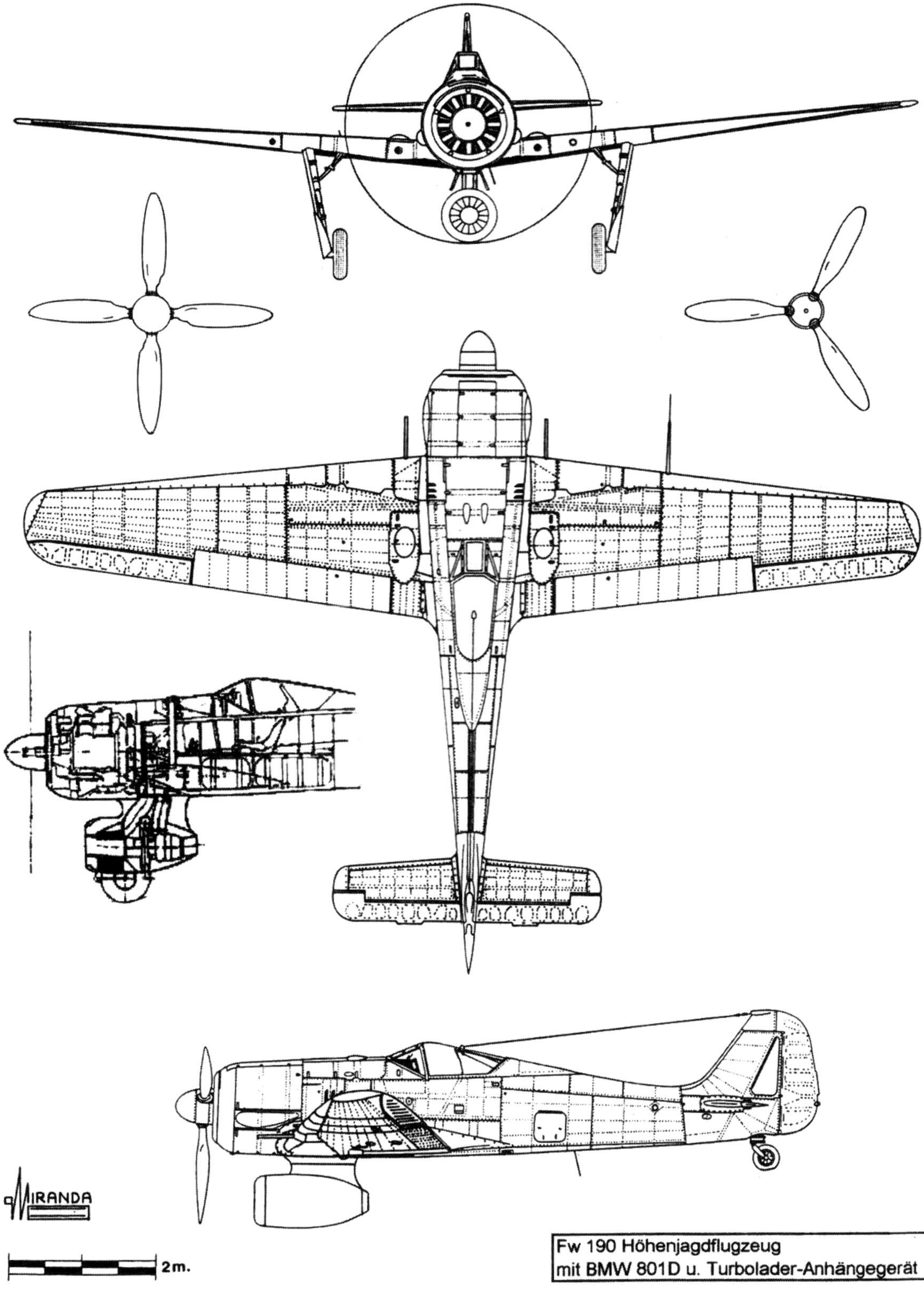

Fw 190 Höhenjagdflugzeug
mit BMW 801D u. Turbolader-Anhängegerät

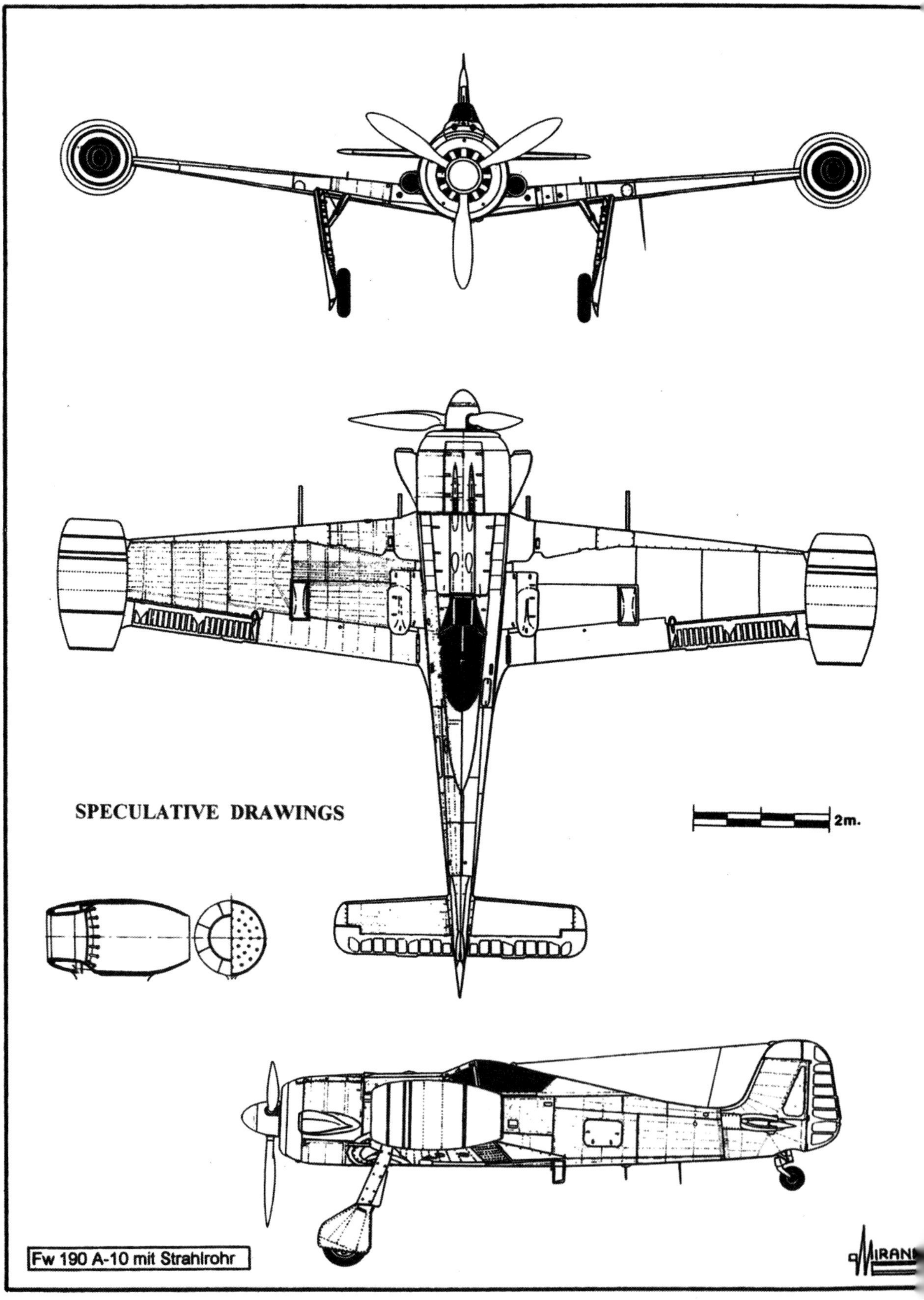
SPECULATIVE DRAWINGS
2m.
Fw 190 A-10 mit Strahlrohr

2

Focke-Wulf Fw 190 TL

In the late 1930s, Max A. Mueller, engineer of the firm Junkers AG, patented a ducted-fan device that greatly improved the performance of the conventional propellers. In 1938, a team of technicians of the company BMW GmbH, under the leadership of Dr.-Ing. Hermann Oestrich, modified a Bramo 325 radial engine fitted with a four-bladed ducted-fan with a diameter of 1 m. The modified engine, which was named motorjet, was installed in a trainer Focke-Wulf Fw 44 and successfully tested in flight by Hanna Reitsch.

In 1939, Max A. Mueller joined the Heinkel-Rostock team, working at the time on the development of the HeS 8 centrifugal turbojet, which was expected to be used to propel the He 280 fighters. With a planned thrust of 700 kp and a diameter 20 per cent shorter than the HeS 3, the new turbojet required a great research effort and an extensive test program. Numerous technical problems had to be solved before starting its large-scale production and the HeS 8 suffered numerous delays. By March 1941, it only produced 500 kp static thrust, 550 kp by early 1942, and 600 kp in early 1943.

The root cause was the reduction of the diameter, recommended by the aerodynamicists to minimise the drag produced by the engine nacelles when installed under the wings of the He 280. Trials experience revealed that the most effective way to increase thrust in this type of turbojets was to also increase their diameter, to improve the performance of the centrifugal compressor. In 1939, the HeS 3B, 93 cm in diameter, produced 450 kp. In May 1941, the British Power Jets W.1, 107 cm in diameter, produced 387 kp and in 1943, the de Havilland Halford H-1, 127 cm in diameter, produced 1,225-kp static thrust. With this power, it was possible to build a single engine jet fighter, with the centrifugal turbojet installed inside the fuselage. In 1943, the British chose the Halford to propel their new fighters Gloster E5/42 and de Havilland E.6/41 Vampire. The Americans used the same turbojet to power the Lockheed XP-80 prototype, in early 1944.

In Germany, Max A. Mueller proposed to build the ZTL version of the HeS 8, with a ducted-fan of 1-m diameter and a planned thrust of 900 kp. Focke-Wulf engineers also proposed to modify a HeS 8 to be used as a nose-mounted power plant in an Fw 190. The modification would consist of replacing the radial inflow turbine with another of 122-cm diameter and the exhaust nozzle by three outlets located underneath and on both sides of the cowling. The outlets were equipped with deflectors to prevent hot gases from damaging the airframe. The new turbojet, called T.1, would have had a thrust of 600 kp by the end of 1942.

The jet version of the Fw 190 A-3 was named 'TL' (Turbolader); it would have had an overall length of 9.4 m, an estimated maximum weight of 4,865 kg and an estimated maximum speed of 850 kph. The ceiling was expected to be of 10,300 m and the range of 1,370 km. Its endurance, with 1,400 litres of J2 heavy kerosene, would have been seventy minutes. As for the armament, would have consisted of two machine guns MG 17 and two MG 151/20 cannon in the standard positions.

In the spring of 1943, the OKL decided to cancel all research work with centrifugal turbojets to focus on the development of axial-flow type engines.

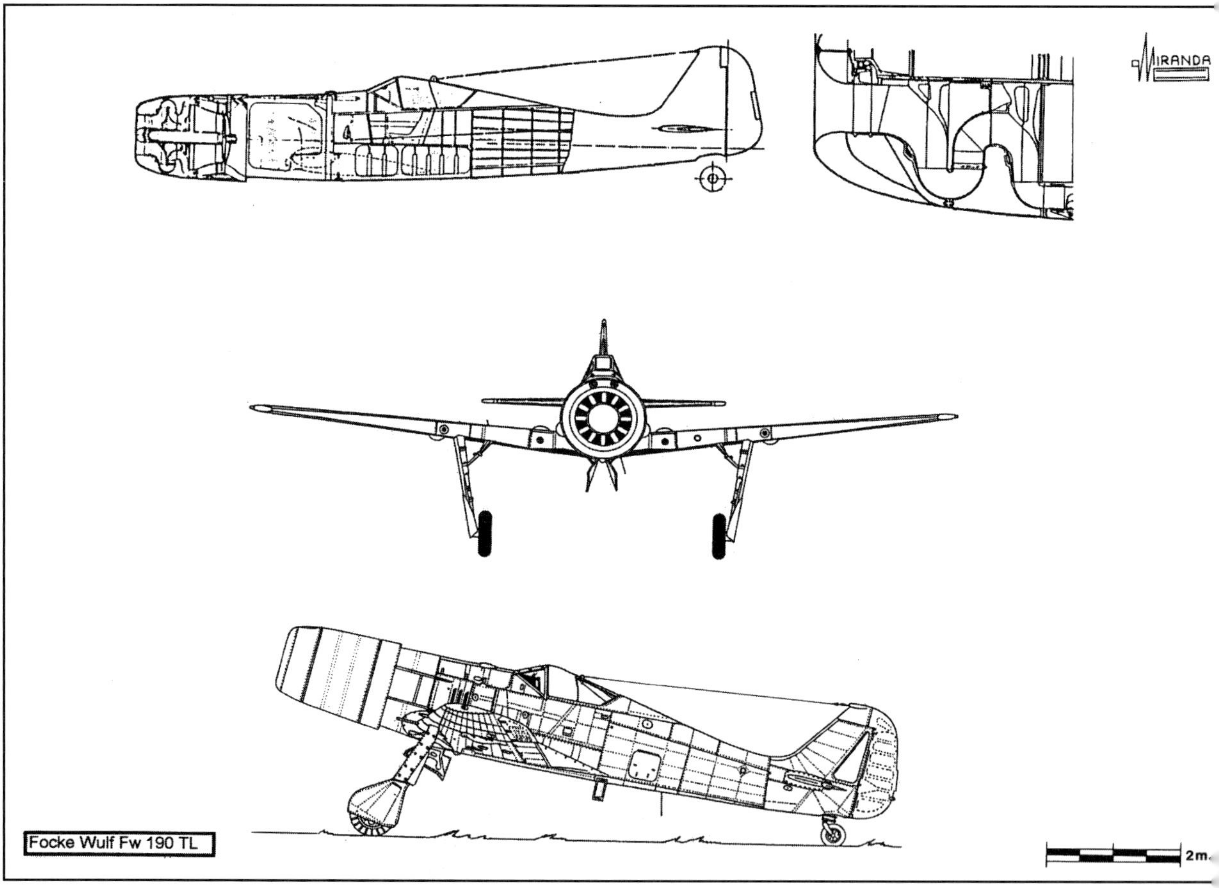

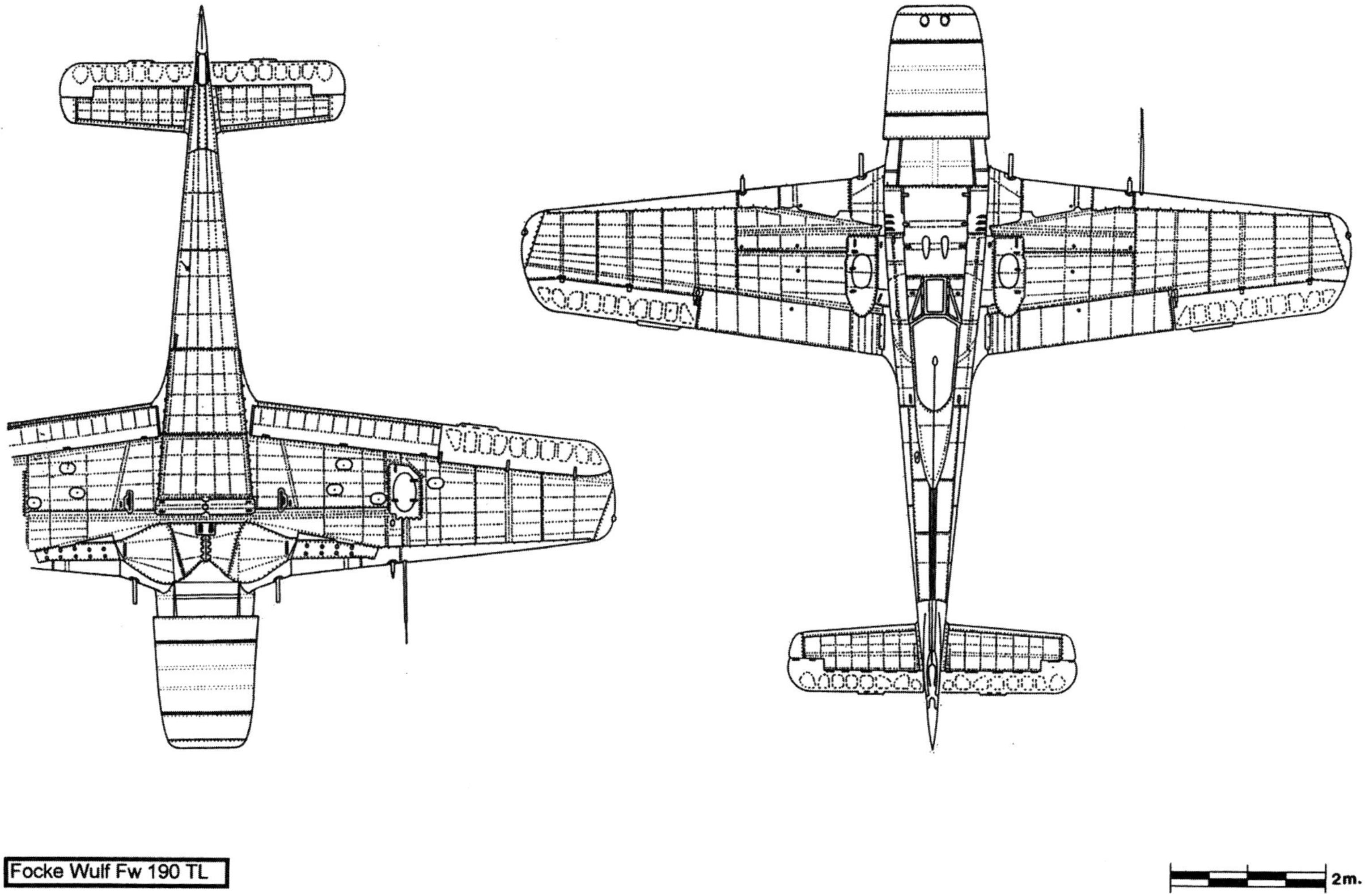

Focke Wulf Fw 190 TL

BMW Motorjet

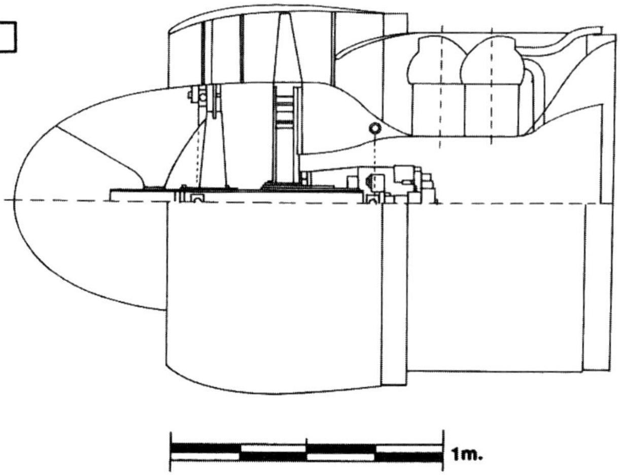

Focke Wulf Fw 44J

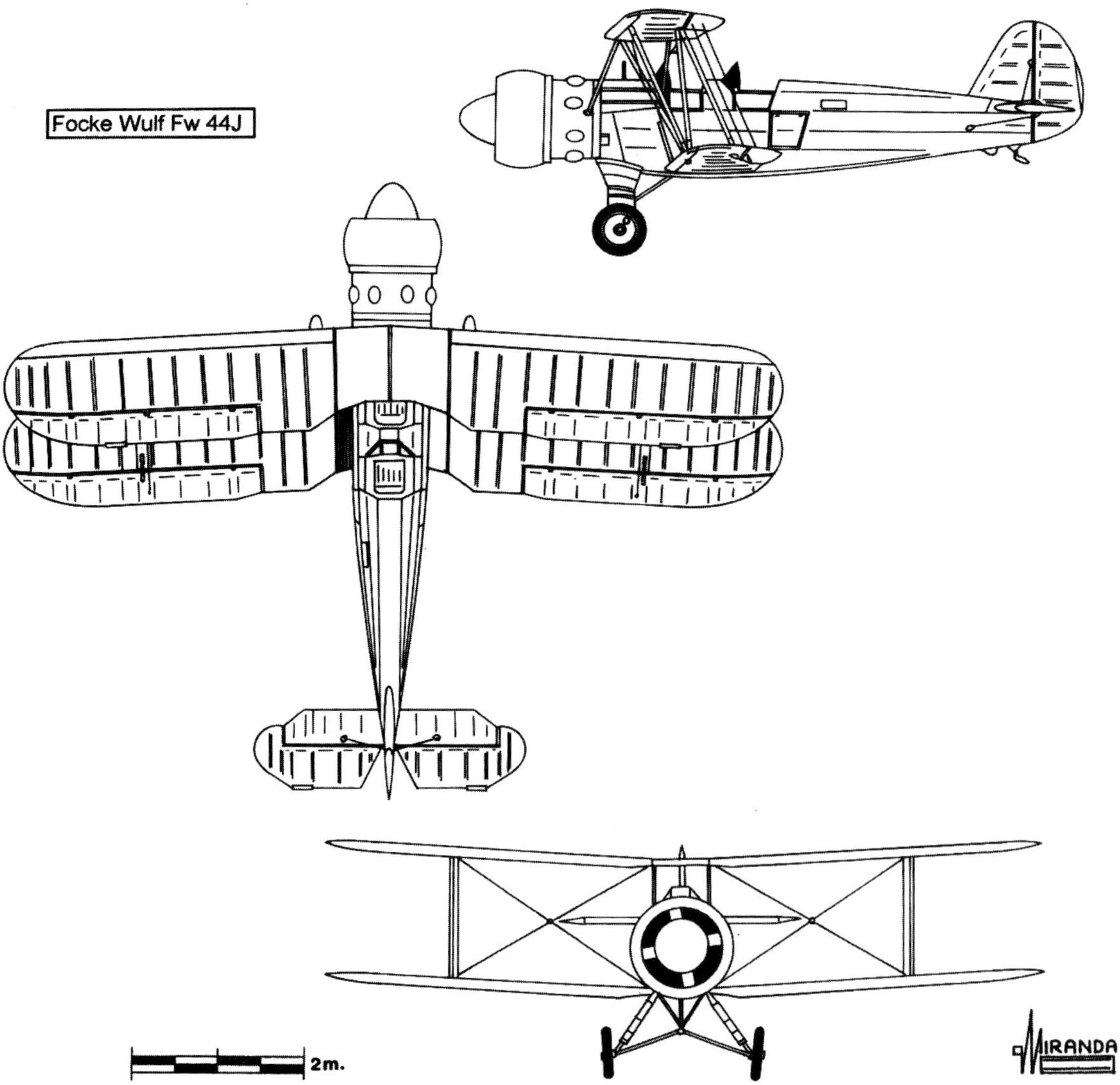

3

Focke-Wulf 1-TL *Jäger Projekt I*

Flying trials with the Messerschmitt Me 262 V2 prototype were conducted at the end of 1942. The test programme included high-altitude combat, revealing unexpected compressibility effects during high-speed dives between 7,600 and 5,500 m. The Me 262 had been designed in 1940, before the aerodynamicists discovered the destructive effects associated with the transonic flux. The turbulent airflow generated in the junction between the engine nacelles and the wing undersurface generated some tailplane buffeting and elevator flutter.

Like its predecessors, Bf 110 and Me 210, the Me 262 proved to be an easy prey in dogfight against the single-engine Allied fighters, demonstrating the correctness of the Latin sentence *errare humanum est, sed perseverare diabolicum* (to err is human, but to persist is diabolical). It was also expensive, requiring a lot of strategic materials during its construction and thrice the man-hours that a standard Bf 109 G required. What the Luftwaffe needed in 1943 was a single-engine air-superiority jet fighter to replace the old '0-Nine', the only successful fighter built by the firm, whose basic design dated back to 1934.

Early in 1943, the *Technisches Amt* (RLM Technical Office) asked Messerschmitt if the Bf 109 G could be adapted to take one Jumo 004 turbojet. The answer was negative. In fact, the firm had all the necessary resources to comply with the RLM requirement: using the wing of the Me 209 and the nosewheel of the Me 309, it would only have been necessary to design a new central wing section so that the attachment points of the undercarriage would not interfere with the jet exhaust. However, the *Sofortprogramm* (interim solution) proposed by the RLM was contrary to the plans of Messerschmitt who at that time had already decided to continue the development of the Me 262. This situation gave the firm Focke-Wulf the opportunity to participate in supplying turbojets that until then had only been available for the Me 262 and the Arado Ar 234.

In February 1943, the Bad Eilsen design team envisaged the study of several possible fuselage-turbojet-air intake configurations and their integration with different types of wings, tail surfaces, and landing gears for the construction of a future single jet fighter. The simplest solution was to replace the BMW 801 radial engine of an Fw 190 with a Jumo turbojet, mounted under the nose to not altering the position of the centre of gravity of the aircraft. Unfortunately for the firm, the new engine turned out to be too long, so the jet nozzle would interfere with the retraction of the main wheels of the Fw 190. It was necessary to design a new type of wings capable of housing the mainwheels of 660 × 160 mm. The greater consumption of J2 heavy kerosene of the turbojet required the installation of two fuel tanks of 390 litres each in the fuselage, making necessary to advance the location of the cockpit 170 cm.

It was planned to mount two Mauser MG 151/20 cannon in the wing roots and two Rheinmetall-Borsig MK 108/30 cannon under the cockpit floor. The *Projekt I* was introduced to the OKL in March 1943 as a realistic solution that would have allowed the *Jagdwaffe* to have an interceptor that would be faster than the Mustang, better armed than the Tempest and the Meteor, and able to overcome the Thunderbolt in dive. It could have been mass manufactured by late 1944, but the *Technisches Amt* rejected the project claiming that the position of the turbojet (whose axis was located 86 cm lower than that of the BMW 801) would substantially decrease the rolling properties, and it was feared that the Jumo 004 would suffer serious damage at belly landing. Also taken into consideration was the risk that jet exhaust gases would cause damage to the tailwheel or burn the airfield surface.

In April 1946, the Soviets demonstrated with their Yak-15 that these precautions were unfounded. The new Yakovlev fighter was based on the same formula as the *Projekt I* and was powered by the same turbojet, being mass-produced and entering into service smoothly in May 1947.

The integration of the turbojet in the airframe of a Yak-3 piston fighter was relatively simple. It was only necessary to modify the wing spar central section, replace the tailwheel with another metal shield, protected by a blast deflector, and to cover the lower part of the fuselage with steel plates. The Soviets successfully used the same formula on the experimental prototypes Lavochkin La-152 (October 1946), La-156 (March 1947), and La-160 (June 1947), all propelled by copies of the Jumo 004. The Italians also used this aerodynamic solution in their prototypes Ambrosini Sagittario (January 1953) and their first supersonic aircraft Aerfer Sagittario 2 (May 1956).

Technical Data

Airframe: light alloy
Wing span: 10.33 m. Length: 9.8 m. Height: 2.6 m. Wing area: 16 sq. m
Engine: one Jumo 109-004 B turbojet rated at 890 kp static thrust
Estimated maximum weight: 3,400 kg. Maximum speed: 780 kph. Ceiling: 12,000 m. Estimated endurance: thirty-five minutes.
Armament: two MG 151/20 cannon with 175 rounds per gun (rpg) and two Mk 108/30 cannon with electro-pneumatic cocking, electrical firing and 70 rpg.

Fw 1-TL Jäger Projekt I

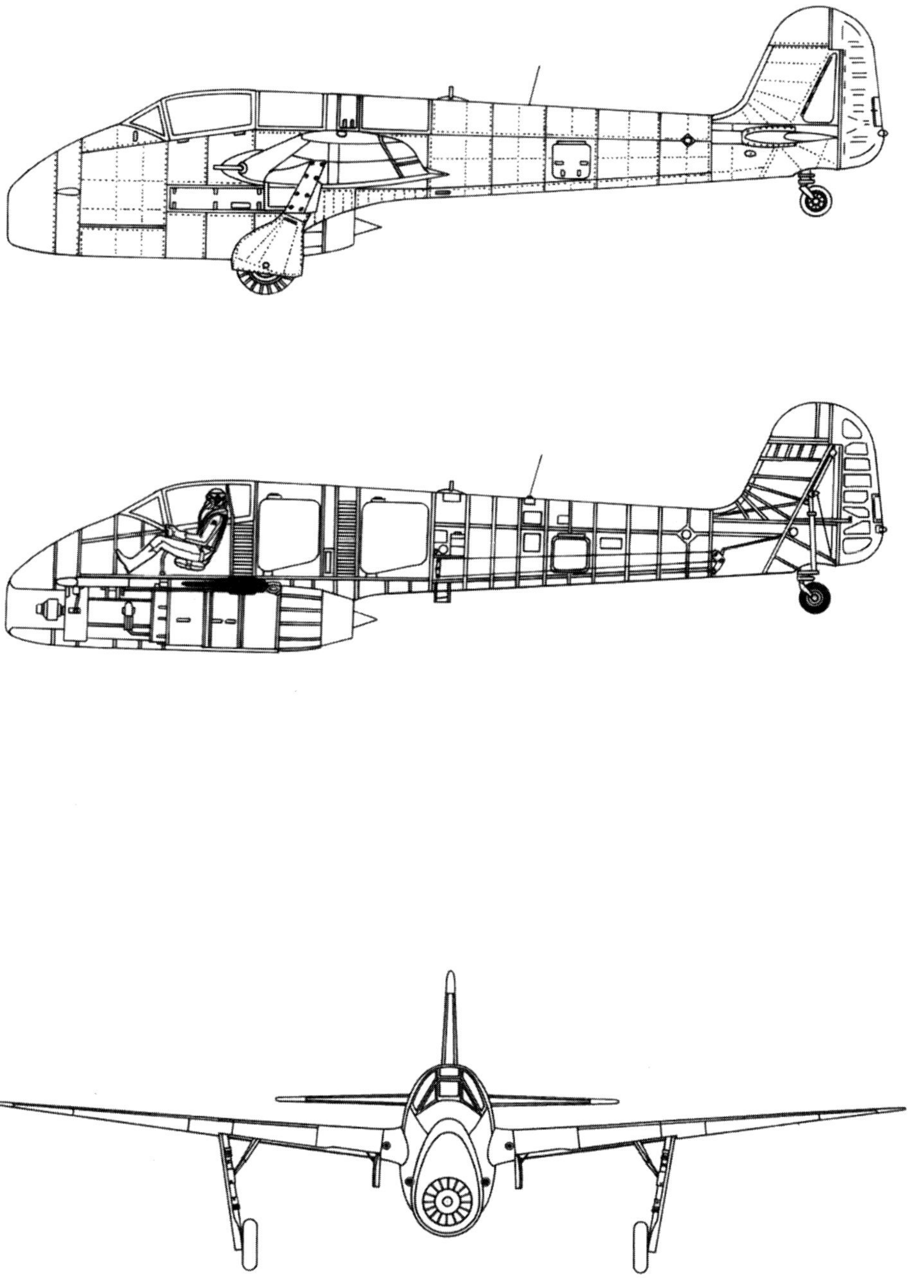

2m.

MIRANDA

Fw 1-TL Jäger Projekt I

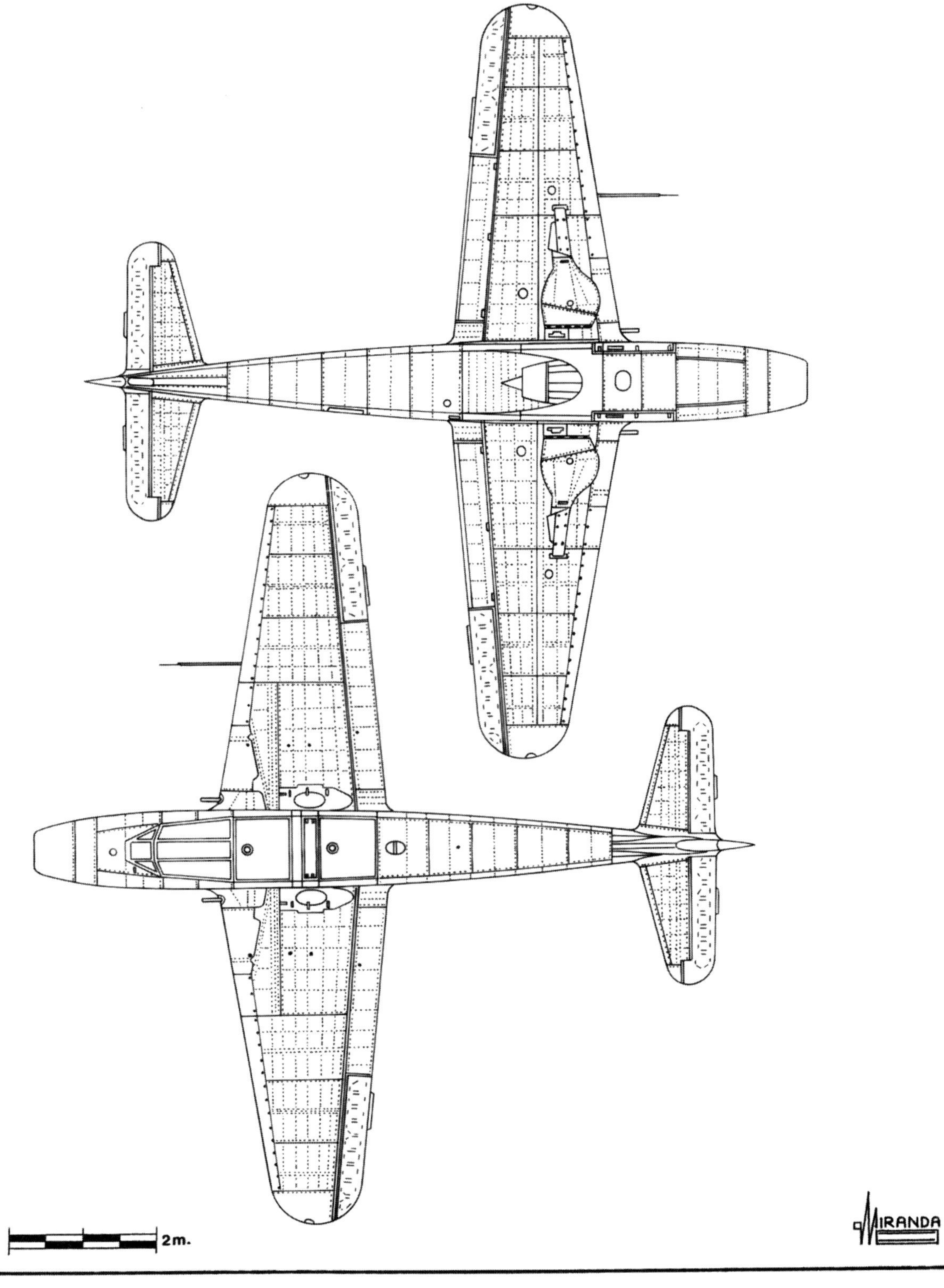

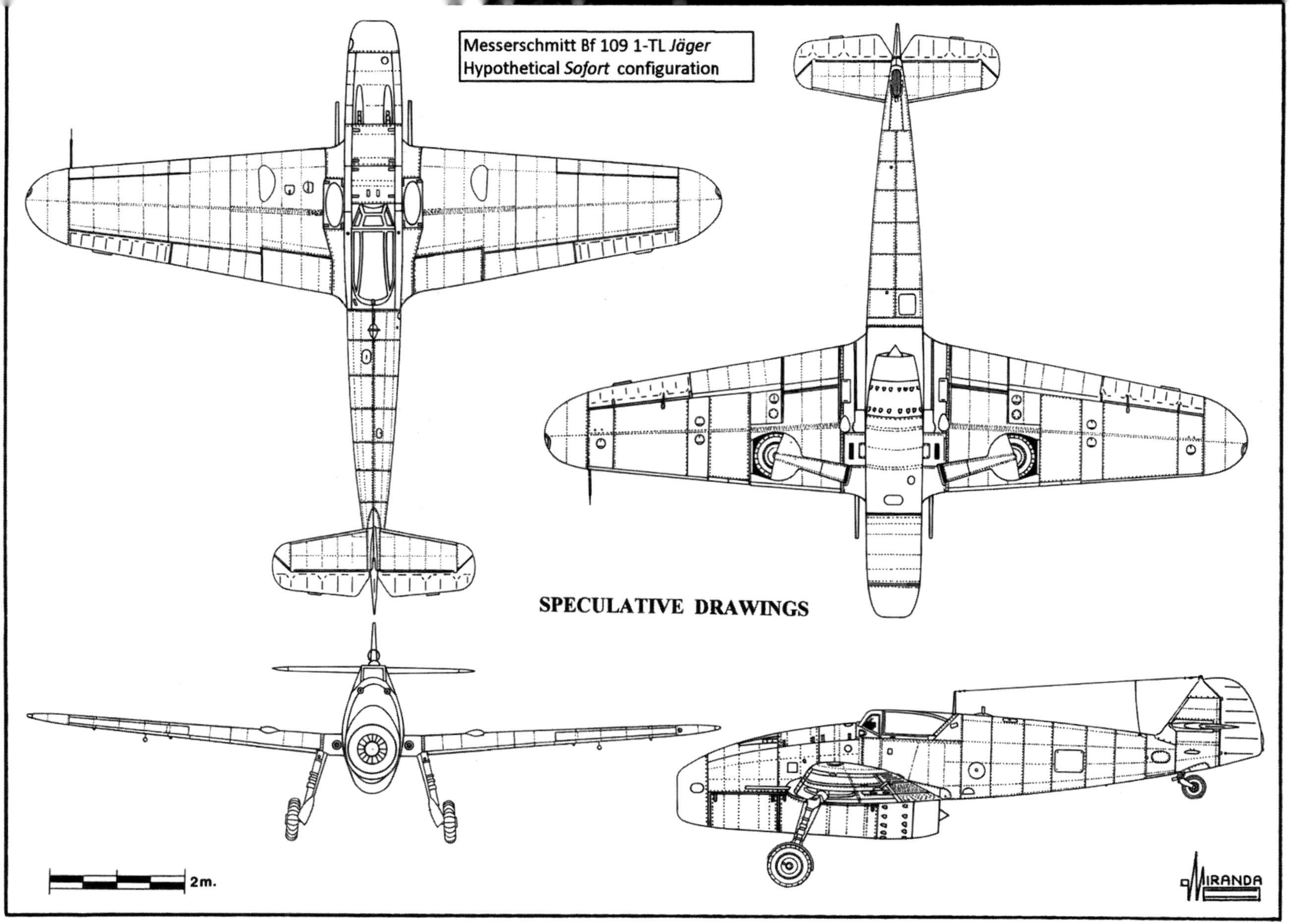
Messerschmitt Bf 109 1-TL Jäger
Hypothetical Sofort configuration
SPECULATIVE DRAWINGS
2m.
MIRANDA

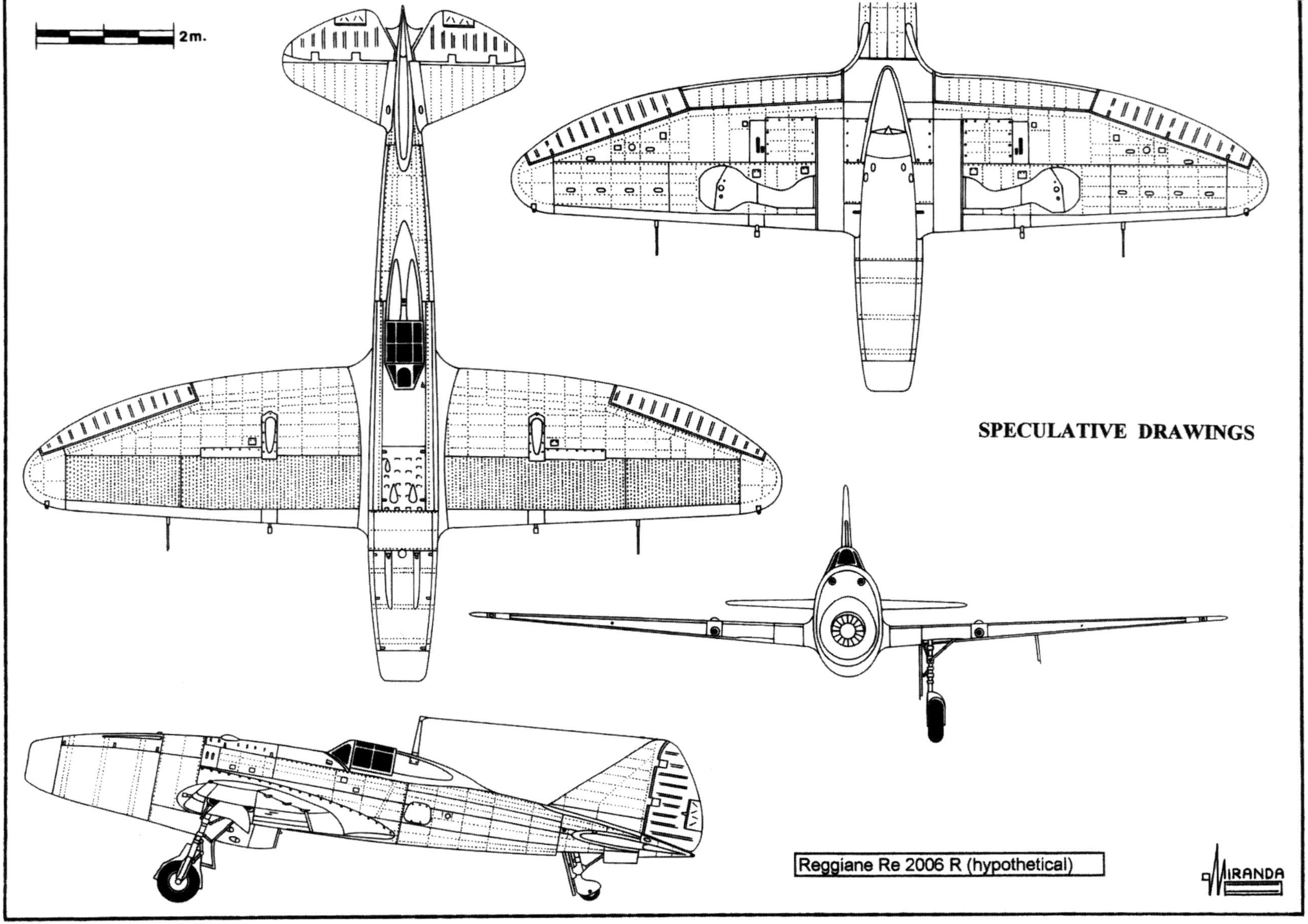
2m.
SPECULATIVE DRAWINGS
Reggiane Re 2006 R (hypothetical)
MIRANDA

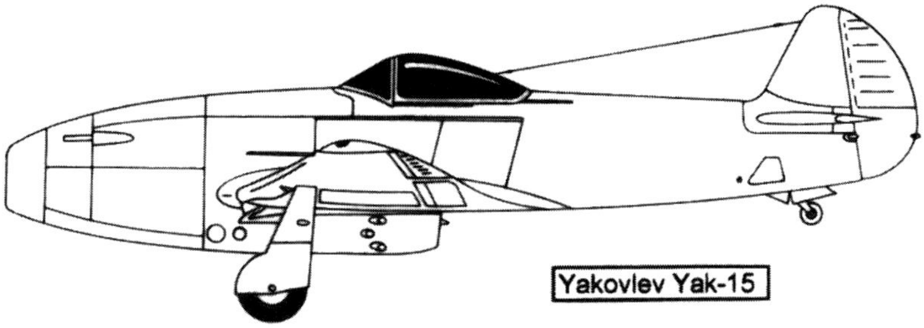

Yakovlev Yak-15

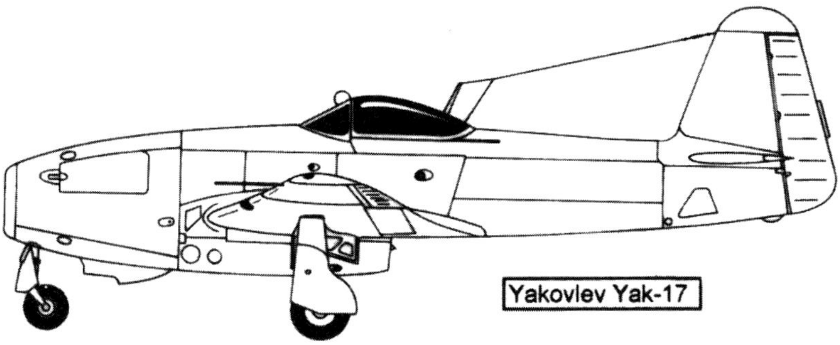

Yakovlev Yak-17

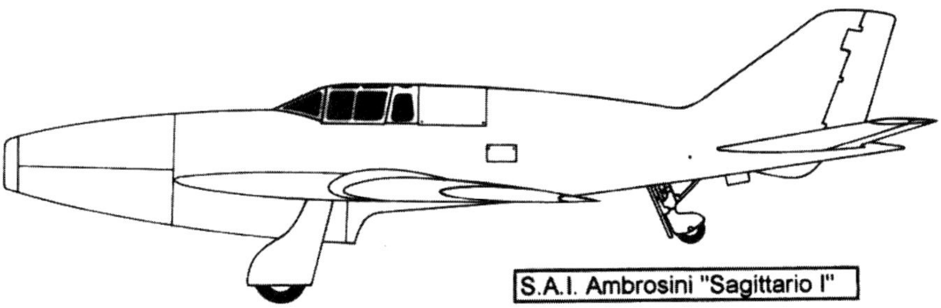

S.A.I. Ambrosini "Sagittario I"

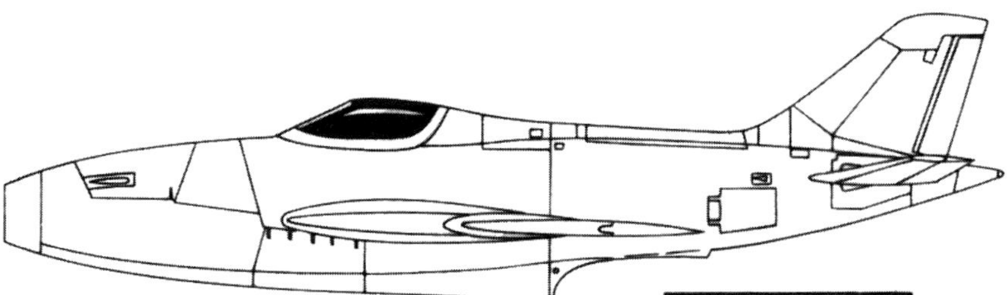

Aerfer "Sagittario II"

2m.

4

Focke-Wulf 1-TL *Jäger Projekt II*

At the beginning of 1943, the OKL had serious doubts about the viability of the Messerschmitt Me 163. To the several crashes occurred during the flight testing, it must be added the delay in the availability of the HWK RII-211 rocket motor, which first approved samples for flying (still far from being safe) would not arrive at Peenemünde research establishment until July.

The Allies offensive of bombers increased by the day. Their escort fighters repelled the Bf 109 and Fw 190 and more devastating incursions were expected with the arrival of good weather. The Me 262 jet fighters did not seem the best solution. Its performances in dogfights were not brilliant, its combat ceiling was insufficient, its engines were not safe, and its airframe suffered from compressibility buffeting.

In the spring of 1943, an internal document of the firm named 'Technical Report Number 90/43' specified that a future single engine jet fighter would require less fuel per hour of flight than the Me 262 and could be built using only 55 per cent of materials and 85 per cent of the man-hours. After inquiries and encouragement from the RLM, the Messerschmitt and Focke-Wulf design teams began to work with single-engine jet fighters. The *Technisches Amt* finally received four projects: Lippisch P.20 (April 1943), Messerschmitt P.1092 (June 1943), Messerschmitt P.1095 (October 1943) and Focke-Wulf 1-TL *Jäger Projekt II* (June 1943).

In all these designs, the turbojet was placed in a ventral position.

Lippisch P.20

On 22 October 1941, the OKL approved the construction of seventy airframes of the Me 163 B series in the Regensburg plant. Production started on 1 December 1941. At that time, the delivery of the RII-211 engines started to suffer delays, putting at risk the whole program. Officially known as HWK 109-509 A, it was a 'hot' double combustion engine, able to operate at 1,750 °C with 1,500 kg in the A-0 version, 1,600 kg in the A-1, and 1,700 kg in the A-2.

Its mass production was slow as it represented an excessive technological jump for its time. It was not until August 1943 that the Me 163B V2 prototype made its first flight, powered by the RII-211. The first seventy airframes of the Komet, urgently needed in combat, were uselessly expecting their engines at the Regensburg factory. The *Abteilung L* (Alexander Lippisch design team) proposed the construction of two alternative versions *parallelenwürfe* in April. The first project was named Lippisch P.20 on 16 April 1943. Basically, it was a Me 163 with a Jumo 004 turbojet installed under the pilot, 36 degrees sweepback angle wing and tricycle type undercarriage. The second project (Lippisch 8-334) never received the RLM official designation. Due to the strong personal disagreement between Alexander Lippisch and Willy Messerschmitt, the *Abteilung L* was disbanded on 28 April and Lippisch himself left the company on 1 May.

Messerschmitt P.1092

On 8 June 1943, Messerschmitt Project Group I, under the leadership of the Dipl.-Ing. Hans Hornung, designed an air-superiority fighter propelled by a Jumo 004 C turbojet that could use the tail surfaces and several components of the Me 262.

The planned armament would consist of two MK 103/30 heavy cannon to attack the bombers and two MG 151/20 rapid-fire cannon to fight the escort fighters. The development of the project, named P.1092 was extended until 10 July 1943, resulting in six versions, which included a high-altitude interceptor, and was cancelled in autumn.

Messerschmitt P.1095

In late May 1944, Göring and Milch met with representatives of the Heinkel and Focke Wulf firms to decide what would be the future of the engines produced by the German aircraft industry. As a result, on 27 May, all test establishments of the Reich were ordered to cease research and testing of pulsejets. To keep the Me 328 project alive, Messerschmitt proposed the construction of the Me 328 C as emergency fighter.

The new aircraft, with 6.4-m wingspan, would be powered by a Jumo 004 B turbojet located in ventral position, a solution that had already been investigated in the P.1092/4 (3 June 1943). The original wings of the Me 328 did not allow the installation of a retractable undercarriage and it was necessary to use other of fixed type and of archaic appearance. The designers felt that the drag generated by this would be amply compensated with the excess of power provided by the turbojet in such a light aircraft. It was expected that the fighter could be launched from a ramp using rocket boosters. The proposed armament for this version was of two MK 103 30-mm cannon.

In September, the design team led by the Dipl.-Ing. Rudolf Seitz proposed some modifications consisting in extending the wingspan to 9.3 m and installing a retractable landing gear from a Me 309. The new design could be interchangeably with the cockpit and tail surfaces of Me 328 or Me 262 and an armament of two MK 108 30-mm cannon located in the nose. With a maximum speed of 860 kph, it could not compete with P.1092's 925 kph. To avoid the cancellation of the project, Seitz proposed a new 'collage' version, with the tail of the Me 209, the landing gear of the Me 309, and the cockpit of the Me 262.

Focke-Wulf 1-TL *Jäger Projekt II*

To dodge the shortcomings of *Projekt I*, Bad Eilsen's team modified the original design. On 7 June 1943, they presented the dossier Baubeschreibung Nr. 264 to the OKL.

An internal document of the firm contained the drawings and calculations that defined the Focke-Wulf 1-TL *Jäger Projekt II* as a new air-superiority fighter propelled by a Jumo 004 B turbojet and with the same armament as the *Projekt I*. The new tricycle type landing gear provided the pilot with a much-improved forward view at take-off and rendered the use of brakes unnecessary in order to bring the elevators into the airstream.

The wing, with 13-degree rear sweep angle at the leading edge and 6.2: 1 aspect ratio, had been developed in 1942 for a high-altitude interceptor propelled by a Jumo 222 piston engine and housed the main landing gear and two MG 151 20-mm cannon. The nosewheel had a mudguard to keep foreign matter from being stuffed into the air intake.

The position of the turbojet was pushed back 230 cm with respect to the previous project to create the room where the nose leg would be housed. These modifications were expected to improve rolling properties by bringing the centre of gravity from the engine to the airframe.

After several tests with a partial pressure suit Dräger Watanzug, it was decided to install a pressurised cockpit in the 9 June 1943 version, with Revi 16 C gunsight, ejector seat and two explosive cartridges to facilitate the separation of the hood at high speed. The pilot protection from 20-mm shells from the rear and 12.7 mm from the front would consist of 100-kg armour plates and one 50-mm thick bullet-resisting windscreen.

Technical Data

Airframe: built of light alloy and steel
Fuel tanks: two of 390 litres of J2 each, in the fuselage.
Oil tank: one with 18 litres of *Schmierstoff*, over the turbojet.
Landing gear: tricycle type with nosewheel of 500 × 180 mm and mainwheels of 660 × 160 mm.
Armament: two MG 151/20 rapid-fire cannon in the wing roots with 175 rounds each and two MK 108/30 heavy cannon with seventy rounds each under the cockpit floor.
Engine: one Jumo 109-004 B turbojet rated at 890-kp static thrust or one 109-004 C rated at 1,015 kp.
Electronic equipment: FuG 16 Zy and FuG 25a.
Wingspan: 9.7 m.
Length: 9.85 m.
Height: 3.6 m.
Wing area: 15 sq. m.
Rate of climb: 20 m/sec.
Maximum speed: 870 kph at 4,000m.
Ceiling: 12,400 m.
Maximum take-off weight: 3,300 kg.
Range: 620 km.

The four projects were rejected by the *Technisches Amt*, arguing the danger of bursting the turbojet during belly landing (something that could also happen with the Me 262 but did not veto its manufacture), the possibility of ingesting foreign matter during take-off, and the degradation of the roll rate. There was also fear that the throttle would result in unacceptable trim changes because of the excessive distance between the axis of the turbojet and the fuselage.

In this way, the continued meddling of the OKL in the designer's work and the excessive zeal demonstrated by the *Technisches Amt* in the search for the perfect weapon ruined the last German opportunity to obtain an air-superiority jet fighter during the Second World War. In 1945, the *Jagdwaffe* still struggled with a handful of antiquated Bf 109 and Fw 190 against thousands of Allied airplanes manufactured following the 'third quality' principle, because the second would take too long and the first would never be available.

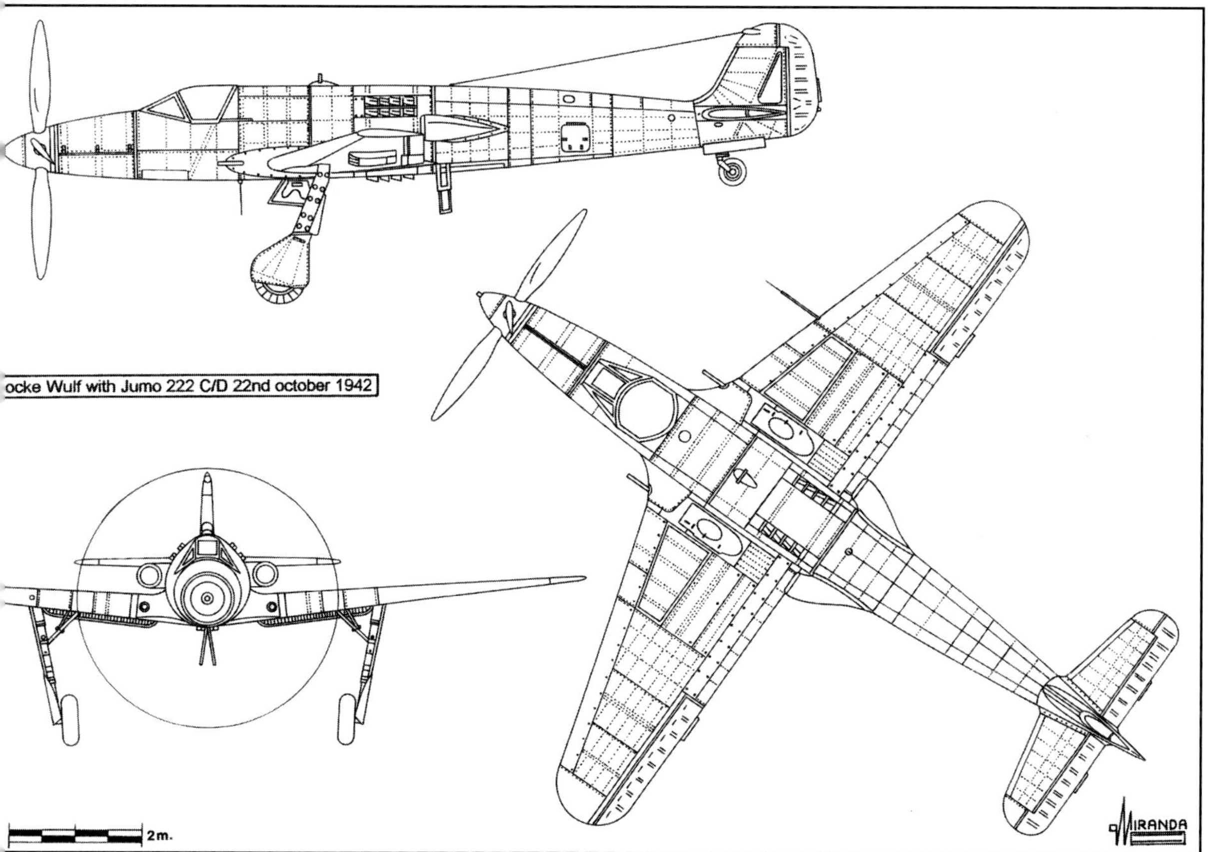

Fw 1-TL Jäger Projekt II

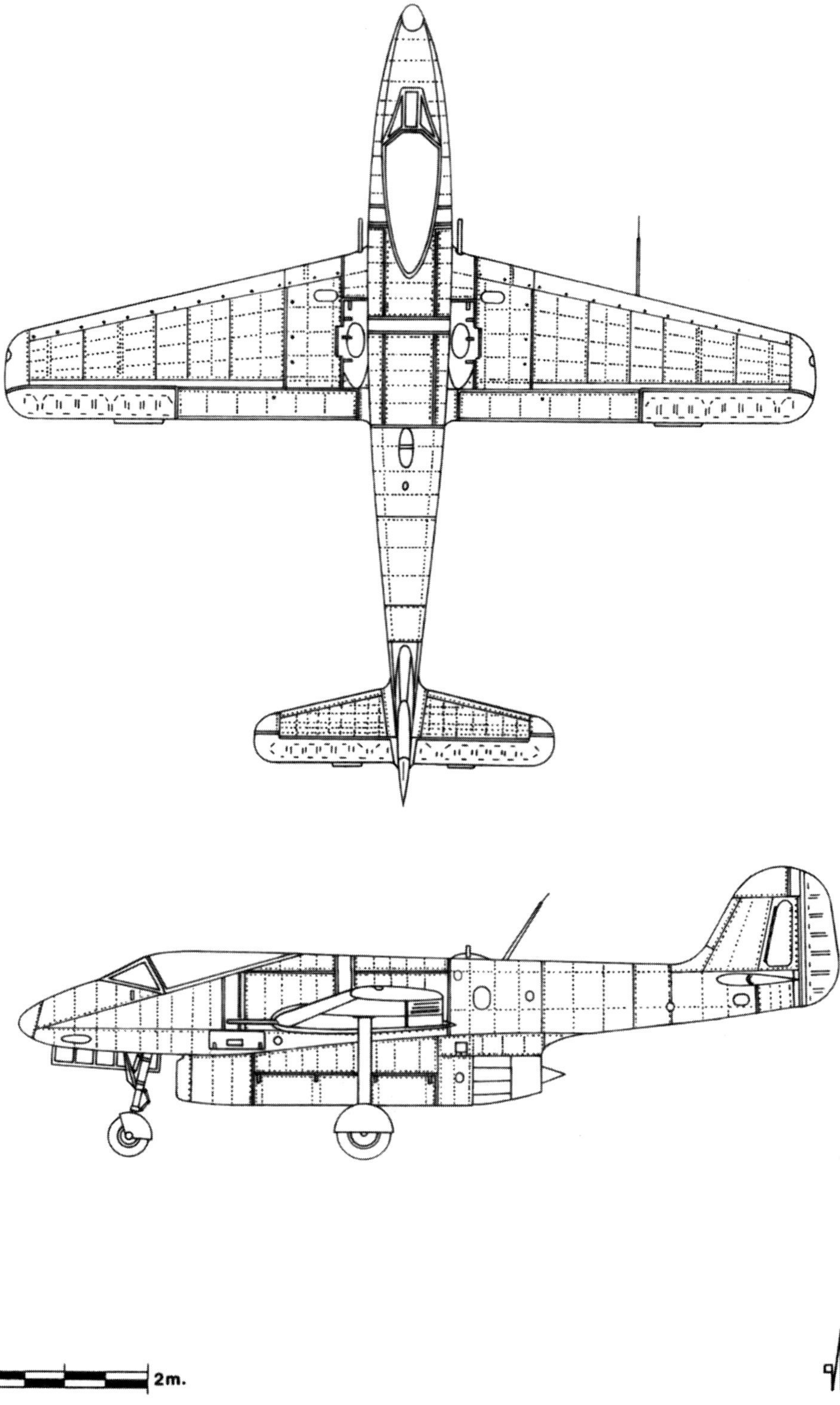

2m.

Fw 1-TL Jäger Projekt II

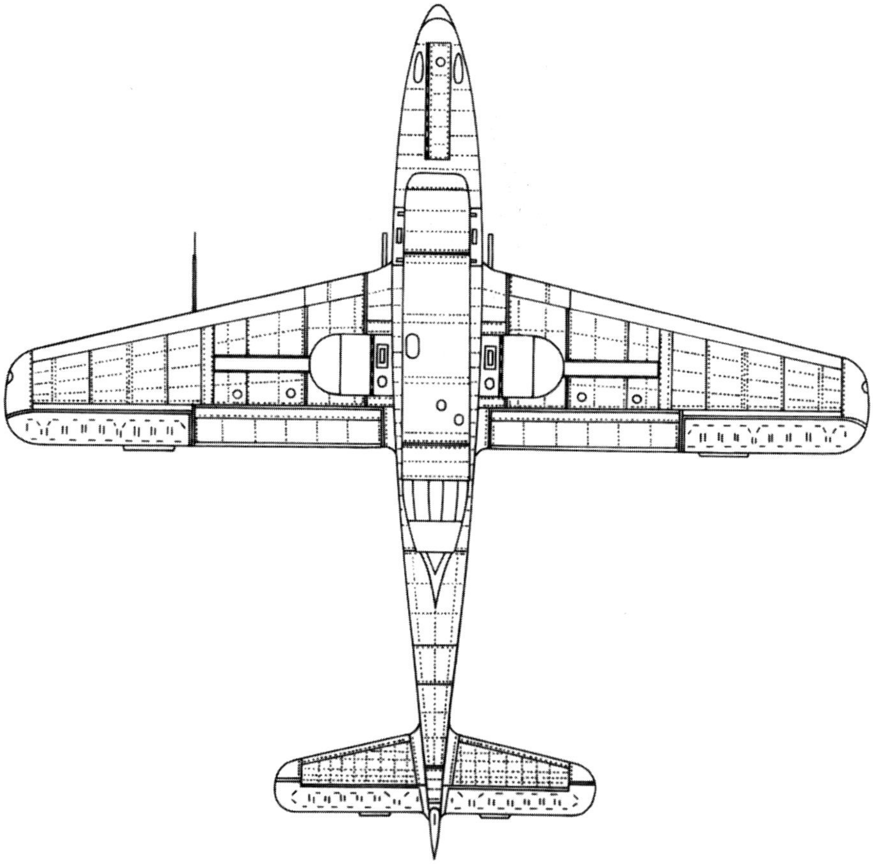

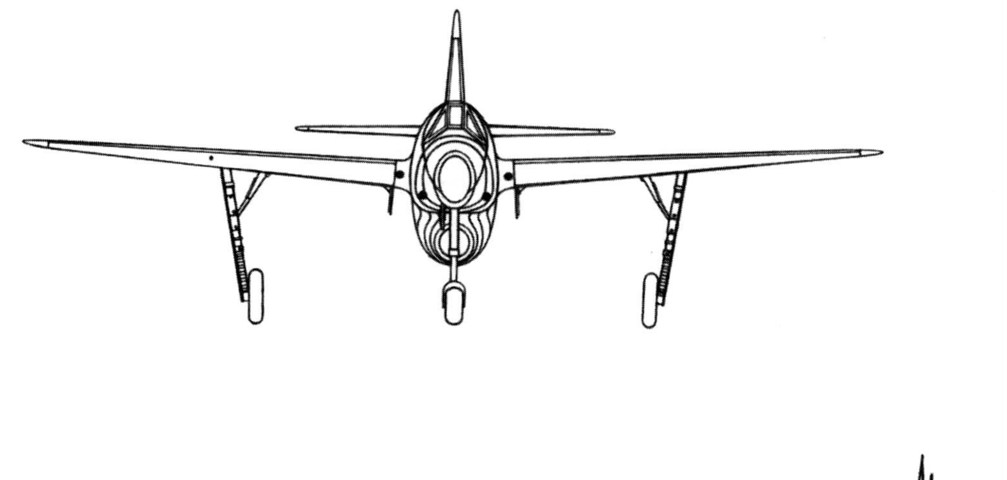

Gewichtsverteilung Jäger mit Junkers-Sondertriebwerk, 20. 7. 1943

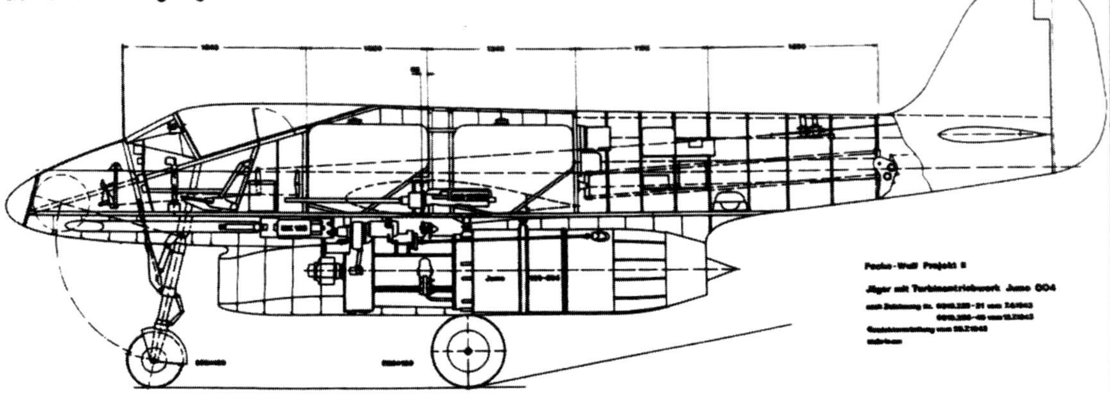

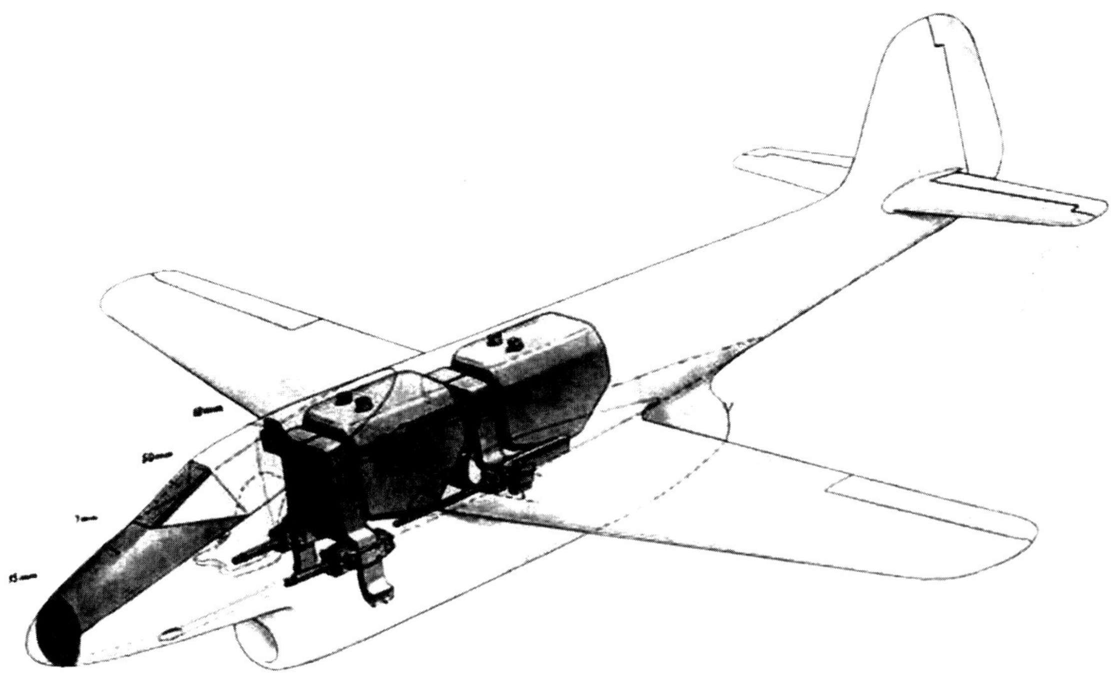

Lippisch P.20

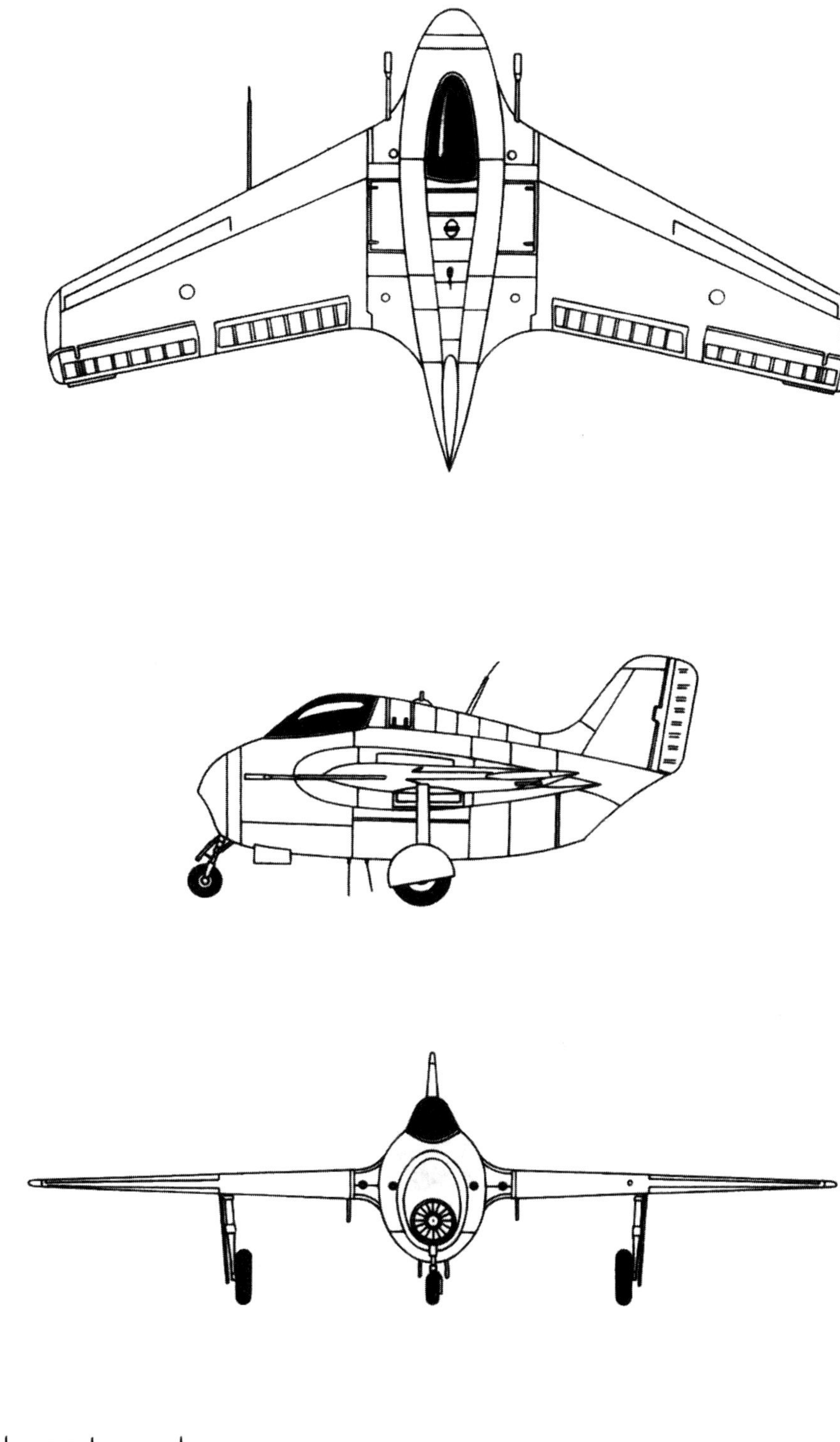

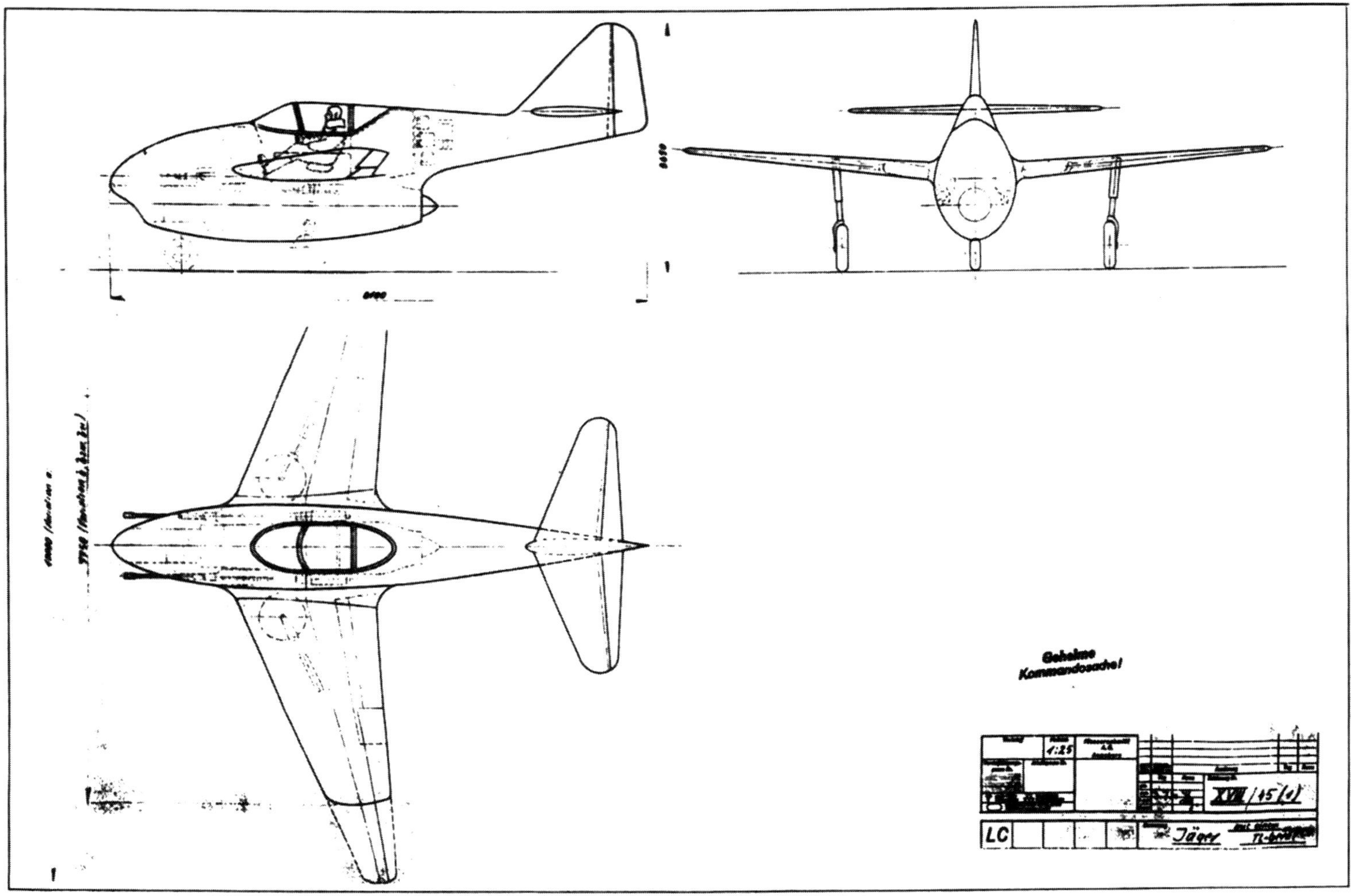

Messerschmitt P 1092 a/bH (July 3, 1943)

Me 328 C with
Jumo 004B

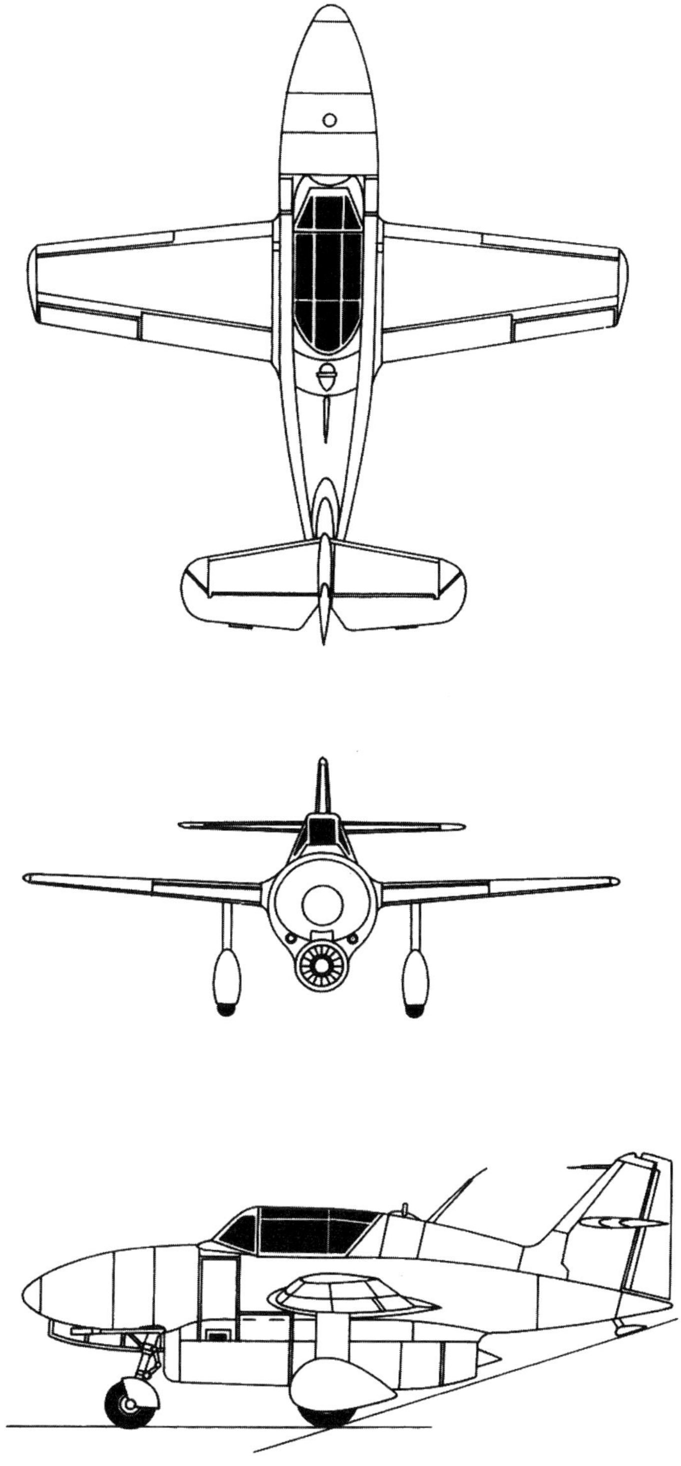

2m.

MIRANDA

Messerschmitt P1095

October 1943

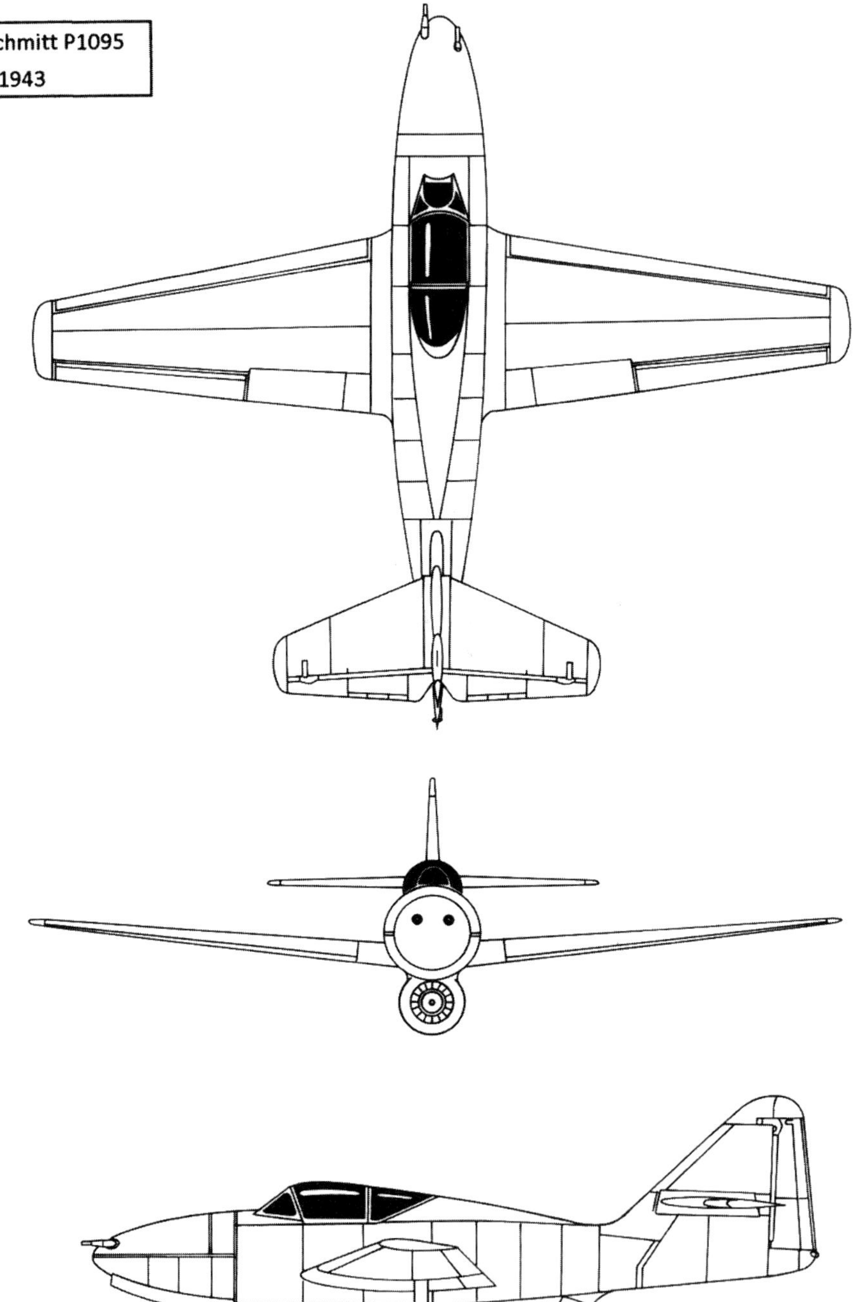

5

Focke-Wulf 1-TL *Jäger Projekt III*

The simplest solution to avoid the OKL objections to the *Projekt II* was to install the turbojet in a back position, but in November 1943, Kurt Tank preferred to place it directly behind the cockpit with side-mounted air intakes.

This new configuration allowed the use of shorter landing gear legs, also improving roll rate and manoeuvrability. The adoption of twin tailfins and a short fuselage permitted them to build a more compact airframe using fewer materials and avoided the loss of thrust associated with a long tailpipe. The wingspan was also reduced, with a wing of greater chord at the root and 16-degree sweep angle at the leading edge. The cockpit was very much like that of *Projekt II*, with the same armour and ejector seat. The armament consisted of four Mauser MG 213 20-mm cannon located under the cockpit floor. A new space was created under the turbojet to house three fuel tanks.

Unfortunately for the Germans, the design of air intakes and air ducts proved inadequate due to the lack of experience of the firm with turbojets. The wind tunnel tests discovered the existence of turbulences between the air scoops and the upper wing surface that would considerably reduce the maximum speed because of the excessive drag. *Projekt III* was cancelled at the end of 1943.

Technical Data

Airframe: light alloy and steel.
Wingspan: 9.10 m. Length: 9.5 m. Height: 2.8 m.
Power plant: one Jumo 004 C turbojet rated at 1,015 kp static thrust.
Armament: four Mauser MG 213 20-mm rapid-fire cannon.

British designers also faced similar problems when they began to work on the design of the first single-engine jet fighters because the entire future of the Gloster Meteor programme seemed in doubt at that time. The large diameter of the Halford H-1 gas turbine, which was then available, made it necessary to install it inside the fuselage and the designers also decided to use lateral air intakes, an aerodynamic solution that allowed the installation of armament and ammunition in the nose.

In 1943, the British firm Gloster Aircraft Co. was asked to proceed with the design of a single-jet fighter named E5/42, with triangular air intakes in the wing roots and tailplane, to keep the elevators away from jet exhaust interference. However, the Allies had not yet developed the ejector seat technology and the survival of the pilot during a high-speed bail out was considered an impossibility because of the position of the tailplane. After constructing a wooden mock-up, the E5/42 was cancelled and the research was continued with the E1/44 fitted with conventional tail planes.

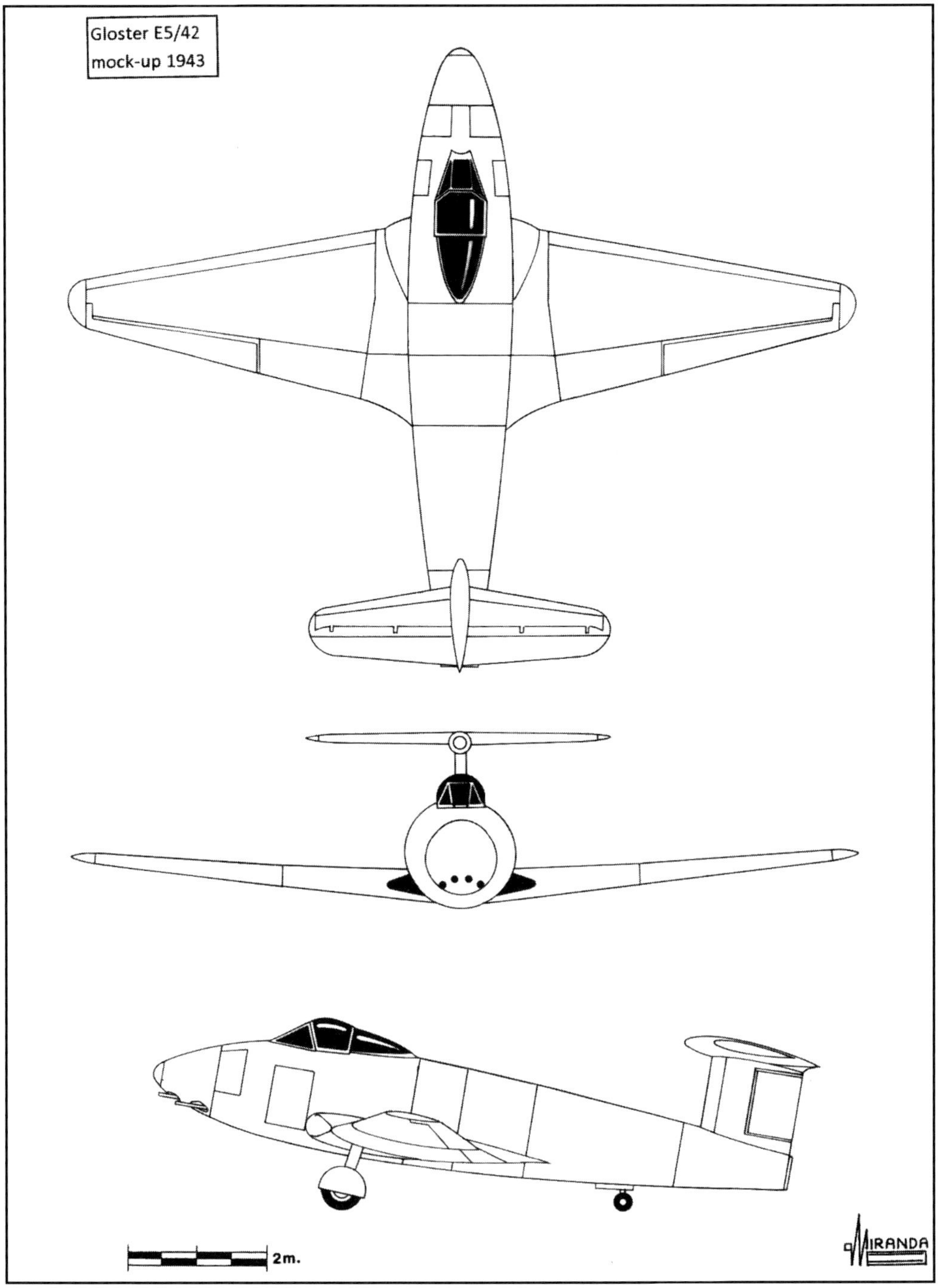

Fw 1-TL Jäger Projekt III

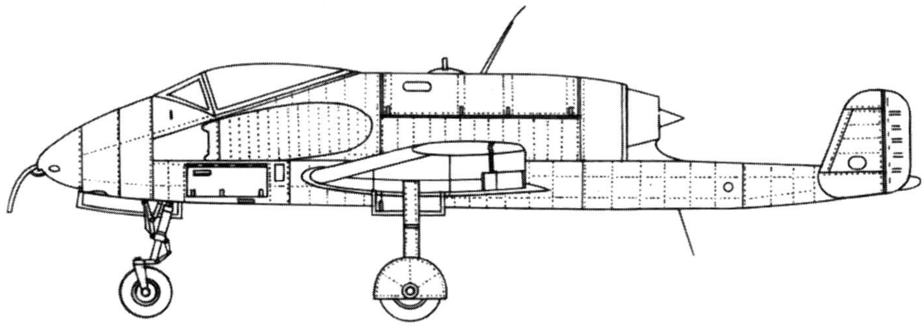

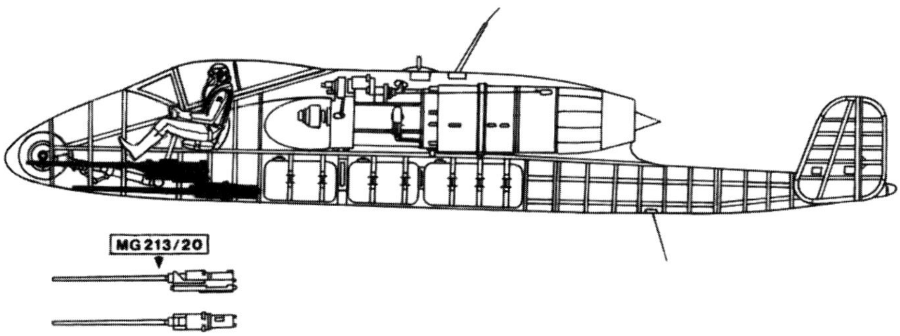

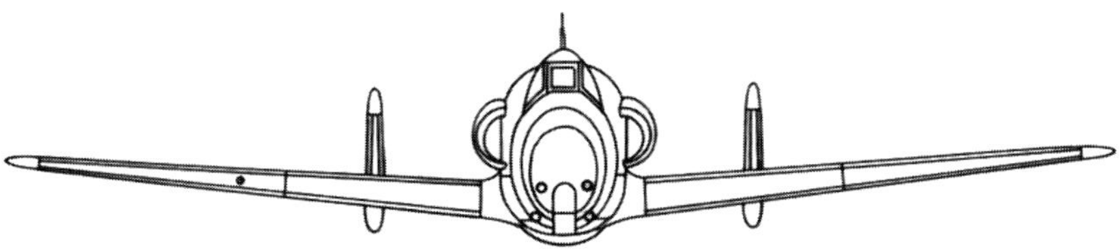

2m.

Fw 1-TL Jäger Projekt III

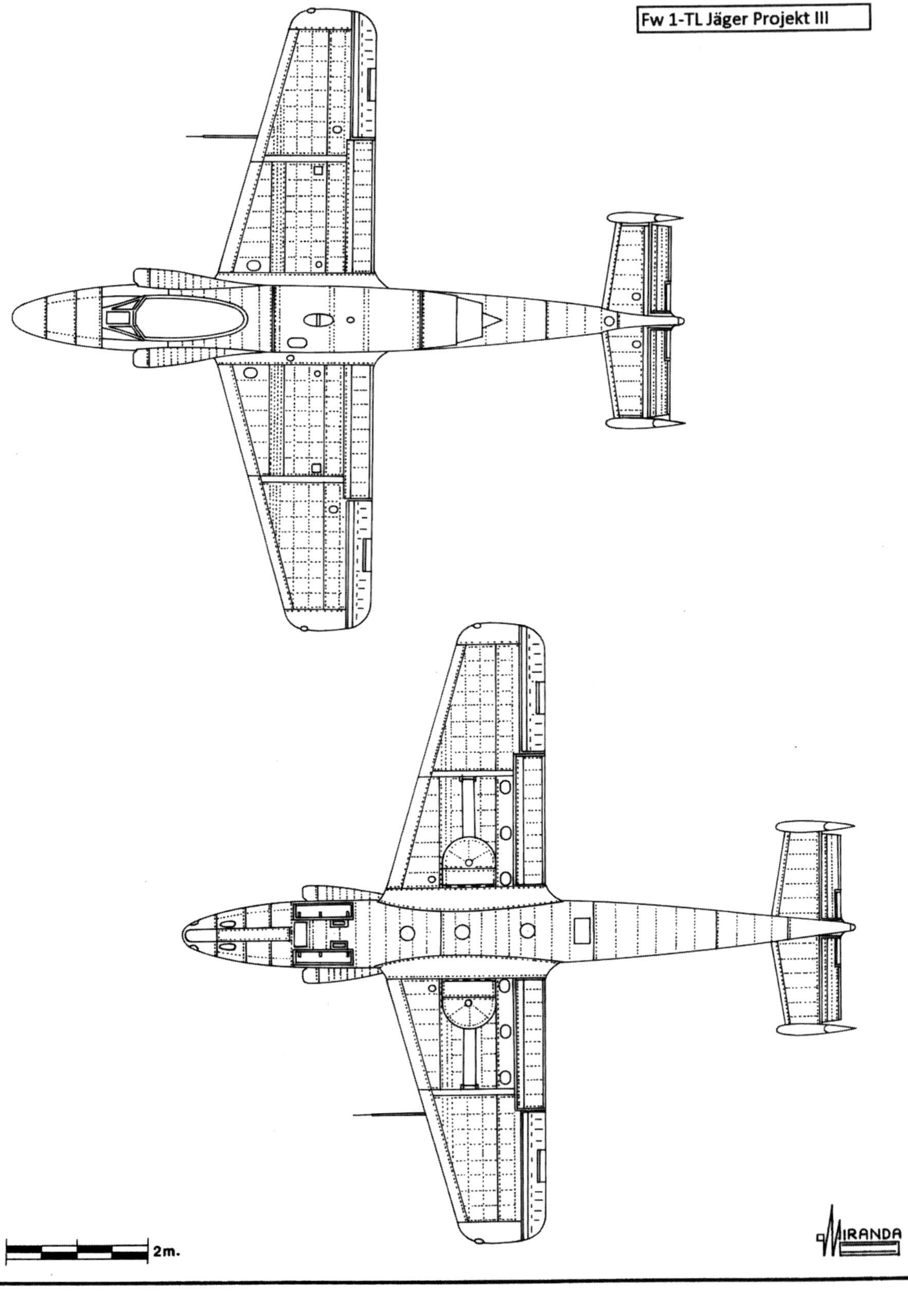

6

Focke-Wulf 1-TL *Jäger Projekt IV*

This variant of the *Projekt III* was designed in December 1943 with important aerodynamic modifications to reduce the drag coefficient. Air intakes shifted 10 cm down and the S-shaped air ducts were gradually integrated into the sides of the fuselage, covered by aerodynamic fairings of greater length.

The twin tailfins were transformed into twin tail booms, a configuration based on the experience acquired by the firm during the construction of the Fw 189. The wingspan was also reduced by 30 cm, increasing the chord at the wing root by 15 cm and the sweep angle of the leading edge up to 19 degrees.

These modifications allowed the installation of two cannon at the wing roots, simplifying the maintenance and reducing the weight of the nose. The main undercarriage legs were shortened even more and the wheels were housed in a ventral bay that also contained four J2 fuel tanks. The low power of the Jumo 004 turbojet would have required the use of long take-off runways that did not abound in the Reich. The Bad Eilsen *Projektabteilung* decided to install two RATO solid-propellant rockets of the type R109-502, with 771 kp peak thrust each, on the back of the ventral bay.

The modifications were considered insufficient by the RLM, which demanded to reach a maximum speed superior to that of the new types of Allied fighters that were expected to enter service by the beginning of 1945. *Projekt IV* was cancelled in January 1944.

Ironically, in September 1942, the enemy had used the same aerodynamic solution in the design of the de Havilland Vampire, one of the most successful post-war fighters; it came to be manufactured in sixteen versions and used by the air forces of thirty countries.

Technical Data

Airframe: light alloy and steel

Wingspan: 8.8 m. Length: 9.5 m. Height: 2.6 m.

Power plant: one Jumo 004 C turbojet rated at 1,015 kp static thrust.

Armament: four Mauser MG 213 20-mm rapid-fire cannon.

Fw 1-TL Jäger Projekt IV

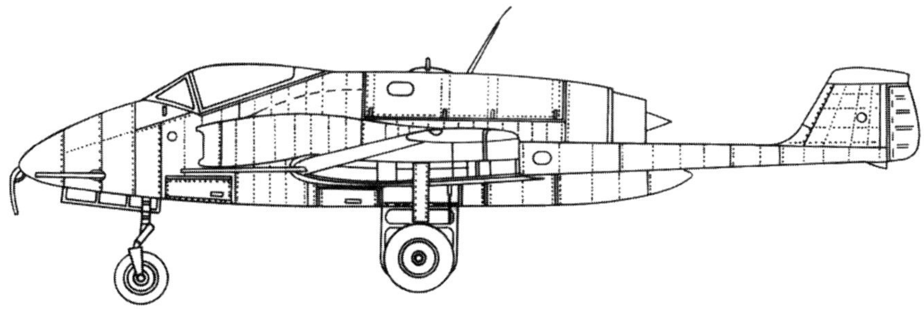

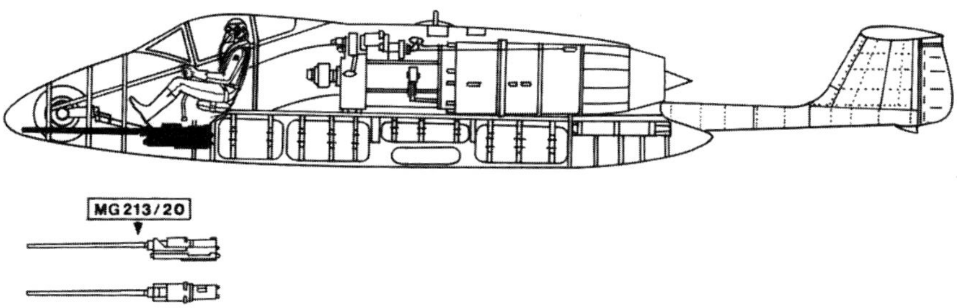

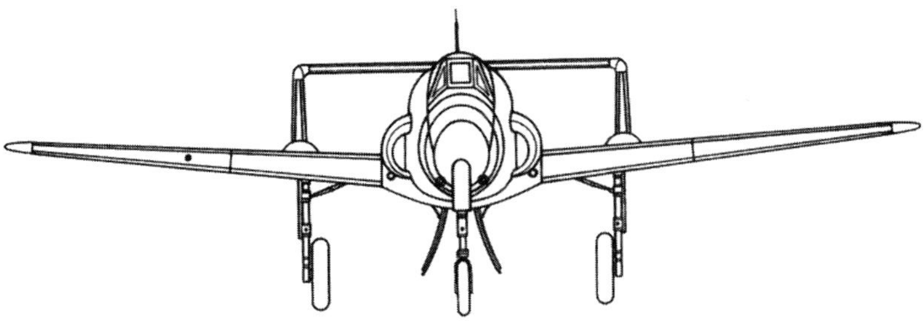

Fw 1-TL Jäger Projekt IV

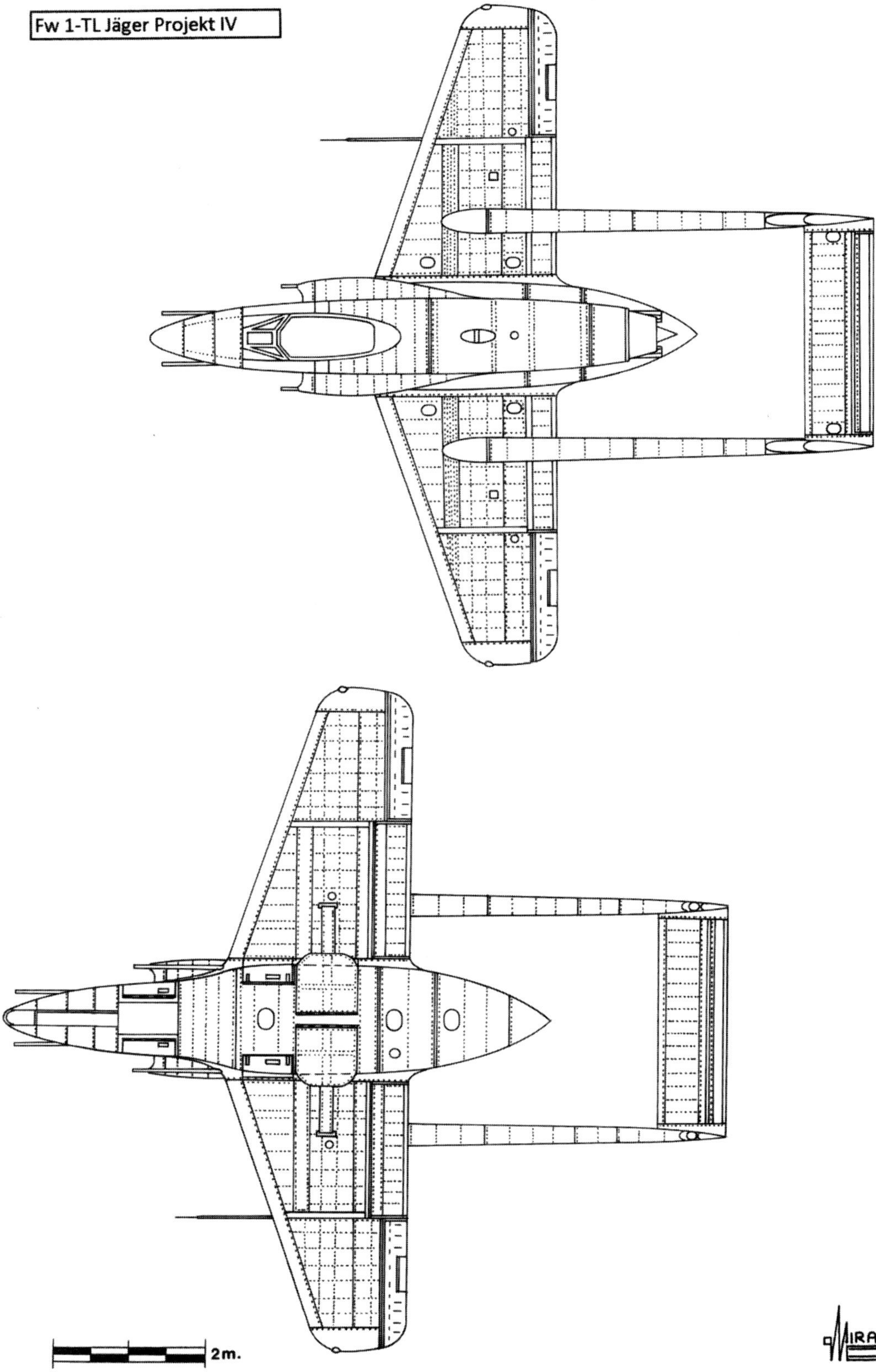

De Havilland E.6/41
Wind tunnel model
September 1942

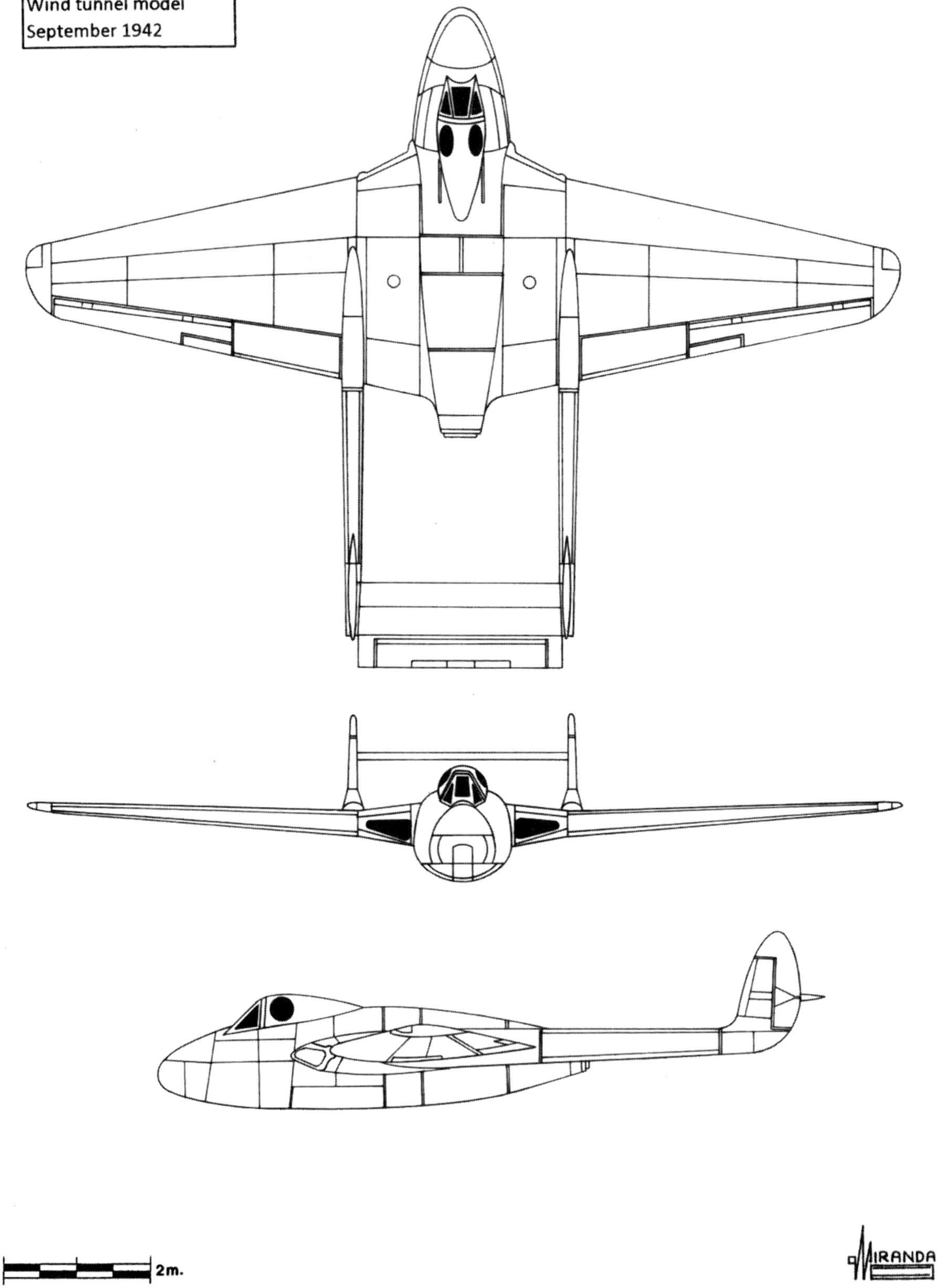

7

Focke-Wulf 1-TLR *Jäger Projekt V*

Early in 1944, Kurt Tank concluded that the performances demanded by the OKL for the future air-superiority jet fighter could not be reached using neither the Jumo 004C nor the HeS 011A, at a time when British turbojets already generated over 2,000 kp. The solution seemed to be a compound power plant that combined the endurance of the turbojet with the bi-propellant rocket punch.

Combining the use of both types of engines, the new fighter would have great operational flexibility: it could act as a point-defence interceptor, using the full power of the two engines, to reach the combat ceiling in the shortest time possible; it could also carry out air patrol missions equipped with droppable fuel tanks for increasing endurance; and it could use the extra speed of the rocket to quickly reach the interception area or get away from a numerically superior enemy by climbing above the operational ceiling of the fighters of the Allies.

The twin-boom configuration with short fuselage, to avoid the thrust loss in the turbojet tailpipe, also limited maximum speed due to the drag penalty generated by the tailplane. To solve the problem, Dipl.-Ing. Hans Multhopp proposed the adoption of a T-shaped tail unit, a radical configuration that was the object of criticism by the *Technisches Amt*. Its main objection was based on the danger posed by the tailplane to a pilot attempting to bail out at high speed. The ejector seat designed in 1942, to equip future versions of the Fw 190, could launch the pilot at a height of 2 m above the cockpit floor, with a margin of 43 cm over the tailfin. However, the T-tailplane, designed to avoid the turbulent airflow generated by the cockpit hood, had to be installed more than 3 m high above the level of the cockpit floor to be effective.

The *Technisches Amt* calculated that during an ejection at critical Mach number, the T-tailplane would reach the pilot in only 0.018 seconds. In 1944, the most effective ejector seat in the world was the Heinkel-Kartusche, propelled by an explosive cartridge with 30 grams of powder, with an ejection speed of 11 m/sec and 12 *g*. It was designed for speeds not exceeding 700 kph. At 1,000 kph and using a T-tailplane, it was necessary to increase the ejection acceleration of 200 g, with equally lethal effects for the pilot.

In January 1944, the firm Focke-Wulf proposed to the OKL a first transonic design called P.011.001, described in the Baubeschreibung Nr. 279 dossier as *Projekt V*. It was a high-altitude interceptor of the *Moskitojäger* class (de Havilland Mosquito hunters) with light armament and a compound power plant formed by a HeS 011A turbojet, with 1,115 kp static thrust, and a bi-propellant rocket motor Walter HWK 109-509 B-0 with 350 kp peak thrust. This was the first design of the firm in which the phenomena of compressibility buffeting, local transonic flux, air viscosity in the boundary layer, and Mach critical number (as defined by the aerodynamicist of the Institut LFA) were taken in account. A frontal air intake was adopted to delay the appearance of vibrations, and a 37 to 43-degree double-swept wing, with 9 to 13 per cent chord to thickness ratio, served to delay the back displacement of the lift centre of pressure and aileron reversal. To facilitate manoeuvrability at high speeds, the tips of the ailerons were clipped.

To avoid that, the 38-degree-swept T-tailplane was affected by the fuselage turbulence at critical Mach numbers; it was installed on a long tailfin with a 60-degree rear sweep. This configuration worsened the usual lateral stability on short-fuselage aircraft. During the Korean War, the Soviet MiG-15, which was nearly two meters longer than the P.011.001, suffered directional snaking problems at high speeds, affecting weapon precision during combat manoeuvres.

Several attempts made to eradicate this problem included the extension of the tailfin up to 3.5 m and the total length of the plane to 8.9 m, as well as increasing the dihedral angle of the tailplane up to 11 degrees, which made the ejection problem even worse.

To reduce the height of the tailplane, wind tunnel tests were carried out with a scale model equipped with an inverted-V tailplane. However, it was verified that the new configuration increased drag because of the vortex generated in the junction between the tailfin and the tailplane.

The P.011.001 should be built in light alloy using the well-proven technology of the Fw 190. The wings, spanning 8.7 m with an area of 17 sq. m and a chord of 306 cm at the root, contained 1,400 litres of K1 heavy kerosene for a 600-km endurance using the turbojet. The fuselage, with egg section, housed the landing gear, the pressurised cockpit with ejector seat and Revi 16C gunsight, two MG 17 machine guns, two MG 151/20 rapid-fire cannon, one rocket propellant tank (containing 1,800 litres of T-Stoff for 210 seconds of rocket powered flight), one rocket propellant tank (containing 800 litres of C-Stoff), the turbojet, the rocket engine, and the electronic equipment.

Designed as a *Moskitojäger*, the P.011.001 was insufficiently armed to combat the four-engine heavy bombers. In 1944, the standard armament of an Fw 190 A-7/R2 *Sturmböck* (assault rammer) were two MG 17, two MG 151/20, and two MK 108/30 heavy cannon. Despite offering an estimated maximum speed of 925 kph and one absolute ceiling of 12,600 m, the propulsion system was a victim of the *Technisches Amt* criticism, who had gone through very bad experiences with the Messerschmitt Me 163 and its rocket propellants, which were dangerous substances.

They argued that the new fighter should only be propelled by one turbojet. Therefore, on February 1944, the project was redefined as P.011.018a, a jet fighter propelled by a HeS 011 A-0 turbojet with 1,300-kp static thrust, with the armament of a *Zerstörer* (bomber destroyer) and four MK 108/30 heavy cannon with 100 rounds per gun.

To maintain the performance of the P.011.001 at heights above 11,000 m, it was necessary to design a new type of wings, spanning 10 m, constructed in duraluminium and plywood, with 40 degrees rear swept, 8 per cent thickness, 24 sq. m surface, and sharper aileron tips to facilitate manoeuvrability in the rarefied air.

Each wing panel held six fuel tanks, totalling 1,440 litres of K1 heavy kerosene, with the elevons and hydraulically operated flaps. The tailplane sweep angle was increased to 35 degrees and the tailfin swept to 66 degrees, bringing the overall length to 9.5 m. The tailplane dihedral angle was also increased to 15 degrees to improve longitudinal stability. The windshield was moved forward 25 cm to increase the visibility of the pilot during take-off, reducing the length of the nose leg, so that the ground incidence would change from 8 to 5 degrees. The cockpit hood was extended 76 cm to reduce the dorsal turbulence and a fuel tank of 170 litres was installed in the space behind the ejector seat.

It was an aerodynamic design far superior to that of its British contemporaries Gloster E5/42, de Havilland Vampire, and Martin-Baker MB 6. The P.011.018a was also too advanced for the mentality of the OKL. Coming ahead of the predictable objections of the *Technisches Amt*, Kurt Tank designed a more conservative version as well with reduced armament and a conventional tailplane. This new configuration, described in the dossier Baubeschreibung Nr. 252, was presented to the OKL at the same time than the P.011.018a to avoid the total rejection of the project. Both designs received the official designation Ta 183, been described in the specialised literature as Ta 183-I/Ta 183 A and as Ta 183-II/Ta 183 B.

On 15 July 1944, the *Technisches Amt* requested the design of an air superiority fighter, powered by a HeS 011 A-0 turbojet, in the *Jägernotprogramm* (emergency fighter program) contest through Proposal 222/I. The new aircraft should reach a maximum speed of 1,000 kph at 7,000 m, with a service ceiling of 14,000 m, an armament of two MK 108/30 heavy cannon with sixty rounds per gun and a fuel capacity of 1,000 litres. A high proportion of *Sparstoffe* (non-strategic materials), such as steel, wood, and plastics, would be used for its construction.

The OKL ordered that large-scale production should start in February 1945 and reach a monthly production rate of 5,000 fighters in June. Initially, the projects presented were the Blohm und Voss P 213.03, Heinkel P.1078 C, Junkers EF 128, Messerschmitt P.1101, P.1110/I, and P.1111, as well as the Focke-Wulf Ta 183 A, Ta 183 B, and *Flitzer III*. Also presented out of date, the projects Arado E.581–5, Heinkel He 162 D, Henschel P.135, Messerschmitt P.1116, and the prototypes Horten Ho 229 and Junkers Ju 388 J, which did not compete for the HeS 011 but for the industrial resources associated with the *Jägernotprogramm*.

In August, the RLM expanded these standards requesting that the new fighter could be easily modified into a twin seat configuration for tasks of night fighter and conversion training. It should also be structurally feasible to install a bi-propellant rocket motor. At the end of the same month, the *Technisches Amt* recommended the installation of nose air intakes and 40 degrees swept wings, a requirement that eliminated Heinkel and Junkers projects, the Messerschmitt P.1110/I and P.1111 and the Focke-Wulf *Flitzer III*. In September, it was decided to expand the fuel capacity up to 1,400 litres, when required to fly for thirty minutes at full throttle.

Failure of the tests carried out with the Dräger Watanzug pressure suit necessitated the installation of a pressurised cockpit with ejector seat and frontal protection against 12.7-mm shelling and against 20-mm shelling from the rear. In October, only two contestants remained: the Focke-Wulf Ta 183 A and the Messerschmitt P.1101, a design capable of reaching transonic speed during combat diving without losing manoeuvrability. The wind tunnel test on the P.1101 models, performed by the AVA in Göttingen during the autumn of 1944, revealed that the maximum speed would still be lower than their expectations.

The reason was the turbulence generated in the joint of the rear fuselage and the engine nacelle, which had a section shaped like the number eight. It was discovered that the airframe generated a triple shockwave at transonic speed. The first one was formed around the cockpit hood, the second over the wing, and the third one over the tailplane. The shockwaves overlapped among each other with a braking effect similar to an arrow going through three discs of felt launched in the air.

The Messerschmitt designers tried to solve the problem replacing the cockpit hood with another with low drag type *Rennkabine*, originally designed for a high-speed version of the Me 262. Wind tunnel test performed with a 'V' and T-shaped tailplanes revealed that such modifications did not substantially improve aerodynamic performance and the P.1101 was cancelled at the end of 1944.

During the selection process, the Ta 183 A suffered numerous modifications, giving way to the version Ta 183 A-0, which was winner of the contest. The 'razorback' dorsal spine was replaced by a triangular-section dorsal structure, which served as the basis for the tailfin, thus providing the necessary space for electronic equipment and a 215-litre fuel tank. The wing chord was reduced from 252 to 235 cm and the wing area to 22.5 sq. m. The tailfin sweep was of 60 degrees, the overall length 9.2 m, and the height 3.5 m. The tailplane sweep angle was increased to 45 degrees and the ground incidence to 7 degrees. The rear section of the hood received a metal coating as additional protection for the pilot head and shoulder.

The position of the armament was also modified by positioning the cannon of the lower level further to the rear and increasing the ammunition tank capacity to 120 rounds per gun. The curvature of the nose was reduced to improve the pilot visibility and a new windscreen was designed with 50-mm thick armoured glass and two triangular, electrically heated, 30-mm thick side panels. The reflex gunsight was replaced by a new gyroscopic gunsight of the type EZ 42 (Adler) and it was proposed to the OKL that the turbojet be replaced by a HeS 011 A-1 with 1,600-kp static thrust. The nose leg was retractable backwards after rotating 90 degrees. The main undercarriage legs were retractable forwards, and were housed to both sides of the air duct. The estimated maximum speed for this version was set at 960 kph and the service ceiling at 14,400 m, with an initial climb rate of 20 mps.

The specifications of the Ta 183 A-1 *Huckebein* production version were published on 28 March 1945. The main innovation was the addition of five weapons racks, mounted beneath the wings and fuselage belly, which could also be used to carry the standard droppable fuel tanks of 300 litres. The ventral rack was located inside a cavity that housed the upper half of the tank to reduce the drag. The capacity of the dorsal fuel tank was increased to 260 litres with the maximum take-off weight up to 5,100 kg. The weight gain required extending the wing area to 23 sq. m and the chord wing up to 248 cm.

The ailerons tips were clipped to improve the rolling at high speed. The expected electronic equipment consisted of a FuG 15/ANF2 direction finder, a GEMA FuG 25a Erstling IFF device, and a Lorenz FuG 125a/EBL 3F Hermine radio navigation device. For the projected installation of a radar, necessary room was provided for the electronic equipment ahead of the instrument panel. The nose radome of the parabolic mirror would reduce the pilot visibility, a defect that was attempted to be compensated by reducing the ground incidence to only 3 degrees.

With 1,700 litres of internal fuel, the *Huckebein* would have a range of 1,740 km. This range could be extended to 3,200 km with the addition of five external drop tanks. In clean configuration, the take-off run was estimated at 650 m and the landing at 555 m. To operate from short runways, the Ta 183 A-1 could use two Rheinmetall-Borsig RI 502 droppable rocket boosters, with 500 kp peak thrust each and six seconds of life. In day fighter configuration, with only two MK 108/30 heavy cannon, the *Huckebein* could carry under four wings air-to-air Ruhrstahl X-4 missiles or three *Trommelanlage* containers with thirty air-to-air R4M unguided rockets each. In the *Zerstörer* (bomber destroyer) configuration he could carry a Rheinmetall-Borsig MK 112/55 heavy cannon in the ventral rack capable of dismantling a B-29 with a single hit.

In the *Schlechtwetterjäger* (all weather fighter) configuration, it could carry four Rheinmetall-Borsig R100 BS unguided rockets, but its use required the installation of a FuG 217 J *Neptun Liliput* rangefinder radar. In *Nachtjäger* (night fighter) configuration, it would use a radar FuG 222 *Pauke S* with a parabolic mirror of 45-cm diameter and one radar operator seated in tandem behind the pilot. In *schlacht* (ground attack) configuration, it could carry forty-five anti-tank 88-mm *Panzerblitz II* rockets, in three containers slung under the wings and fuselage belly, or six WK 14 BS incendiary rockets of 280 mm slung under the wings. In *Jabo* (anti-ship) configuration, it could carry one SD 500 bomb or one BT200 torpedo-bomb under the belly.

On 30 August 1944, the Messerschmitt Project Bureau decided to build a prototype of P.1101 powered by a Jumo 004B turbojet. This experimental aircraft was expected to be used to test the behaviour of the swept wings in flight and compare it with the data obtained in the wind tunnel by the scientists of the *Deutsche Versuchsanstalt für Luftfahrt* (DVL), who had recommended the cancellation of the project. Doubts about possible discrepancies between the behaviour predicted by theorists and actual flight at transonic speeds also affected the designers of the *Huckebein* project.

In December 1944, Kurt Tank decided to build four prototypes called *Rechnerische Ankündigung* (Ra) to test in flight the basic airframe of the Ta 183 powered by different engines. The program was to start in January 1945 with the construction of the Ta 183 Ra-1, an advanced version of the P.011.001 powered by a HeS 011 A-0 turbojet and a HWK 109-509 B-1 bipropellant rocket engine. For safety reasons, the rocket propellants were stored in two detachable tanks under the wings.

The 350-litre T-Stoff oxidant tank was positioned asymmetrically to the C-Stoff fuel tank, which had a capacity of only 180 litres and a shorter diameter to compensate for the drag braking effect. The K1 heavy kerosene for the turbojet was stored in a rear tank of 290 litres, with an additional 1,300 litres inside the wings. To improve the longitudinal stability, with respect to P.011.001, the tailfin chord was increased by 10 cm and the sweep angle of the tailplane was reduced to 37 degrees. The tailplane span was increased by 36 cm. The wing span was reduced by 6 cm and the sweep angle to 40 degrees, but the wing surface remained unchanged. When the nose leg was shortened, the ground incidence was reduced by two degrees and the length of the cockpit hood was increased by 68 cm to reduce turbulence on the rudder. The weaponry proposed for this version was two MG 151/20 rapid-fire cannon and two MK 108/30 heavy cannon.

The Ta 183 Ra-2 (20 March 1945) should be powered by a Jumo 004 B turbojet with only 890 kp static thrust. To compensate the reduction of power with respect to the *Huckebein*, it was decided to increase the chord of the wing up to 248 cm, the wingspan to 11 m, and the wing area to 24.7 sq. m. The tips of the ailerons, the tailplane, and the rudder were also modified, giving them a rounded shape. The overall length was reduced by 30 cm and the ground incidence became of 5 degrees, thus the height being reduced by 35 cm. The Jumo turbojet normally operated with heavy kerosene of type J2, although if necessary, a mixture of B4, 87-octane petrol and motor oil could also be used. The specific fuel consumption was 1.38 kg/hp per hour, higher than that of HeS 011. Therefore, it was necessary to increase the capacity of the dorsal fuel tank by 30 litres. The proposed armament was four MK 108/30 cannon.

The Ta 183 Ra-3 of January 1945 was to be powered by a HeS 011 A-0 turbojet with 1,300 kp static thrust. The main dimensions were the same as those of the *Huckebein*, except for the chord wing at the root, which was 235 cm, and the wing area of 22.5 sq. m. Differences with the production version affected the retraction system of the nosewheel, the shape of the windshield side panels, and the position of the armament. The capacity of the dorsal tank was reduced to 240 litres.

The Ta 183 Ra-4 of February 1945 was to be powered by a HeS 011 A-1 with 1,600 kp static thrust. Basically, it was a Ra-3 with the wing of a *Huckebein*, a 540-litre dorsal fuel tank protected by armoured plates, and a single access panel to the guns on each side of the fuselage. The *Technisches Amt* considered the swept wings of the Ta 183 to be potentially dangerous during landing at low speeds. However, most of the criticism was directed against the T-tailplane configuration. They argued that it was too heavy for a fighter, it did not provide enough lateral stability, and it could not be built with wood. They also considered the front section of the fuselage, which was 13 per cent bigger than that of the standard Fw 190, to be excessive.

In February 1944, Kurt Tank sent a set of drawings and calculations to the RLM contained in the dossier Baubeschreibung Nr. 252, describing the 'soft' version of the Ta 183, denominated Ta 183 B (P.011.037a). The cross section of the fuselage was 24 per cent lower than that of the Ta 183 A, the armament was reduced to only two MK 108/30, the cockpit was moved back 1.5 m and the tailplane was placed at the same height as the head of the pilot. The wing span was reduced by 50 cm and the sweep wing angle to 34 degrees, the wing roots were moved to the rear by 90 cm, and the tailplane was moved forward by 72 cm. The internal fuel capacity did not change.

This basic design evolved throughout 1944 trying to adapt to the changing demands of the *Jägernotprogramm*. In its P.011.039a version (February 1945), the cockpit had been advanced 36 cm to improve the visibility of the pilot at landing, the wings had been advanced 11 cm to preserve the longitudinal stability, and the weight of the new fuel tank of 250 litres installed over the air duct had been altered. The entire tail section was designed in a way that could be constructed in wood and was interchangeable with that of the *Huckebein*. The Ta 183 B was superior to all versions of the Ta 183 A in ceiling and maximum speed, thanks to its smaller front section and the lower structural weight of the airframe.

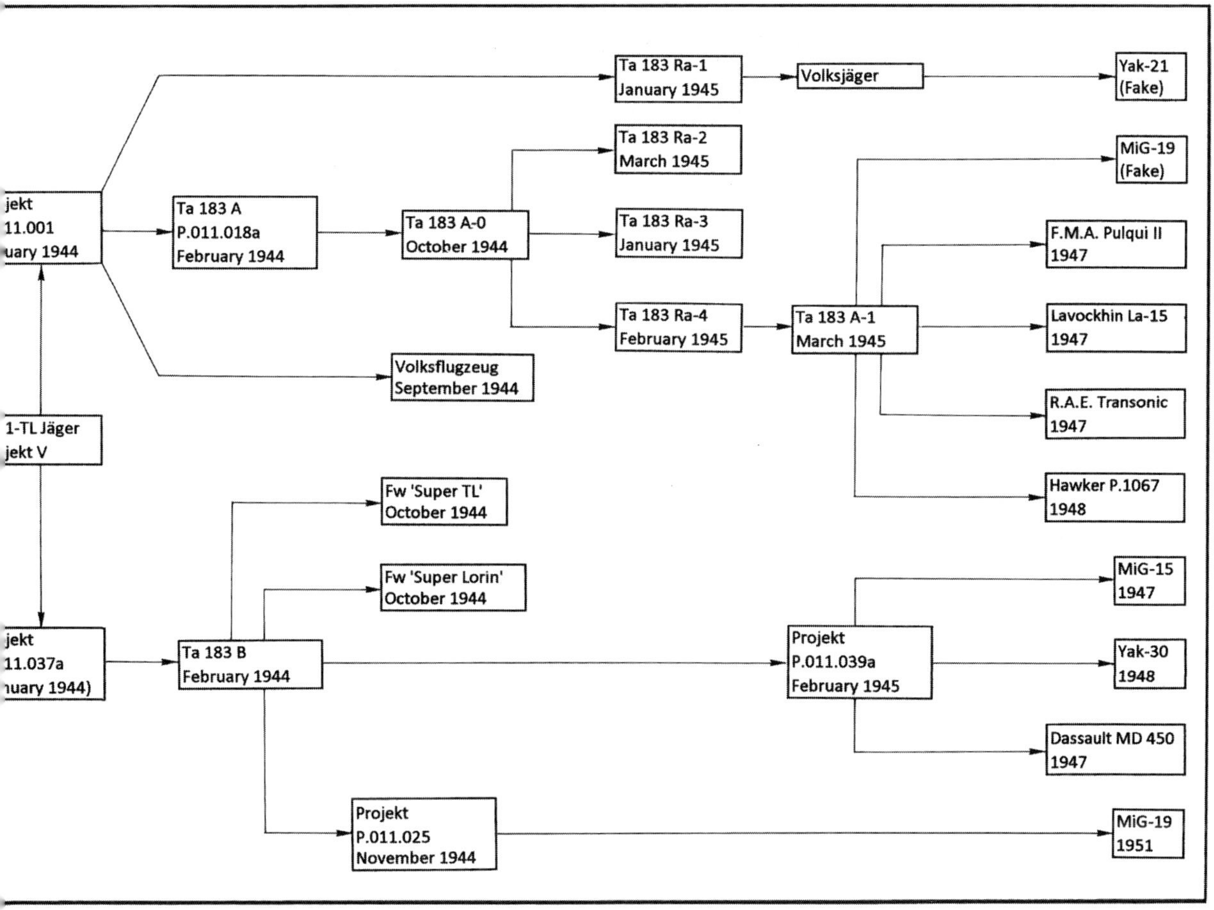

Projekt
P.011.001
January 1944

Ta 183 A
P.011.018a
February 1944

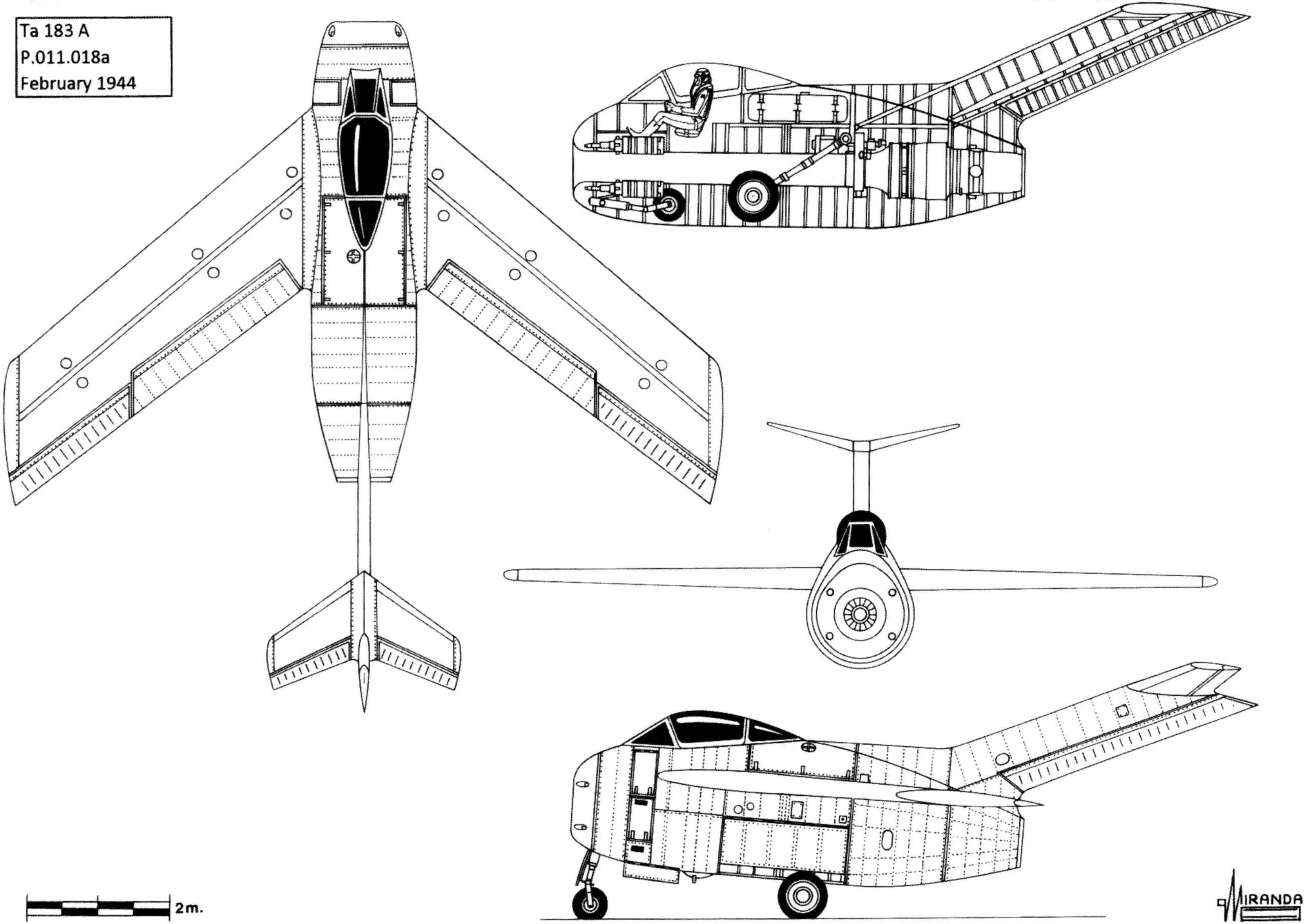

Ta 183 A-0
October 1944

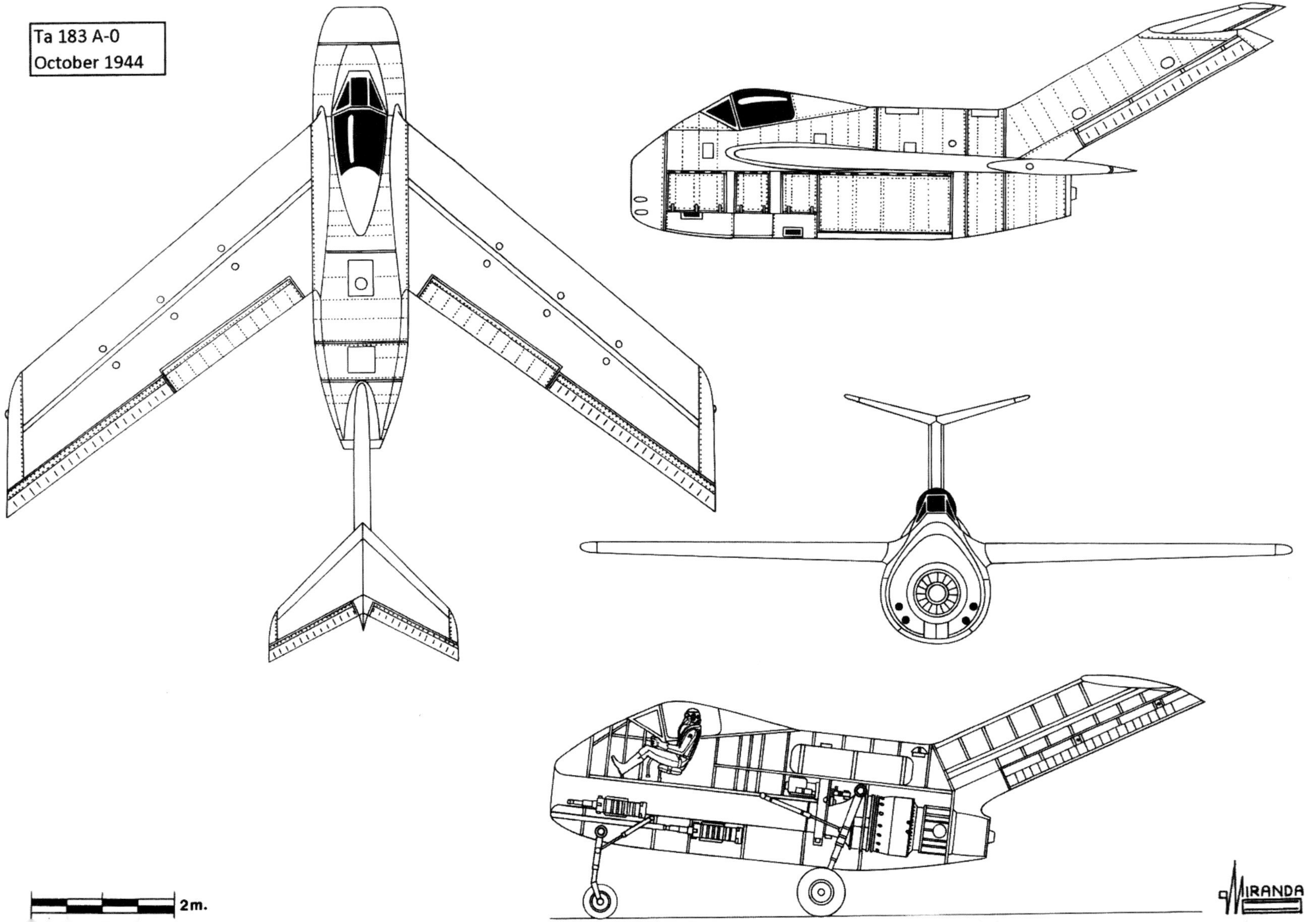

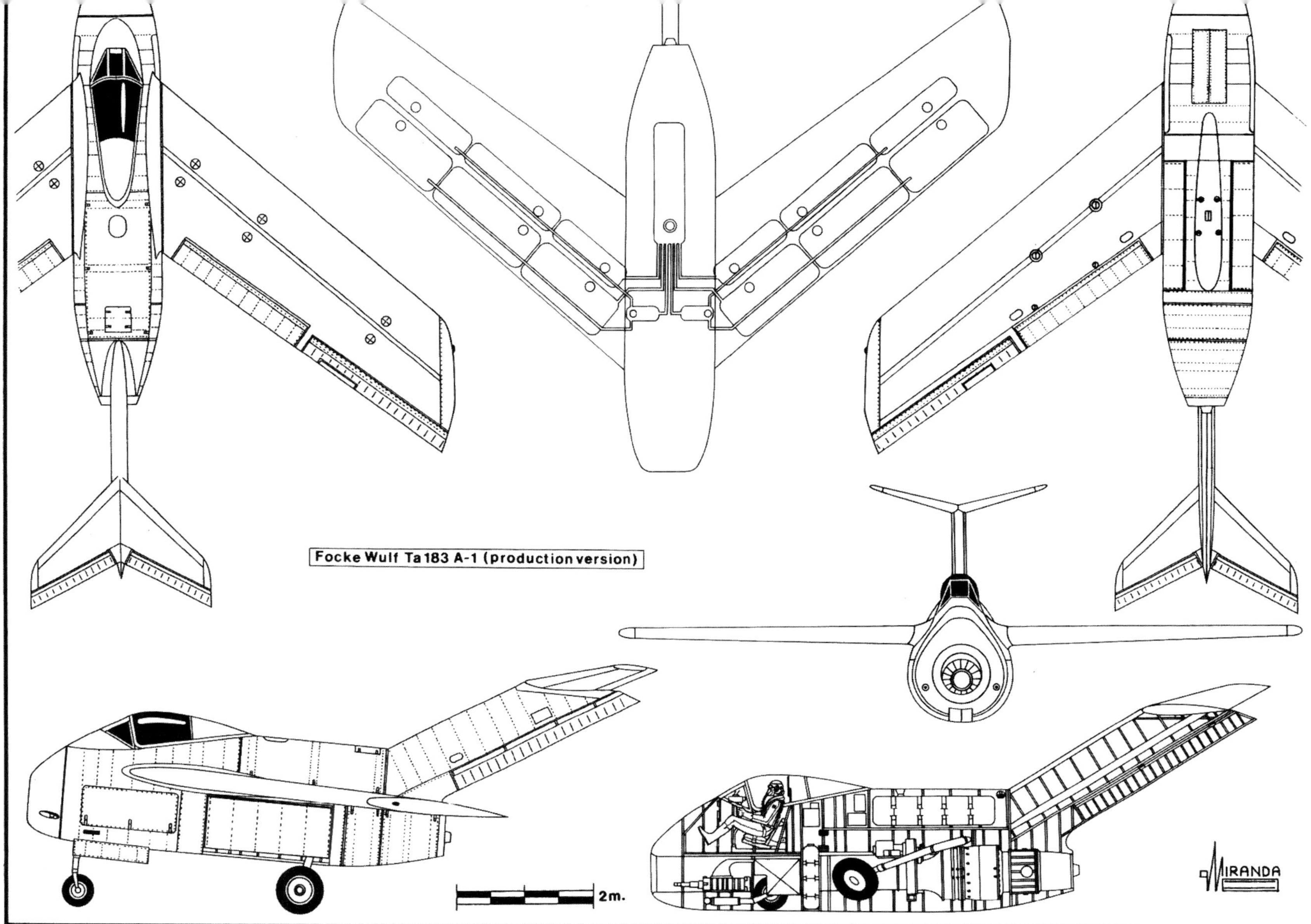

Focke Wulf Ta 183 A-1 (production version)

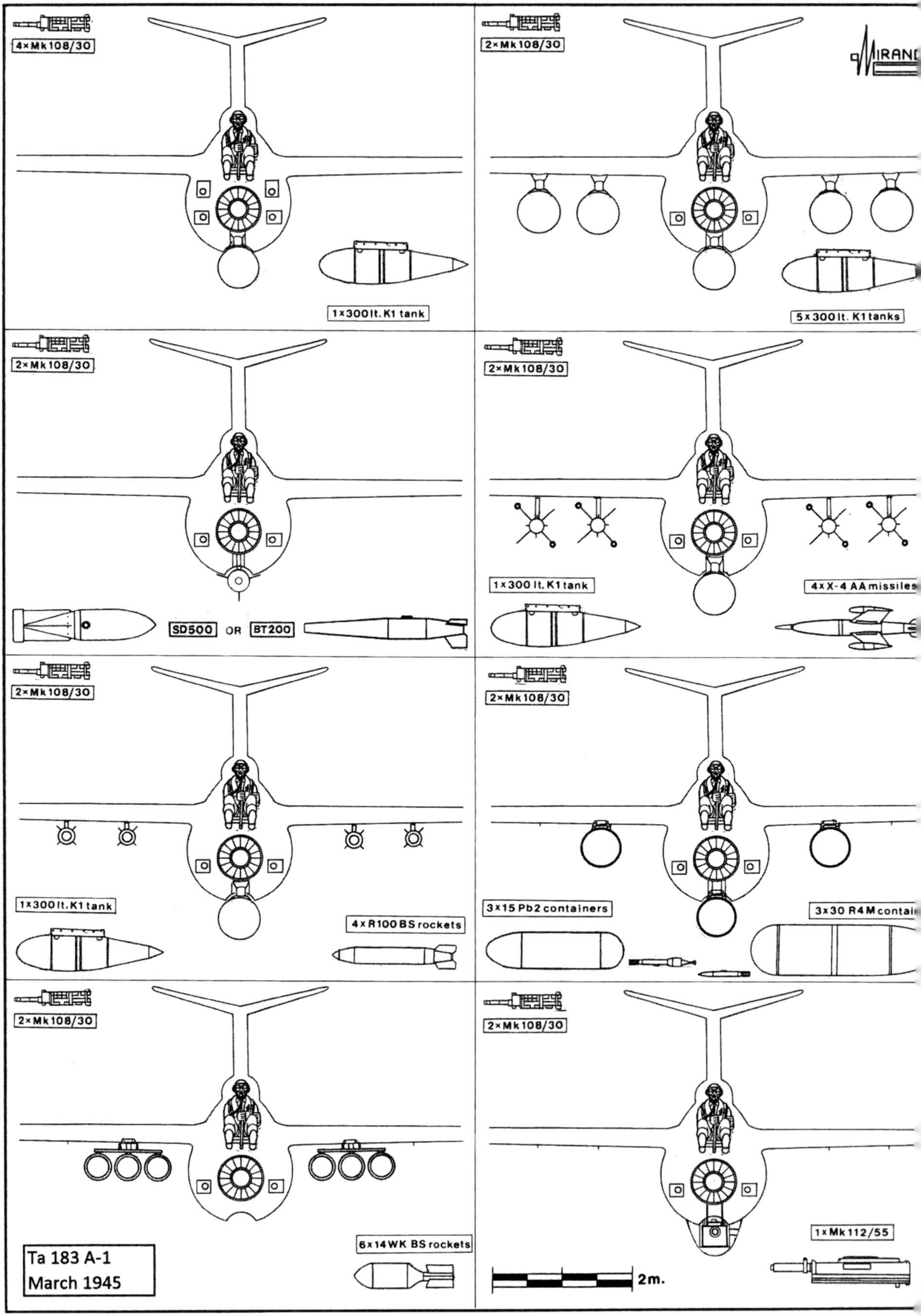

Ta 183 A-1
March 1945

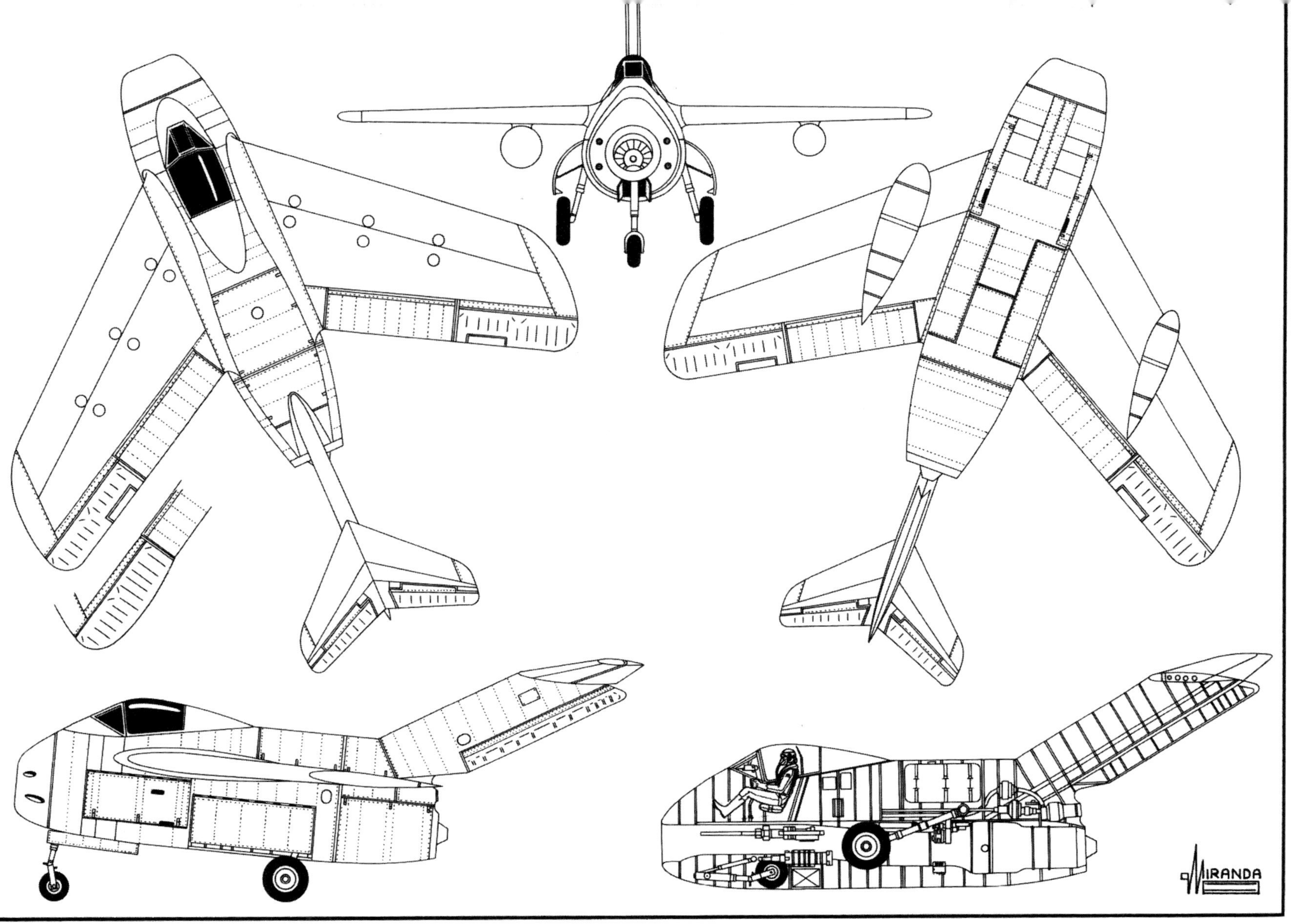

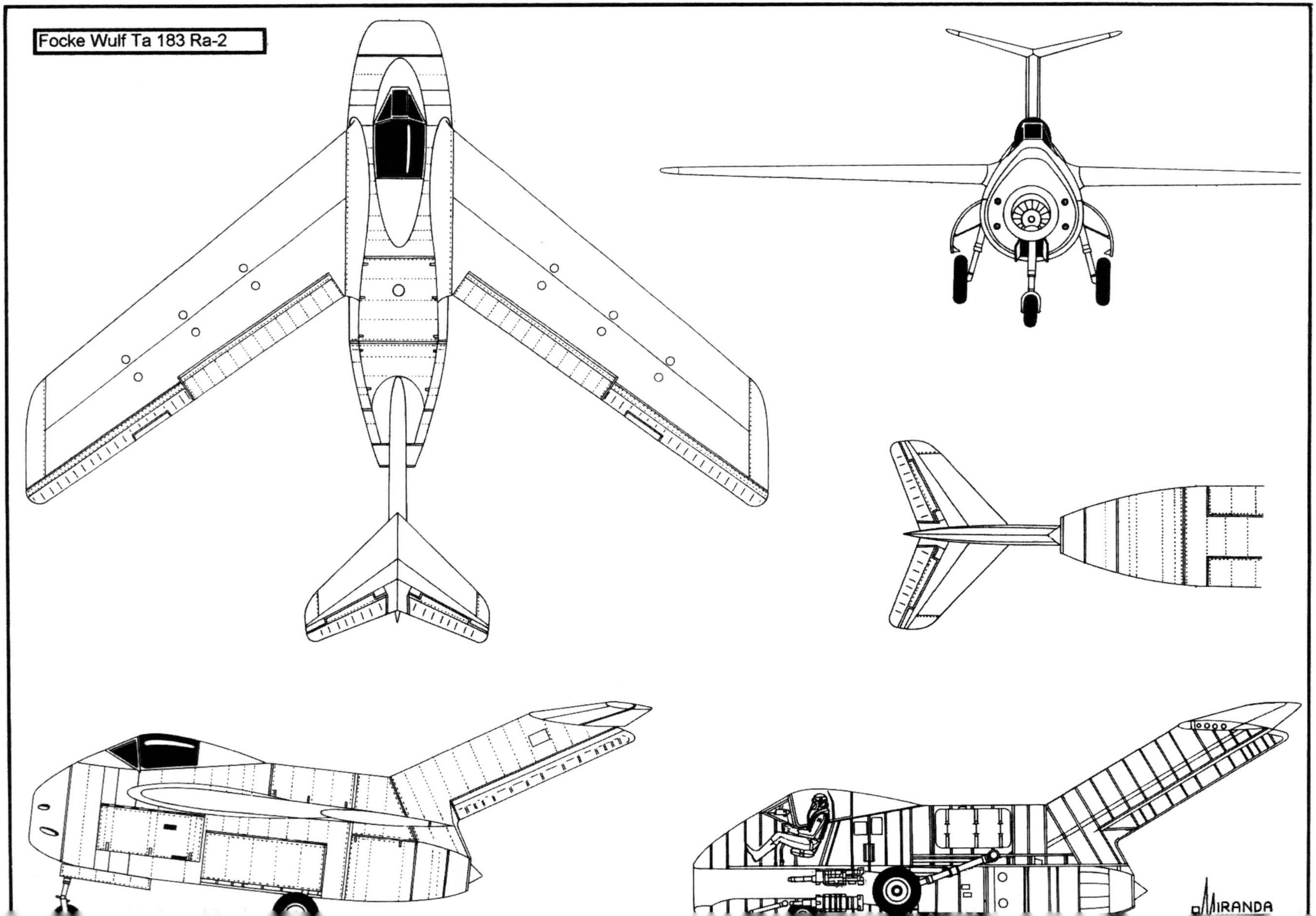
Focke Wulf Ta 183 Ra-2
MIRANDA

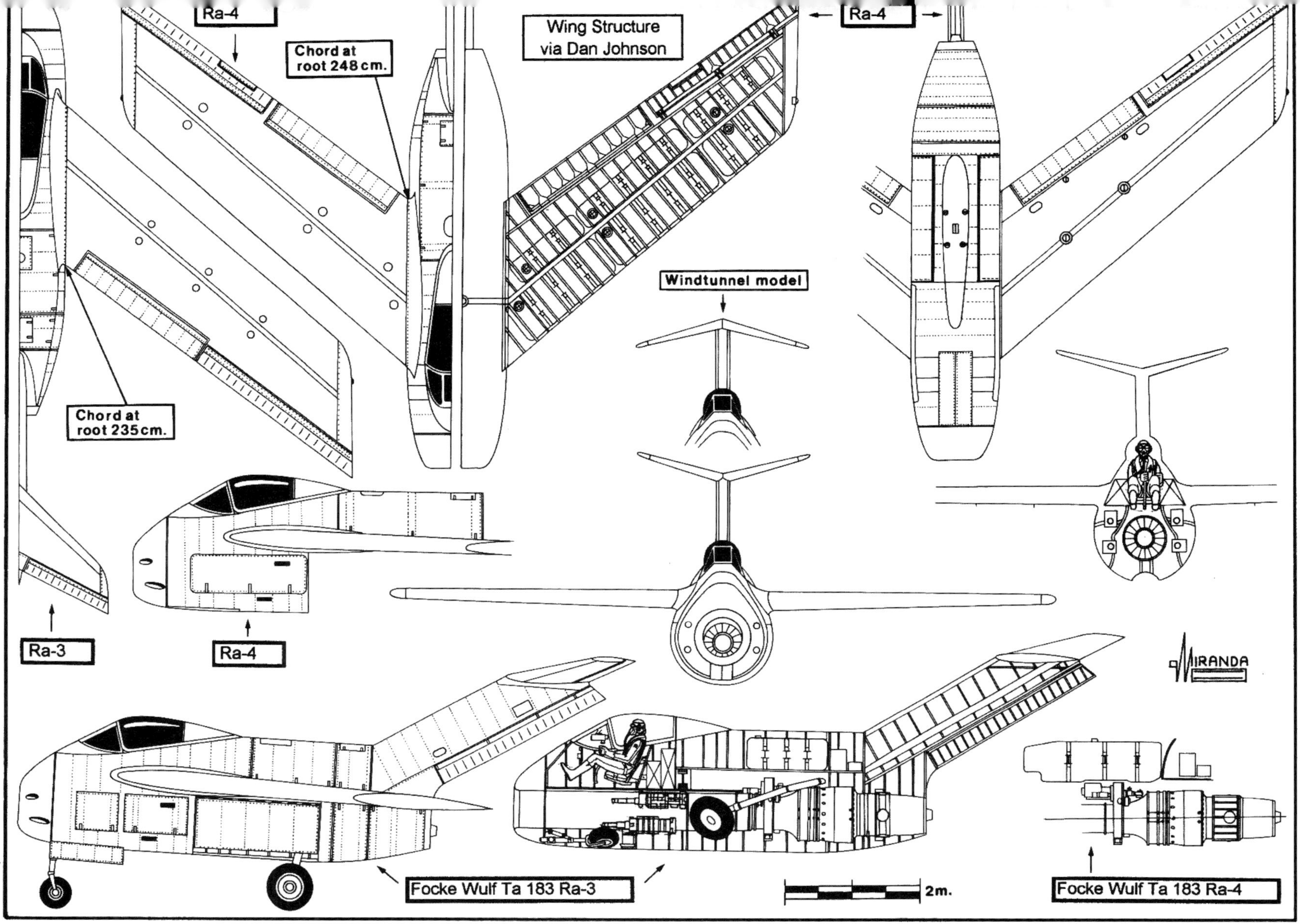
Ra-4
Chord at root 248 cm.
Wing Structure via Dan Johnson
Ra-4
Windtunnel model
Chord at root 235 cm.
Ra-3
Ra-4
MIRANDA
Focke Wulf Ta 183 Ra-3
2m.
Focke Wulf Ta 183 Ra-4

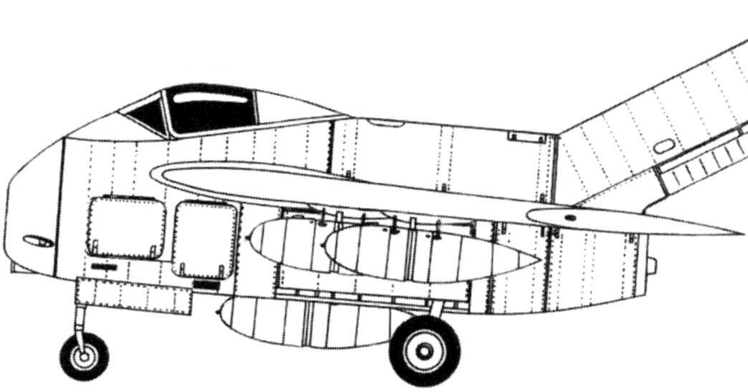

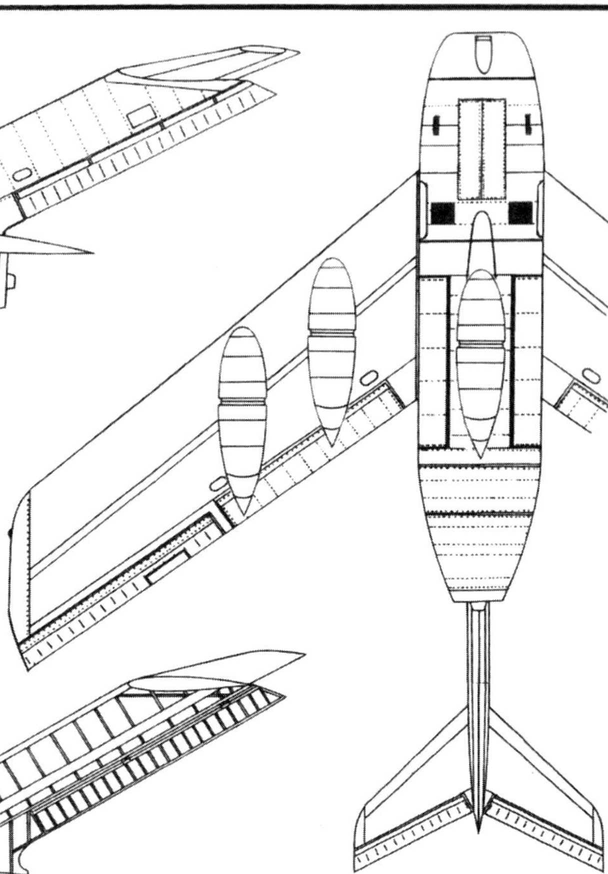

SPECULATIVE DRAWINGS

Ta 183 R
Reconnaissance Aircraft

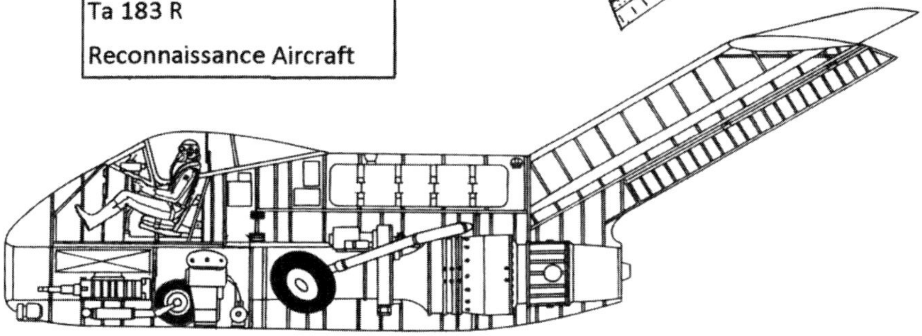

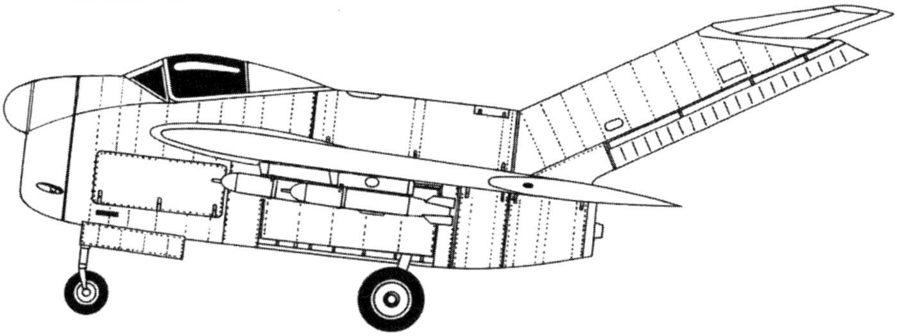

Ta 183 N with FuG 248 radar and 4 x R100BS rockets

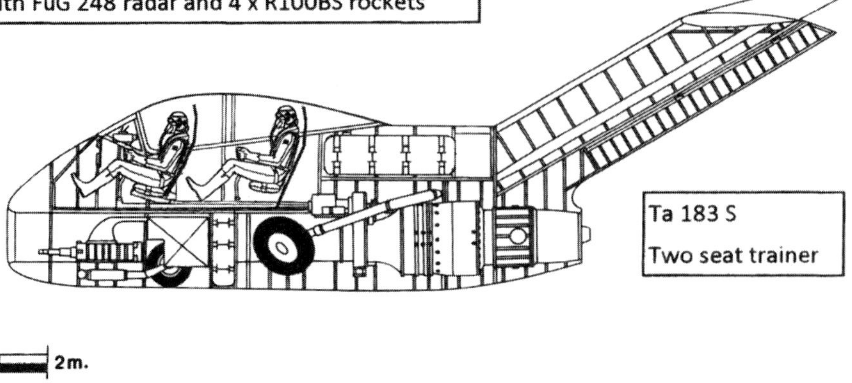

Ta 183 S
Two seat trainer

2m.

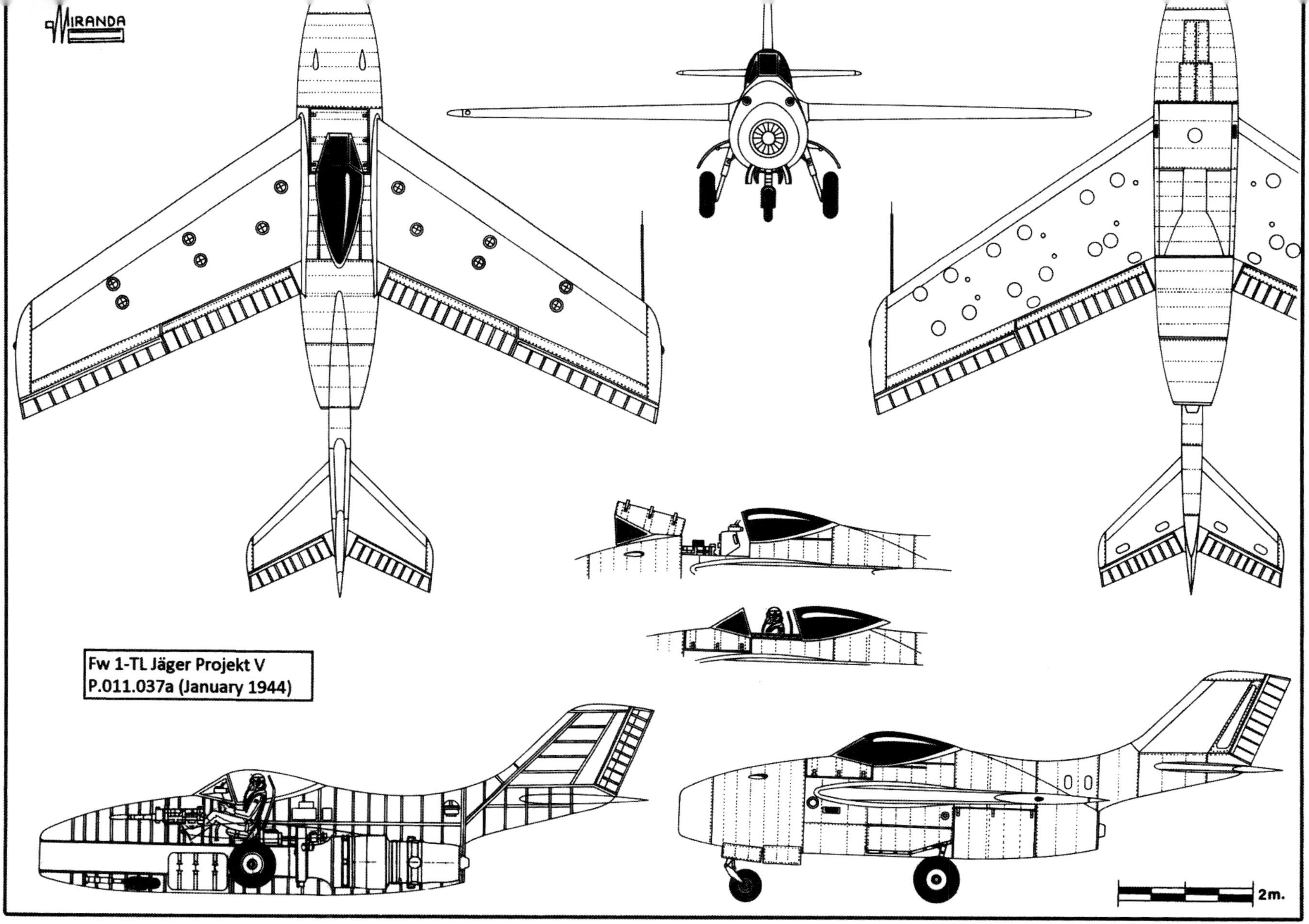

Fw 1-TL Jäger Projekt V
P.011.037a (January 1944)

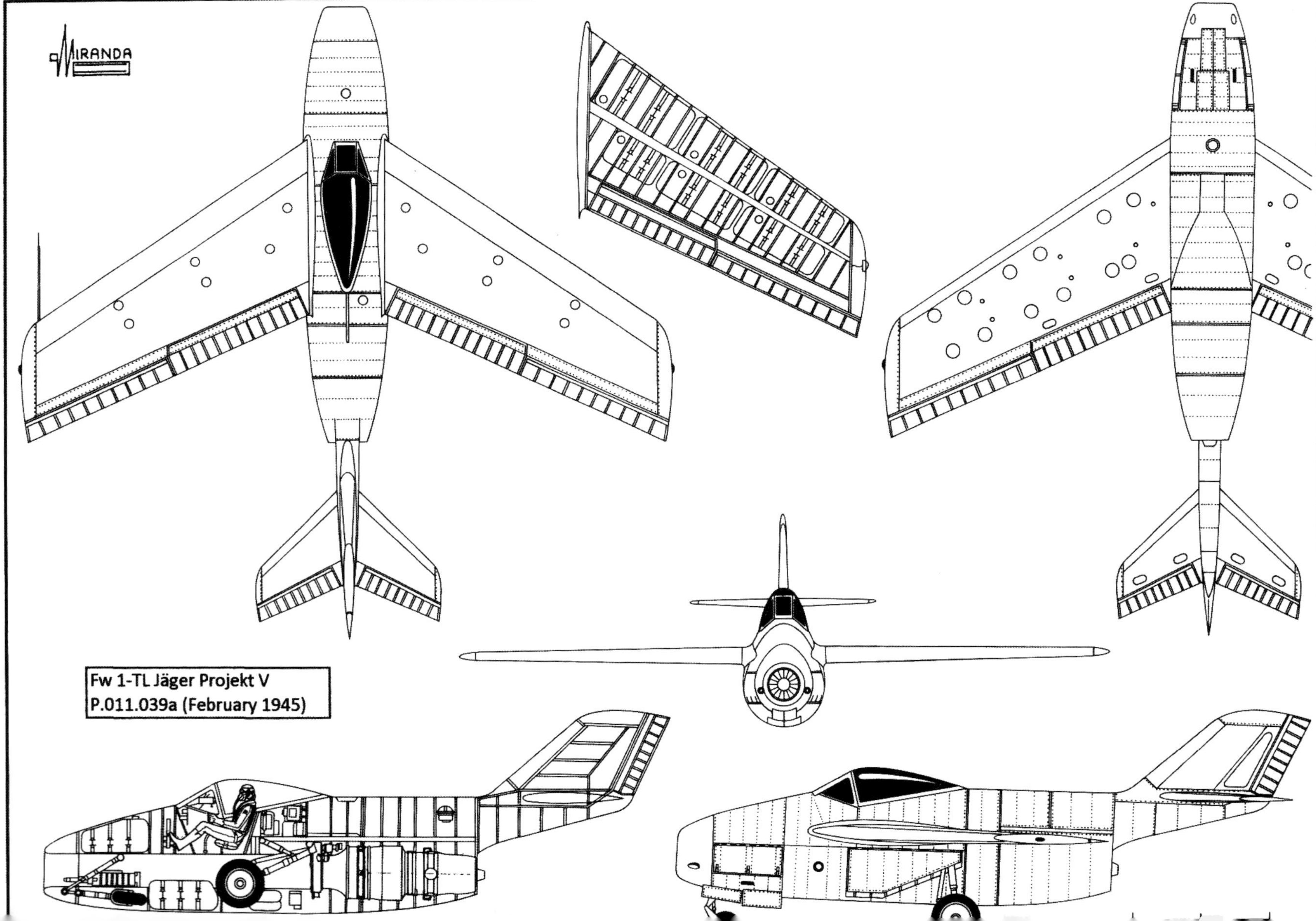

Fw 1-TL Jäger Projekt V
P.011.039a (February 1945)

EVOLUTION

Fw 1-TL Jäger Projekt I

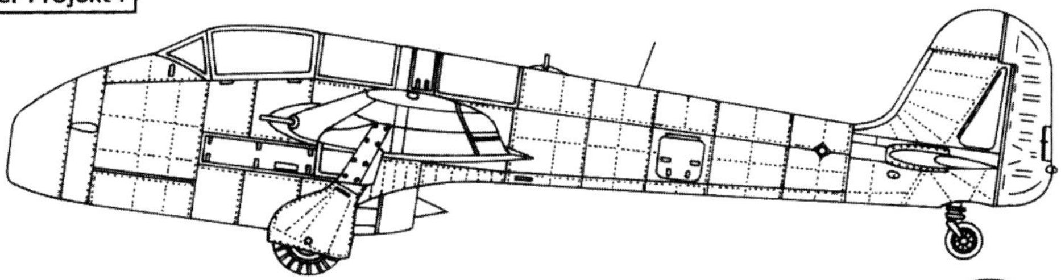

Fw 1-TL Jäger Projekt II

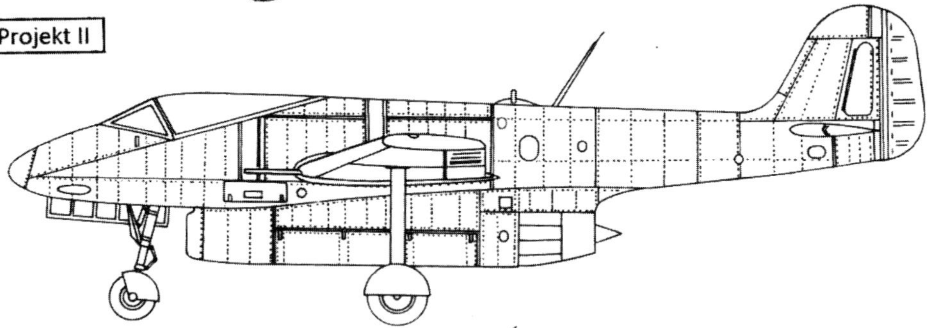

Fw 1-TL Jäger Projekt III

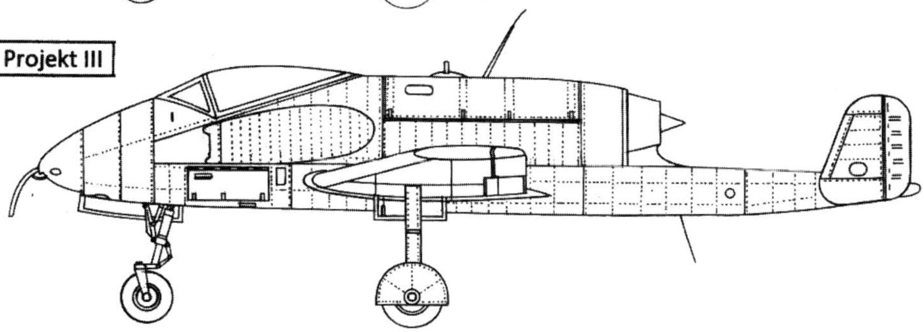

Fw 1-TL Jäger Projekt IV

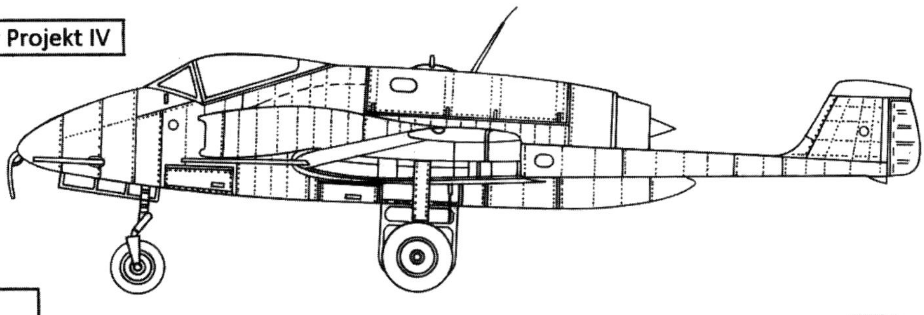

Projekt
P.011.001
January 1944

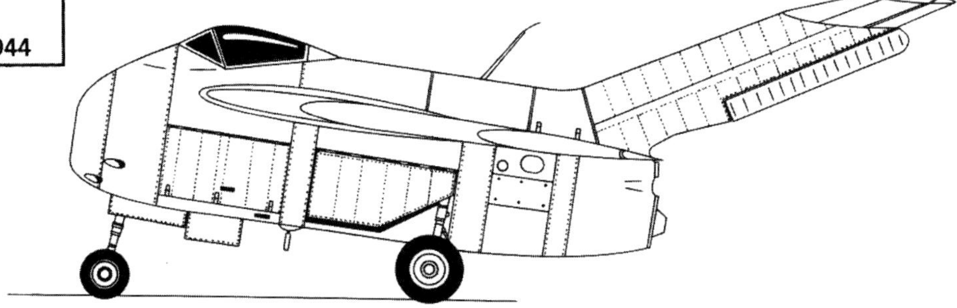

2m.

MIRANDA

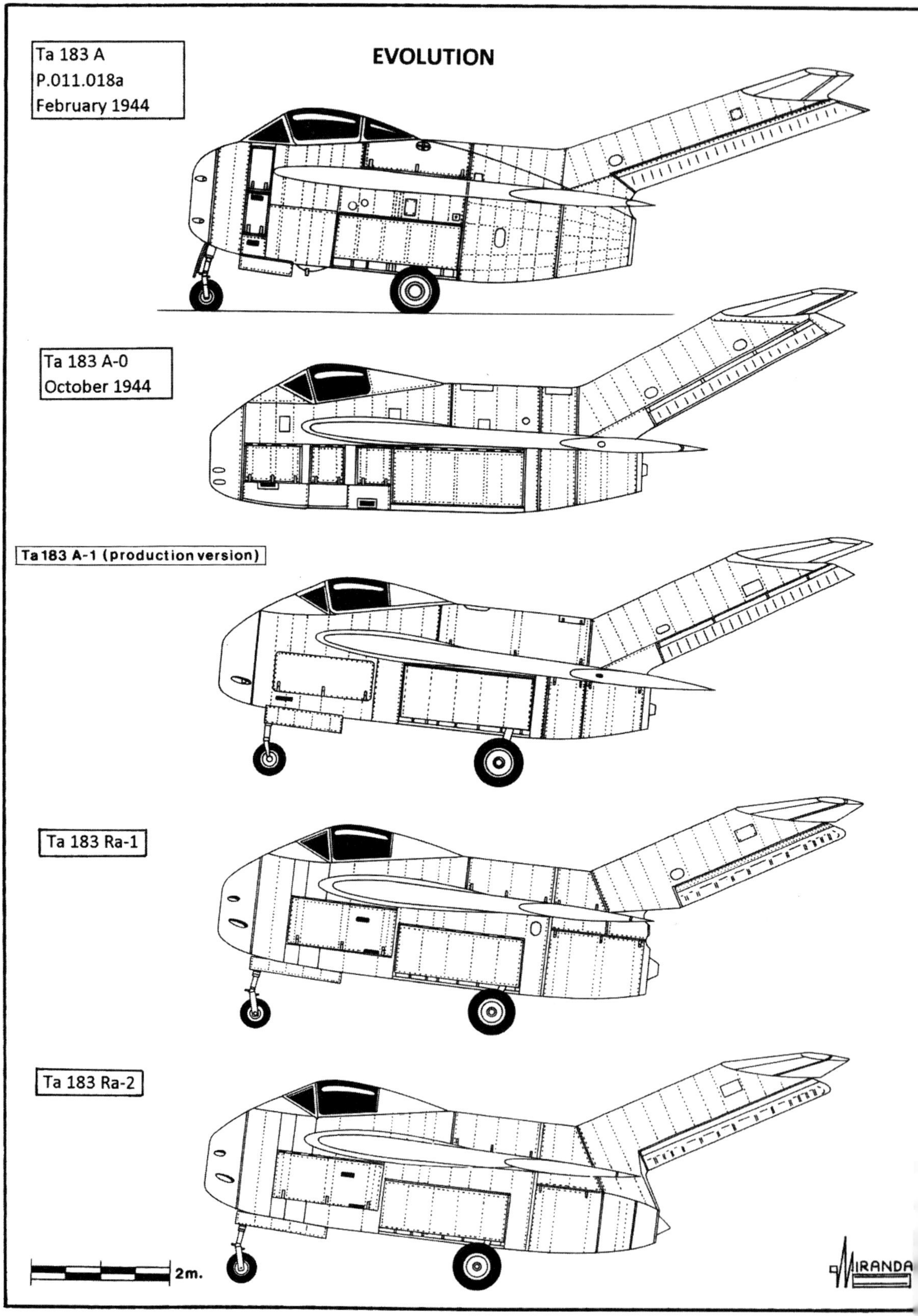
EVOLUTION
Ta 183 A
P.011.018a
February 1944
Ta 183 A-0
October 1944
Ta 183 A-1 (production version)
Ta 183 Ra-1
Ta 183 Ra-2
2m.
MIRANDA

EVOLUTION

Ta 183 Ra-3

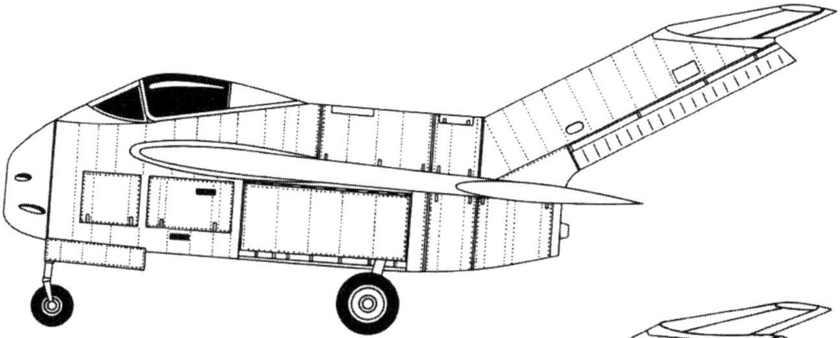

Ta 183 R
Reconnaissance Aircraft

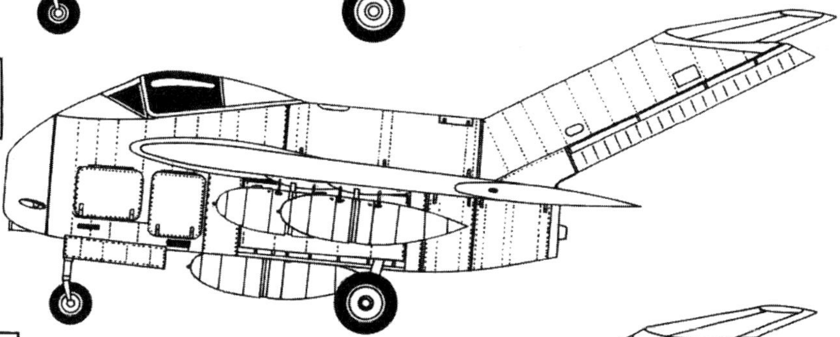

Ta 183 N with FuG 248 radar

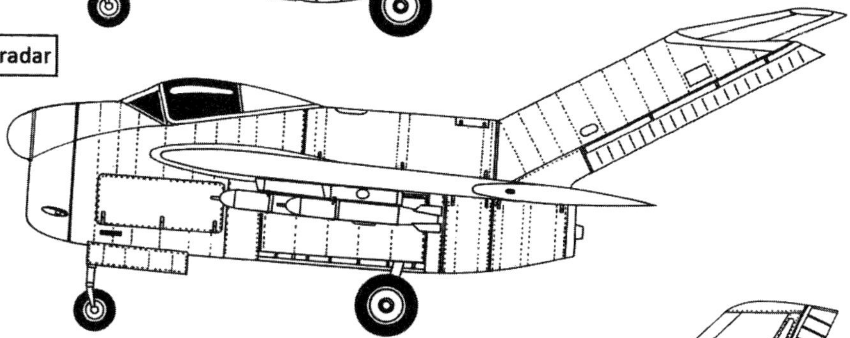

Fw 1-TL Jäger Projekt V
P.011.037a (January 1944)

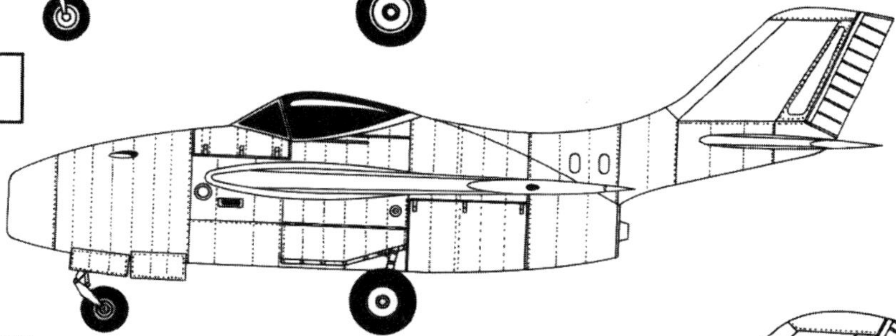

Fw 1-TL Jäger Projekt V
P.011.039a (February 1945)

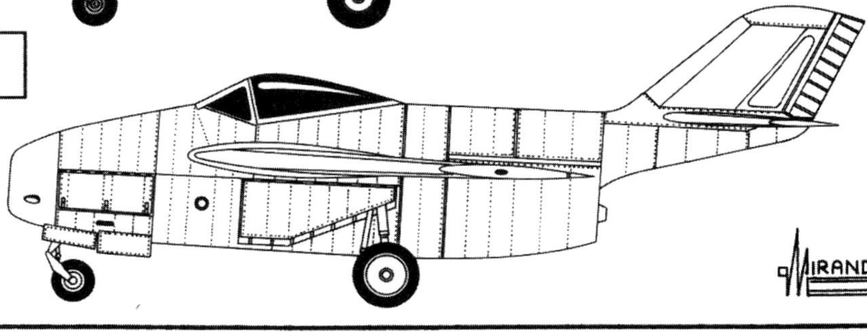

2m.

MIRANDA

Messerschmitt P1101
Experimentation Aircraft
with a T-shaped tailplane
end of 1944

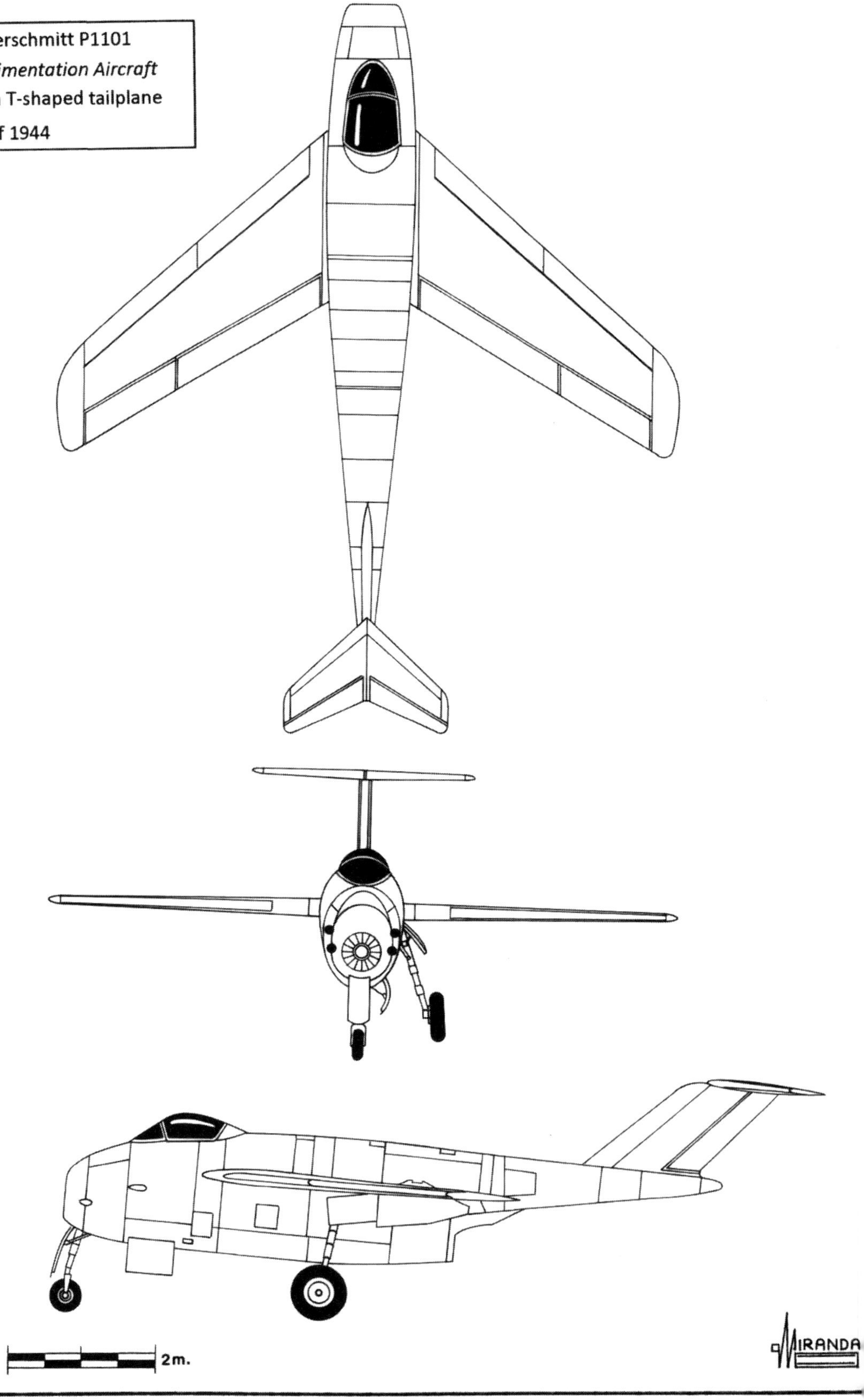

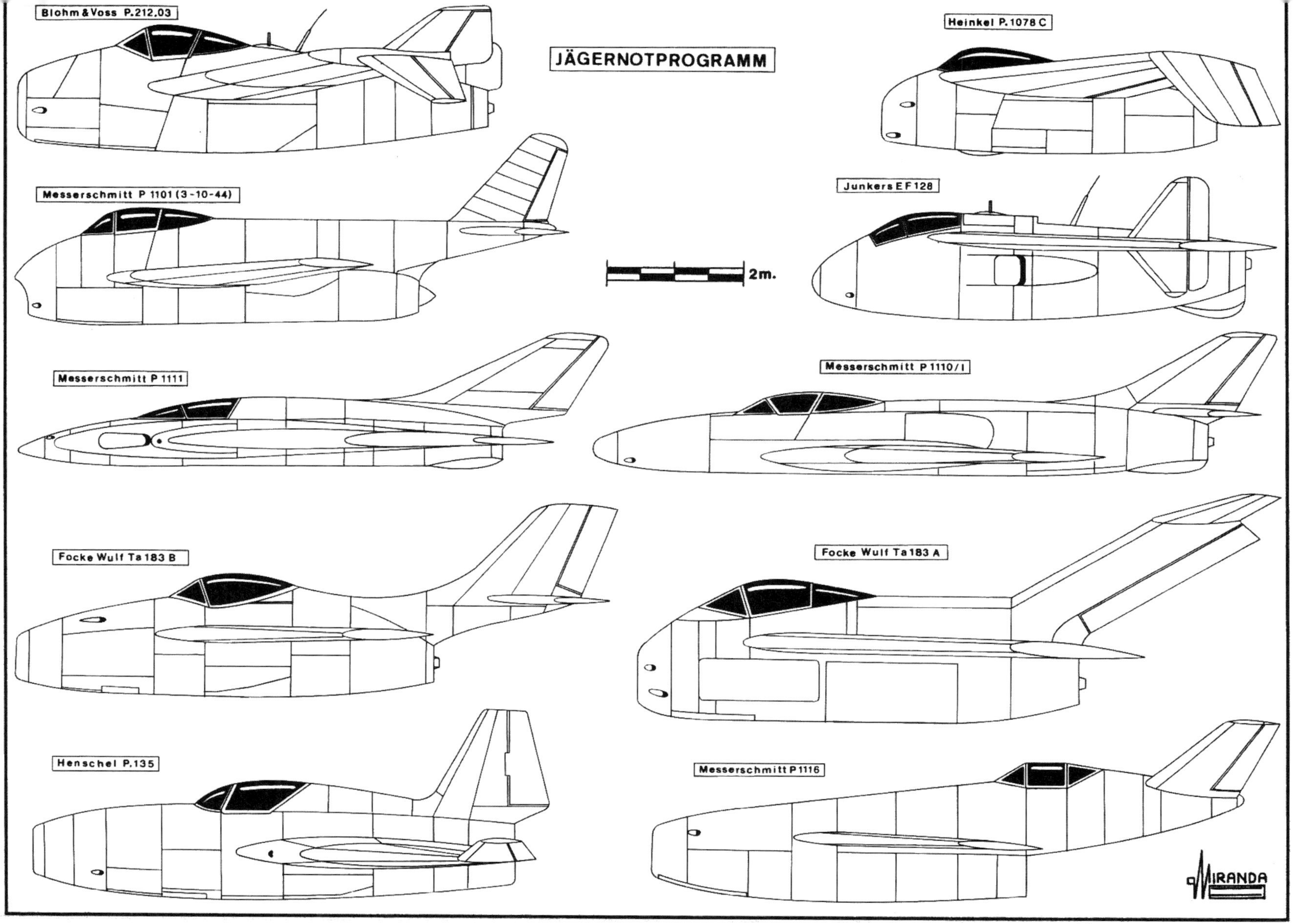
JÄGERNOTPROGRAMM
Blohm & Voss P.212.03
Heinkel P.1078 C
Messerschmitt P 1101 (3-10-44)
Junkers EF 128
2m.
Messerschmitt P 1111
Messerschmitt P 1110/I
Focke Wulf Ta 183 B
Focke Wulf Ta 183 A
Henschel P.135
Messerschmitt P 1116
MIRANDA

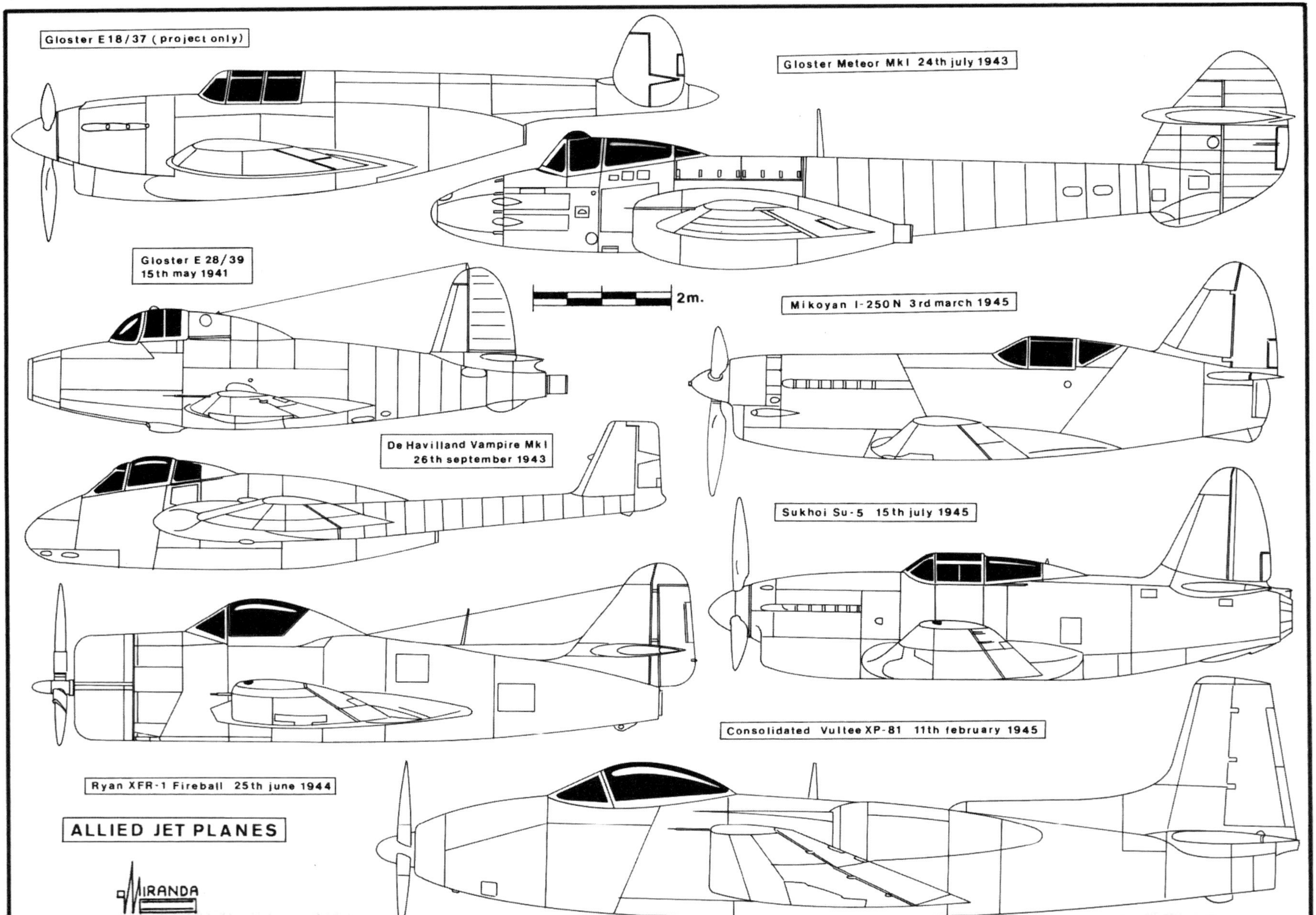

ALLIED JET PLANES

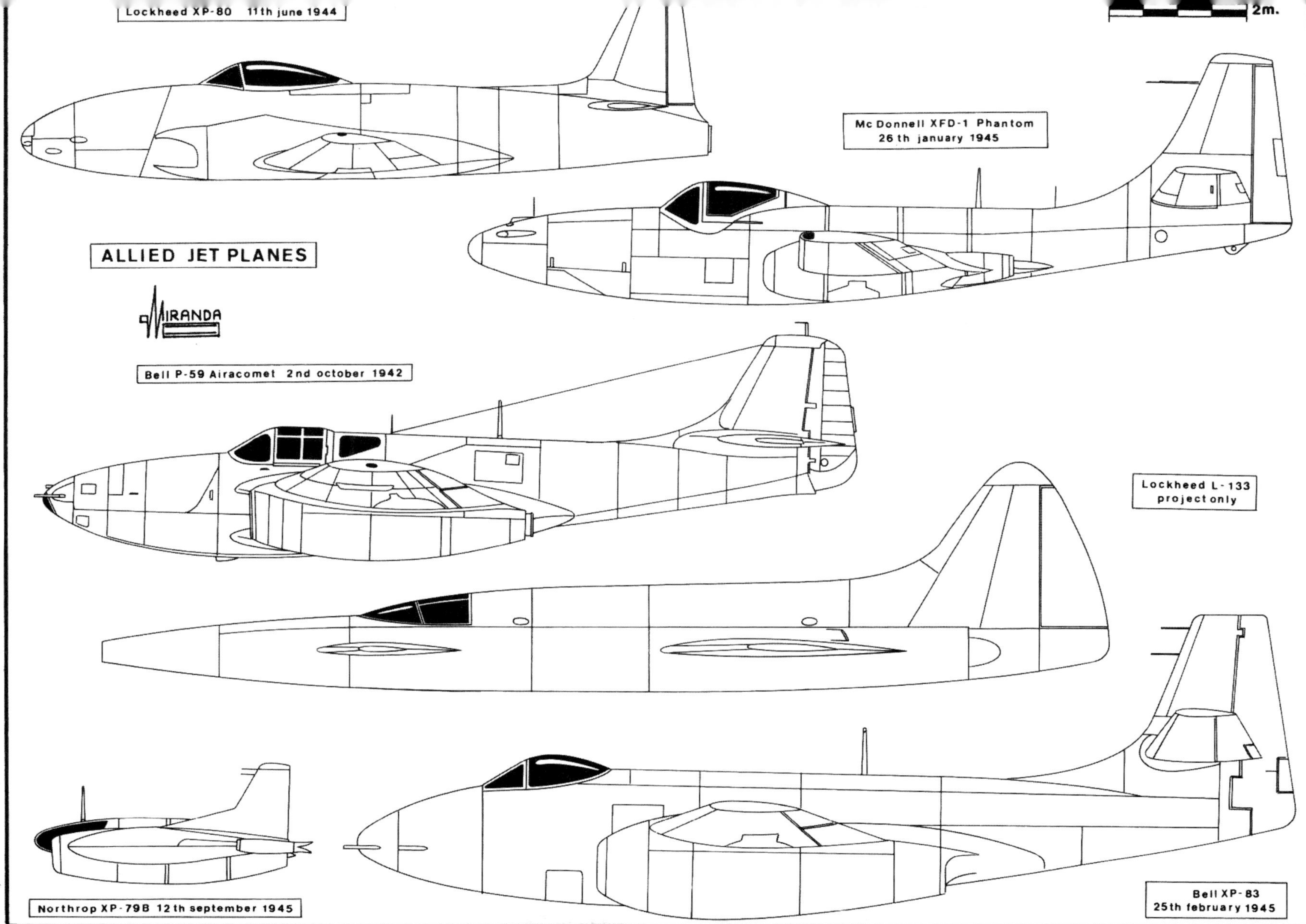
Lockheed XP-80 11th june 1944
2m.
Mc Donnell XFD-1 Phantom 26 th january 1945
ALLIED JET PLANES
MIRANDA
Bell P-59 Airacomet 2nd october 1942
Lockheed L-133 project only
Northrop XP-79B 12th september 1945
Bell XP-83 25th february 1945

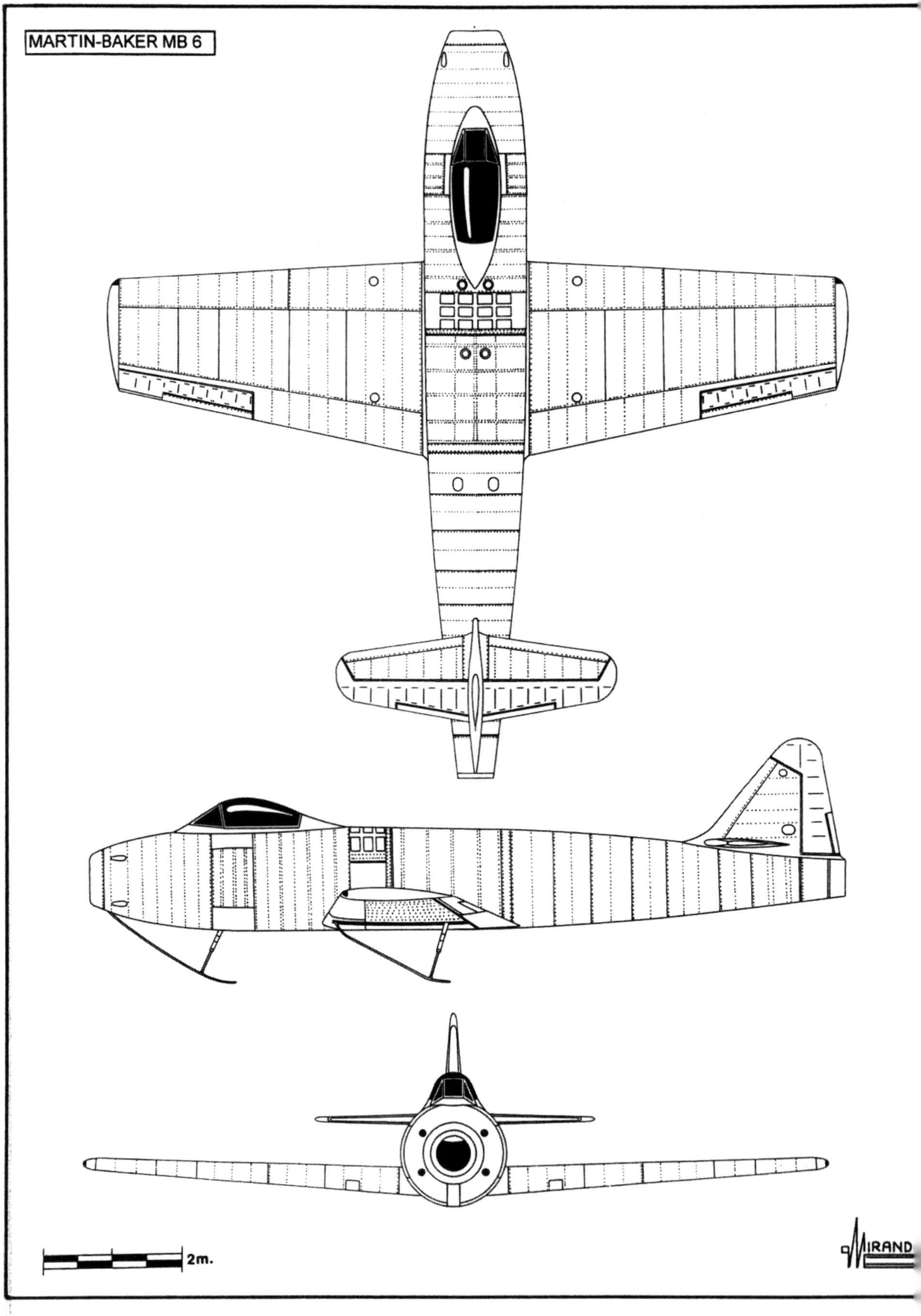
MARTIN-BAKER MB 6
2m.
MIRAND

8

Focke-Wulf 1-TLR *Jäger Projekt VI*

Anticipating that the *Technisches Amt* would reject Baubeschreibung Nr. 279 (Proposal P.011.001) because of its T-tail configuration, Kurt Tank proposed to the RLM the construction of a more conservative, twin-boom design fighter called the Flitzer (1 February 1944).

The Flitzer was described in the Baubeschreibung Nr. 280 dossier as an air-superiority *Moskitojäger*, with turbojet and rocket mixed power plant, which could be constructed using a mixture of 52 per cent steel, 45 per cent light alloy, and 3 per cent plastics. Its estimated performances were slightly higher than the T-tail design, with an initial rate of climb of 18.2 m/sec, an absolute ceiling of 13,000 m, and a maximum speed of 955 kph.

The wing span was only 8 m, with wing area reduced to 15.5 sq. m and the height to 2.35 m. The twin-boom formula required an increase of the overall length up to 10.55 m to maintain longitudinal stability. The wings, newly designed and with a 3.77: 1 aspect ratio, had a 280-cm chord at the root, 29 degrees swept at the leading edge, and 4 degrees swept at the trailing edge. They were fitted with fixed leading-edge slots, split flaps, and double ailerons to optimise roll rate at different speeds. Each wing panel housed one fuel tank with 210 litres of K1 heavy kerosene, one landing gear leg with a 240 × 210 wheel, one MK 108/30 cannon with sixty rounds, and one air intake/air duct ensemble.

The fuselage had a design like that of *Projekt IV*. It housed the nose leg, with a 560 × 200 wheel, the pressurised cockpit with standard armour, seat ejector and Revi 16C gunsight, two MK 151/20 rapid-fire cannon with 175 rounds each, two T-Stoff rocket propellant tanks with 560 and 350 litres (sufficient for 400 seconds of powered flight), one Heinkel HeS 011A turbojet with 1,115 kp static thrust, one Walter 109-509 B-0 bi-propellant rocket with 350 kp peak thrust, one FuG 15ZY, and one IFF transponder FuG 25a.

For safety reasons, the rocket propellant C-Stoff was stored in the tail-booms, in two 160-litre tanks. The estimated range, with 1,071 litres of rocket propellants and 420 litres of K1, was 890 km, with a maximum take-off weight of 4,750 kg. The estimated maximum speed was 810 kph, using only the turbojet. The Mauser MG

151/20 were very effective against Tempests and Thunderbolts, but they lacked the punch needed to destroy a four-engine heavy bomber.

In February 1944, the Fw 190 A-6 of the *Sturmstaffel I*, armed with four MG 151/20 rapid-fire cannon, were forced to perform risky head-on passes against the B-17 and B-24, trying to achieve some hits in the cockpit or in the unprotected engines (the only places where the low destructive capacity of the 20-mm ammunition could achieve results). In April, the new Fw 190 A-7/R2 of the 5/JG1 was armed with 30-mm Rheinmetall-Borsig MK 108 cannon, a weapon capable of destroying a heavy bomber with only five impacts of its powerful ammunition 30 × 90RB of the Minengeschoß class. However, the MK 108 had prematurely entered into service, with a low effective range and high dispersion fire factor that forced the *Sturmjägern* to shoot from less than 100 m from the target to obtain results.

There was another 30-mm cannon that used a much more powerful 30 × 184B type munition, with a muzzle velocity that doubled to that of the MK 108 and an effective range of 1,000 m. It was the Rheinmetall-Borsig MK 103, derived from an anti-tank cannon, which was very difficult to integrate into the single engine fighters because of its powerful recoil and its weight, equivalent to three MK 108.

On 20 June 1944, Kurt Tank proposed to the RLM the construction of a *Zerstörer* version called *Flitzer II*. Basically, it was the same airframe armed with two MK 103/30 in the nose. The main modification consisted of reducing the amount of rocket propellants to only 663 litres, enough for 250 seconds of powered flight, and extending the wing area up to 17 sq. m and the wing chord at the root up to 307 cm, with the trailing edge sweep angle being decreased by one degree. The estimated range was reduced to only 570 km but was considered sufficient for the defence of important targets.

Each wing panel contained 210 litres of K1 and a MG 151/20 cannon with 350 rounds. The two MK 103/30s were installed under the cockpit floor, with eighty rounds per gun. The Revi 16C gunsight was replaced by a Zeiss ZFR 4a *Zielfernrohr* (telescopic gunsight). The fuselage housed a tank with 560 litres of T-Stoff and another with 330 litres of K1. The C-Stoff was reduced to 100 litres, and was stored in the twin-booms.

The new turbojet proposed for this version was a HeS 011 A-0 with 1,300 kp static thrust and the rocket engine, a HWK 109-509 B-1 with 400 kp peak thrust. The take-off weight was increased by 100 kg and the absolute ceiling up to 13,800 m due to the increase in power and the modification of the wings. The maximum speed, with turbojet only, was estimated of 830 kph; with both engines, this was 965 kph.

Flitzer II was proposed to the RLM as a conservative alternative to the Ta 183 A (P.011.018a), although neither project was sufficiently advanced to reach the production phase. In July, a good opportunity was presented with the publication of the *Jägernotprogramm* contest and the firm Focke-Wulf presented three projects: Ta 183 A, Ta 183 B, and *Flitzer III* (20 July 1944).

The latter consisted of a *Flitzer II* modified to meet the contest specifications by suppressing the rocket engine, replacing the MK 103/30 with two MK108/30 with eighty rounds per gun, and raising the capacity of the fuel tanks up to 1,000 litres of K1. The low density of the K1 compared to the rocket propellants decreased the overall weight to 3,650 kg. When using only the turbojet, the absolute ceiling fell to 13,000 m and the estimated maximum speed to 830 kph.

In September, the *Technisches Amt* decided to extend the internal fuel capacity of the *Jägernotprogramm* fighter to 1,400 litres and the designers of Bad Eilsen succeeded by installing six K1 tanks in the *Flitzer III*: two of 210 litres each in the wings, one of 480 and one of 330 litres in the fuselage, and two of 85 litres each in the tail booms. The estimated range was 1,100 km, but the excessive drag generated by the tailplane/tailfin ensemble lowered the maximum speed to a value that was unacceptable for the RLM, declaring the Ta 183 A-0 the winner of the contest.

The Flitzer project had another chance when the *Volksjäger* specification was published on 8 September. Focke-Wulf responded by presenting two projects: the *Volksflugzeug*, a simplified version of Ta 183 and the *Volksflitzer* (18 September 1944), a light version of *Flitzer I* with a maximum weight of 3,150 kg as described in the dossier Baubeschreibung Nr. *272*. The main modification consisted of reducing the wing area to 14 sq. m, reducing the chord at the root to 237 cm, and increasing the trailing edge sweep angle to 11 degrees.

The fuselage was modified to allow the installation of a turbojet BMW 109-003 A-2 with only 705 kp static thrust, eliminating one of the fuel tanks. The capacity of heavy kerosene of the type J2 was reduced to 790 litres and the range to 600 km. The lower power of the turbojet reduced the service ceiling to 10,700 m and the maximum speed to 770 kph, while the *Volksflugzeug* could fly at 820 kph with the same engine. Kurt Tank proposed to the OKL the installation of a HeS 011 A-0 that would make the *Volksflitzer* an excellent light fighter to complement the Ta 183. The new project, named *Flitzer IV*, had 1,120 litres of K1 fuel, 870 km of range, and 10,800 m of ceiling.

However, even with the higher power of HeS 011, it was estimated that the maximum speed would be the same as that of the *Volksflugzeug* powered by the BMW 003; the *Flitzer* programme was definitively cancelled on 3 October 1944.

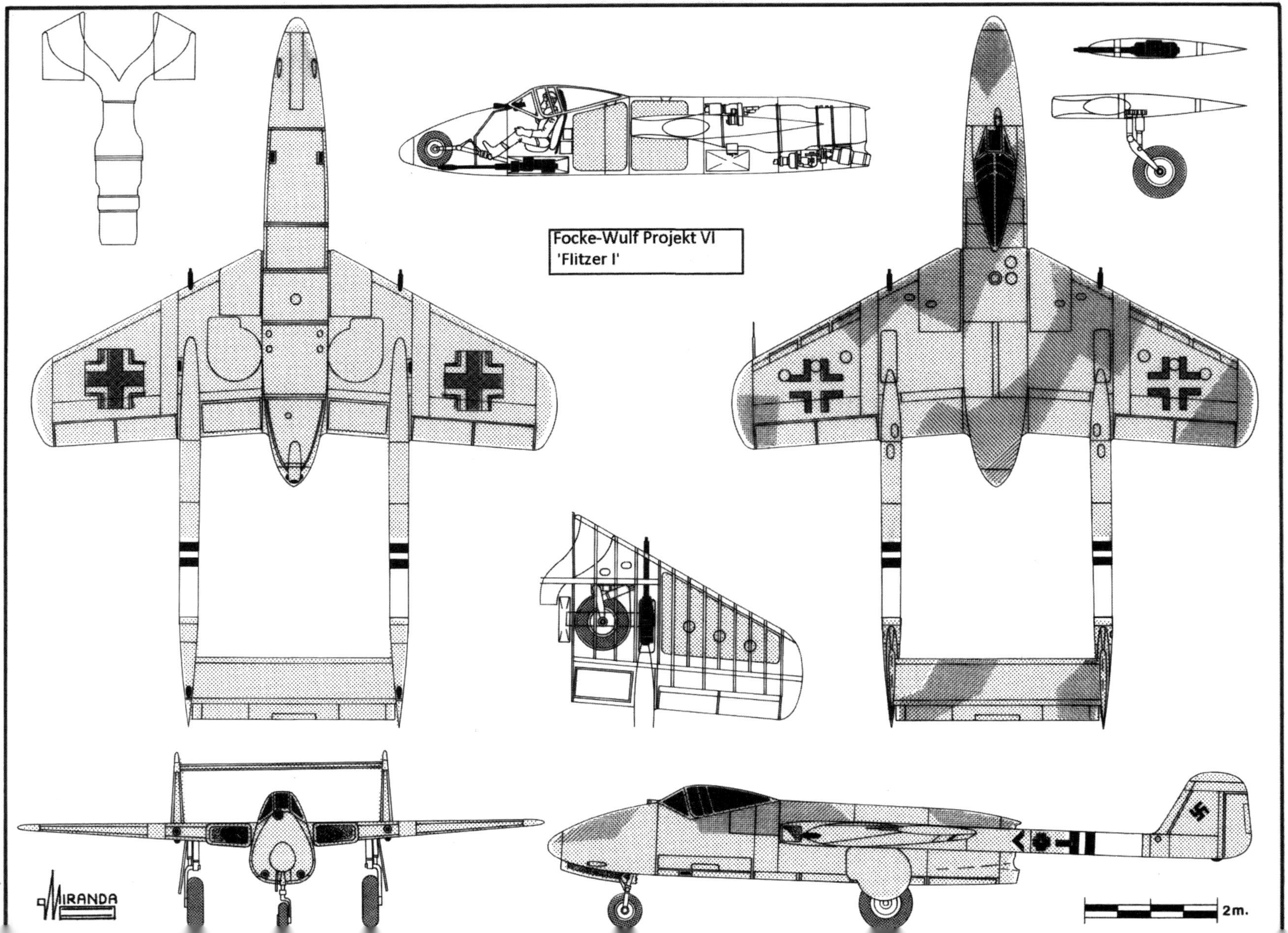

Focke-Wulf Projekt VI
'Flitzer I'
2m.
MIRANDA

Focke-Wulf Projekt VI

Flitzer III July 20, 1944

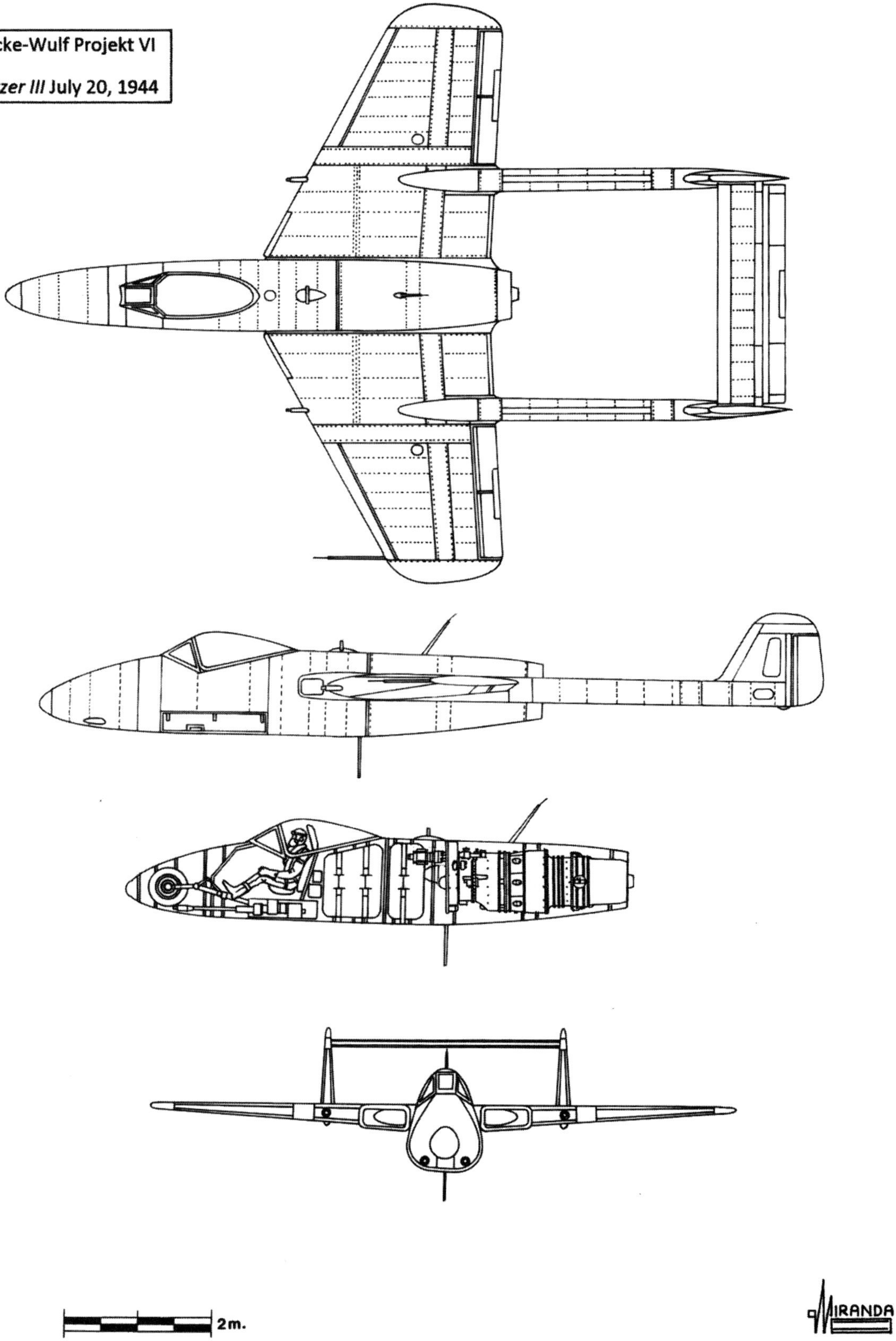

Focke-Wulf Projekt VI

Flitzer IV September 8, 1944

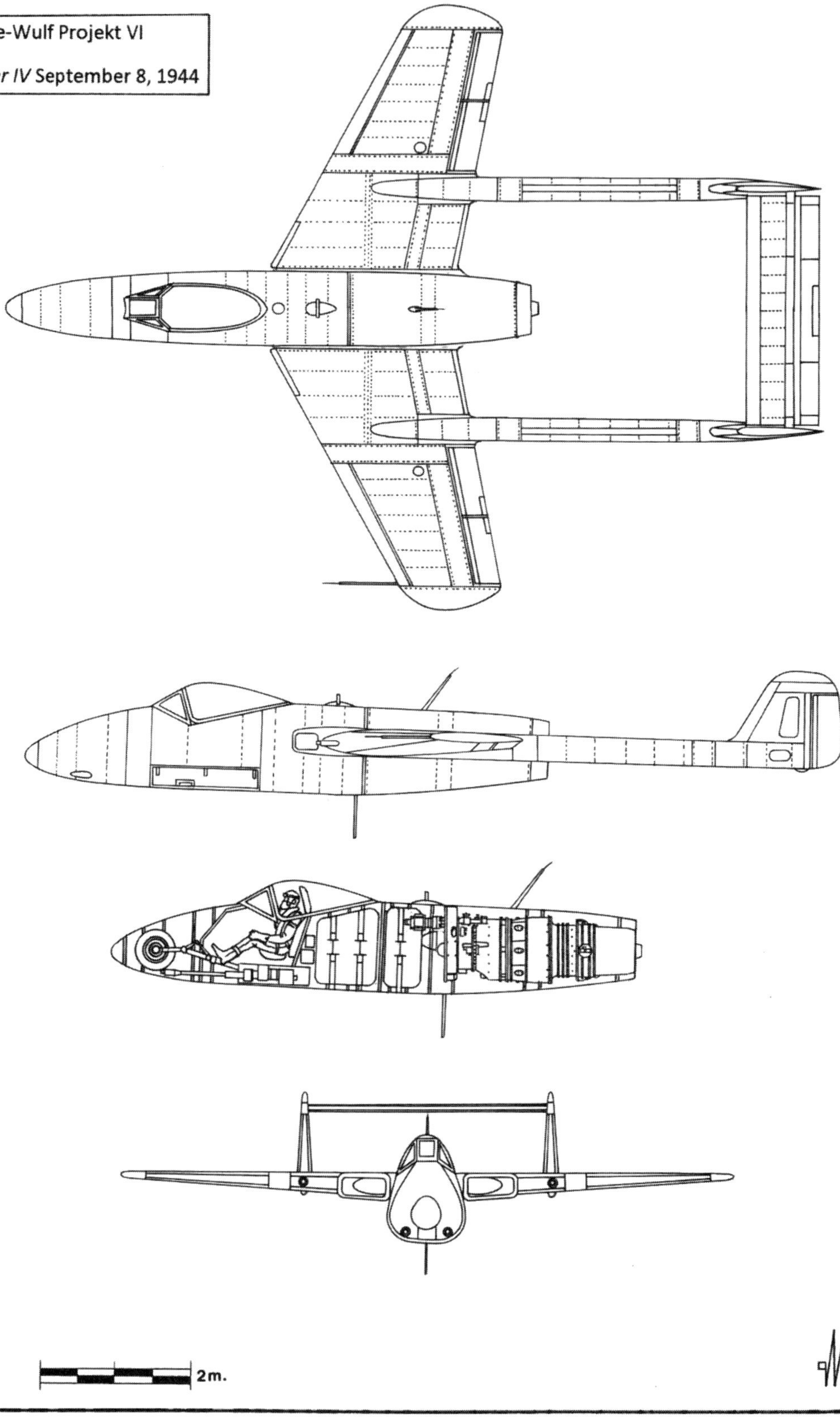

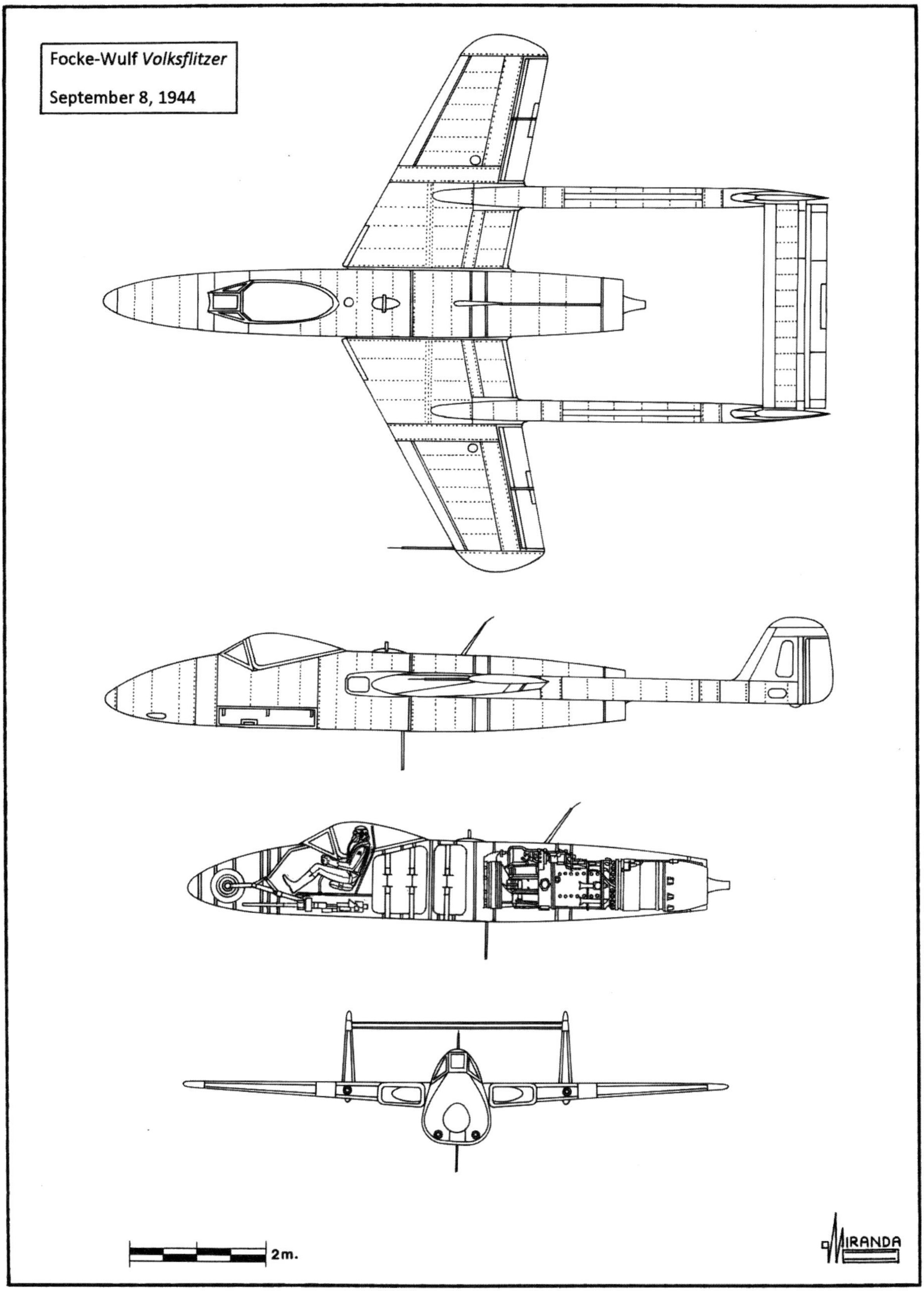
Focke-Wulf *Volksflitzer*
September 8, 1944
2m.
MIRANDA

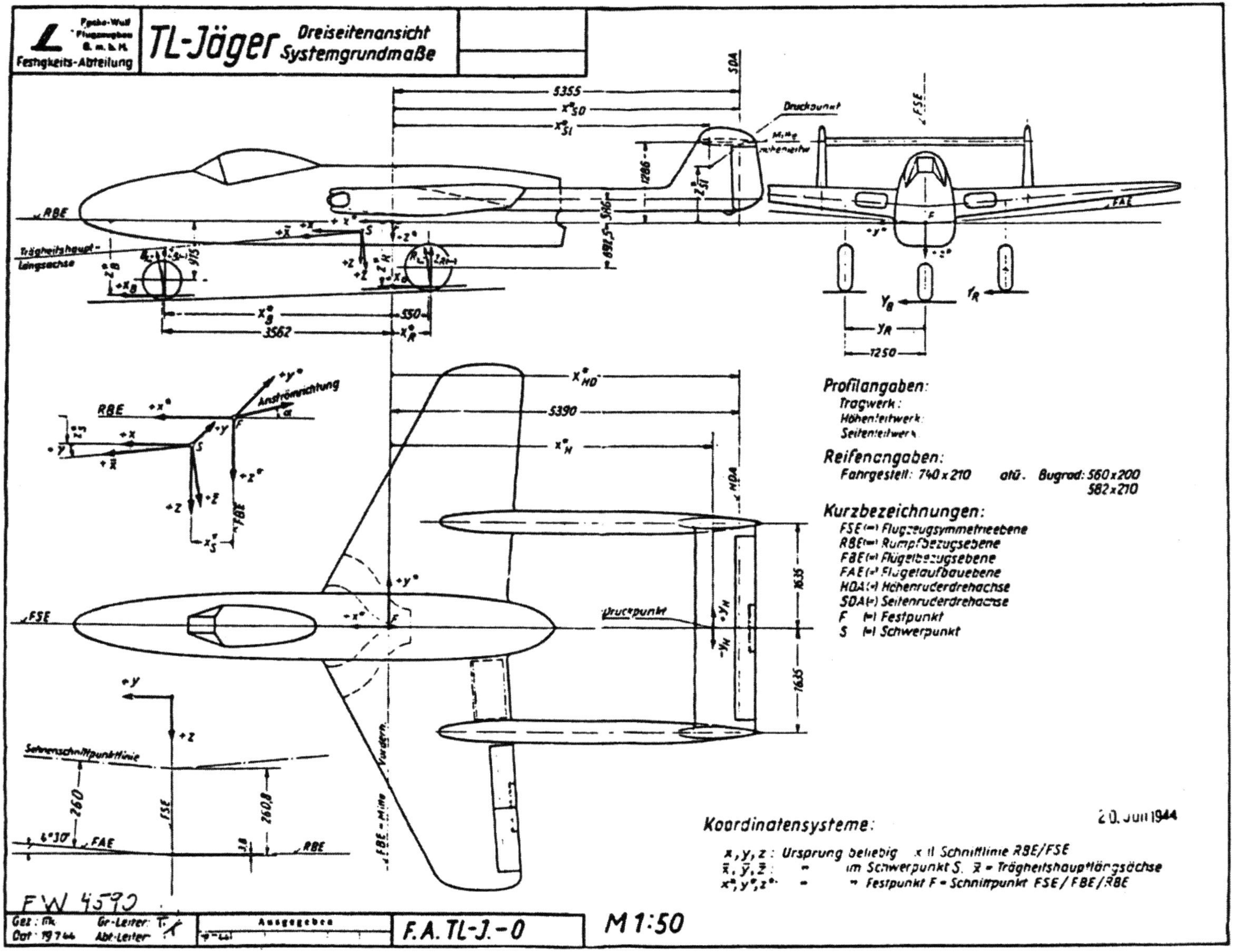
Focke-Wulf Flugzeugbau G.m.b.H.
Festigkeits-Abteilung
TL-Jäger Dreiseitenansicht Systemgrundmaße
Profilangaben:
Tragwerk:
Höhenleitwerk:
Seitenleitwerk:
Reifenangaben:
Fahrgestell: 740 x 210 alü. Bugrad: 560 x 200
582 x 210
Kurzbezeichnungen:
FSE (=) Flugzeugsymmetrieebene
RBE (=) Rumpfbezugsebene
FBE (=) Flügelbezugsebene
FAE (=) Flügelaufbauebene
HDA (=) Höhenruderdrehachse
SDA (=) Seitenruderdrehachse
F (=) Festpunkt
S (=) Schwerpunkt
Koordinatensysteme:
x, y, z : Ursprung beliebig x ‖ Schnittlinie RBE/FSE
x̄, ȳ, z̄ : " im Schwerpunkt S, x̄ = Trägheitshauptlängsachse
x°, y°, z° : " Festpunkt F = Schnittpunkt FSE/FBE/RBE
20. Juni 1944
FW 4590
F.A. TL-J.-0
M 1:50
Gez.: Mk.
Dat.: 19.7.44
Gr.-Leiter:
Abt.-Leiter:
Ausgegeben

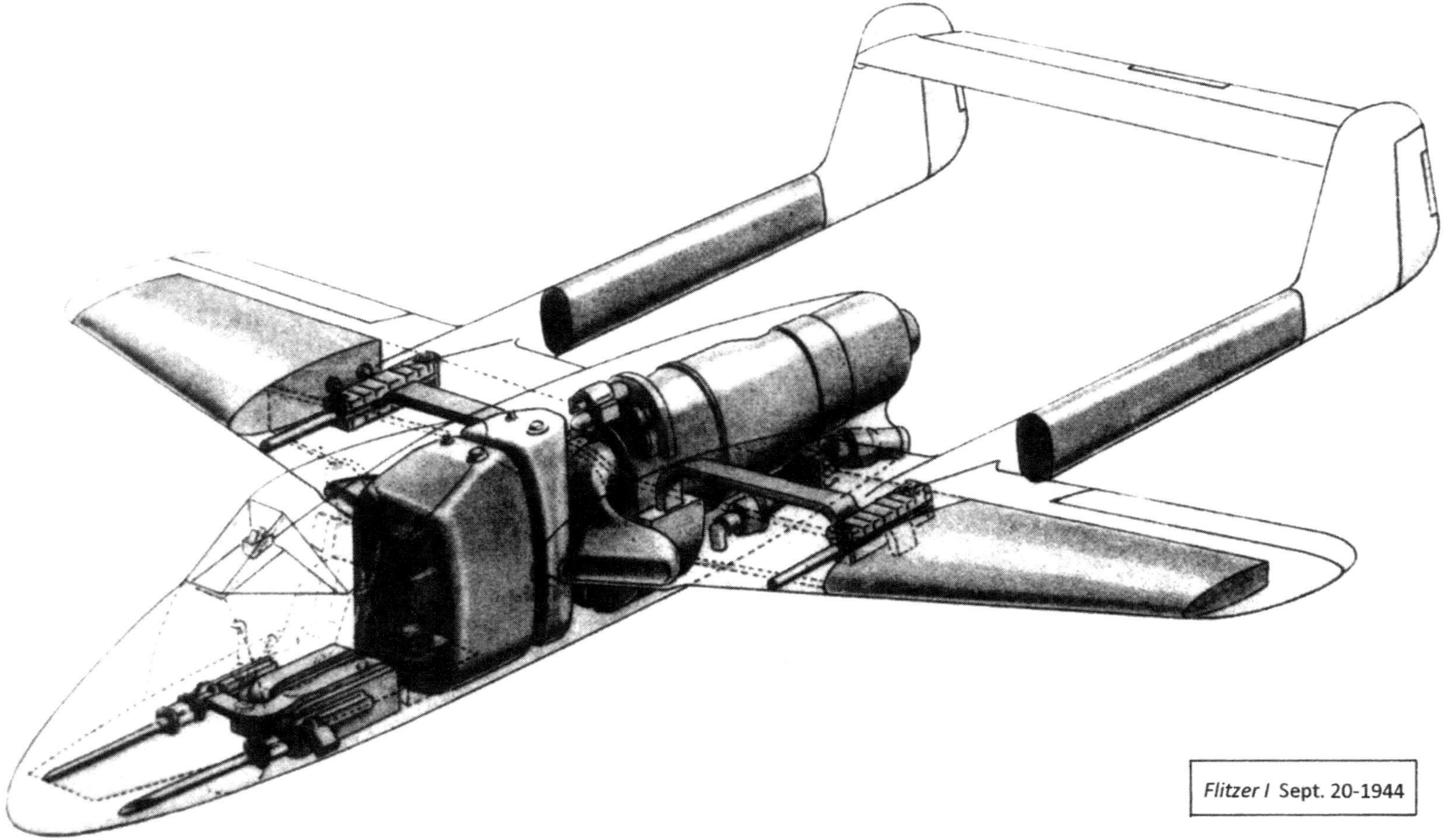

Flitzer I Sept. 20-1944

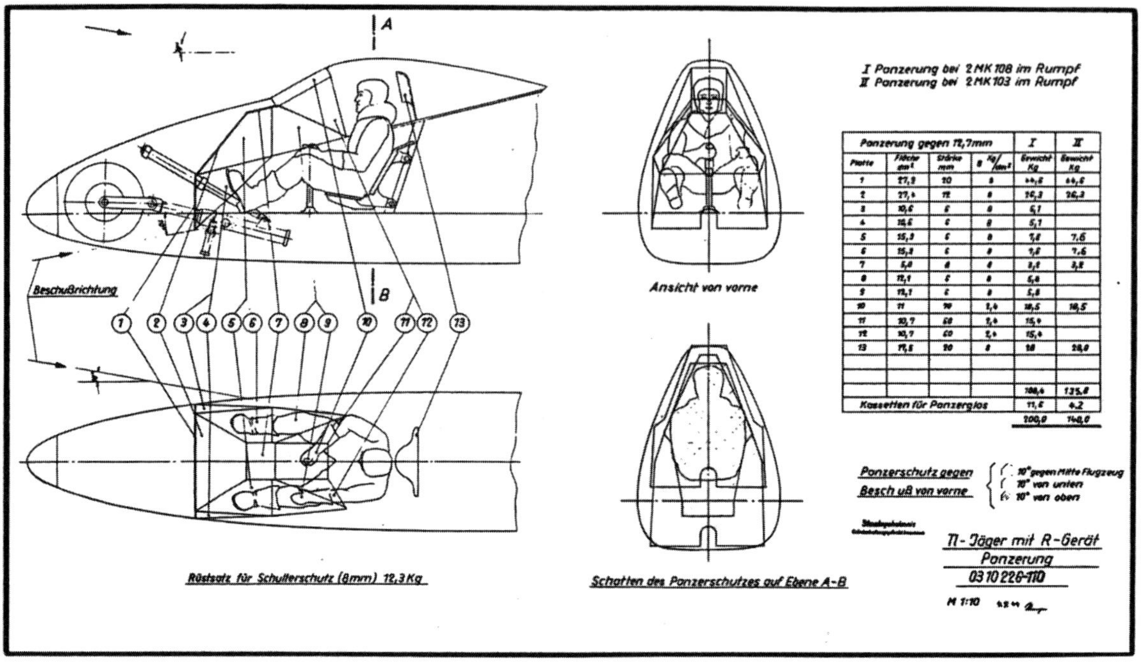

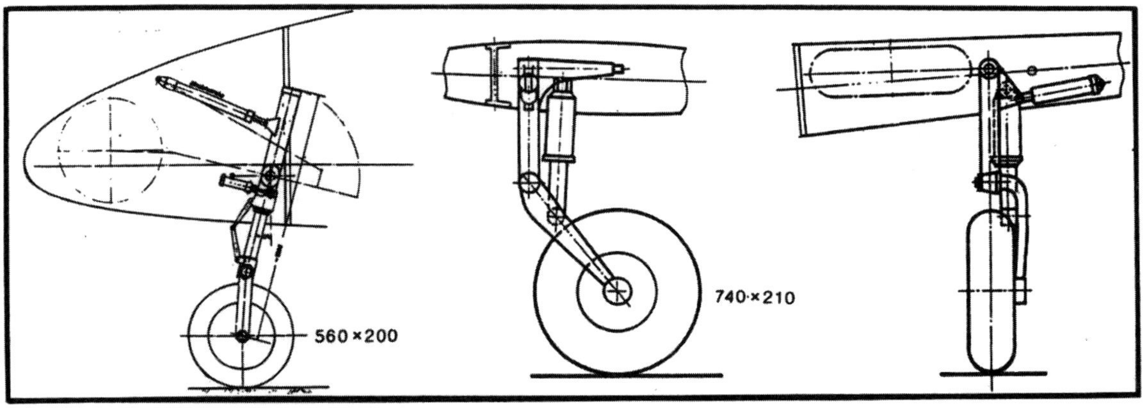

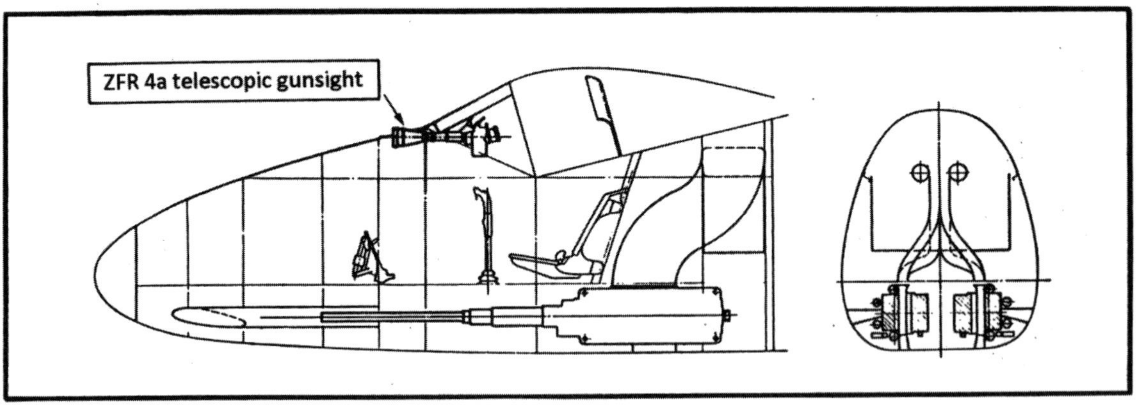

Flitzer II with 2 x 103/30 Rheinmetall cannons

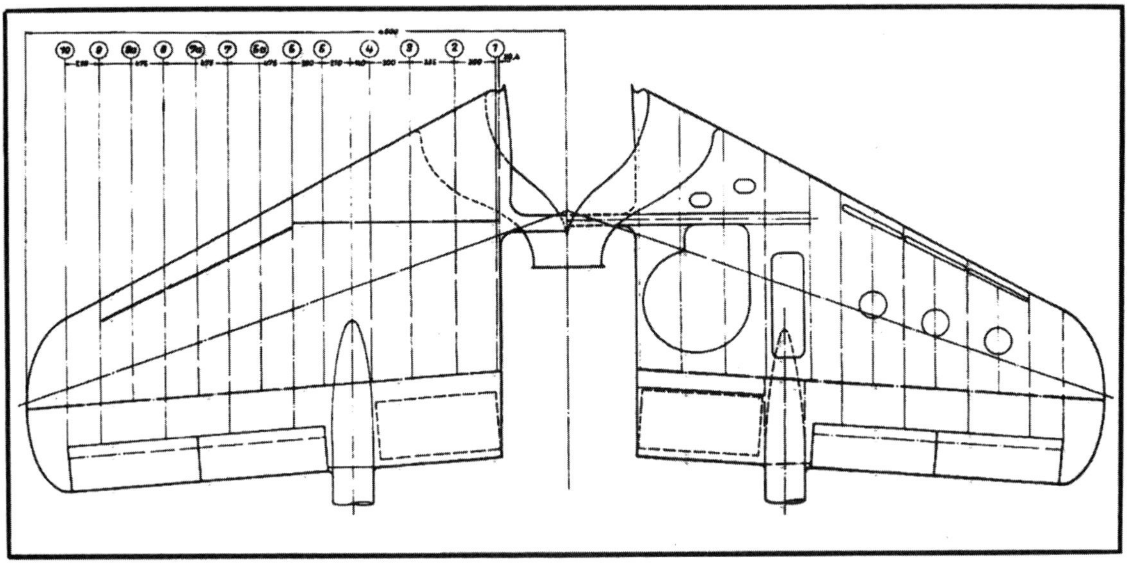

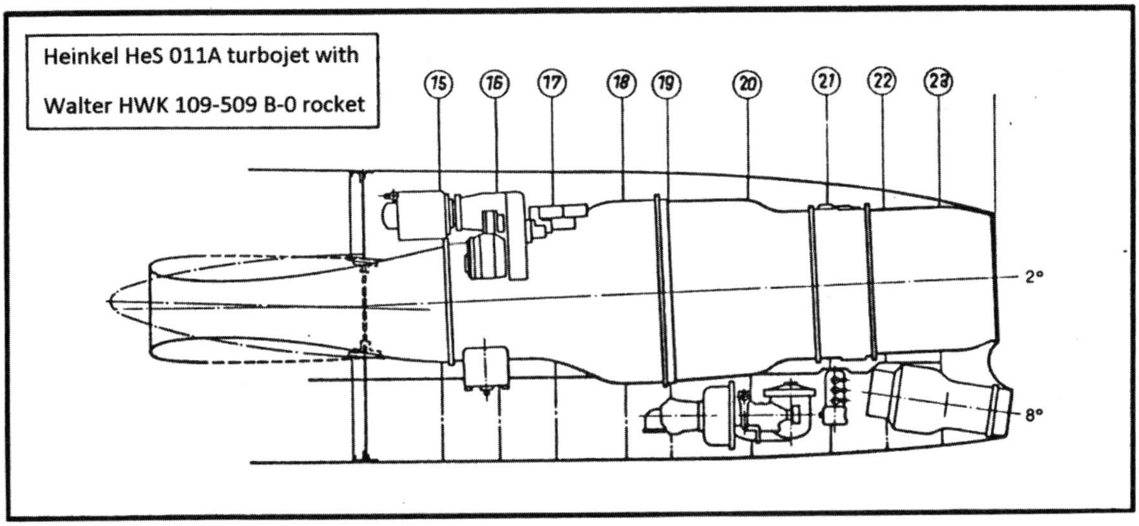

Heinkel HeS 011A turbojet with Walter HWK 109-509 B-0 rocket

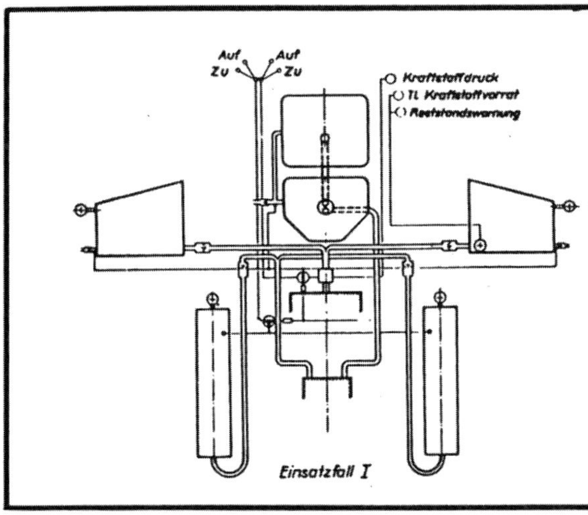

Flitzer I fuel system

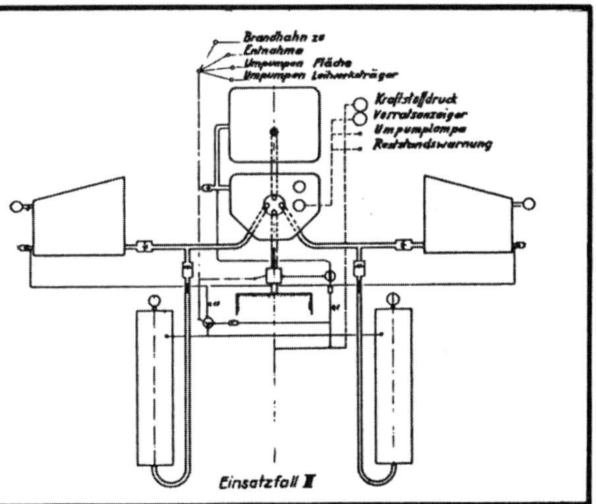

Flitzer III fuel system

9

Focke-Wulf 1-PTL *Jäger Projekt VII*

In May 1944, the RLM commissioned Daimler-Benz to develop the turboprop DB 109-021 *Pollux*, based on the Heinkel HeS 011 turbojet.

The engines of this type allowed to regulate the fuel flow with adjustments in the airscrew pitch, which, together with its low specific fuel consumption of 0.45 kg/hp per hour, made them very suitable to propel long-range airplanes. Turboprops were lighter and more powerful than the conventional piston engines and could work with heavy kerosene.

Version Sk.021.50-0008.10 (2 August 1944) was designed to propel a future variant *Aufklärer* (reconnaissance) of Arado Ar 234. It consisted of a HeS 011A turbojet to which had been added an extra third turbine stage and a 2.5-m diameter variable-pitch six-bladed airscrew that could be driven through reduction gearing of the epicyclic planetary type, giving an airscrew speed ratio of 1 to 5.82 (1,800 rpm). The whole assembly had a length of 3.7 m and was suitable for installation under the wings of Arado Ar 234. At least 50 per cent of the turbojet power was diverted to airscrew thrust.

Version Zeich.Nr.109-021.6008 (17 October 1944) was designed to propel the Messerschmitt Me 262 B-2 *Nachtjäger* (night fighter). It had a length of 4.1 m and was based on the HeS 011 A-0 turbojet. Compared with pure jet fighters, the PTL airplanes were superior in take-off, climb, acceleration, and endurance, but the power of the turboprops rapidly declined with height and were not adequate to propel high-altitude interceptors.

In general, the jet versions were 107 per cent faster and 87 per cent lighter, with the service ceiling 130 per cent higher and a 34 per cent longer range compared with the turboprops versions. When the future performances of the 109-021 turboprop were known in July 1944, Kurt Tank decided to use it to propel a *Flitzer schlacht* version (ground attack), called *Projekt VII*, capable of taking off using the smallest forward landing strips with heavy loads.

The adaptation of the turboprop to the airframe of a single-engine fighter required the use of a long power shaft to connect the airscrew, in the extreme nose, with the turbojet installed in the rear section of the fuselage. On 2 August 1944, modification

Zeich.Nr.0310 226-114, described in the dossier Baubeschreibung Nr. 226, was proposed to the OKL. The power plant would be a version of the 109-021 named Sk.021.50-0008, with a power shaft of 3 m and an airscrew built with wide, wooden blades (*Holzblättern*) from the VDM 9-12157 H-3 used by the Fw 190 D-9.

To compensate for the loss of power in the shaft, the diameter of the propeller was increased to 2.7 m. The complete turboprop averaged 6.8 m in length and produced 2,400 hp shaft power at 800 kph and sea level, with a residual jet thrust of 585 kp. The planned armament for this version consisted of two Mauser MG 151/20 cannon (synchronised variant) under the cockpit floor and two Mauser MG 151/15 heavy machine guns in the wings.

The dimensions were the same as those of the *Flitzer III* (20 July 1944) except the overall length was reduced to 9.9 m. The internal fuel capacity was 1,354 litres of heavy kerosene K1, enough to fly 1,460 km. Each wing panel housed one 210-litre fuel tank; the fuselage housed one tank with 597 litres of capacity and another with 337 litres. Take-off weight amounted to 5,000 kg, the maximum speed was estimated at 845 kph, and the initial rate of climb was 40 m/sec.

On 8 September, the OKL received a proposal to construct the *Zerstörer* (bomber destroyer) version, described in document Zeich.Nr.0310 226-113a, which was named Peterle, derived from the acronym PTL. The power plant consisted of a HeS 011 A-0, a power shaft of 4.6 m, and a conventional reduction gear box that allowed the installation of a Rheinmetall-Borsig Mk 103/30 heavy cannon in the nose, which fired through the propeller hub. The shaft power at 800 kph and sea level was 3,300 hp with a residual jet thrust of 770 kp.

The main modifications made in the design of the Peterle consisted of the adoption of a single fuselage fuel tank of 720 litres, an asymmetric nose leg that did not interfere in the operation of the shaft when retracting, and an armament consisting of a MK 103/30 heavy cannon in the nose. Two Mauser MK 213/20 (synchronised variant) rapid-fire cannon were positioned under the cockpit floor and two MG 151/15 machine guns were located in the wings. The Revi 16C gunsight was replaced by a ZFR 4a telescopic gunsight and the overall length increased to 10.5 m.

According to some authors, the Peterle had a reverse thrust system for a short landing run consisting of constant speed airscrew control with a quick blade pitch reverse mechanism.

Focke-Wulf PTL Jäger

Zeichnung Nr. 0310226-114

vom 8.9-1944

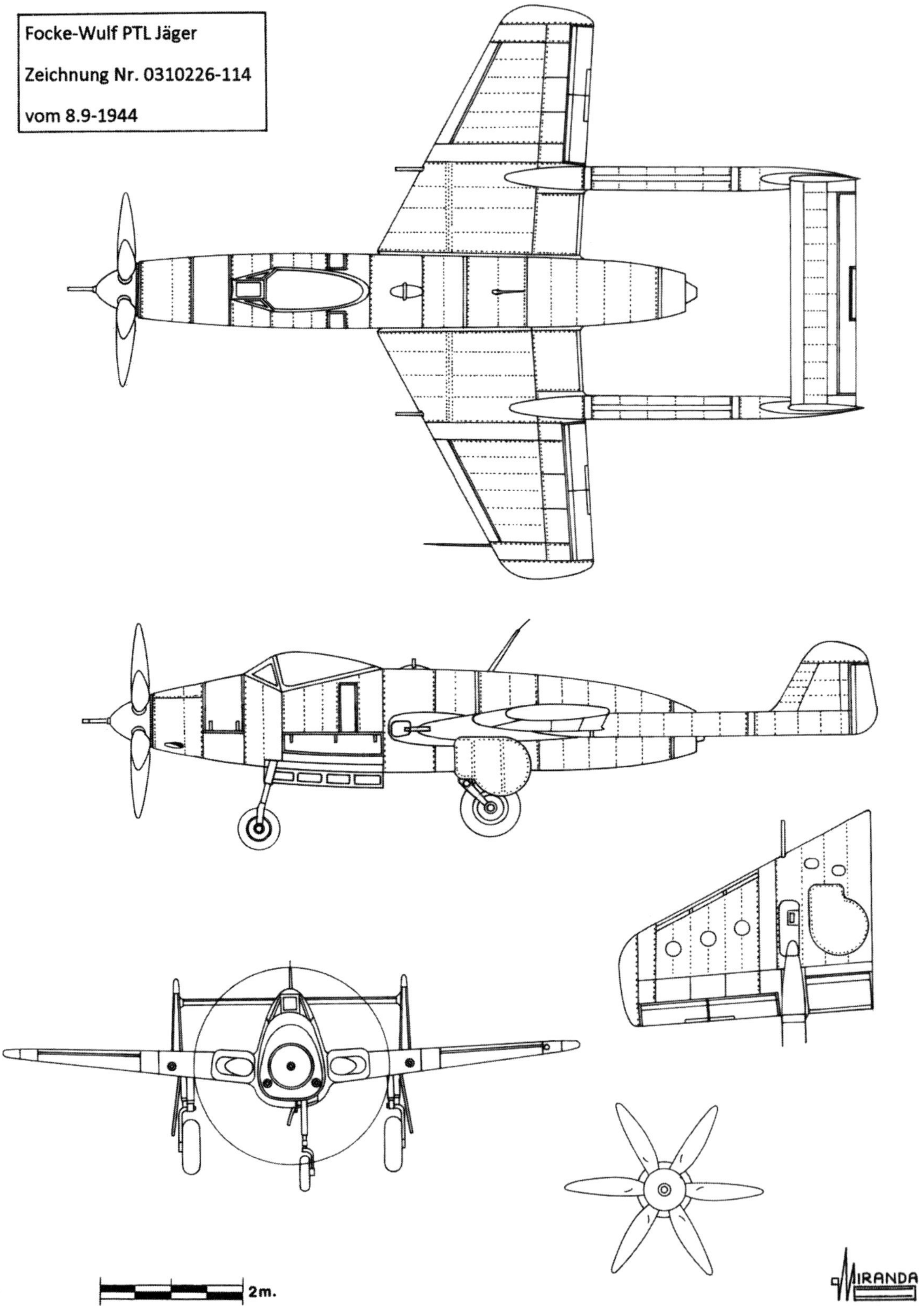

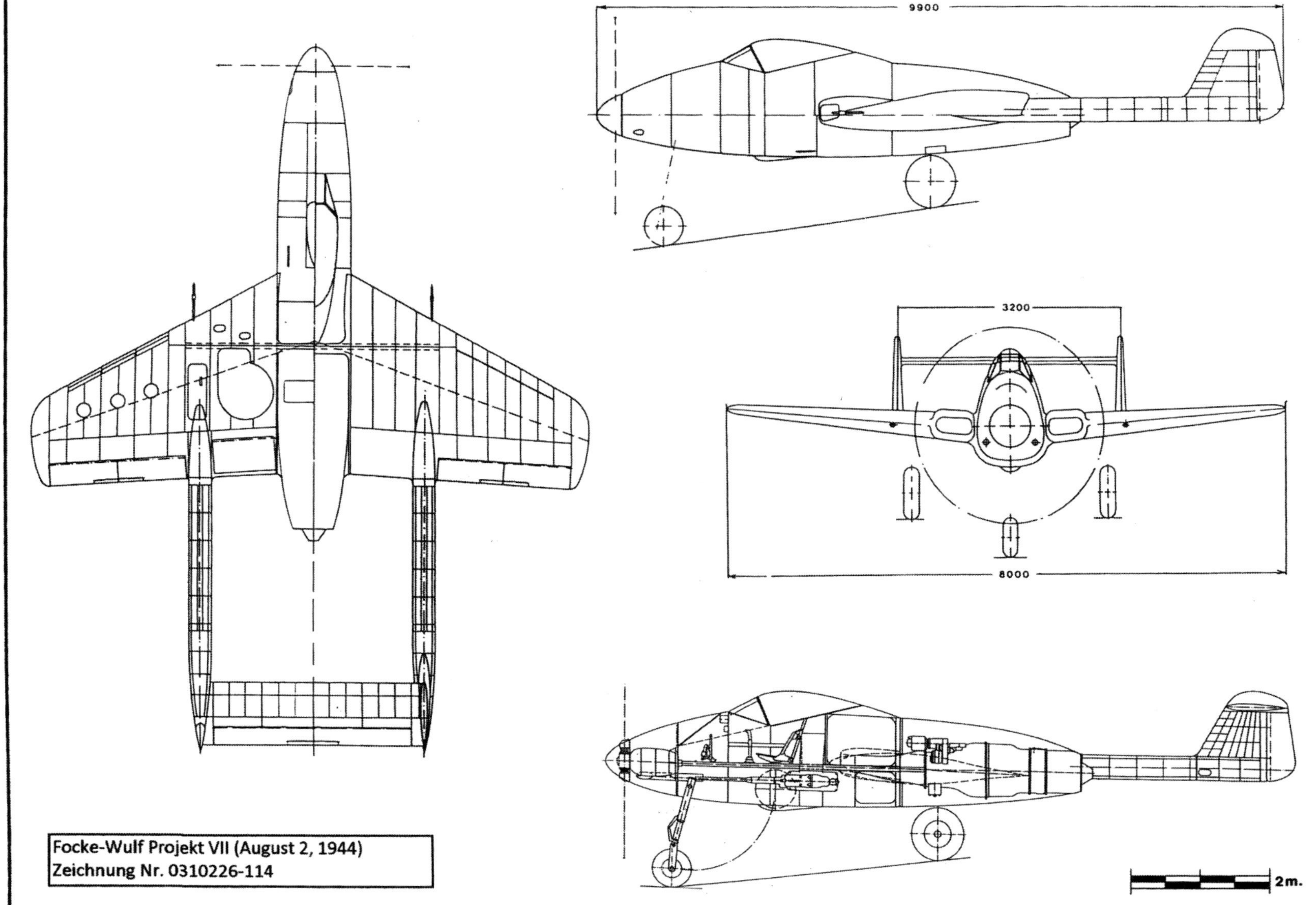

Focke-Wulf Projekt VII (August 2, 1944)
Zeichnung Nr. 0310226-114

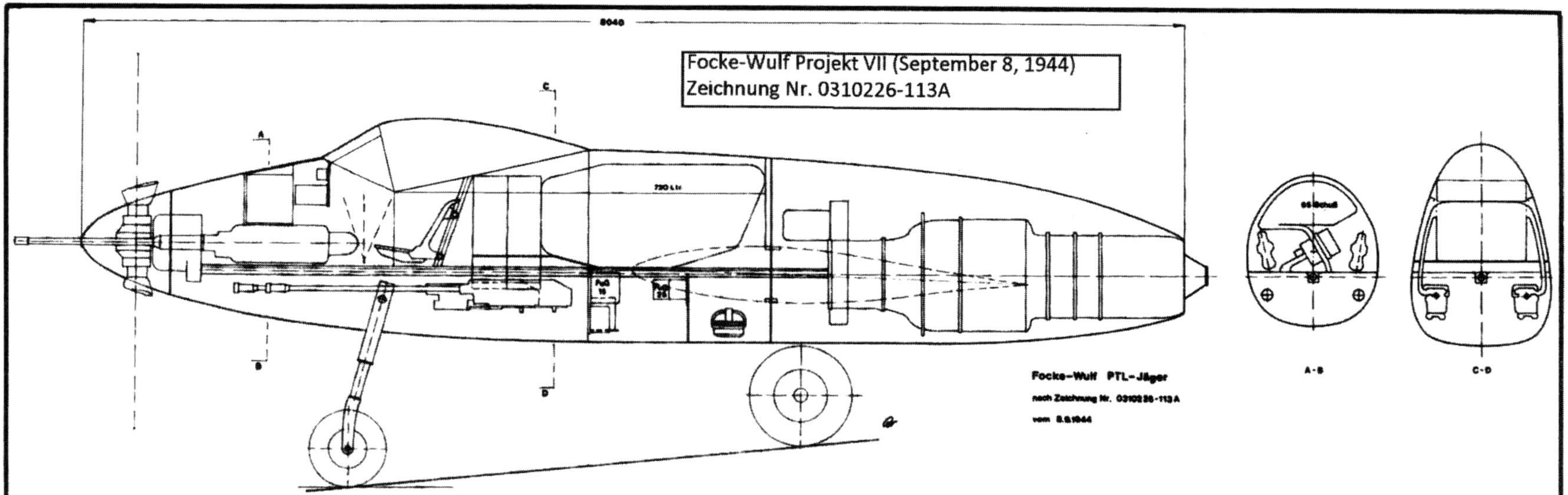
8040
Focke-Wulf Projekt VII (September 8, 1944)
Zeichnung Nr. 0310226-113A
720 Ltr.
Focke-Wulf PTL-Jäger
nach Zeichnung Nr. 0310226-113A
vom 8.9.1944
A-B
C-D

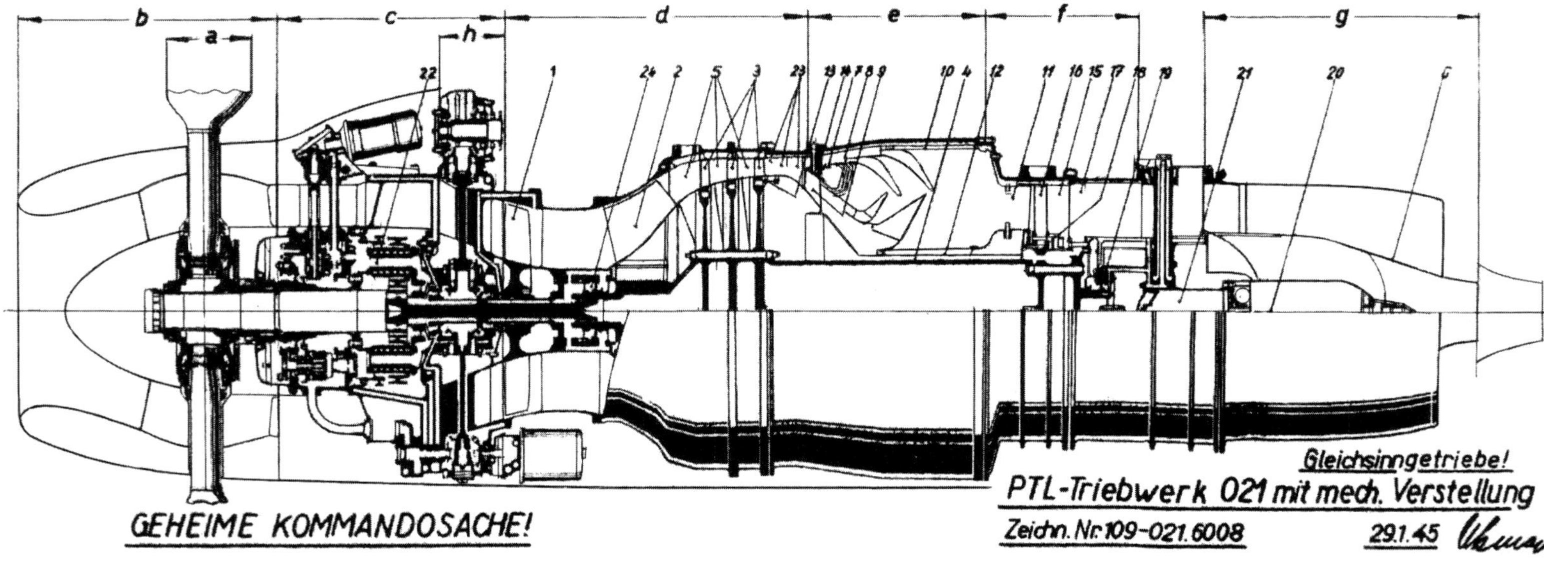
b
a
c
h
d
e
f
g
22
1
24
2
5
3
23
13
14
7
8
9
10
4
12
11
16
15
17
18
19
21
20
Gleichsinngetriebe!
PTL-Triebwerk 021 mit mech. Verstellung
Zeichn. Nr. 109-021.6008
29.1.45
GEHEIME KOMMANDOSACHE!

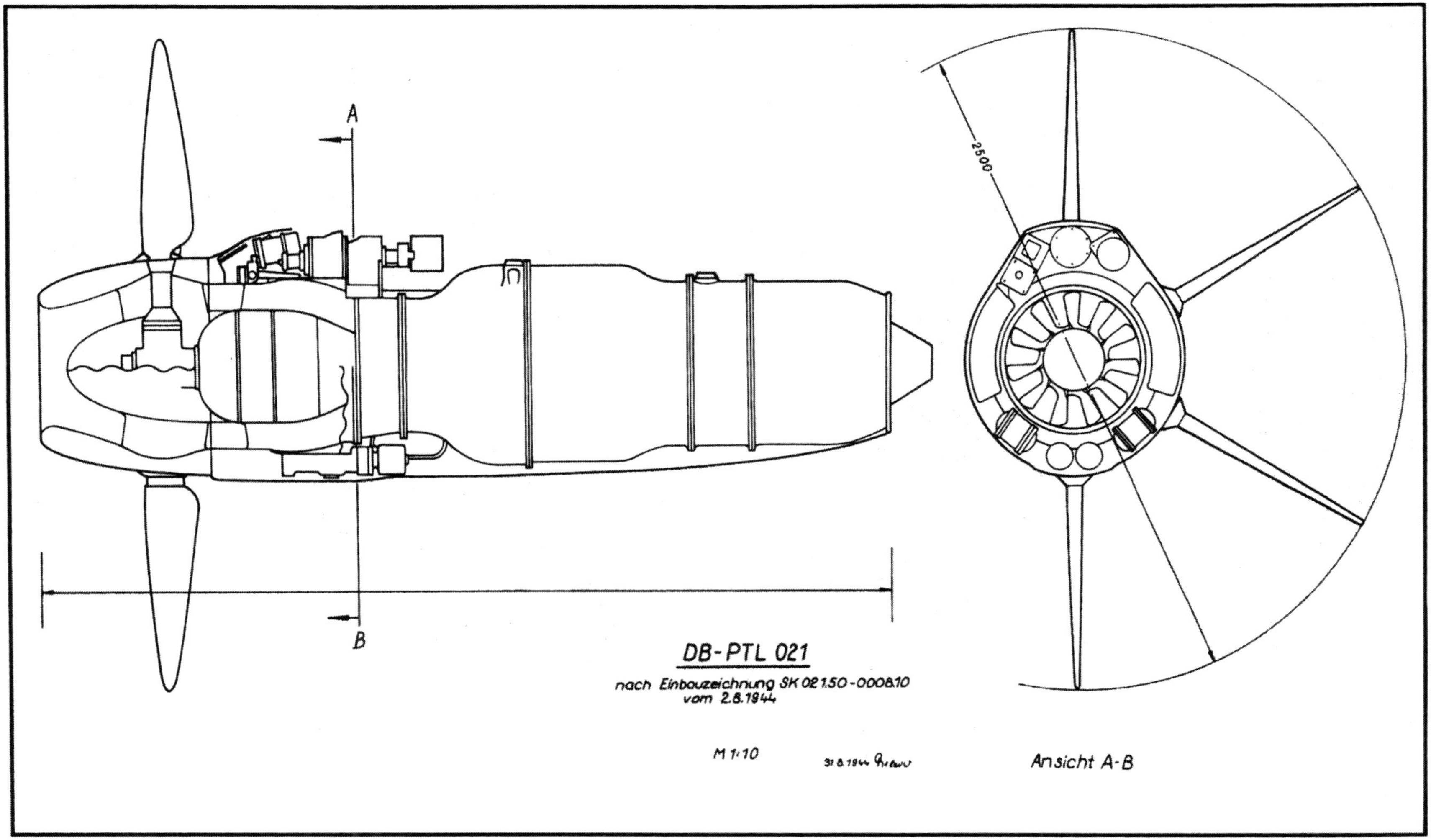
A
B
2500
DB-PTL 021
nach Einbauzeichnung SK 021.50-0008.10
vom 2.8.1944
M 1:10
Ansicht A-B

Arado Ar 234 PTL (August 17, 1944)

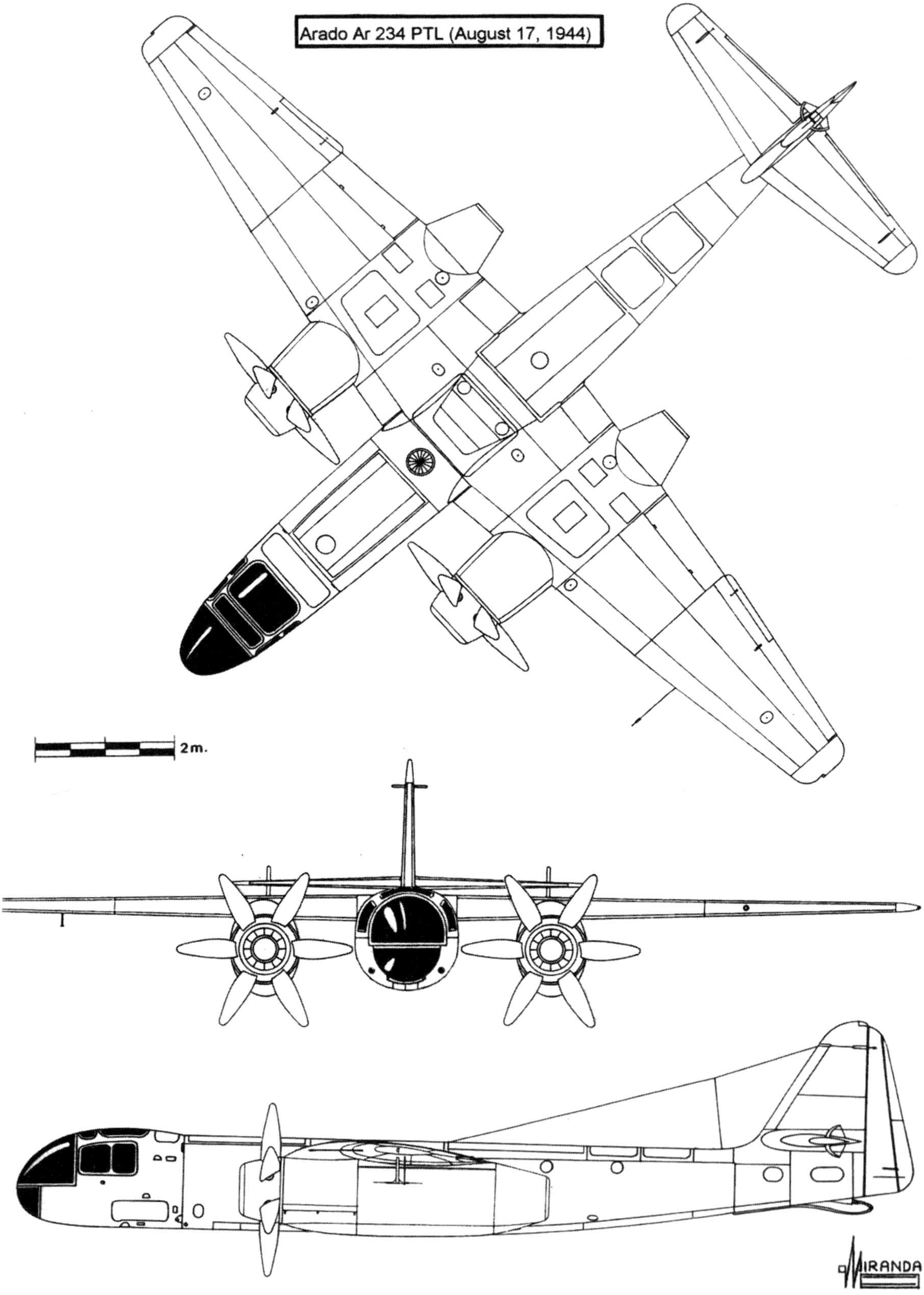

10

Focke-Wulf 1-PTL *Kampfjäger mit* PTL-021

Continuing its strategy of combining different types of airframes with all available power plants, on 14 November 1944, Kurt Tank proposed to the OKL the construction of a *Kampfjäger* (strike fighter) turboprop based on the airframe of the P.011.037a. The new project weighed less than the Peterle, and eliminating the tail-boom improved the roll rate and reduced the drag. It was expected that these changes would allow it to achieve a maximum speed of 900 kph, an initial rate of climb of 39 m/second, and a ceiling of 13,800 m.

Described in dossier Baubeschreibung Nr. 281 as P.0310 226-127 and in the specialised literature as *Projekt VIII*, the *Kampfjäger* would be propelled by a turboprop Daimler-Benz Sk.021.50-0008, with a power shaft of 6.7 m and a variable-pitch six-bladed airscrew with 2.7-m diameter. The proposed armament consisted of a Rheinmetall-Borsig MK 108/30 cannon, firing through the propeller hub, and two Mauser MG 213 20-mm (synchronised) cannon under the cockpit floor. A bomb rack with capacity for a SC 250 bomb would be installed under the fuselage belly. Each wing panel, with 35 degrees swept and 10 per cent thickness ratio, housed one fuel tank with 280 litres of K1 heavy kerosene, one main undercarriage leg, and one air intake/air duct ensemble. The wing span was 8.2 m and the wing surface 17.5 sq. m. The fuselage, with 10.8 m of length, housed the turboprop, the armament and ammunition, the pressurised cockpit, with armour protection, the ejector seat and reflector gunsight, the electronic equipment, four fuel tanks with 880 litres of K1 and the asymmetric nose leg. With 1,440 litres of fuel, its range would be 1,020 km, with an endurance of 1.17 hours and a maximum take-off weight of 4,900 kg.

In August 1950, the United States company McDonnell decided to modify the prototype of the XF-88 installing an Allison XT38 A-5 turboprop to study the performance of this type of engines at high speeds. The modification was completed in early 1952 and the first flight was made on 14 March 1953 under the designation XF-88B. First flying tests revealed that the weight of the ensemble of power shaft, gearbox, and propellers did not compensate for the fuel savings and that this type of power plant could not be used successfully in long-range escort fighters. Between 1954 and 1957, the XF-88B was used by NACA to test up to twenty-seven types of supersonic propellers in flight.

In 1951, the Republic Aviation Corporation started two research programmes using the Allison XT40 A-1 turboprop. The first programme consisted of the design of a research aircraft to test supersonic propellers. The second was a study of the possibilities of turboprop to propel a strike fighter for the USAF and one high-performance carrier fighter for the US Navy. The decision to construct two prototypes XF-84H based on the airframe of an F-84 fighter was taken in December 1952. The first flight took place on 22 July 1955. During the flying test program, it was discovered that the sonic waves generated by the propeller caused injury to the ground crews within several hundred feet of the aircraft. This unexpected circumstance, along with numerous problems experienced with the hydraulic system and gearbox malfunction, led to the cancellation of the programme in October 1956.

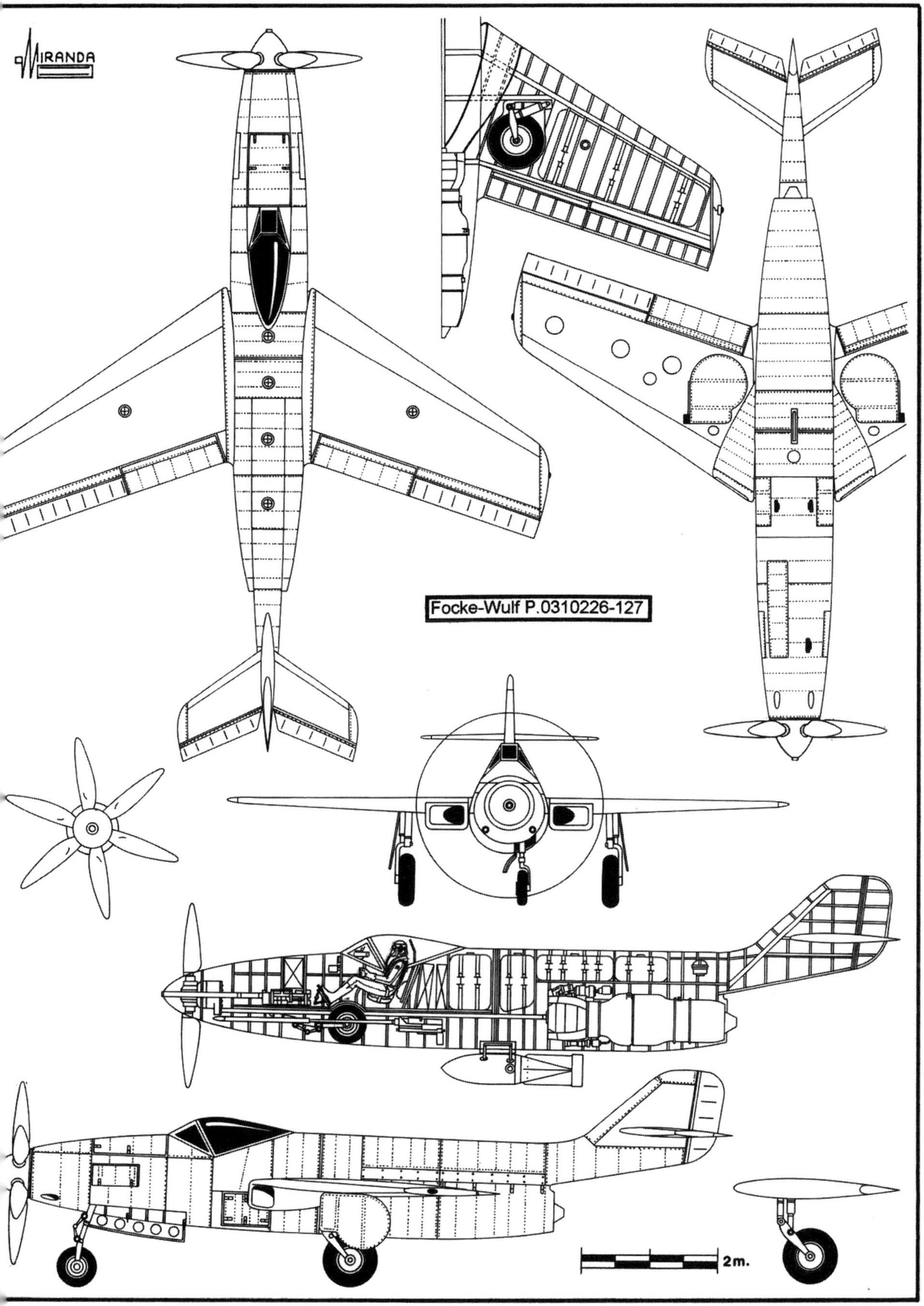
MIRANDA
Focke-Wulf P.0310226-127
2m.

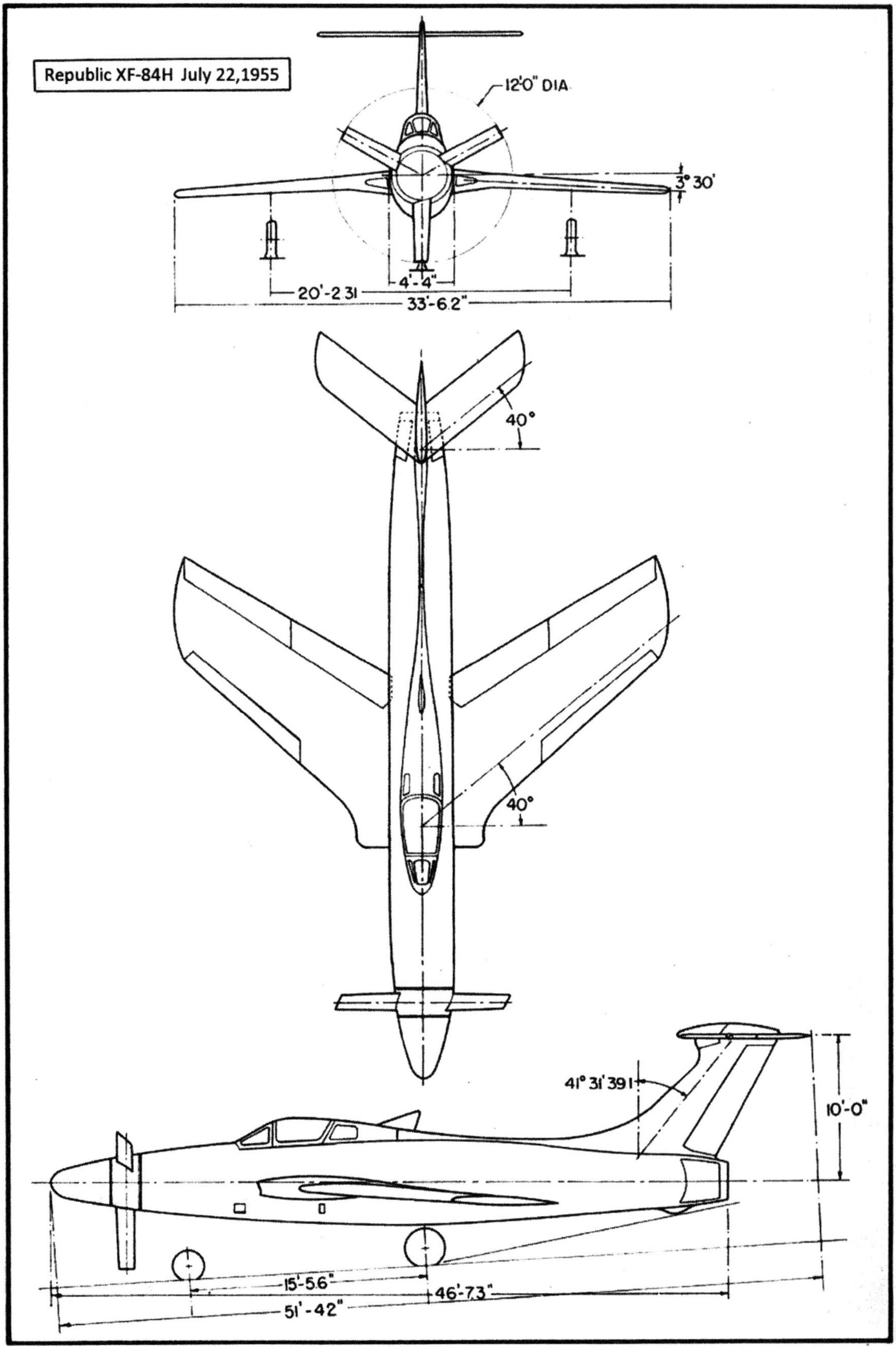

Republic XF-84H July 22,1955

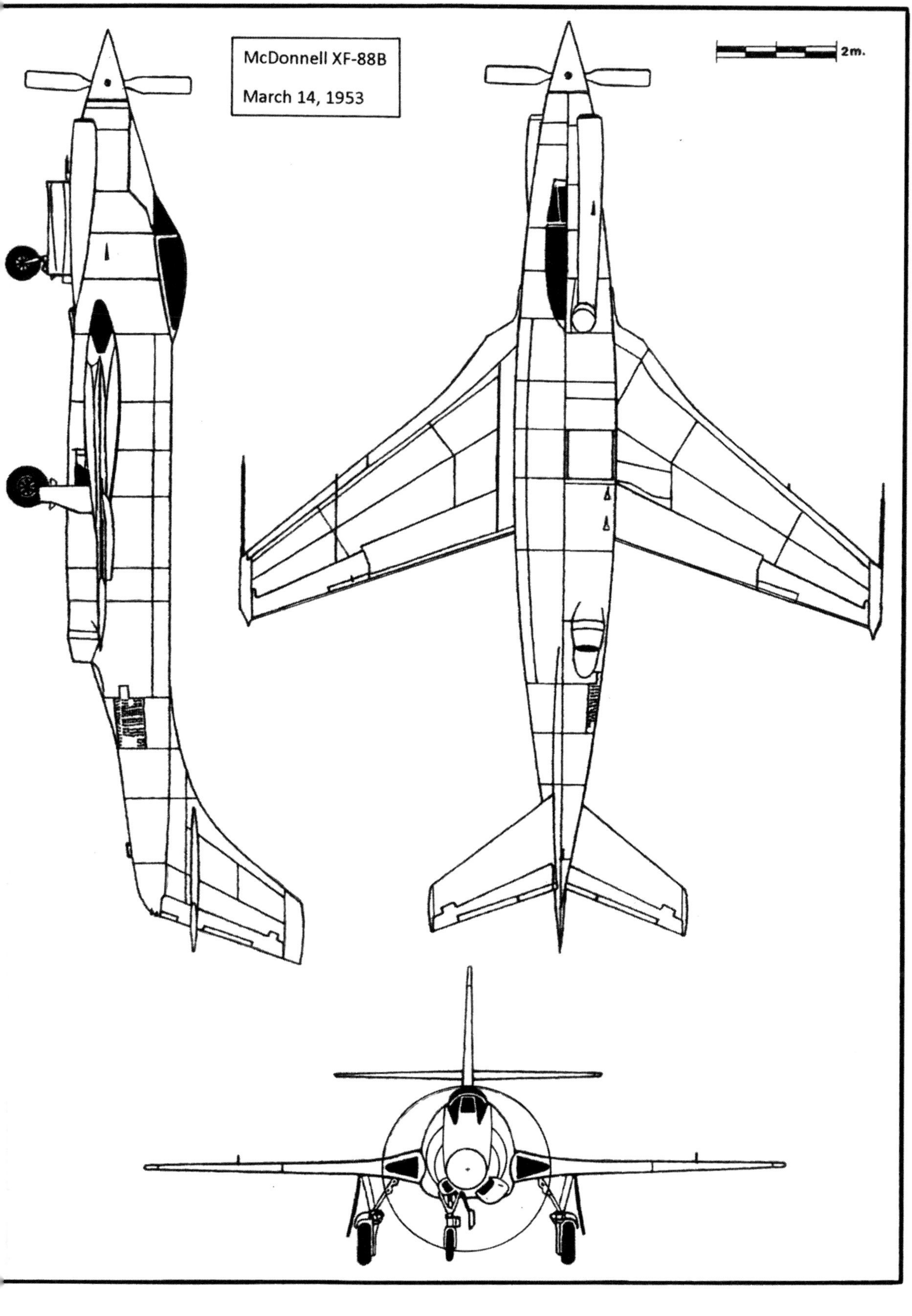
McDonnell XF-88B
March 14, 1953
2m.

11

Focke-Wulf 1-TL *Höhenjagdflugzeug mit* BMW 018 (Super TL)

Except for the Heinkel AG and Junkers AG, the German manufacturers of aircraft engines lacked the necessary infrastructure to build airframes. However, there is information from that time about projects of airplanes designed by BMW and Daimler-Benz. They were mainly simple ideas to promote some of their less demanded products.

From 1943, it was evident that Germany did not have the required resources to manufacture big fleets of strategic bombers. Therefore, the projected heavy engines that the designers of fighters tended to ignore needed to adapt or die.

BMW had developed the powerful turbojet BMW 109-018, a monster that was 4.95 m long, 1.25 m wide, and with 3,400 kp static thrust. It was intended to power the *Strahlbomber Projekt II*, a flying wing able to fly at 985 km/h with 5,000 kg of bombs—a luxury that Germany could not afford. When *Projekt II* was cancelled by the end of 1944, there were not many projects of airplanes under study that would have been able to house such a huge engine.

The firm Blohm und Voss designed a 125 per cent scaled-up version of the P.202 fighter, named P.198. It was a high-altitude interceptor with a BMW 018 suspended under the fuselage.

In November 1944, the EZS design team of BMW, led by Dipl.-Ing. Huber, proposed a 65 per cent scaled-down version of the *Strahlbomber Projekt II* powered by a single BMW 018. It was a flying wing of 23-m span, able to fly at 1,040 km/h; carrying heavy armament, it was able to destroy a B-29 with a single shot of its four 55-mm cannon. It was a design with huge potential and was known as the BMW *Strahljäger Projekt V*.

The solution chosen by the Bad Eilsen design team, under the leadership of the Dipl.-Ing. von Halem, consisted of increasing the dimensions of the Ta 183 B by 115 per cent, replacing the HeS 011A turbojet by a BMW 109-018. The new engine used the same type of fuel J2 as the BMW 003, but had a specific fuel consumption of only 1.10 kg/hp per hour and a much higher power to weight ratio.

The Focke-Wulf project, described in the Baubeschreibung Nr. 252 dossier in October 1944 and frequently cited in the specialised literature as Focke-Wulf Super

TL, was a high-altitude interceptor far superior to *Huckebein* but it did not surpass the design phase, with the BMW 109-018 being cancelled in December 1944.

Technical Data

Wings: built of wood, plywood, and steel, with 42 degrees rear swept and 12 per cent thickness, housing twelve fuel tanks, ailerons, and flaps.
Tail surfaces: made of light alloy
Fuselage: Egg section, built with light alloy, housing the pressurised and armoured cockpit with ejector seat, three fuel tanks, two heavy cannon, and the turbojet.
Landing gear: The main legs could retract forwards and the wheels were housed on both sides of the air duct. The nose leg could retract backwards after rotating 90 degrees.
Engine: one BMW 109-018 turbojet with 3,400 kp static thrust.
Armament: Two Mk 108/30 heavy cannon and the possibility to transport different combinations of R4M rockets, 300-litre droppable fuel tanks, X-4 missiles, or one SC/SD 500 bomb under the fuselage.
Take-off weight: 5,600 kg.
Estimated maximum speed: Mach 0.98
Estimated service ceiling: 13,000 m.
Wingspan: 11 m.
Length: 10.87 m.
Height: 4.75 m.
Wing area: 25 sq. m.

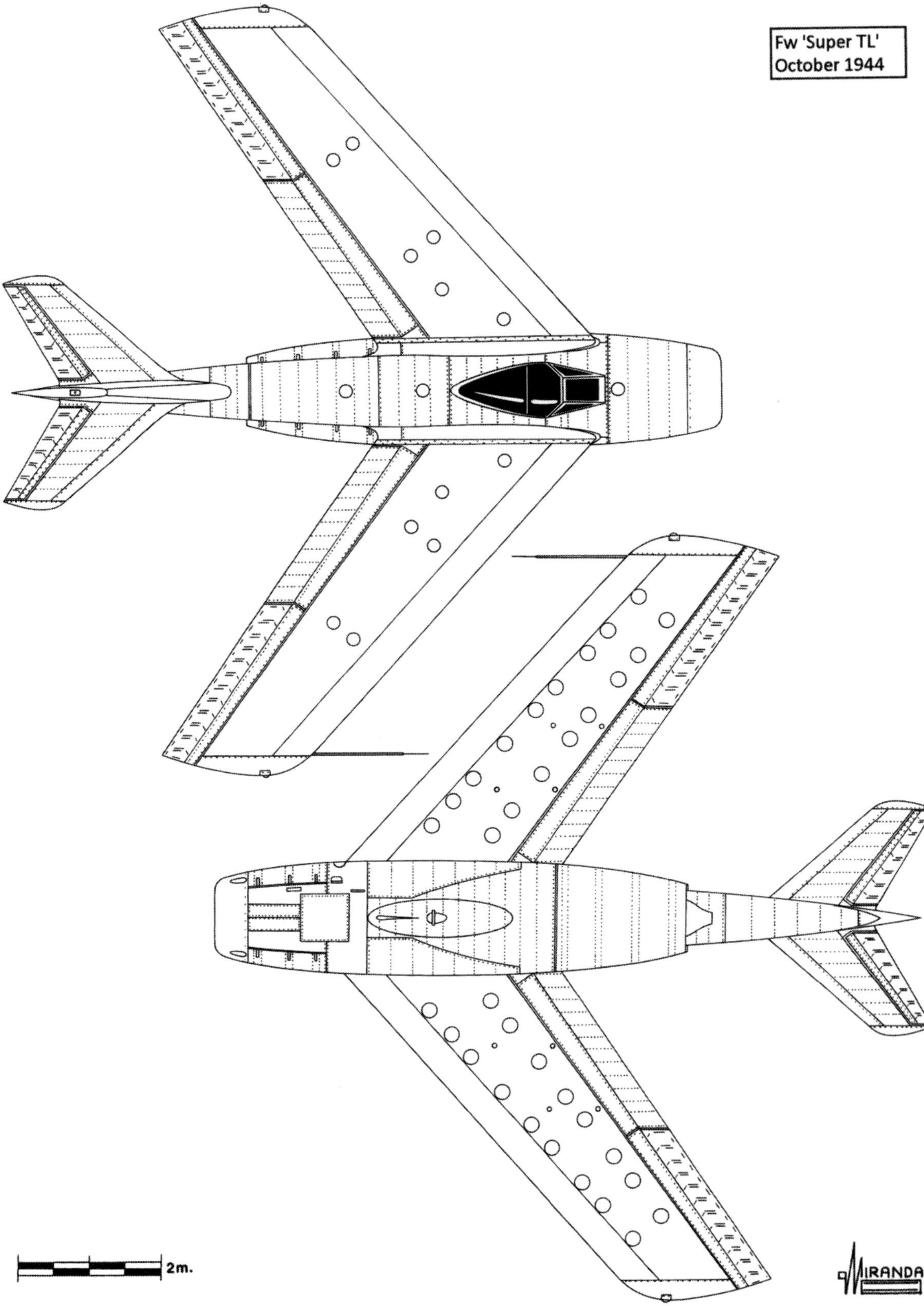

Fw 'Super TL'
October 1944

Fw 'Super TL'
October 1944

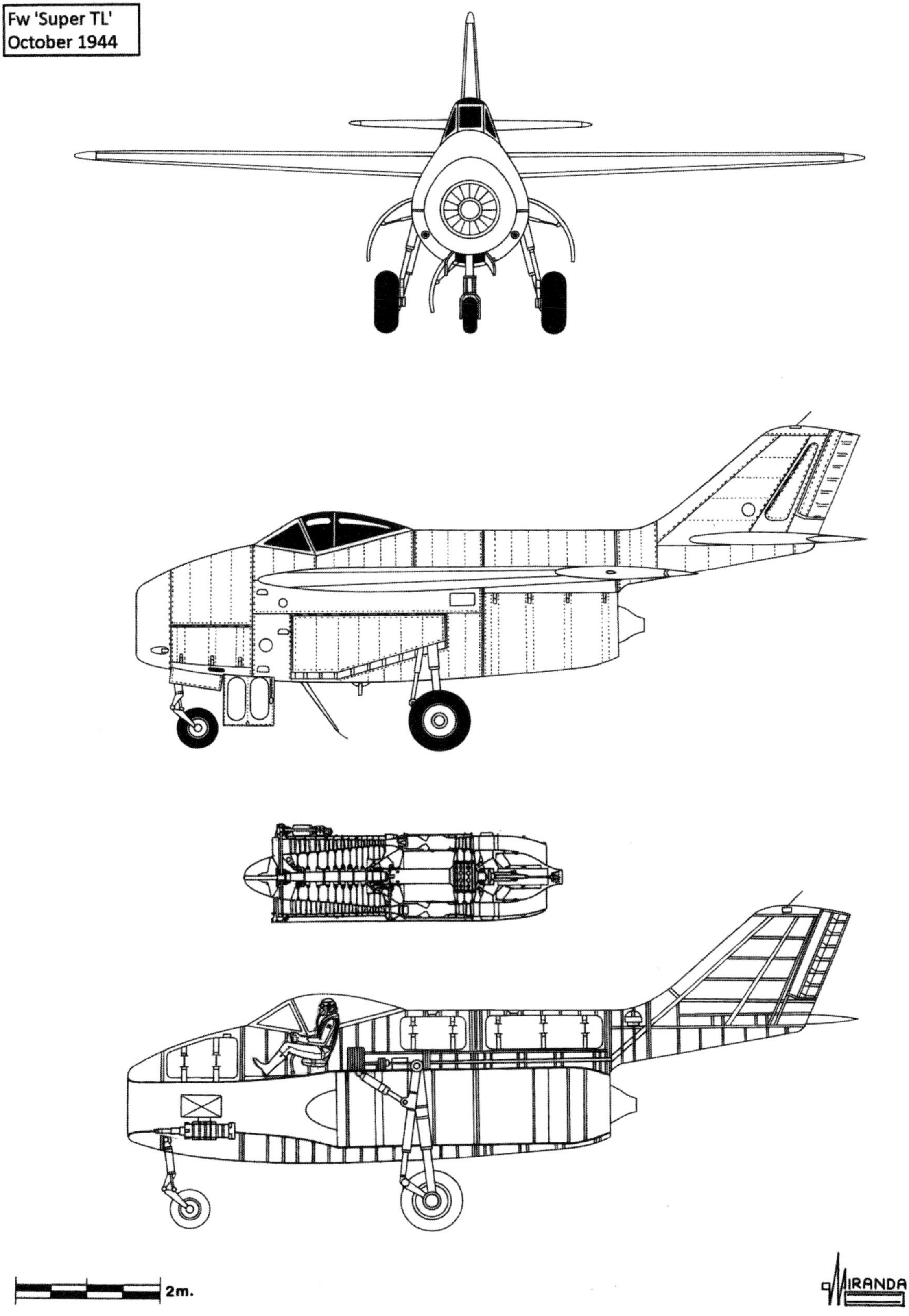

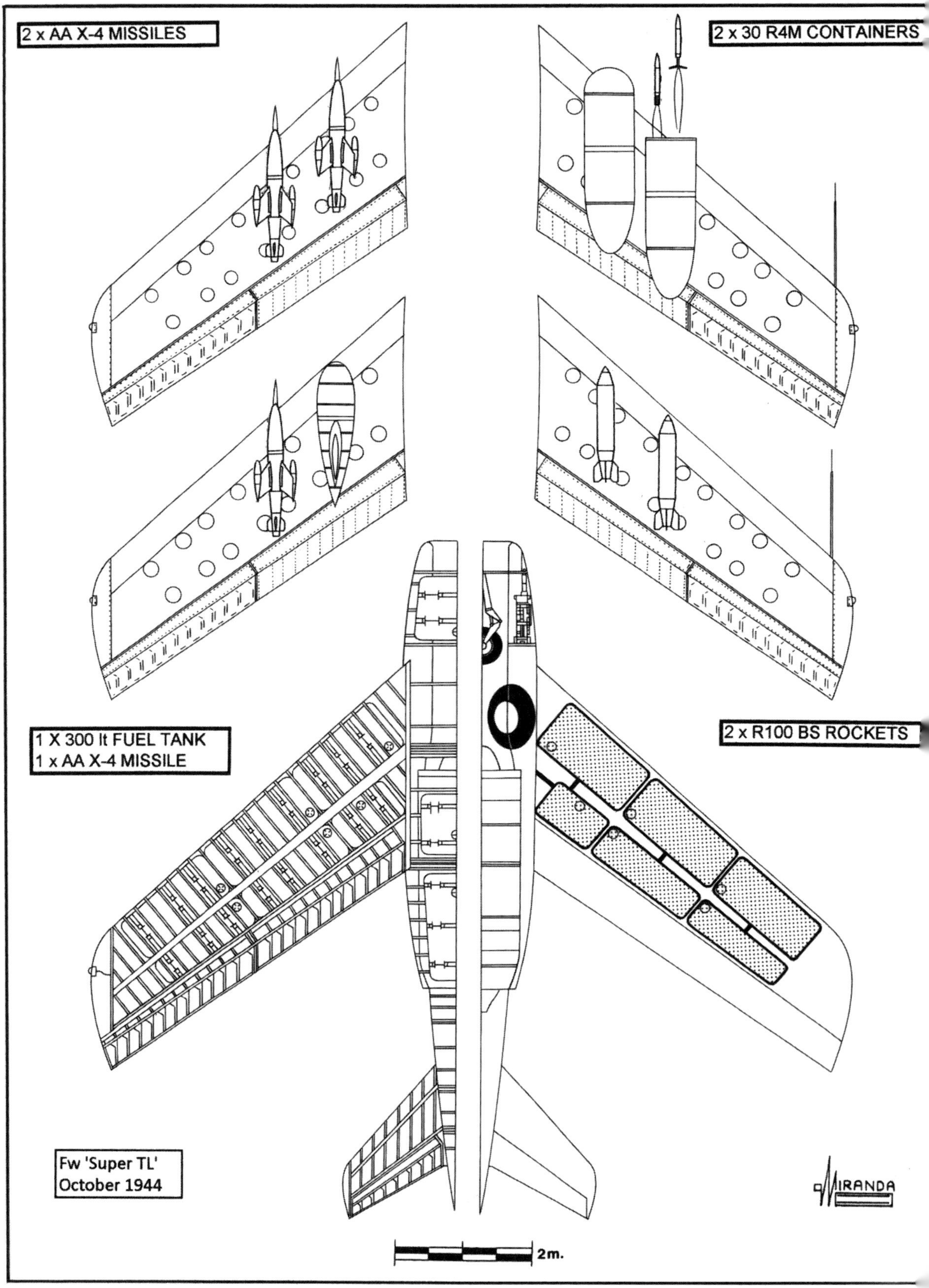

2 x AA X-4 MISSILES
2 x 30 R4M CONTAINERS
1 X 300 lt FUEL TANK
1 x AA X-4 MISSILE
2 x R100 BS ROCKETS
Fw 'Super TL'
October 1944
2m.
MIRANDA

12

Focke-Wulf 1-TL *Volksflugzeug*

During the winter of 1943–1944, the USAAF day-bombing offensive against the *Reich* cities and industry grew in intensity, both in the frequency of attacks and in the number of aircraft employed. In February 1944, the Luftwaffe began using *Sturm* (assault) tactics as a desperate measure to try to break the self-defensive formations of the four engine American bombers.

The Fw 190 fighters of the *Sturm* units carried out almost suicidal frontal attacks against the 'boxes' of B-17 and B-24, suffering heavy losses. When the fighters began escorting the bombers in the summer of 1944, some *Staffeln* lost a third of its members in each combat. In August, the *Sturmgruppen* lost a fighter for each destroyed bomber. In the autumn, the life expectancy of a *Sturm* pilot was ten hours of flight.

During the very short-range attacks, the *Sturmjägern* had to be exposed to the defensive fire of hundreds of heavy machine guns and it became necessary to gradually increase the armour to protect the pilot. In November, the armour of an Fw 190 A-8 weighed 256 kg. These aircraft needed a special propeller and a droppable fuel tank to reach the level of flight of the bomber stream and were easy prey for the Mustangs in a dogfight. By the end of 1944, the *Sturmjägern* were escorted by conventional fighters Fw 190 D and Bf 109 G. However, the Luftwaffe did not have enough airplanes and the shortage of the B4 87-octane fuel for the piston fighters had already began in Germany. By contrast, the Thunderbolts operated with 100-octane gasoline and the Mk III Mustangs of the 129 Sqn. RAF used 130-octane to intercept the V-1 missiles.

The battle for supremacy in German airspace had already been lost by the Luftwaffe. As in France in 1939, the USSR in 1941, and Australia in 1942, the Germans began to consider the mass construction of a 'panic fighter' to stop the advance of the invader. On 8 September 1944, the *Technisches Amt* requested the design of an easy-to-build light fighter to start mass production on 1 January 1945. It was expected to reach a production rate of 1,000 aircraft per month in May. The contest was called *Volksjäger* for political reasons, with the deadline for proposals on 20 September 1944.

The new aircraft would be powered by a BMW 003 A-2 turbojet, with 705 kp static thrust and the largest possible proportion of non-strategic materials should be used in its construction. It needed a maximum speed of 750 kph, with thirty minutes endurance at sea level, a maximum take-off weight of 2,000 kg, wing loading not more than 200 kg /sq. m, and a take-off run of 500 m. Its air superiority version would be armed with two MG 151/20 rapid-fire cannon, with 120 rounds per gun. In *Zerstörer* configuration, it would use two MK 108/30 heavy cannon with fifty rounds per gun. The electronic equipment would consist of an R/T device FuG 24 and a GEMA IFF discriminator FuG 25 Erstling.

Seven companies were invited to produce designs: Arado, Blohm und Voss, Fieseler, Focke-Wulf, Heinkel, Junkers, and Messerschmitt. Initially, both Focke-Wulf and Messerschmitt, whose fighters fought daily, refused to take part as the *Volksjäger* would deplete the industrial resources reserved for *Jägernotprogramm.*

The project EF 123 presented by Junkers was quickly rejected because of the *Technisches Amt* manifest aversion to the designs with the turbojet positioned in ventral position. The E-580 proposed by the firm Arado was also rejected on 12 September due to the position of the air intake, located in the aerodynamic shadow region generated by the cockpit hood. On 15 September, a conference was held in which the RLM discarded all projects except the Heinkel P.1073 (11 September 1944) and Blohm und Voss P.211-01 (14 September 1944). Focke-Wulf's representatives attended for information purposes only. On the 19th of the same month, another meeting took place to evaluate the new projects presented by Arado, Junkers, and Siebel. On this occasion, Focke-Wulf decided to participate with the designs *Volksflugzeug* and *Volksflitzer*, lightened versions of *Projekt V* and *Projekt VI*. No data is known about the Siebel project or about the Fieseler project, except that it had a maximum weight of 2,900 kg and a take-off run of 580 m.

The Blohm und Voss project was considered unsafe for inexperienced pilots because of its swept wing. On 29 September, the firm proposed to change the wing of the P.211-00, but the *Technisches Amt* had already decided on the Heinkel P.1073. On the 30th of the same month, the OKL declared it winner of the contest announcing that it would be manufactured under the denomination He 162 *Spatz*.

By this time, all aircraft manufacturers had already learned to fight the continuous interference of the *Technisches Amt* always proposing two versions of the same project: one of advanced aerodynamics and high performance and another more conventional and easy to build. Heinkel, who had already suffered the rejection of their He 100, He 112, and He 280 fighters as well as two years of delay in accepting the He 219, decided to first present the straight wing version and won the contest.

The RLM used to favour the multi-purpose option to the detriment of the specialised versions. According to this philosophy, it was demanded that night fighters could carry bombs and interceptors photo-reconnaissance cameras. All projects submitted to the *Volksjäger* contest had a straight wing version (Arado E-580, Blohm und Voss P.211-00, and Heinkel He 162 A) and another with a swept wing (Arado E-581-2, Blohm und Voss P.211-01, and Heinkel He 162 D).

Focke-Wulf also presented two versions of *Volksflugzeug*: *Entwurf I* (Configuration I) with straight wing and *Entwurf II* with 38-degree swept wing, both with 7.5-m wingspan, 13.5-sq. m wing area, and 4 to 1 aspect ratio. Both versions shared an overall length of 8.8 m, a height of 2.85 m, an initial climb rate of 14.5 m/sec, a range of 550 km, a service ceiling of 10,500 m, and a take-off run of 1,000 m. They could internally transport 790 litres of J2 fuel in a tank located in the fuselage and two more in the wings. The armaments consisted of two MK 108/30 heavy cannon, with sixty rounds per gun, in the fuselage.

The pressurised cockpit, with ejector seat, would be protected by armour plates and armoured windscreen. *Entwurf I* had a maximum speed of 750 kph and a maximum take-off weight of 2,900 kg. *Entwurf II* had a maximum speed of 820 kph and a maximum take-off weight of 3,050 kg.

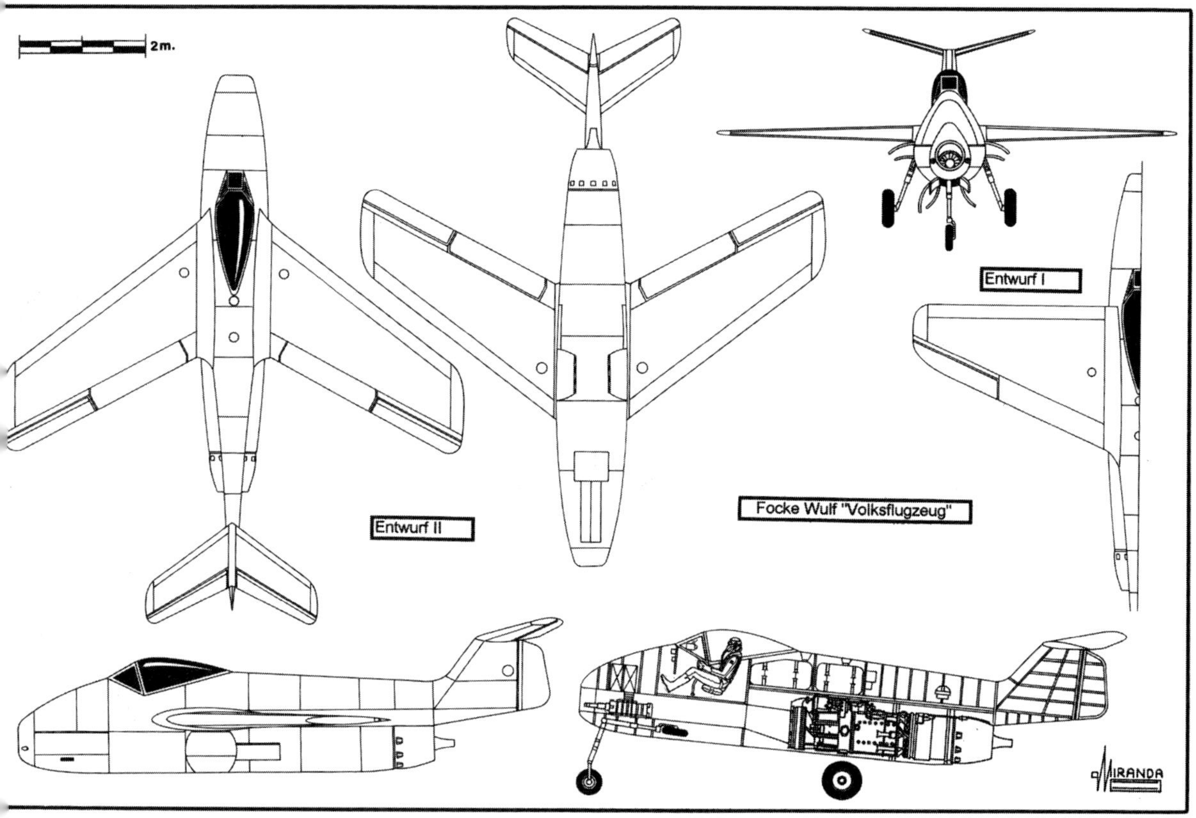

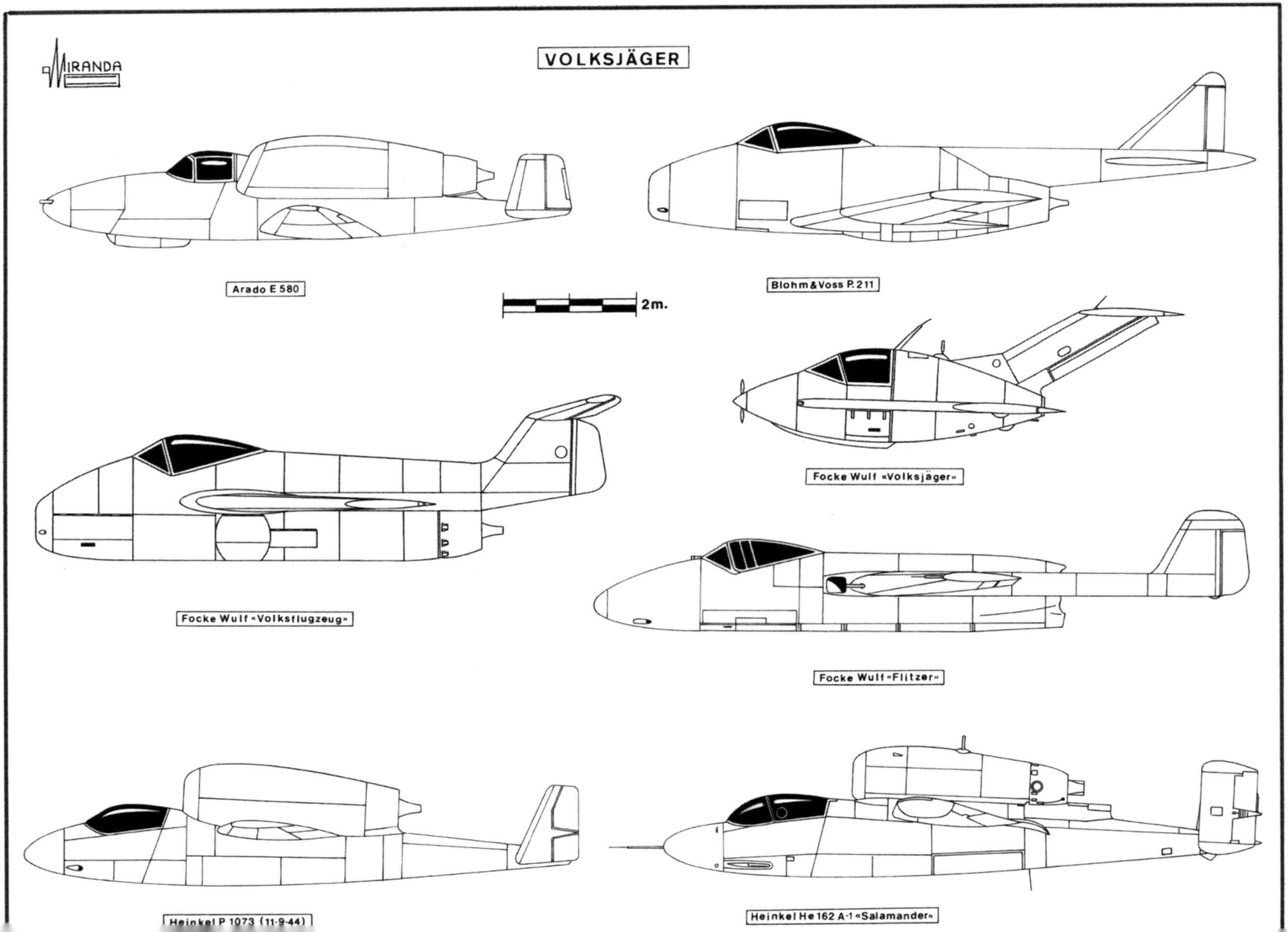
VOLKSJÄGER
Arado E 580
Blohm&Voss P.211
2m.
Focke Wulf «Volksjäger»
Focke Wulf «Volksflugzeug»
Focke Wulf «Flitzer»
Heinkel P 1073 (11·9·44)
Heinkel He 162 A-1 «Salamander»

13

Focke-Wulf 1-TL *Berich Nr.03028* (4 January 1943)

By mid-1942, Kurt Tank commissioned an advanced design study for a future air-superiority fighter powered by one of the new axial-type turbojets developed by BMW and Junkers from Dipl.-Ing. Julius Rotta. The result was an internal document of the firm entitled Berich Nr. 03028, *Grundlagen zum Entwurf eines Jägers mit Turbinentriebwerk* (Study No. 03028, Basic principles for the design of a turbojet-powered fighter) in which three possible configurations were described.

The first configuration was the *Jäger mit Turbinentriebwerk* BMW P.3302 *Entwurf I* (7 December 1942). This was a very advanced design for its time, with 21-degree negative forward swept wing, 45-degree rear swept butterfly tail surfaces, and 3,000-kg maximum take-off weight. The asymmetric main undercarriage legs folded in, the port leg had a slope of 22 degrees, and the starboard leg a slope of 10 degrees. The mainwheels were hidden in tandem in the fuselage belly to minimise the front section of the plane. The BMW P.3302 turbojet, rated at 600 kp static thrust, was in a back position. It was a first version of the BMW 109-003 and operated with B4 87-octane petrol stored in the fuselage in two tanks of 550 and 300 litres, enough for forty-five minutes of powered flight at 6,000 m.

The armament would consist of two MG 151/20 rapid-fire cannon, with 300 rounds per gun, located under the cockpit floor, and two MK 108/30 heavy cannon, with 200 rounds per gun, located behind the nose wheel bay. At the time of the study, the turbojet, the 30-mm cannon, and the ejector seat (required for an emergency bail-out, due to the dangerous position of the air intake) only existed as prototypes.

Being only an aerodynamic study, Berich Nr. 03028 did not include data on construction materials, electronic equipment, or armour or cockpit pressurisation system. However, it contained some technical data on dimensions and estimated performances. The wings, spanning 8.2 m, had an aspect ratio of 4.8:1, 14 sq. m surface area, and 214 kg/sq. m maximum load. The overall length was 10.5 m and the height, 2.75 m. The estimated maximum speed was 800 kph and the absolute ceiling, 10,800 m.

The second configuration was the *Jäger mit Turbinentriebwerk* Jumo 004 *Entwurf I* (22 December 1942). It only differed from the previous version by the improvement of some performances: maximum speed was 900 kph, the absolute ceiling was 13,600 m, and the maximum take-off weight was 3,350 kg.

The conservative version of the first design was the *Jäger mit Turbinentriebwerk BMW P.3302-Entwurf II* (22 December 1942). It had straight wings and tail surfaces, an overall length of 9.25 m, and a lower maximum speed. Until the mid-1930s, the interest of designers in forward swept wings consisted of their ability to delay stall at low speed and high angles of attack. Low speed controllability assured full aileron control until total loss of lift, and the wingtips remained uninstalled to high angles of attack. In 1921, Willy Messerschmitt built the S9 glider to study the behaviour of this type of wing and in 1936, Alexander Lippisch used the DFS 42 *Kormoran* for the same purpose.

The appearance of turbojets during the forties allowed the design of airplanes capable of flying at Mach 0.7, although only Germany had carried out theoretical studies on the behaviour of swept wings at high speeds. In 1942, Dipl.-Ing. Hans Wocke, who carried out aerodynamic studies for Junkers, concluded that the forward-swept wings generated less negative pressure on their upper surface and helped delay shockwave formation to higher subsonic Mach numbers. In this type of wing, the air drifted towards the wing root and did not affect wingtips, making the use of leading-edge slots unnecessary.

Unfortunately for the Germans, the scale model wind tunnel tests carried out in 1942 did not reveal the existence of two dangerous defects that would prevent their use in high speed fighters. Aircrafts with forward-swept wings suffered a pronounced tendency to Dutch roll during a turn with heavy *g* loads. However, the appearance of aeroelastic divergence phenomena was much more serious. When the dynamic pressure is greater than the structural elastic restoring forces, a change in lift caused by the wing deformation exceeds the structural limits and the wing fails. This phenomenon has limited the use of forward sweep to angles less than 15 degrees in the construction of the prototype Ju 287 bomber in Germany, the Cornelius XFG-1 glider in the USA, and Romeo Ro.57 heavy fighter in Italy. None of these aircraft exceeded 550 kph.

Above a certain speed and degrees of forward sweep, the wing would bend and twist its leading edge up. An increased forward sweep angle required higher strength to resist the twisting and delay the divergence phenomena. The wing needed to be extremely stiff, but the technology of the time and the available materials were inadequate to build such a wing. All-metal wings are effectively limited to 15 degrees, but a high-performance fighter requires a much greater degree of forward swept.

After knowing the results of vibration tests carried out with the wing of a Ju 287 in July 1944 and the flight behaviour of the prototype Ju 287 V1, the OKL ordered the cancellation of two projects with forward-swept wings: Blohm und Voss P. 209-02 and Heinkel He 162 D, as well as the construction of the prototypes Ju 287 V3 and Ju 287 V4. Following the war, the state-of-the-art materials technology was unable to resolve the wing rigidity problem and the forward-swept versions of the North American P-51, Bell XS-1, Douglas D-558-1, and Convair XB-53 did not come to be built.

The Soviets did not have much success with the information captured by the Germans in the archives of the DVL-Institut. In 1948, they limited themselves to studying the aerodynamic behaviour of the forward-swept wings with the rocket research airplane Tsybin LL-3 up to Mach 0.95. Until the advanced composite structures boron-graphite matrixed into epoxy resins in the 1970s, it was not possible to achieve sufficient stiffness to control the aeroelastic divergence at supersonic speeds.

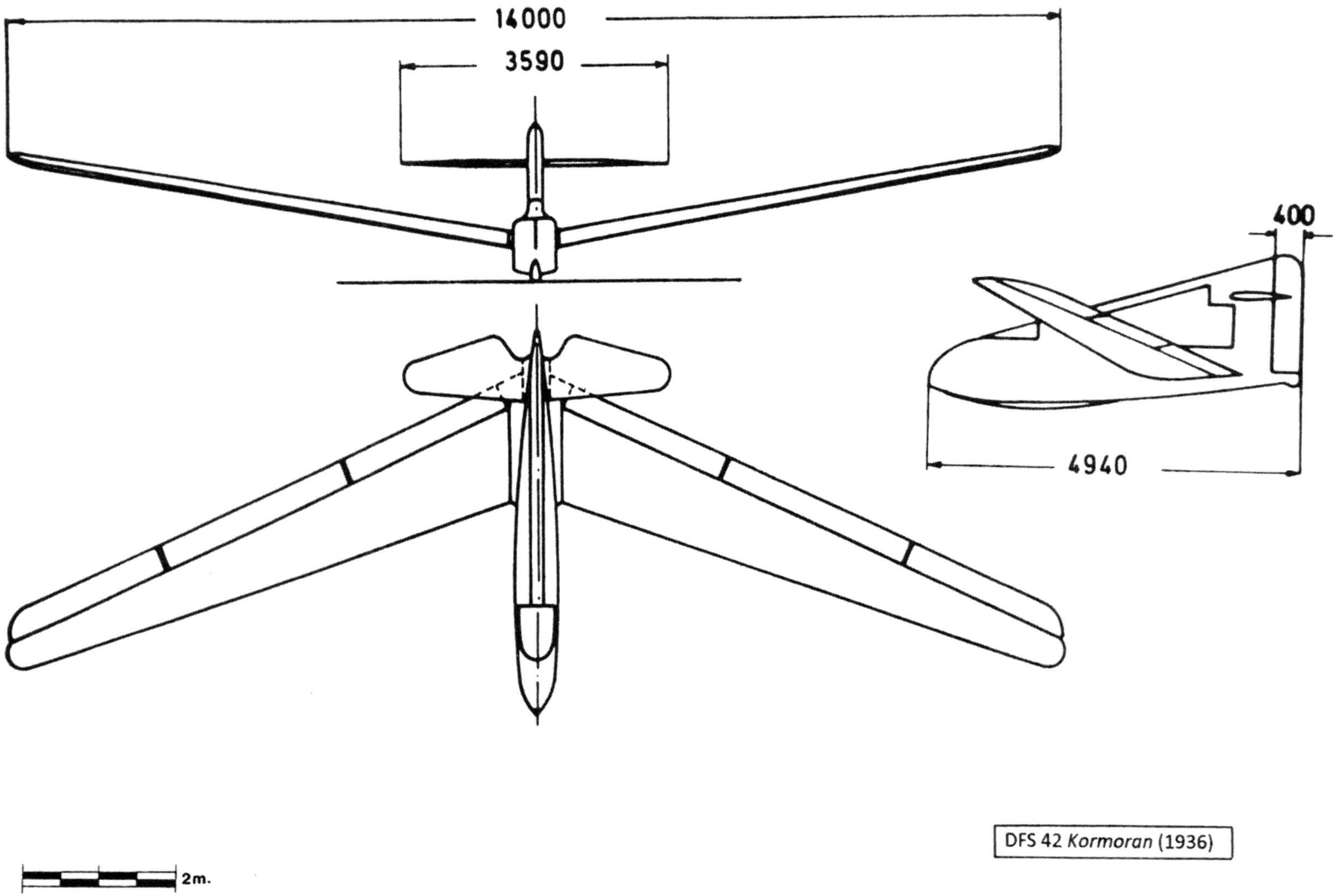

DFS 42 *Kormoran* (1936)

Focke-Wulf *Berich Nr.03028* (December 7, 1942)

Jäger mit Turbinentriebwerk BMW P.3302-Enwurf I

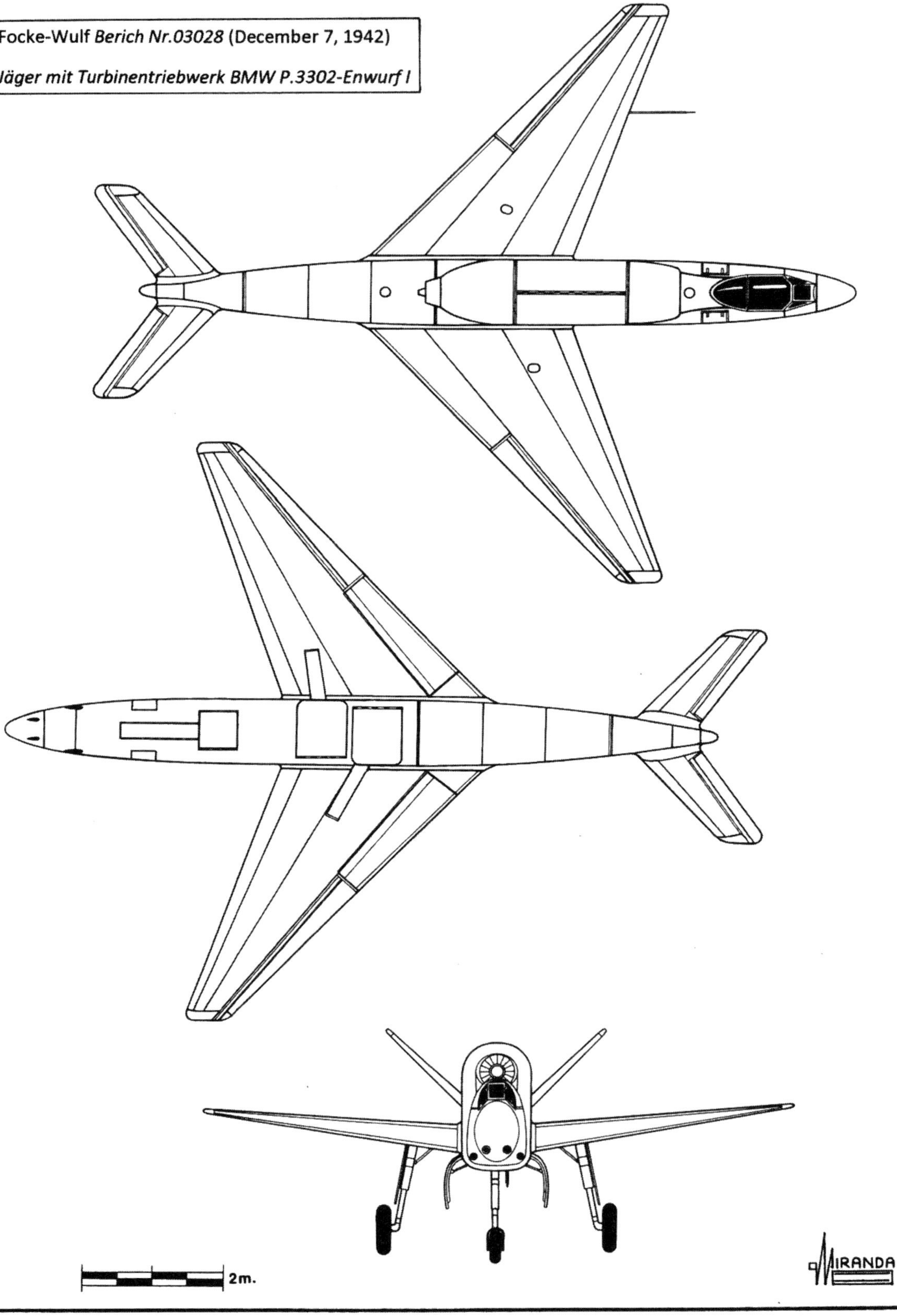

Focke-Wulf *Berich Nr.03028* (December 22, 1942)

Jäger mit Turbinentriebwerk BMW P.3302-Entwurf II

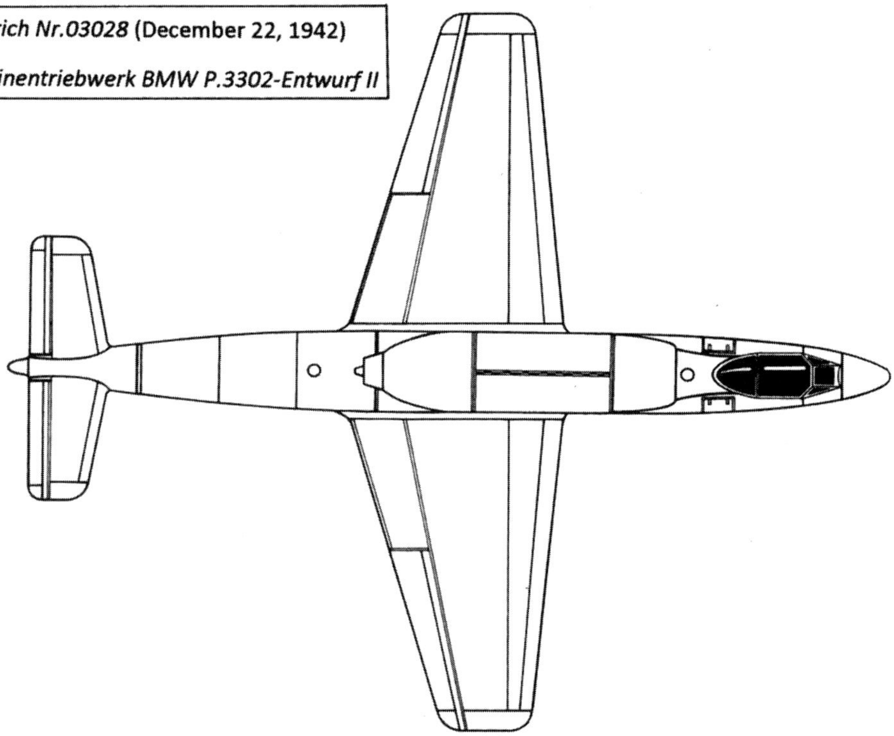

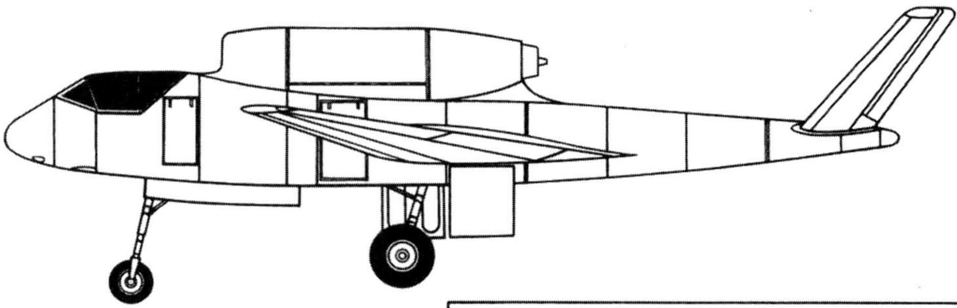

Focke-Wulf *Berich Nr.03028* (December 7, 1942)

Jäger mit Turbinentriebwerk BMW P.3302-Enwurf I

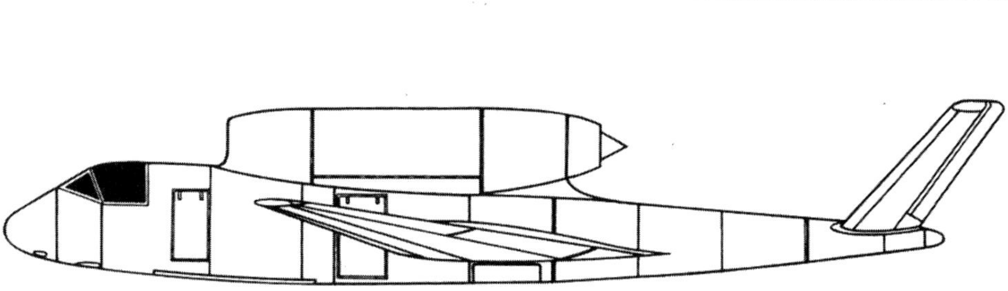

Focke-Wulf *Berich Nr.03028* (December 22, 1942)

Jäger mit Turbinentriebwerk Jumo 004-Entwurf I

2m.

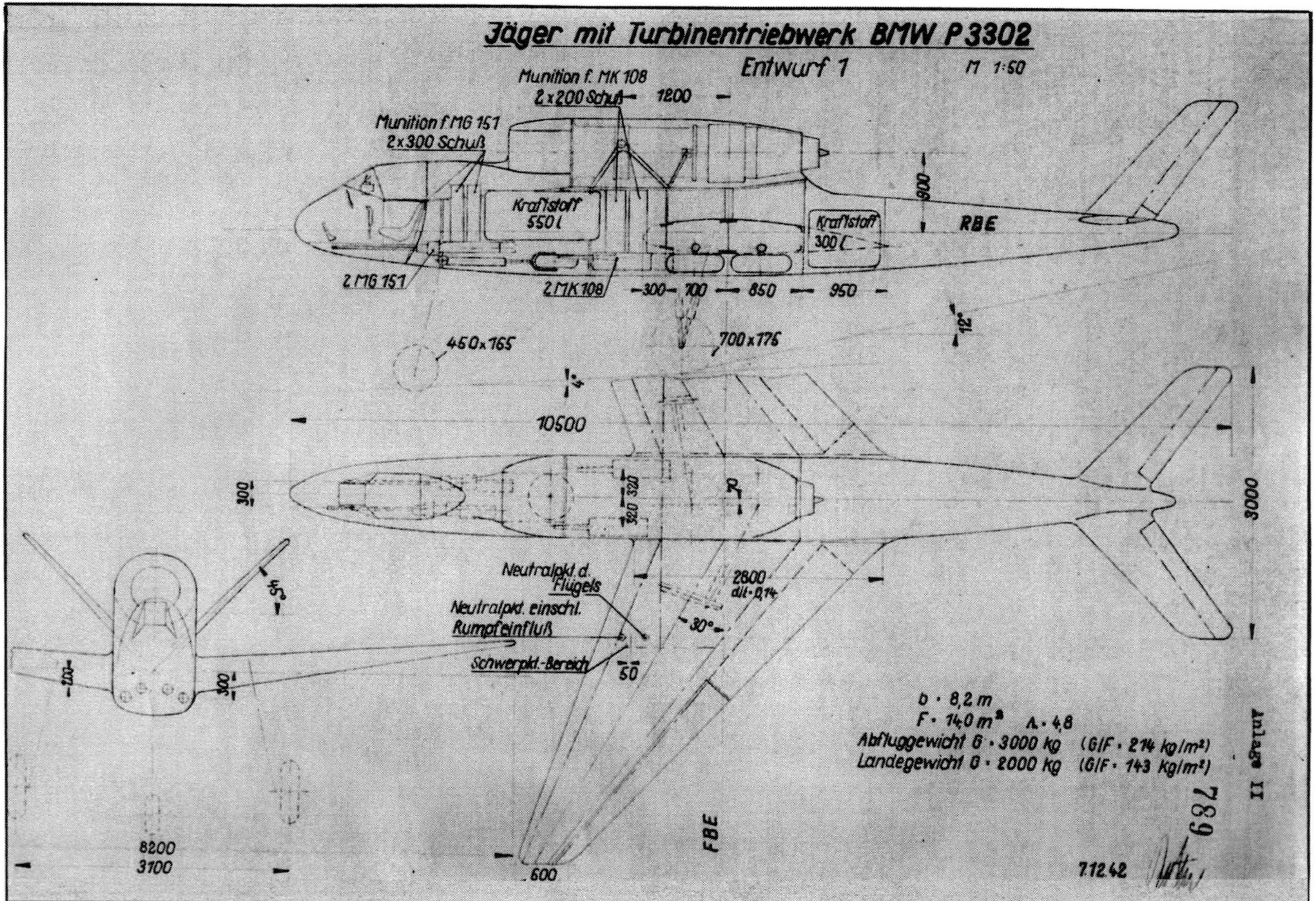
Jäger mit Turbinentriebwerk BMW P 3302
Entwurf 1
M 1:50
Munition f. MK 108
2 x 200 Schuß
1200
Munition f. MG 151
2 x 300 Schuß
Kraftstoff
550 l
Kraftstoff
300 l
900
RBE
2 MG 151
2 MK 108
300
700
850
950
12°
450 x 165
700 x 176
4°
10500
300
320
320
30
3000
Neutralpkt. d. Flügels
Neutralpkt. einschl. Rumpfeinfluß
Schwerpkt.-Bereich
50
2800
dlt = 0,14
30°
45°
200
300
b = 8,2 m
F = 14,0 m²
Λ = 4,8
Abfluggewicht G = 3000 kg (G/F = 214 kg/m²)
Landegewicht G = 2000 kg (G/F = 143 kg/m²)
Anlage II
789
FBE
8200
3100
600
7.12.42

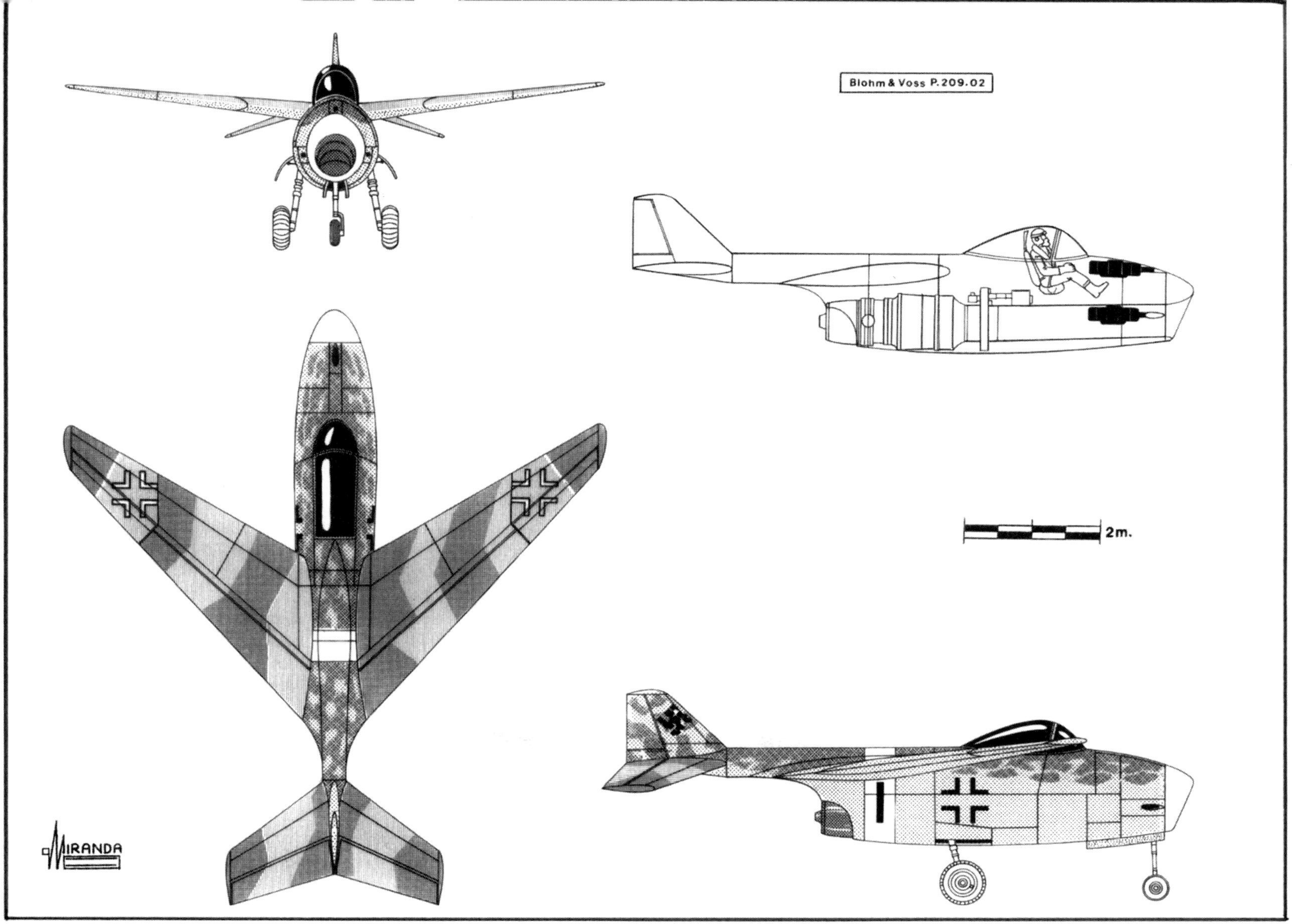
Blohm & Voss P.209.02
2m.
MIRANDA

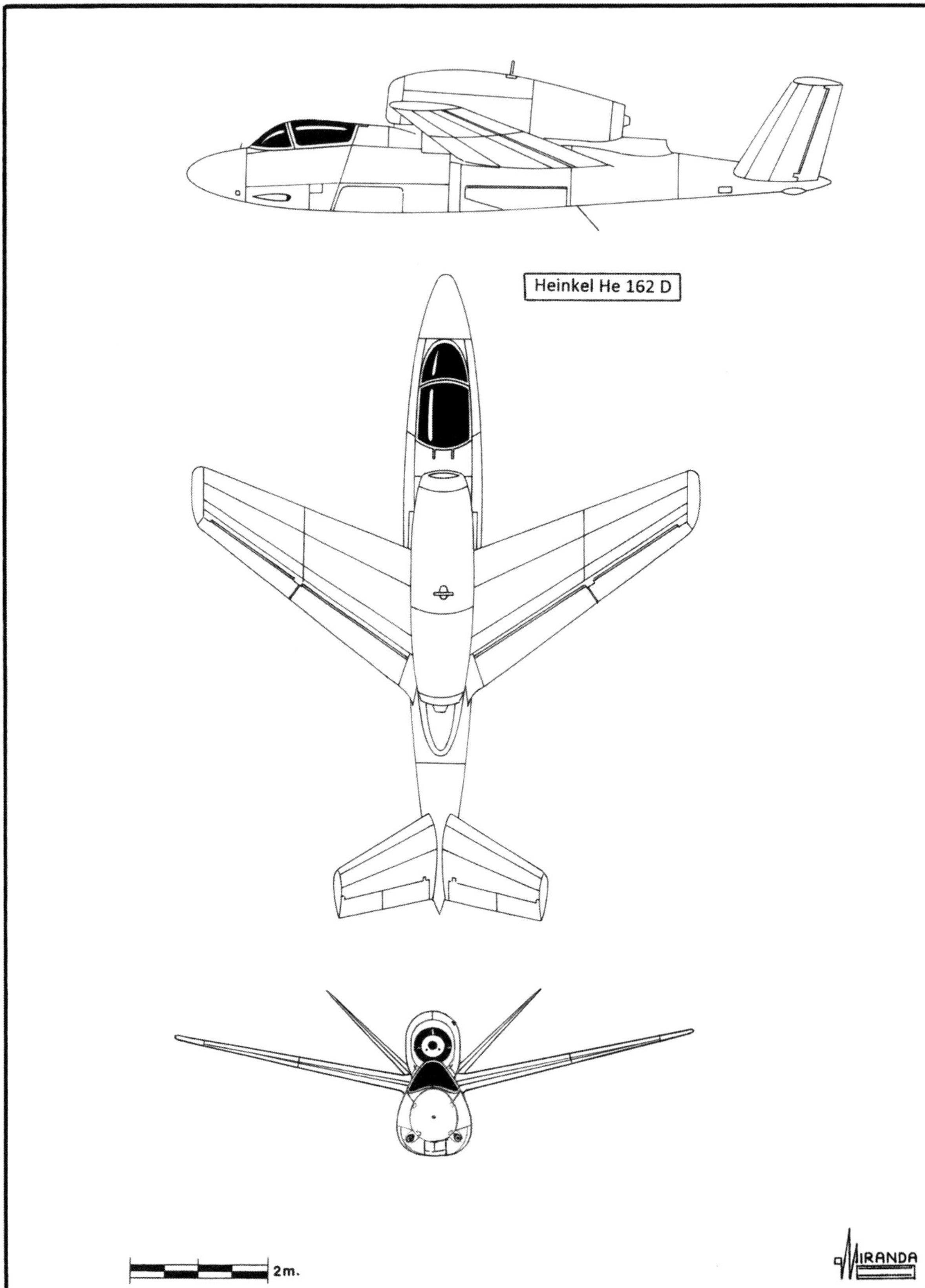

Heinkel He 162 D

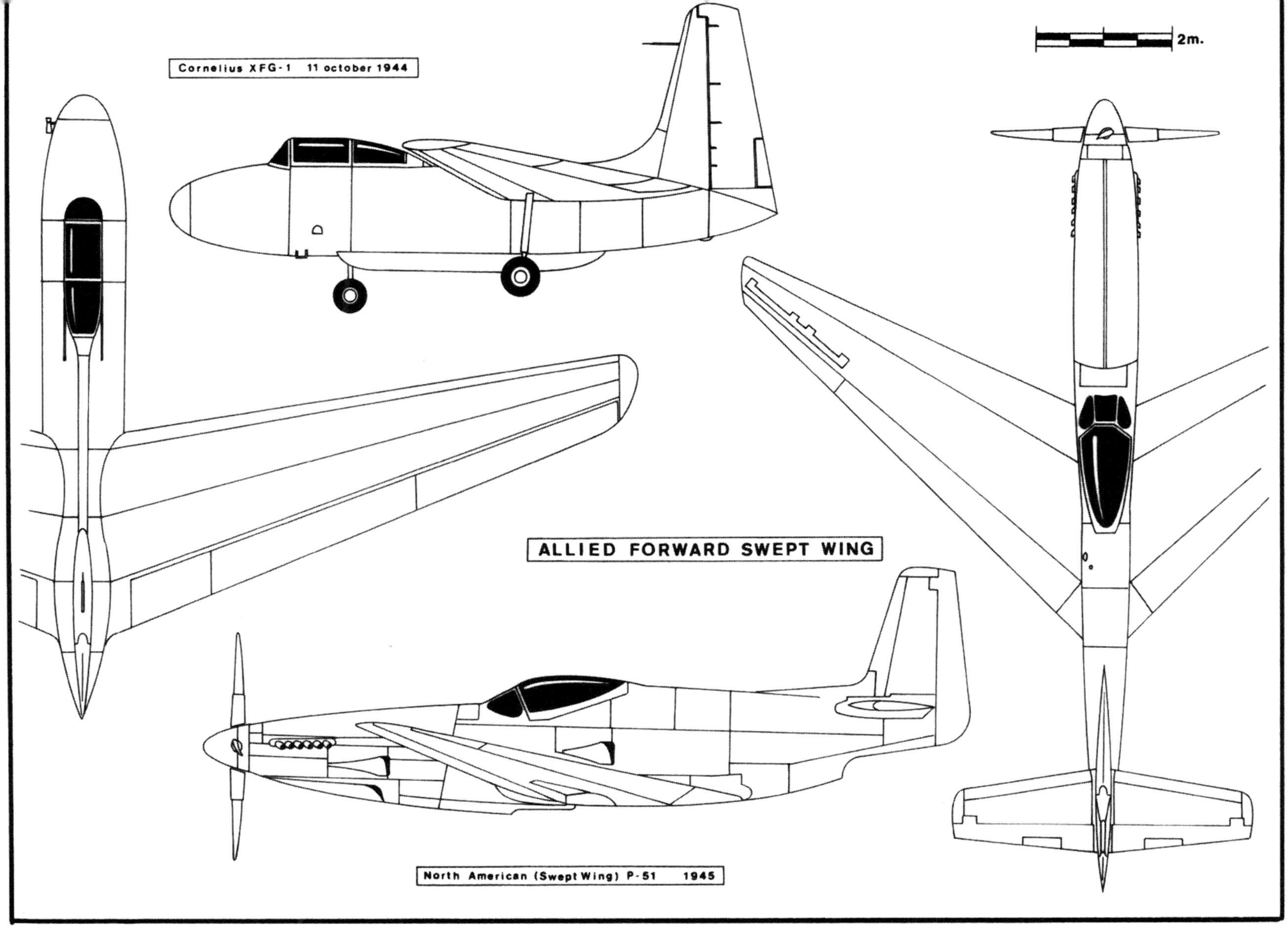

Cornelius XFG-1 11 october 1944
ALLIED FORWARD SWEPT WING
2m.
North American (Swept Wing) P-51 1945

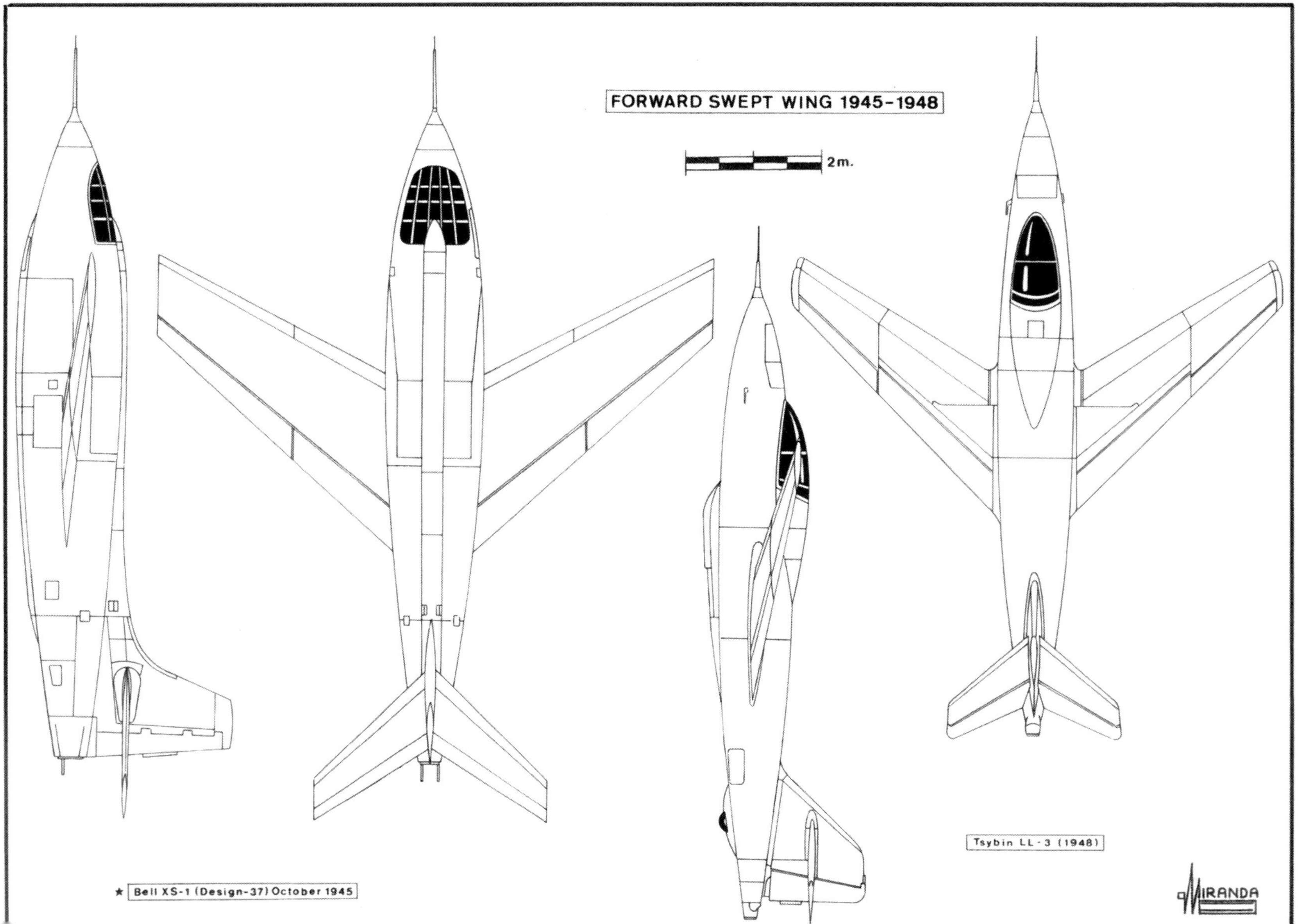
FORWARD SWEPT WING 1945-1948
2m.
★ Bell XS-1 (Design-37) October 1945
Tsybin LL-3 (1948)
MIRANDA

14

Focke-Wulf 1-R *Volksjäger*

During the last year of war in Europe, German industrial capacity had been irreversibly eroded by the long naval blockade and continued bombardment. The situation was particularly serious for the piston engine manufacturers, who had already exhausted the chrome and molybdenum reserves needed to harden the steel. Special *Schmierstoff* lubricants and B4 87-octane fuel were also lacking. The shortage induced aircraft manufacturers to compete for available turbojets and rockets engines, and the OKL was forced to resort to the tender system. *Jägernotprogramm* awarded of the HeS 011 turbojet and *Volksjäger* that of the BMW 003.

The only abundant and inexpensive engine available in 1944 was the VSR-9a pulsejet, with 32,000 units manufactured by the Argus firm to power the V-1 missiles. The Argus *Schmidt-rohr* could transport a ton of explosives to London, running on Br-Stoff crude oil, but produced only 336 kp of thrust. It was not throttleable and totally unsuitable to power a fighter. The extreme pressure from Chief Party Commissioner Dipl.-Ing. Karl Otto Saur forced the *Technisches Amt* to issue a request for the proposal of a pulsejet fighter.

On 8 November 1944, the *Miniaturjäger* specification was published for the construction of a light fighter armed with an MK 108/30 cannon, with a maximum speed of 810 kph at sea level and 710 kph at 6,000 m. The aeronautics industry responded with seven projects: the Blohm und Voss P.213, the Heinkel He-162 B-1 and P.1077 *Romeo I*, the Junkers EF.126 *Lilli*, and the Messerschmitt Me 328 A-1, A-2, and A-3. Only the P.213 and EF-126 were small enough to use one VSR-9a; the others were designed to use two engines.

Messerschmitt had already been working on the Me 328 for two years and had started building prototypes. Flight tests conducted with the Me 328 V3 between September and November 1944 were disappointing as the pulsejets only worked acceptably at low altitude, losing power very quickly above 2,800 m. When the results of the tests were known, the OKL decided to cancel the *Miniaturjäger* contest in December.

Most of the projects presented were reconfigured to *schlachtflugzeug* (ground-attack airplanes) because the simplicity of its design made its construction very cheap: an

EF.126 cost 30,000 Reichsmarks against the 74,000 Reichsmarks of a *Volksjäger*. The projects Heinkel He 162 B-2 and P.1077 Romeo II, the Junkers EF.126A *Elli*, and the Hütter *Jabo* (March 1945), all propelled by the new pulsejet Argus As 044 of 660-kp thrust, were presented to the *schlachtflugzeug* programme.

Some designers were working since late 1943 on projects like the *Bordjäger* (parasite fighter), the kind of plane that would finally give hundreds of available pilots of gliders the opportunity to enter combat.

In its simple version, the *Gleitjäger* (glider fighter) was a small plane with armoured cockpit and minimum frontal section. Towed to the vicinity of the bomber stream by a conventional fighter, it would be launched from a height sufficient to perform a single attack using an MK 108/30 cannon. The first *Gleitjäger* design was the Blohm und Voss BV 40 on 13 December 1943. The DFS Eber, DVL *Jagdsegler*, Gotha P.56, and Zeppelin *Panzerfaust* (having already improved their destruction capacity with the use of unguided air-to-air rockets RZ 65, W.Gr.21 and R4/M) appeared during the following year.

Some *Bordjägers*, such as the Gotha P.54, the Messerschmitt P.1103, or the Zeppelin *Rammer*, were designed as planes specialised in collision tactics, attacking from behind the bombers, and ramming their tail surfaces. To reach the proper impact velocity, they used one or two solid-propellant rockets: Schmidding 109-533/553 or Rheinmetall 515. Other more sophisticated designs aspired to use the Walter HWK 109-509 B, a small bi-propellant rocket engine built with the auxiliary combustion chamber of the HWK 109-509 A/B. With only 350-kp peak thrust, this engine was not enough to perform a conventional take-off but could propel a small *Bordjäger* to more than 900 kph. By mid-1944, at least five *Bordjäger* projects were competing for HWK 109-509 B: Arado E.581, Blohm und Voss BV 40, Focke-Wulf *Rammjäger*, and the Messerschmitt P.1103 and P1103 B.

In June, the *Technisches Amt* issued a requirement for a small and inexpensive point-defence interceptor of the *Objektschutzjäger* type for the protection of important targets, to be powered by a 1,700-kp thrust rocket engine 109-509 A/B or 109-509 A-1. The new *Objektschutzjäger* was manufactured in two versions. The light one, to be launched with the help of four RATO rockets and an acceleration that would not exceed 2.06 *g*, would be launched from a mobile launch ramp with 40 degrees slope. The second version, with greater propellants capacity, could carry out the take-off in only 350 m using a three-wheel dolly (that could be jettisoned) and four Rheinmetall 109-502 RATO rockets. It was expected that the heavy version could replace the 109-509 A/B in the future by the most advanced HWK 109-509 C with 2,000-kp peak thrust.

The *Objektschutzjäger* contest received seven proposals during the summer of 1944. Messerschmitt presented the P.1104 in two versions: ramp-launched (10 August 1944) and trolley-launched (22 September 1944). Heinkel proposed the P.1077 Julia (16 August 1944) with the pilot in the prone position and the P.1077 *Julia II* with the pilot in conventional position. Junkers presented the EF.127/I *Walli* for a mobile launch ramp and the EF.127/II *Elli* with a three-wheeled trolley and landing skid.

Focke-Wulf participated with its *Volksjäger* design, that could use both launch systems with the help of two or four Rheinmetall 109-502 rocket boosters of

770-kp peak each. The airframe consisted of a 67 per cent homothetic reduction of the Ta 183, with 6.77-m wingspan, 6.77-m length, and 10-sq. m wing area. The construction of the fuselage would be in light alloy, with a steel-armoured nosecone and plates behind the pilot. It housed one wind generator, the pressurised cockpit, two Mk 108/30 cannon, the T-Stoff and C-Stoff rocket propellant tanks, one Walter HWK 109-509 A-1 rocket engine with 1,700-kp peak thrust and the compressed-air-operated landing skid.

The electronic equipment proposed was one FuG 16ZY, one IFF discriminator FuG 25a, and one direction finder device FuG 16 Zvg. Each wing panel, with steel structure and plywood cladding, 40 degrees rear swept and 7.4 per cent thickness, housed five C-Stoff tanks and compressed-air-operated flaps. The tail surfaces, with wooden structure and cladding, consisted of a 60-degree swept tailfin and one 45-degree swept T-tailplane. The conventional version, with a maximum weight of 2,133 kg, could take off on a 260-m run, climb 15,000 m, and fly at 1,000 kph.

On 8 September 1944, the RLM declared the Heinkel *Julia II* the winner of the contest, ordering the construction of twenty prototypes and mass producing 300 aircraft per month. At the end of 1944, *Julia II* was also cancelled in favour of the Bachem Ba 349 Natter.

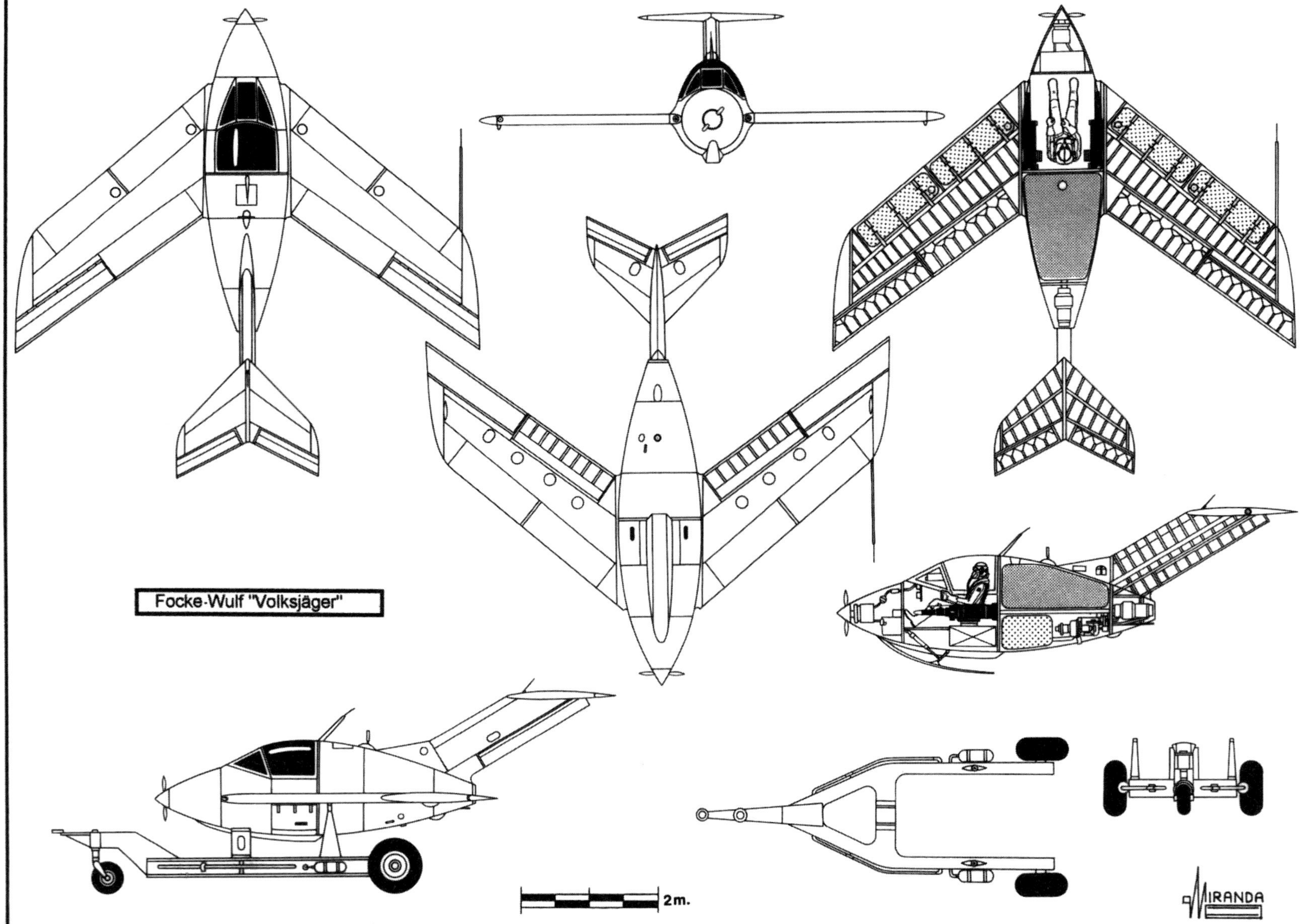

Focke-Wulf "Volksjäger"

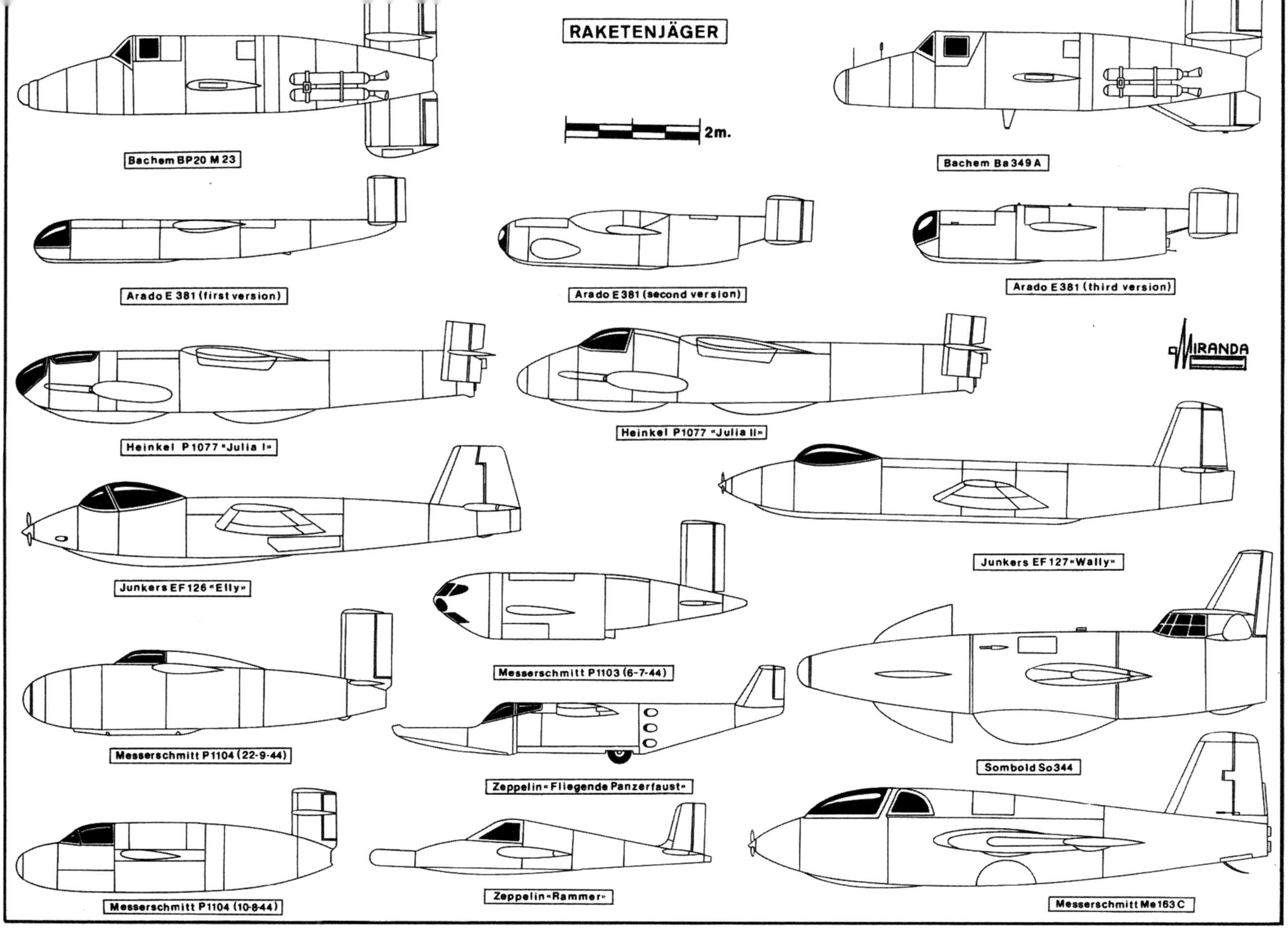
RAKETENJÄGER
2m.
Bachem BP20 M 23
Bachem Ba 349 A
Arado E 381 (first version)
Arado E381 (second version)
Arado E 381 (third version)
MIRANDA
Heinkel P1077 «Julia I»
Heinkel P1077 «Julia II»
Junkers EF 127 «Wally»
Junkers EF 126 «Elly»
Messerschmitt P1103 (6-7-44)
Sombold So344
Messerschmitt P1104 (22-9-44)
Zeppelin «Fliegende Panzerfaust»
Messerschmitt P1104 (10-8-44)
Zeppelin «Rammer»
Messerschmitt Me163 C

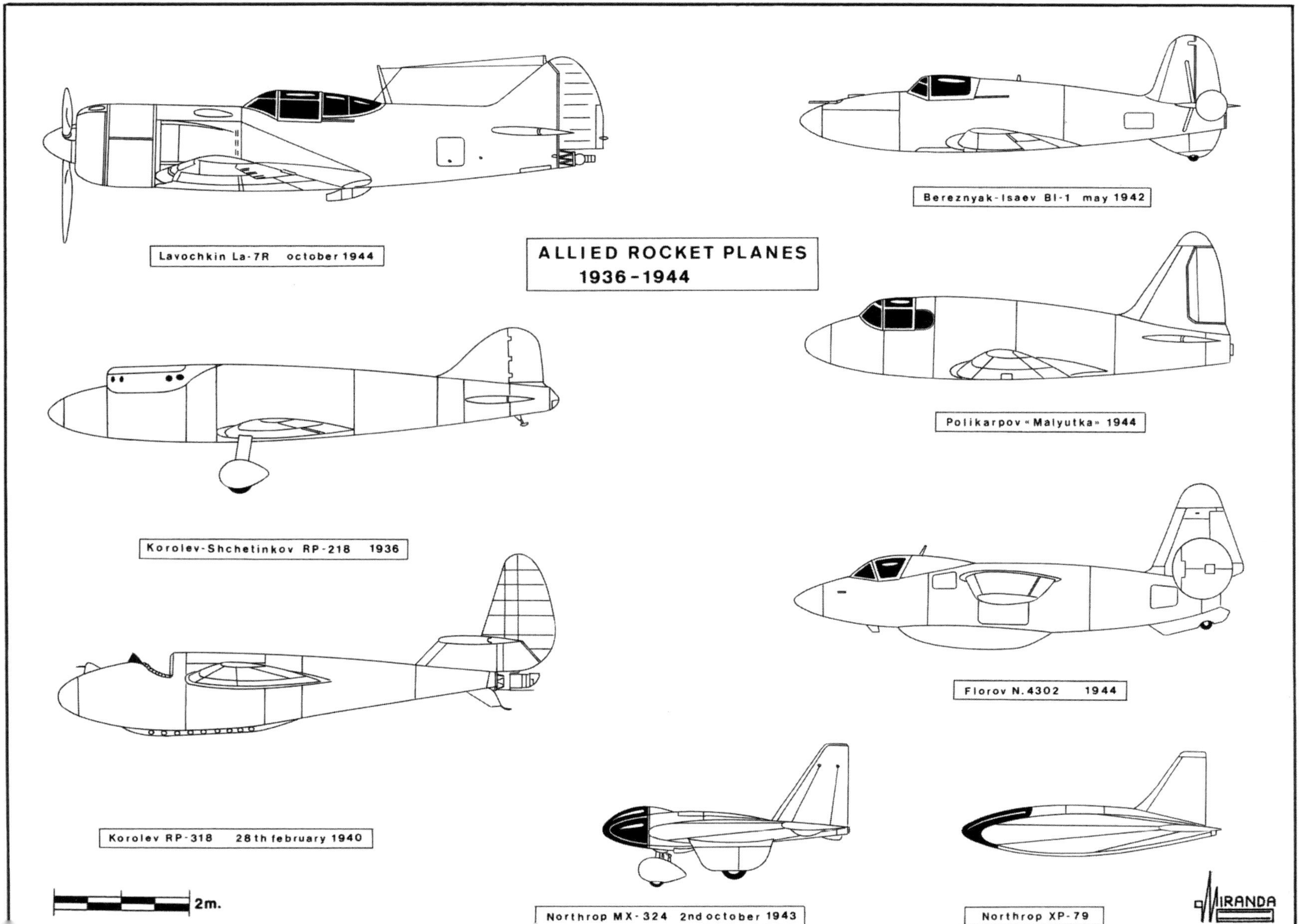
ALLIED ROCKET PLANES
1936-1944
Lavochkin La-7R october 1944
Bereznyak-Isaev BI-1 may 1942
Polikarpov «Malyutka» 1944
Korolev-Shchetinkov RP-218 1936
Florov N.4302 1944
Korolev RP-318 28th february 1940
2m.
Northrop MX-324 2nd october 1943
Northrop XP-79
MIRANDA

15

Focke-Wulf 1-R *Rammjäger*

The mass production of the Fi 103 (V-1) flying bombs, which had been entrusted to the Fieseler and Volkswagen firms, was expected to reach 2,000 units in December 1943, 6,000 in May, and 9,000 in September 1944.

However, it was soon made evident that even giving them the highest political priority, the manufacturing capacity of both firms in their factories at Fallersleben, Meissen, Cham, Kassel, Rothwesten, Wolfsburg, and Mittelwerk would not be enough to achieve the forecasted manufactured units. This circumstance was not ignored by the rest of the aeronautical firms of the Reich that rushed to present their own projects based on the V-1.

The Arado firm presented the *Deichselschlepp, Startwagen*, and *Huckepack* systems for the transport and launch of the V-1 from the Ar 234 C bombers. The DFS Institut used a V-1 airframe to build the SG 5041 fuel tank that could be towed by the Ar 234. Heinkel modified some He 111 H-16 and H-22 to transport and launch both the V-1 and the manned missiles of the Reichenberg series. Blohm und Voss proposed a transport and launch system, to be used from the U-boat Type XXI, able to reach New York. Gotha worked in an anti-ship version with float *Gleitboot*. Porsche designed the Type 300 detachable turbojet with a superior performance than the Argus 109-014.

Messerschmitt designed a *Startwagen* device that allowed the transport and launch of the V-1 by the Bf 109 G-6. Its team also designed the P.1103 and P.1104 rocket interceptors using some parts of the V-1. The Zeppelin firm designed a rammer using the wings and tail surfaces of the V-1. Henschel specialised in the construction of *Reichenberg* prototypes.

Nothing was known about the projects proposed by the Focke-Wulf company until French historian Paul Malmassari published his article '*Découverte de quelques projets autour du V-1*' in *Le Fana de l'Aviation* in September 2000. He describes the *Brummer* project developed by DFS so that an Fw 190 could transport a V-1 in *Startwagen* configuration. He also refers to a rammer design proposed by Professor Conradis of the Bad Eilsen Institute in September 1944. The concept behind this design was to install an armoured nose instead of the warhead of a V-1 and a pilot cockpit with armoured windshield and ejector seat in the space usually occupied by the compressed air bottles.

A bi-fuel rocket replaced the Argus pulsejet, which was not right for high-altitude flight, and the *rammer* would be launched from a He 111 bomber to save rocket fuel. There are no drawings of this project; the author has therefore taken licence to reconstruct this design based on Malmassari's description, with the warning that any error should be credited to the author, and not to him. It also seems reasonable that Focke-Wulf would have used the armoured windshield and clear canopy of the Fw 190 A-8/R2 *Sturmbock* and the control surfaces of the *Reichenberg*. The rocket should have been the compact HWK 109-509 B-0, already used by the firm in the designs of the Fw *Projekt V* and *Projekt VI*. It could be installed behind the cockpit in a light downwards angle without interfering with the control cables of the tail surfaces. The propellant tanks of T-Stoff and C-Stoff could be installed behind the armoured nose.

Some V-1 carried *Kutonase* (cable-cutter) devices in the wing leading edges, possibly also a useful device in the *Rammer*. We do not know about the type of seat used, except that the Focke-Wulf firm had carried over some experiments with an ejector seat installed in an Fw 190 and with a special type of explosives.

Per Malmassari's story, the ejection happened after the impact. This suggests an anti-*g* device installed in the seat like the one in the Gotha P.54.

SPECULATIVE DRAWINGS

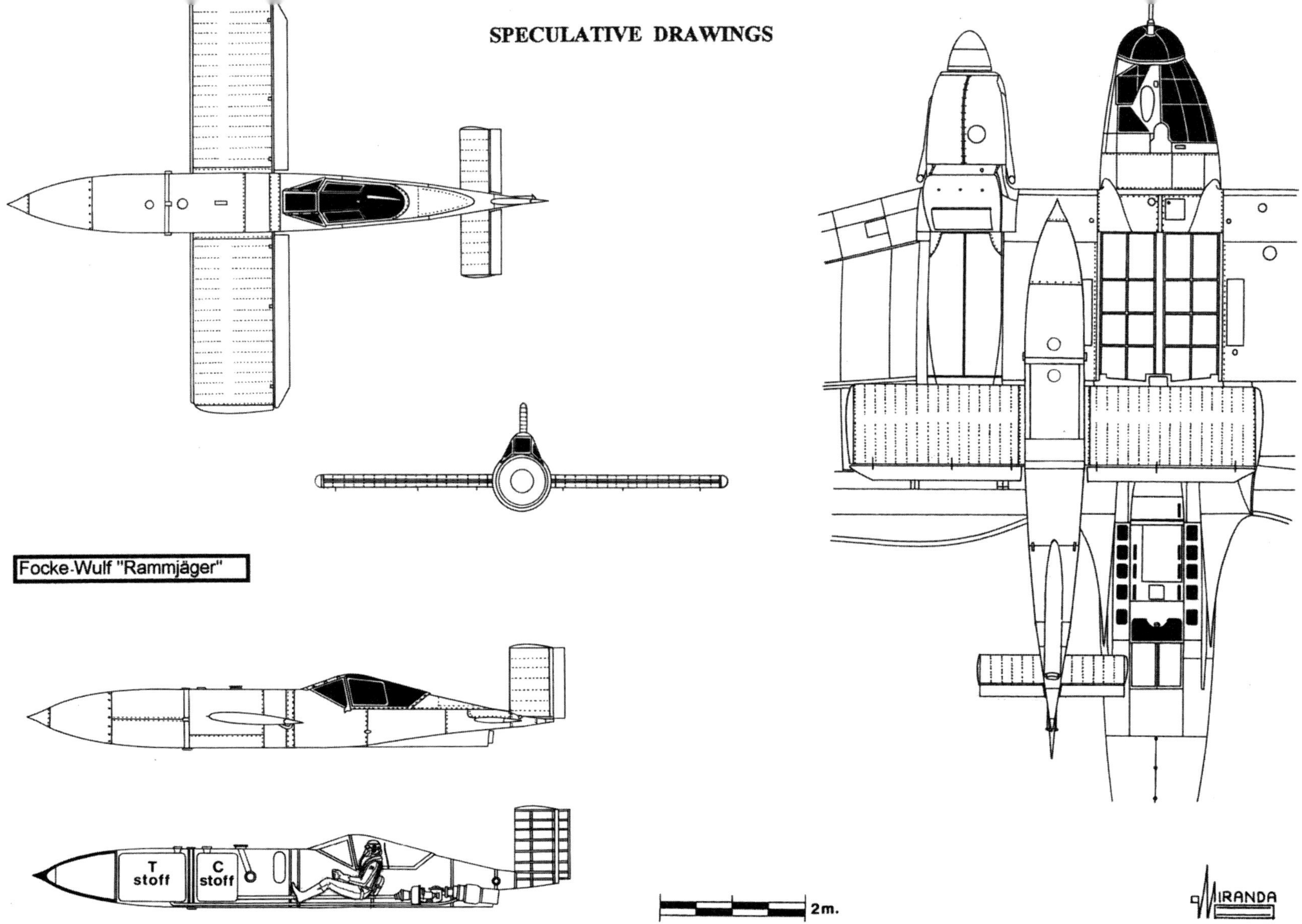

Focke-Wulf "Rammjäger"

16

Focke-Wulf 2-TL *Jagdflugzeug mit* HeS 109-011

During the summer of 1944, the RLM announced plans for the monthly construction of 5,000 fighters powered by the new HeS 011 A-0 turbojet. For some aircraft manufacturers, this large-scale production programme meant the possibility to gain access to a regular supply of turbojets. It also led to the design of a new class of combat airplanes powered by two jet engines.

The excess power allowed them to act indistinctly as *Fernjäger* (long-range fighter), *Zerstörer* (bomber destroyer), or *Schnellbomber* (fast bomber), except with light field modifications of the *Rüstsätze* type. They were big airplanes with enough space for fuel, electronic equipment, and additional crew members, which was very convenient for their future transformation into night fighters.

As an interim solution for the *Sofortprogramm*, the firm Arado proposed to the OKL the construction of a *Zerstörer* based on the airframe of the Ar 234 C. The new aircraft, named Ar 234 E, would be endowed with a heavy armoured cockpit, two HeS 011 turbojets suspended under the wings, and two MK 103/30 heavy cannon in a ventral pack.

The long-term solution *Vorrückenprogramm* was the Arado TEW project 16/43-19, which the designers had been working on since mid-1943. It was a monster of 16 tons and 18 m in length, capable of carrying 2,000 kg of bombs and anti-ship missiles, as well as different combinations of MG 213/20, MK 108/30, and MK 103/30 cannon.

The solution chosen by Kurt Tank was a 130 per cent scaled-up Ta 183 B named *Projekt* P.011.025 in the internal documentation of the firm and Focke-Wulf Fw 250 in the specialised literature. It was presented to the OKL on 21 November 1944, in a dossier called Baubeschreibung Nr. 250. The position of the two HeS 011 A-0 turbojets, placed very close together inside the fuselage, allowed it to fly using only one of them in case of failure or to save fuel without lateral stability problems. This aerodynamic solution also generated less drag than the Arado formula, allowing the plane to reach higher speeds.

It was a multipurpose aircraft, which could be manufactured in at least three versions without changes in the assembly line. One was the *Fernjäger*, a long range heavy fighter designed to hunt down the bombers that, having been damaged, remained behind in the trip of return to its bases, abandoning the protection of the 'box'. It was a very profitable combat tactic that the short-legged interceptors Bf 109 and Fw 190 could not afford. *Fernjäger* could fly at 765 kph with a single engine and had a range of 2,440 km using only the internal fuel. The second was a *Zerstörer*, armed with 30-mm, 50-mm, and even 55-mm cannon, with a clean range of 1,370 km and enough speed to escape the escort fighters. There was also a *Schnellbomber* designed to meet the specifications of the Focke-Wulf 1000×1000×1000. It could internally transport an SC1000 *Hermann* bomb to London, flying to 1,074 kph.

Unfortunately for Focke-Wulf, some ground tests carried out in November with Me 262 W.Nr. 130015 showed that the internal drag in air ducts reduced the turbojet thrust by 45 kp for each metre in length. The Fw 250 used two air ducts of 6.4 m each, which would imply a thrust loss of 576 kp at full throttle. This design defect forced the cancellation of the project on 26 February 1945.

Technical Data: *Fernjäger*

Wings: 43 degrees swept, 4:1 aspect ratio and 39 sq. m area. Each wing panel was built of plywood and steel, housing six fuel tanks, one main undercarriage leg, flaps and ailerons.
Tailplane: 45 degrees swept, built in wood/plywood.
Tailfin: 41 degrees swept, built in wood/plywood.
Fuselage: built in light alloy and steel, it housed two air intakes/air ducts ensembles, two He S 109-011 A-0 turbojets with 1,300 kp static thrust each, the nose leg, the pressurised cockpit with ejector seat and armour, three dorsal fuel tanks, four standard MK 108/30 cannon and one ventral weapons bay that could contain an SC 1000 bomb or an extra fuel tank of 1,600 litres.
Optional armament: four MG 213/20 cannon, with 180 rounds per gun, in a ventral pack. Internally fuel capacity: 3,560 litres.
Wingspan: 12.5 m; Length: 12.75 m; Height: 3.8 m.
Maximum take-off weight: 7,400 kg.
Maximum estimated speed: 1,078 kph
Range: 1,440 km.
Climb rate: 25.4 m/sec.
Ceiling: 15,300 m.

Technical Data: *Zerstörer*

Wings: 43 degrees swept, 4:1 aspect ratio and 39 sq. m area. Each wing panel was built of plywood and steel, housing six fuel tanks, one main undercarriage leg, flaps and ailerons.
Tailplane: 45 degrees swept, built in wood/plywood.
Tailfin: 41 degrees swept, built in wood/plywood.

Fuselage: built in light alloy and steel, it housed two air intakes/air ducts ensembles, two He S 109-011 A-0 turbojets with 1,300 kp static thrust each, the nose leg, the pressurised cockpit with ejector seat and armour, three dorsal fuel tanks, four standard MK 108/30 cannon and one ventral weapons bay that could contain an SC 1000 bomb or an extra fuel tank of 1,600 litres.
Optional armament two MG 213/20 cannon, with 180 rounds per gun, or two MK 103/30 cannon, with 75 rounds per gun, or one MK 214/50 cannon, or one MK 412/55 cannon in a ventral pack.
Internally fuel capacity: 2,000 litres.
Wingspan: 12.5 m; length: 12.75 m; height: 3.8 m.
Maximum take-off weight: 8,850 kg.
Maximum estimated speed: 1,068 kph.
Range: 1,370 km.
Climb rate: 20.6 m/sec.
Ceiling: 14,500 m.

Technical Data: *Schnellbomber*

Wings: 43 degrees swept, 4:1 aspect ratio and 39 sq. m area. Each wing panel was built of plywood and steel, housing six fuel tanks, one main undercarriage leg, flaps and ailerons.
Tailplane: 45 degrees swept, built in wood/plywood.
Tailfin: 41 degrees swept, built in wood/plywood.
Fuselage: built in light alloy and steel, it housed two air intakes/air ducts ensembles, two He S 109-011 A-0 turbojets with 1,300 kp static thrust each, the nose leg, the pressurised cockpit with ejector seat and armour, three dorsal fuel tanks, four standard MK 108/30 cannon and one ventral weapons bay that could contain an SC 1000 bomb or an extra fuel tank of 1,600 litres.
Optional armament four 108/30 cannon, with 120 rounds per gun, and one SC 1000 bomb internally.
Internally fuel capacity: 2600 litres.
Wingspan: 12.5 m; length: 12.75 m; height: 3.8 m.
Maximum take-off weight: 9,000 kg.
Maximum estimated speed: 1,074 kph.
Range 1,640 km.
Climb rate: 20.2 m/sec.
Ceiling: 14,000 m.

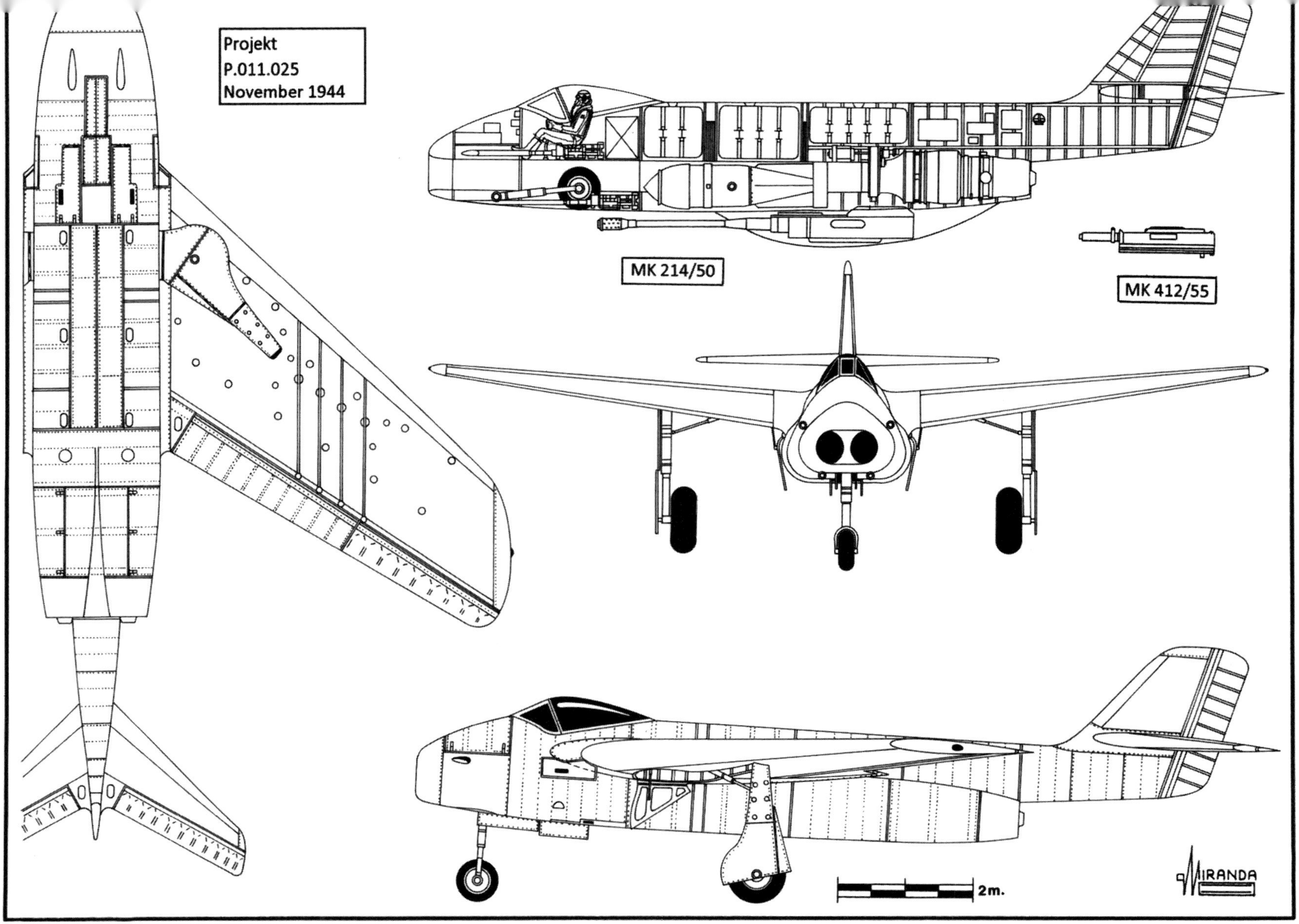
Projekt
P.011.025
November 1944
MK 214/50
MK 412/55
2m.
MIRANDA

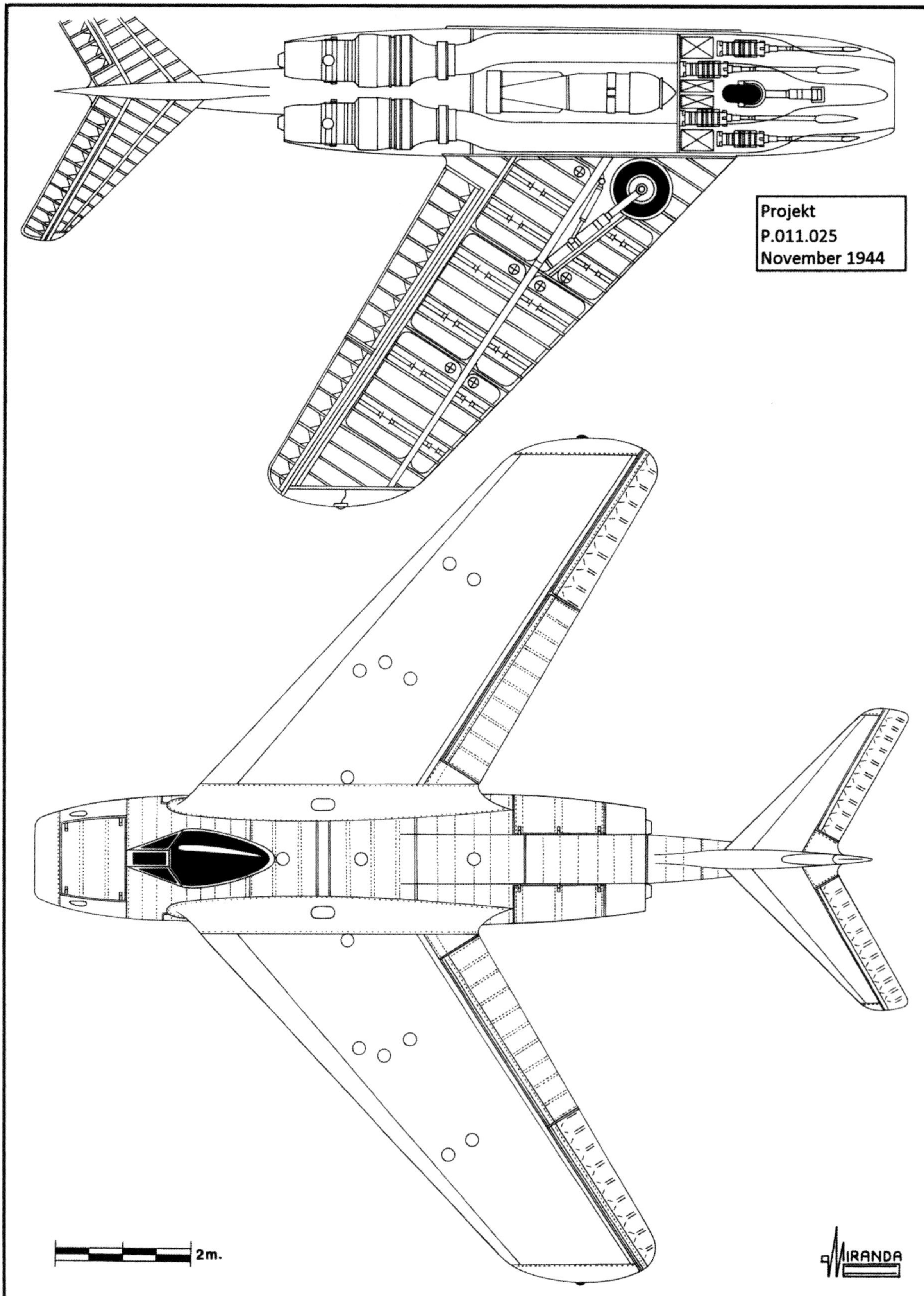
Projekt
P.011.025
November 1944
2m.
MIRANDA

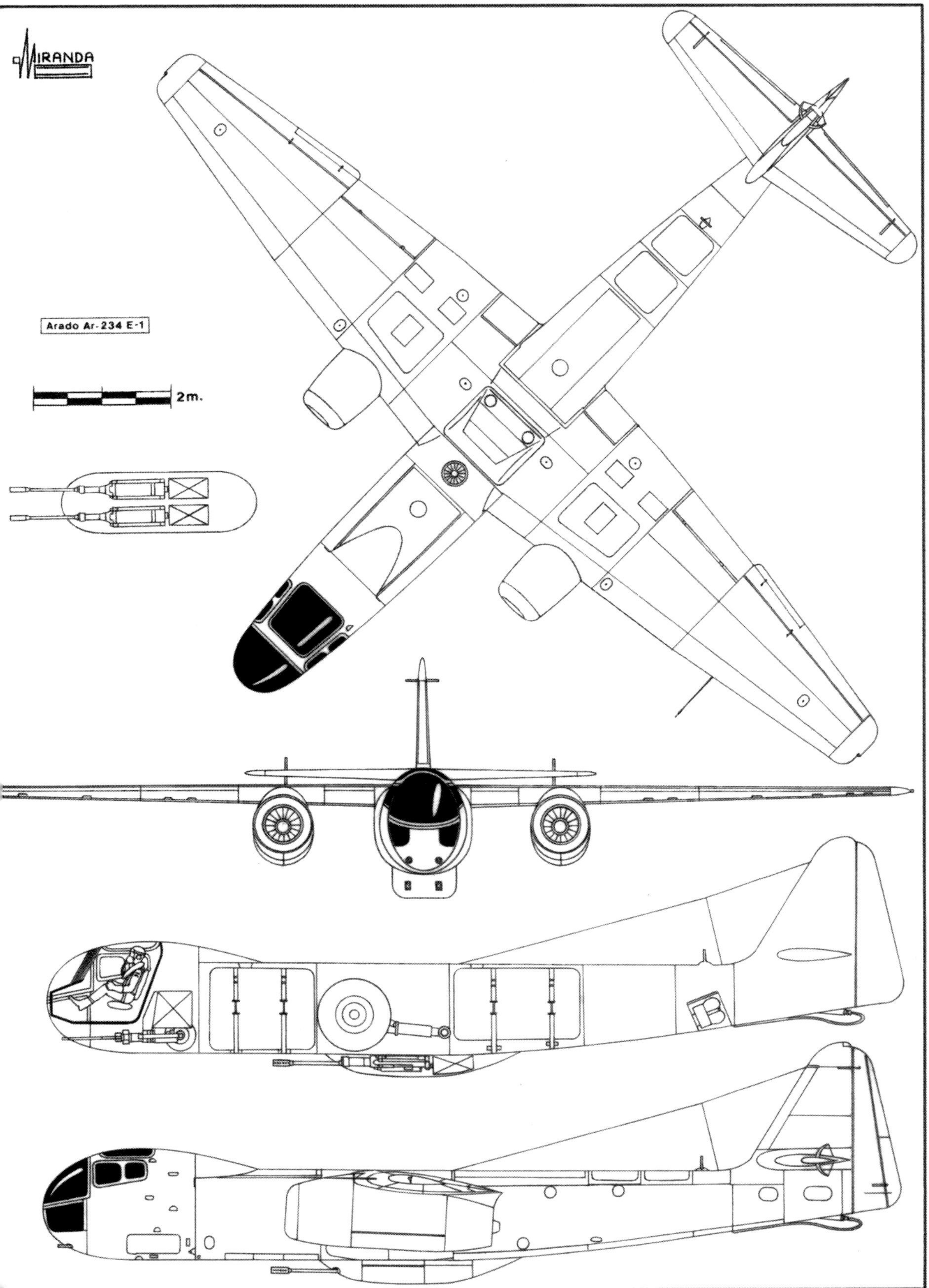

MIRANDA
Arado Ar-234 E-1
2m.

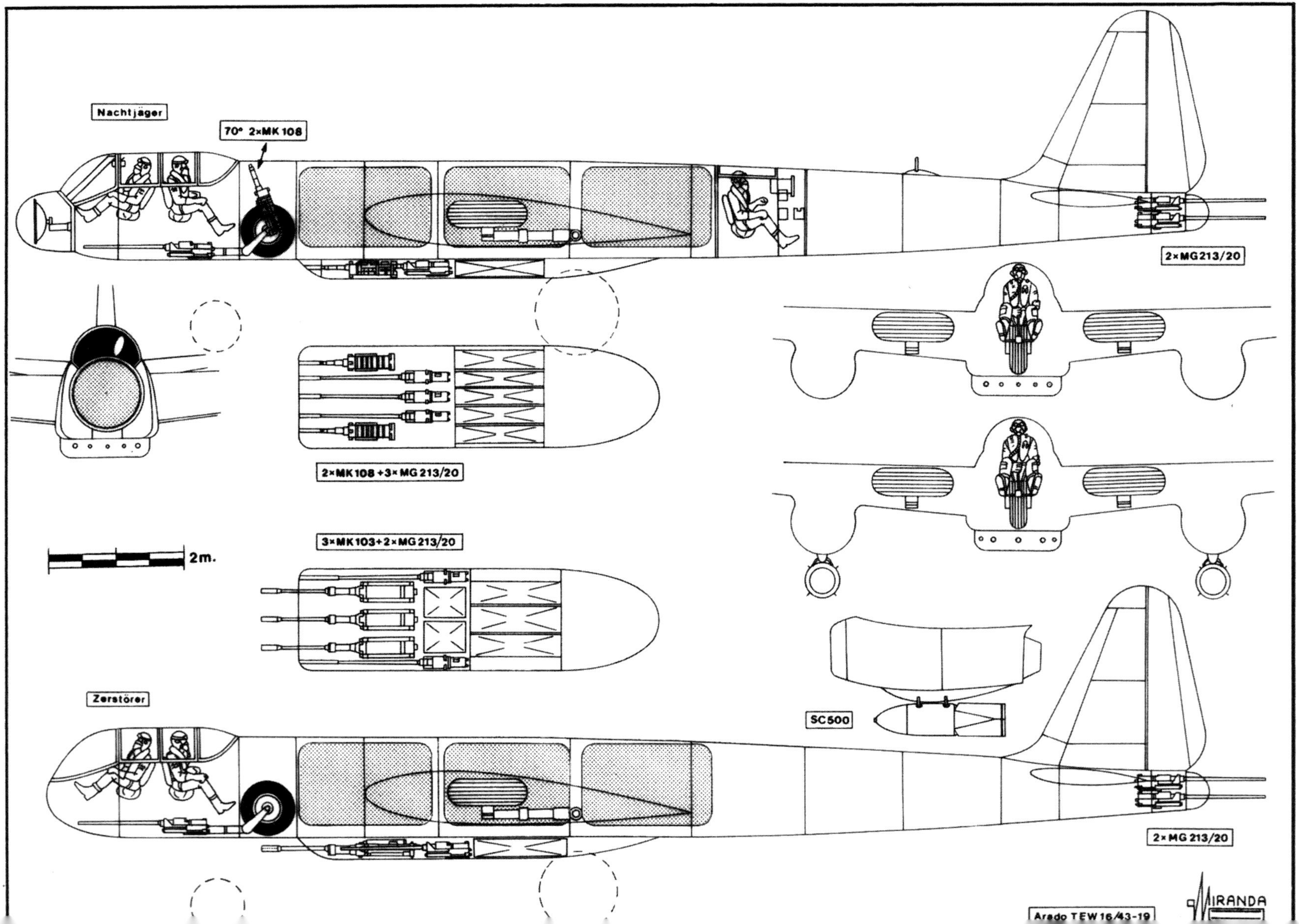

Nachtjäger
70° 2×MK 108
2×MG 213/20
2×MK 108 + 3×MG 213/20
3×MK 103+2×MG 213/20
2m.
SC500
Zerstörer
2×MG 213/20
MIRANDA
Arado TEW 16/43-19

17

Focke-Wulf 2-TL *Nachtjäger Projekt I*

By mid-1944, the RAF night bombing offensive had reached its peak intensity. The Pathfinder Force airplanes had gained much experience locating strategic targets at the heart of the Reich; it marked them with light markers to help the bomber stream that followed with a delay of just a few minutes to accurately launch their bombs.

Many bombers were equipped with the cartographic radar H2S, which could distinguish shorelines, rivers, and lakes very efficiently, thus supporting navigation. However, from a German viewpoint, the worst of all were the small attacks of the Mosquitos made by a dozen of airplanes to mislead the defences of the *Himmelbett* system over the bombing chosen location.

In daylight, they attacked U-boats in the Bay of Biscay and small units of the *Kriegsmarine* from France to Norway with 57-mm cannon fire, bombed administrative centres and Gestapo headquarters, forcing the cancellation of previously announced political meetings of Goebbels and Göring, with timely accurateness. At night, they bombed Berlin with impunity or marked targets with light markers for the big formations of Lancasters and Halifaxes. At its highest provocation point, they started to destroy the Ruhr factories with extremely accurate bombings during the night, even with fog and at an altitude of 9,000 m. The Germans took months to find out that the Allies were being helped by the radar equipment of the Oboe system, which guided them from the southeast of England.

The *Himmelbett* night system of defence of the Reich covered five countries, dozens of radars (even specialised ships abroad), thousands of cannon and searchlights, aerodromes, squadrons, and control and command centres. It ran for thousands of kilometres of cables and was not working. The night fighters obtained by the transformation of the veteran Bf 110, Do 217, and Ju 88 were not good enough. The Luftwaffe was fighting and losing.

Some single-engine fighters of the types Messerschmitt Bf 109 G-6 and Focke-Wulf Fw 190 A-6 used in operations '*Helle Nachtjadg*' and *Wilde Sau* from the summer of 1943 were fast enough to hunt the Mosquitos, but lacked the electronic equipment *Himmelbettaufsatz* necessary to locate them in the dark. In February 1944, some Bf 109 G-6/U4N, equipped with passive radar receivers FuG 350 Naxos Z, began to operate at night with the 1./NJG 10. This equipment was designed to detect the emissions of cartographic radar *H2S* used by the British four-engine bombers, but not those used by the Mosquito.

The NJG 11 was formed as a night fighter squadron specialised in the experimentation with radars. In the summer of 1944, a Fw 190 A-6/R6 was equipped with a FuG 217 L *Neptun Liliput* radar, using it as a rangefinder for launching rockets W.Gr.21. Flying tests were also carried out with a Fw 190 A-8/R11 equipped with a FuG 217/218 *Neptun J3* radar capable of measuring the azimuth and with *Hirschgeweih* antennas on the wings; however, the drag generated by them caused an unacceptable loss of speed. The conclusion was that the most suitable model for night combat was the Fw 190 A-6/R11. It was equipped with a FuG 217 *Neptun J1* radar of inferior performances to those of the J3, but its *Letzler* aerials generated less drag than the *Hirschgeweih* of the most advanced model.

In early 1944, the Fw 190 A-6/R11 began to be used by the night fighter units JG 300, JG 302, 2./NJGr 10, 1./NJG 10, and NJG 101; however, there were few results because its BMW 801 engine lost power over altitudes of 6,000 m. It was also useless to intercept the *Oboe* Mosquitos flying at 9,000 m. Additionally, its armament lacked the punch required to demolish a Lancaster in a single attack. The Messerschmitt Bf 109G series 5 and 6 had the right speed and ceiling to deal with the Mosquito, but their use in night operations was problematic given the fragility of their landing gear and the absence of blind-landing equipment.

However, in the summer of 1943, tests were carried out on two Bf 109 G-6/N, equipped with prototypes of the FuG 217 and *Letzler* aerials radar. The operational version, called the Bf 109 G-5/AS, with pressurised cockpit and DB 605 AS engine, was used in mid-1944 by the II./NJG 11 during high-altitude interceptions. Combat experience showed that single-seat fighters were not suitable for night combat. In addition to the problems experienced with its landing gear, short-range aerials, and the absence of blind landing devices, it was discovered that the glare of radarscope ruined the night vision of the pilot, who also needed to keep an eye on the airspace around him. For this reason, an aircraft of the II./JG 300 rammed a Lancaster on March 1944.

What they needed was a fast aircraft with an extended range and a second crewmember to take care of the radar. After discarding the options represented by the Arado Ar 240 C-2 and the Messerschmitt Me 410 C/N, the Luftwaffe thought to find the solution in the Focke-Wulf Ta 154 *Moskito*, a machine specially designed as a night fighter, which used a wood construction system like that of its British adversary. Unfortunately for the Germans, during the first flying trials carried out with the prototype V2 in September 1943, it was verified that the drag generated by the Matratzen aerials of the radar FuG 212 reduced the maximum speed by 12 per cent. Similar results were obtained in December with the *Hirschgeweih* aerials of the FuG 220 installed in the prototype V3.

It was expected that the *Letzler* aerials installed in the operational version Ta 154 A-4 would improve performance, but after several accidents, it was discovered that this model suffered a structural defect impossible to correct and the Luftwaffe rejected its use on nocturnal operations on 7 November 1944.

The Heinkel He 219 was not considered a good option. Its performances were inferior to those of the *Moskito* due to the excessive weight of the first-generation ejector seats, activated by compressed air, and the *Hirschgeweih* aerials of the radar Lichtenstein SN-2, which generated even more drag than those of the *Neptun J3*.

On 25 October 1944, the OKL ordered the conversion of the fastest available airplanes (Me 262, Ar 234, and Do 335) into emergency night fighters, following the *Sofortprogramm* directive. The modification consisted of installing a *Neptun* radar and a second crew member to operate it. The Me 262 B-1a/U1 and the Ar 234 B-2N, which were thus transformed, could enter service with some success in 1945. However, the air drag generated by the big *Hirschgeweih* antennae installed in the nose, and the removal of one of the fuel tanks to make room for the radar operator, penalised the maximum speed and endurance and partially overrode the advantage of the initial design.

The *Sofortprogramm* did not solve the problem. After dismissing the construction of dozens of night fighter projects and postponing entering the Heinkel He 219 into service for years, the *Technisches Amt* had to recognise its need to have aircraft designed for night combat. The Horten brothers already had a very advanced design of a twin-seat version of the Ho 229, originally projected for pilot training. Under these circumstances, they proposed the construction of a night fighter version, based on the V6 prototype, already in the first manufacturing stages in the Friedrichroda factory, in Gotha. As for the *Sofortprogramm* requirements, the V6 had the advantage of having been originally designed as a two-seat plane, with the provision to have additional fuel tanks in the wings. Initially, they thought to install a FuG 218 *Neptun V* radar, coming from a Messerchmitt Bf 110 G-4, with a Morgenstern aerial and four dipoles in a 'X' formation; this is assumed to be the case, with great aesthetic suffering from the Hortens.

On 27 January 1945, the OKL published the *Vorrückenprogramm* for high performance night fighters, equipped with the new radar Telefunken FuG 222 *Pauke S* with parabolic antenna of 45 cm in diameter. It was installed internally within an aerodynamic container of dielectric material placed in the nose of the aircraft. In this model, the scope was replaced by a Revi device equipped with a red filter that did not affect the night vision of the pilot. It was expected that the new night fighter would reach a maximum speed of 900 kph, with a service ceiling of 9,000 m and an armament of four forward-firing MK 108/30 cannon.

Arado presented the project E.583, a single seat flying wing powered by two HeS 011 A turbojets. The Dornier Project Office of Friedrichshafen designed a *Schlechtwetterjäger* (all-weather interceptor) driven by two DB 603 LA in tandem piston engines. Based on the aerodynamics of the P.247/1, it was equipped with a Bremen 0 radar, *Schräge Musik*, and had a crew of two. It also had a laminar flow wing (with no sweep) originally designed by Heinkel for the Do 335 B-4, modified to reach the 16.44-m span. The vertical tail surfaces were the same as those in the standard Do 435 and they used the horizontal surfaces originally designed for the Do 535. The project was presented to the RLM on 27 January 1945 as Do P.252/1 *Moskitojäger* but its manufacturing was left aside in March 1945 in favour of the faster Messerschmitt Me 262 B-2.

By the end of 1944, the Heinkel engineers designed an advanced system of automatic triggering weapons combining the fire control radar FuG 222 *Pauke S* with the gyroscopic gunsight Askania EZ 42 (Adler). The 1078 project was created to prove that the system could be integrated in single-engine fighters, providing them with additional capacity to act as night fighter or *Moskitojäger* controlled by the ground command by means of the FuG 25a and FuG 125a devices installed onboard.

The P.1078 A was very much like the Messerschmitt P.1101 with swept wings and tail surfaces. It had a small parabolic antenna fixed on the nose and two 30-mm cannon on both sides of the pilot. The P.1078 B had a twin boom type fuselage and a batwing like that of the Blohm und Voss P.209.01, chosen to diminish the compressibility buffeting effect and the roll damping at high speed. It was expected that the anhedral wingtips would perform the function of a tailplane. The radar, the armament, and the nose leg were housed in the starboard fuselage and the cockpit, armoured but without ejector seat, was positioned in the port fuselage.

The P.1078 B received strong criticism from the *Technisches Amt* due to the lack of protection of the fuel tanks and the asymmetric nose leg. The batwing was also considered inefficient during combat turns and it was feared that the shockwaves generated by the twin nose cones would interfere with the operation of the air intakes. The P.1078 project was cancelled on 27 February 1945.

The Heinkel P.1079 was originally conceived as the successor of the He 219. It followed the same working scheme as the P.1078: a classical airframe 'A' version and two flying-wing 'B' series with the same type of batwing than the previous project. By the end of February, the OKL added the requirement that the new fighter should include the FuG 244 radar, which, together with the *Schräge Musik* guns and its ammunition, added 300 kg to the weight of the airplane. Heinkel preferred to continue working on a lighter version of *Entwurf II* without a tailfin, a *Moskitojäger* able to fly at more than 1,000 km/h with a ceiling of 12,900 m thanks to the new Heinkel HeS 011 engines. The flight control of a batwing airplane at high speed was above the technical capabilities of 1945. That was only achieved when having the Boeing computer-controlled Bird of Prey in 1996.

Junkers presented an all-weather version of the EF.128 interceptor with the pilot and the radar operator sitting side-by-side. Focke-Wulf proposed to modify its project P.0310.025-1006, which had originally been conceived as a single-seat high-altitude interceptor. It was able to fly and fight at an altitude superior to the Me 262 B-2a, with a great rhomboid wing and pusher airscrews aircraft, powered by a 4,000-hp Argus As 413 piston engine and armed with four guns of 30 mm. The plan considered a bad-weather *Moskitojäger* two seat variant equipped with one FuG 222 radar and a 45-cm diameter parabolic mirror fixed in front of the radiator. Neither the Argus As 413 nor the Jumo 222 E/F, proposed as a replacement, were available when Göring ordered to stop the development of any type of piston engine on 22 February 1945.

Focke-Wulf also proposed a heavy fighter powered by two HeS 011 A turbojets named *Projekt I*. It was a version of the Baubeschreibung Nr. 250, extensively modified for its use in night operations. Described in the dossier Baubeschreibung Nr. 251–36, it was proposed to the OKL on 27 January 1945. It had a redesigned low wing with a 33-degree rear sweep and larger surface flaps. The chord at the root was reduced by 80 cm and the wingspan was increased by almost 5 m.

To compensate for these changes, the fuselage length was increased by 75 cm and the tailplane was replaced by a larger one. The position of the engines was advanced 1 m to minimise the loss of thrust, reducing the length of the air ducts and eliminating the bomb bay. The pressurised cockpit lengthened to accommodate the radar operator who sat with his back to the pilot in a conventional non-ejecting seat. The OKL proposed two armament configurations. *Zustand I* consisted of two forward-firing MK 108/30 cannon with 120 rounds per gun, located in the nose, and two other MK 108/30 cannon in 80-degree *Schräge Musik* configuration, with 100 rounds per gun. *Zustand II* would have four forward-firing MK 108/30 cannon with 120 rounds per gun.

The estimated maximum speed was of 820 kph at 7,500 m, the service ceiling of 14,000 m, and the endurance (with 5,400 litres of fuel and 11,000 kg take-off weight) of two hours and forty-five minutes. Its main dimensions were a wingspan of 17.3 m, a length of 13.4 m, a height of 5.06 m, and wing area of 50 sq. m. The electronic equipment consisted of a fire control radar Telefunken FuG 222 *Pauke S* with a fixed, 45-cm diameter parabolic mirror located inside the circular air intake, an automatic blind landing system consisting of a Lorenz FuBl 3/AWG 1 calculator in combination with the Siemens/LGW FuG 130 *Funklandegerät* device, and the radio altimeter Siemens FuG 101a, with two inverted 'T' antennae under the left wing and one comb aerial under the fuselage belly. It also had one IFF discriminator GEMA FuG 25a Erstling with a 300-mm rod antenna under the fuselage, shared with the command relay FuG 139 *Barbarossa*, one radio goniometer Telefunken Peil G6 *Ludwig*, one passive radar receiver Telefunken FuG 350 Zc *Naxos* with 25 cm of the diameter dorsal-rotating antenna, and one R/T device Lorenz FuG 24 SE with whip antenna.

Moskitojägern

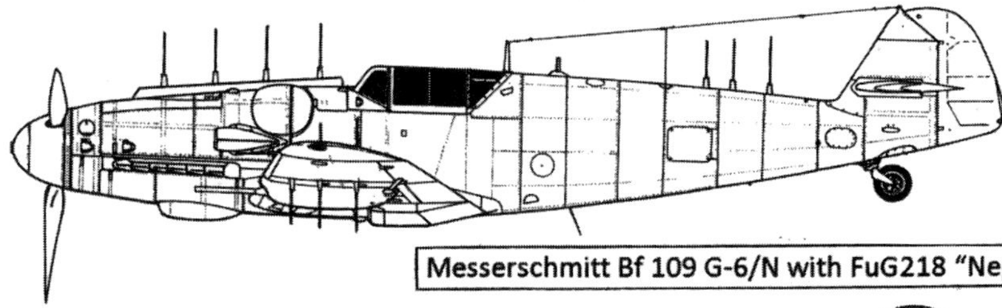

Messerschmitt Bf 109 G-6/N with FuG218 "Neptun V1"

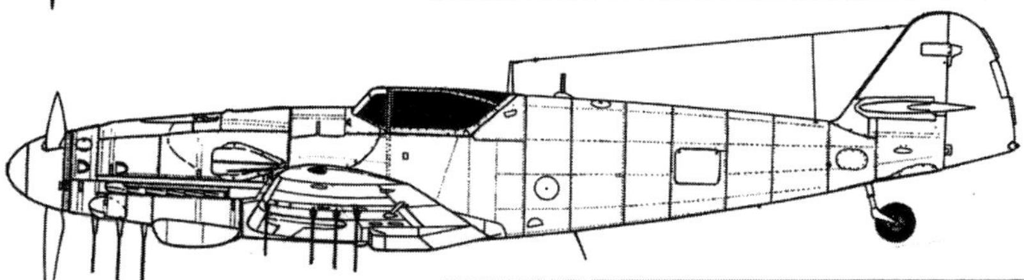

Messerschmitt Bf 109 G-5/AS with FuG 218 "Neptun J3"

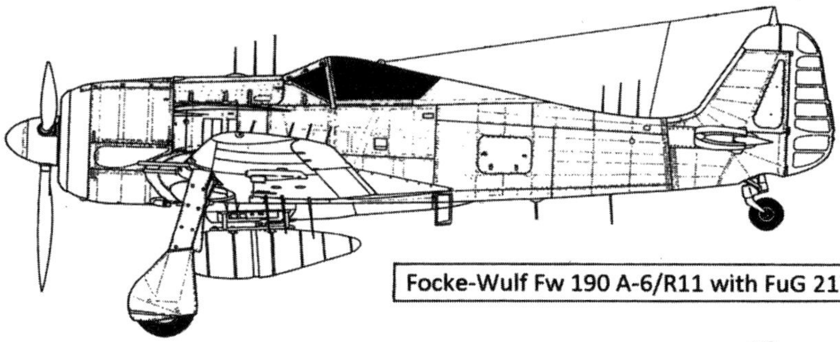

Focke-Wulf Fw 190 A-6/R11 with FuG 217 "Neptun J1"

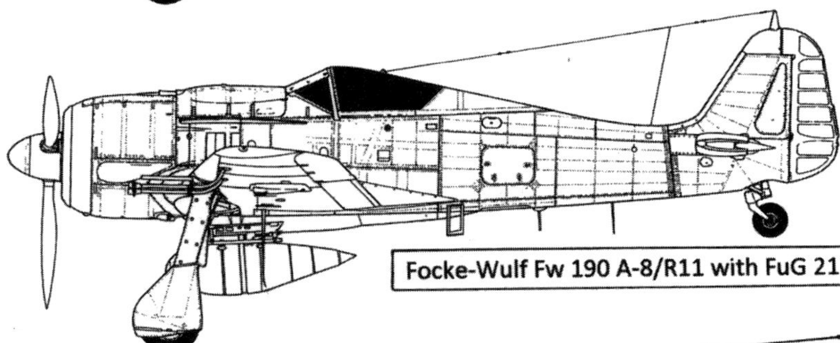

Focke-Wulf Fw 190 A-8/R11 with FuG 217 "Neptun J3"

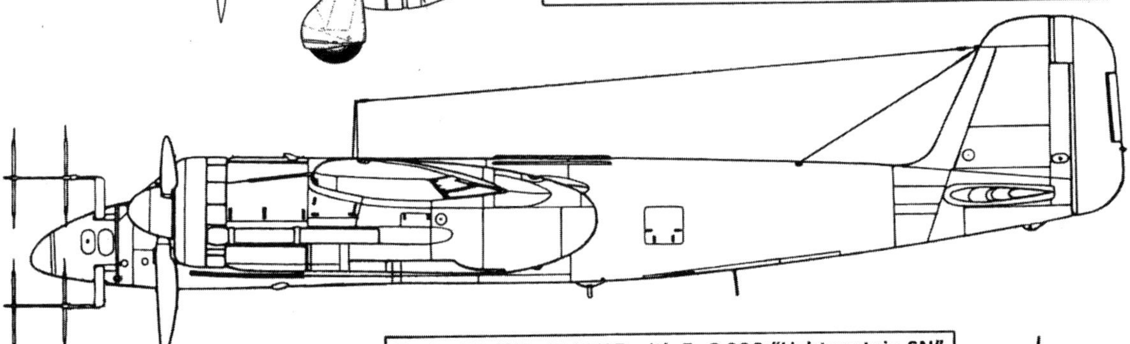

Focke-Wulf Ta 154 V15 with FuG 220 "Lichtenstein SN"

2m.

MIRANDA

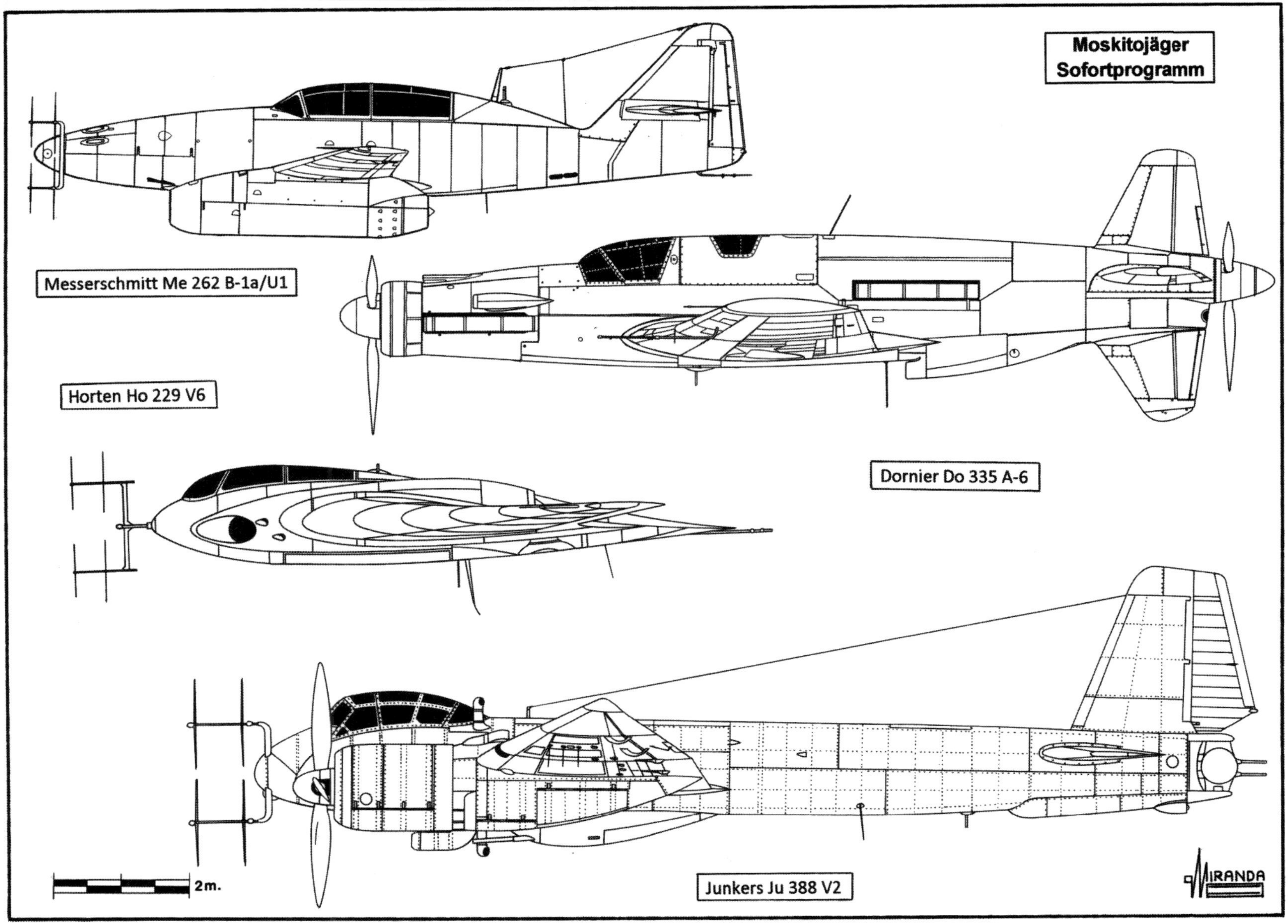
Moskitojäger
Sofortprogramm
Messerschmitt Me 262 B-1a/U1
Horten Ho 229 V6
Dornier Do 335 A-6
Junkers Ju 388 V2
2m.
MIRANDA

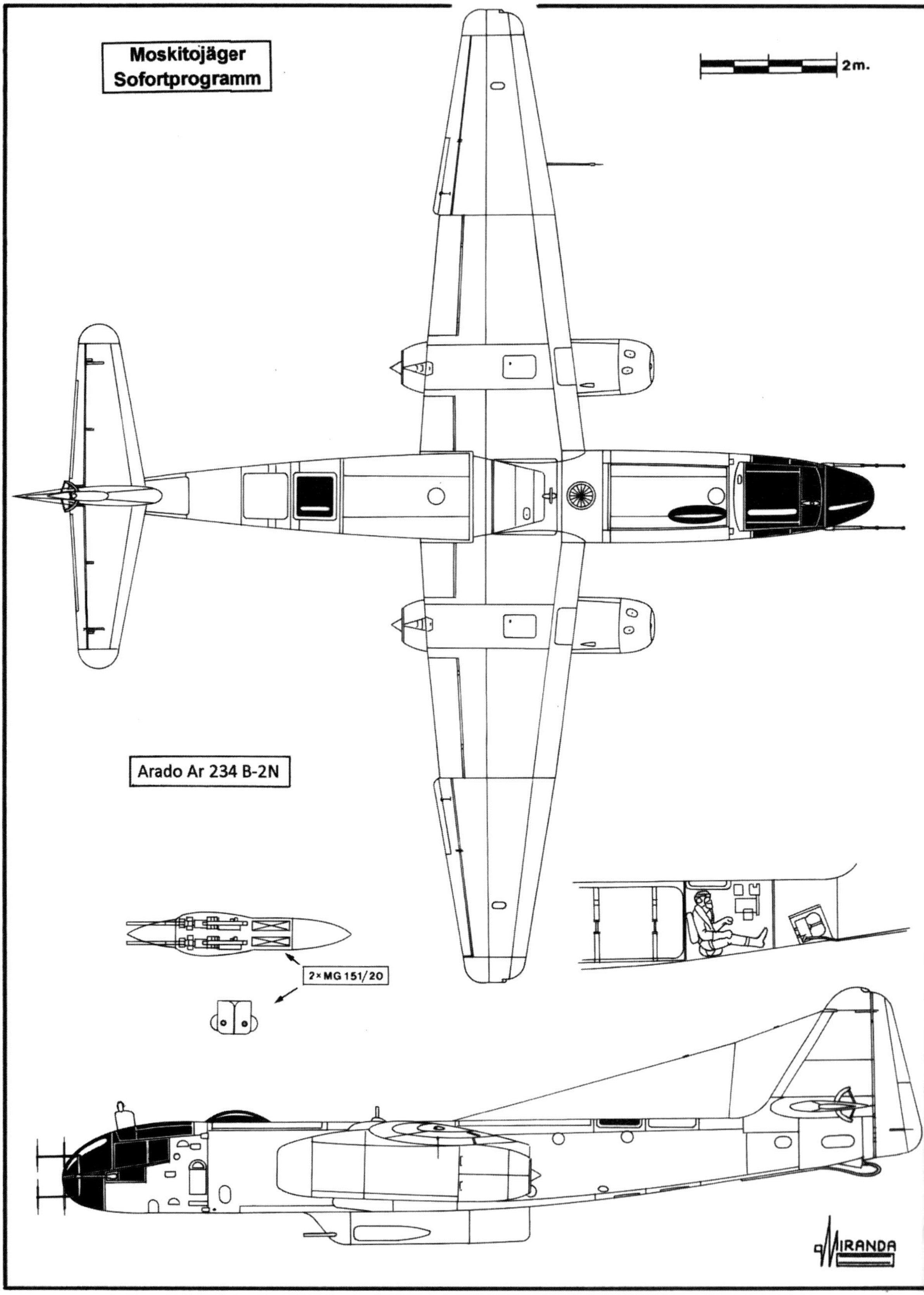
Moskitojäger
Sofortprogramm
2m.
Arado Ar 234 B-2N
2×MG 151/20
MIRANDA

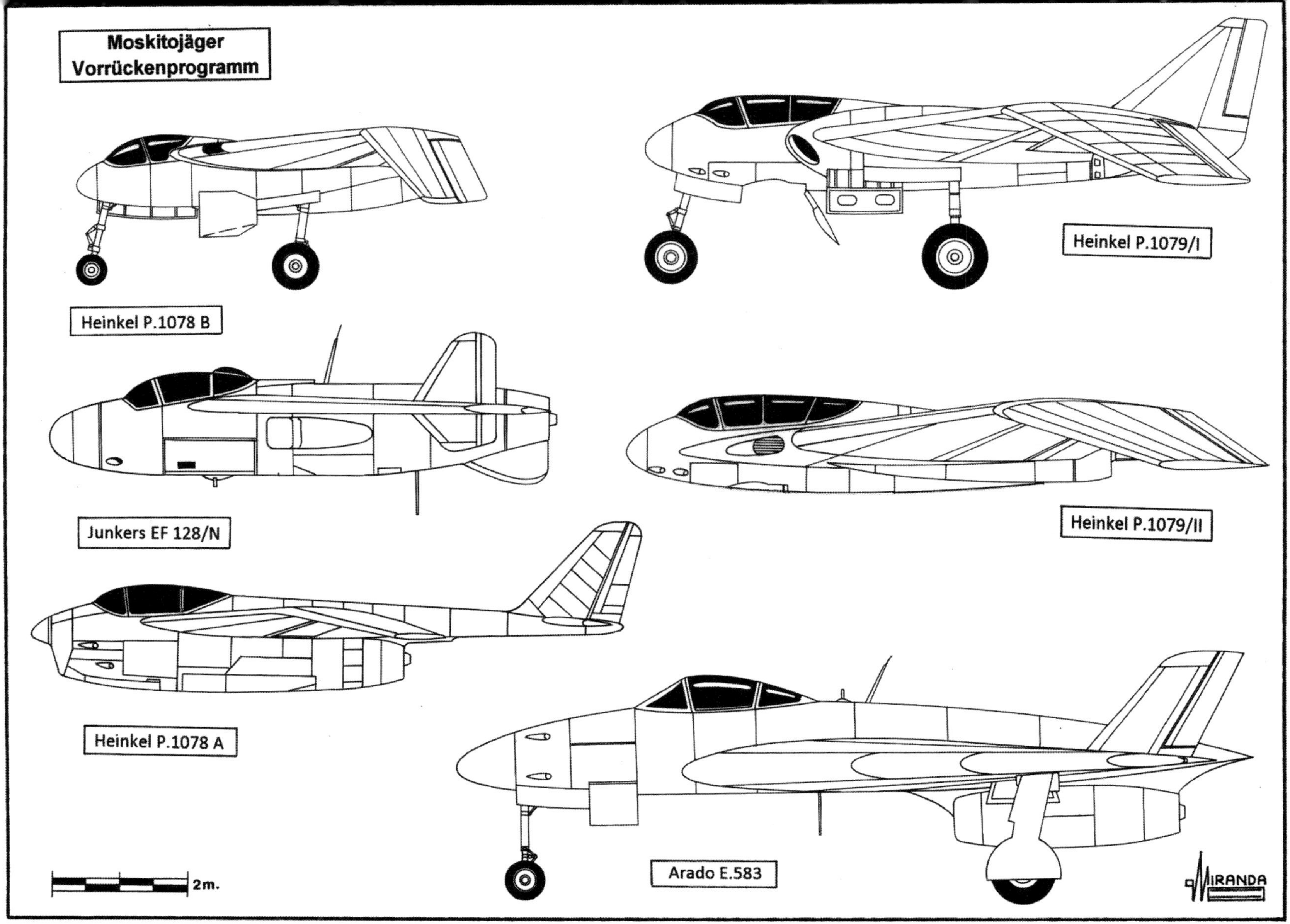
Moskitojäger
Vorrückenprogramm
Heinkel P.1078 B
Heinkel P.1079/I
Junkers EF 128/N
Heinkel P.1079/II
Heinkel P.1078 A
Arado E.583
2m.
MIRANDA

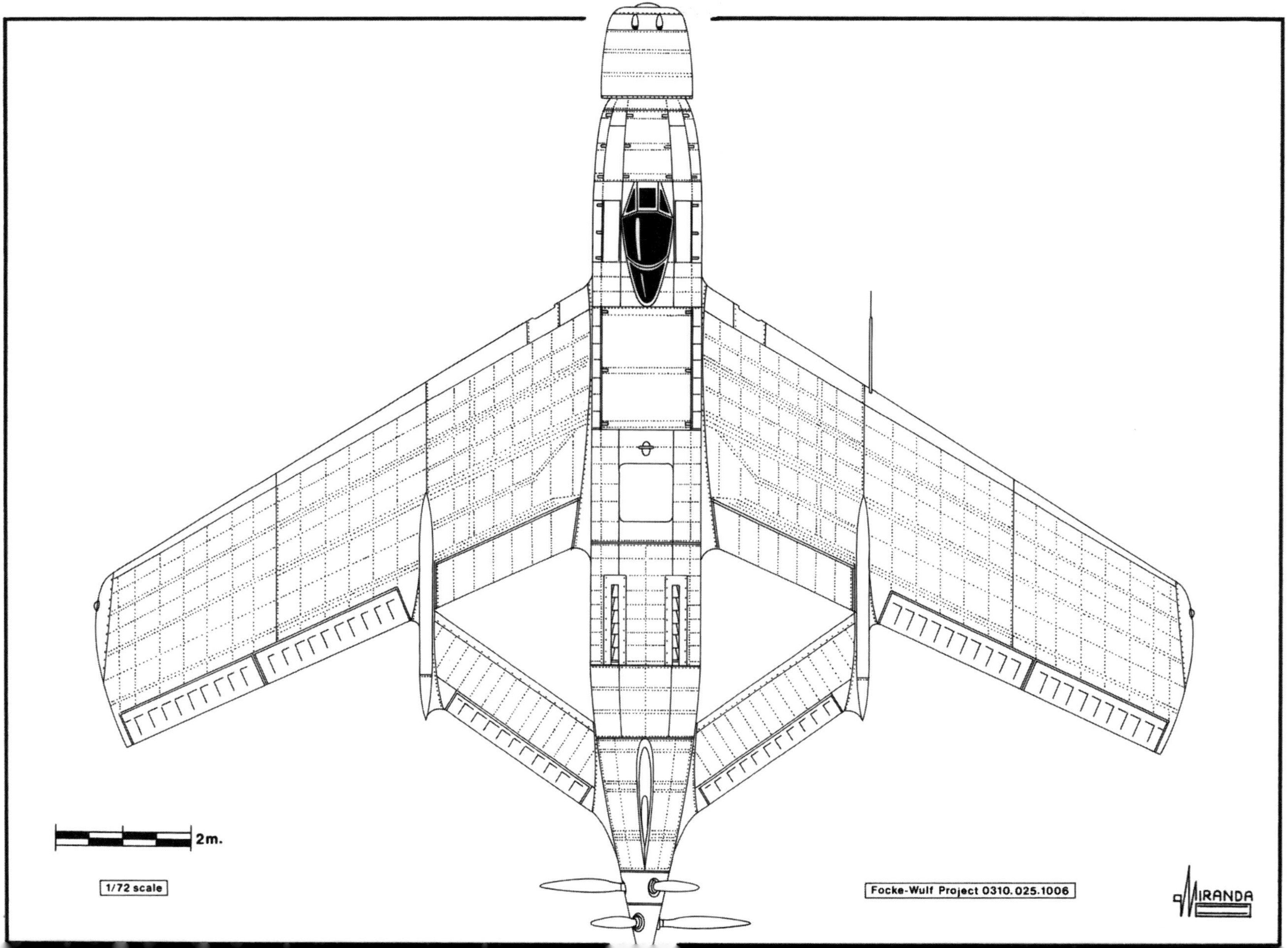
2m.
1/72 scale
Focke-Wulf Project 0310.025.1006
MIRANDA

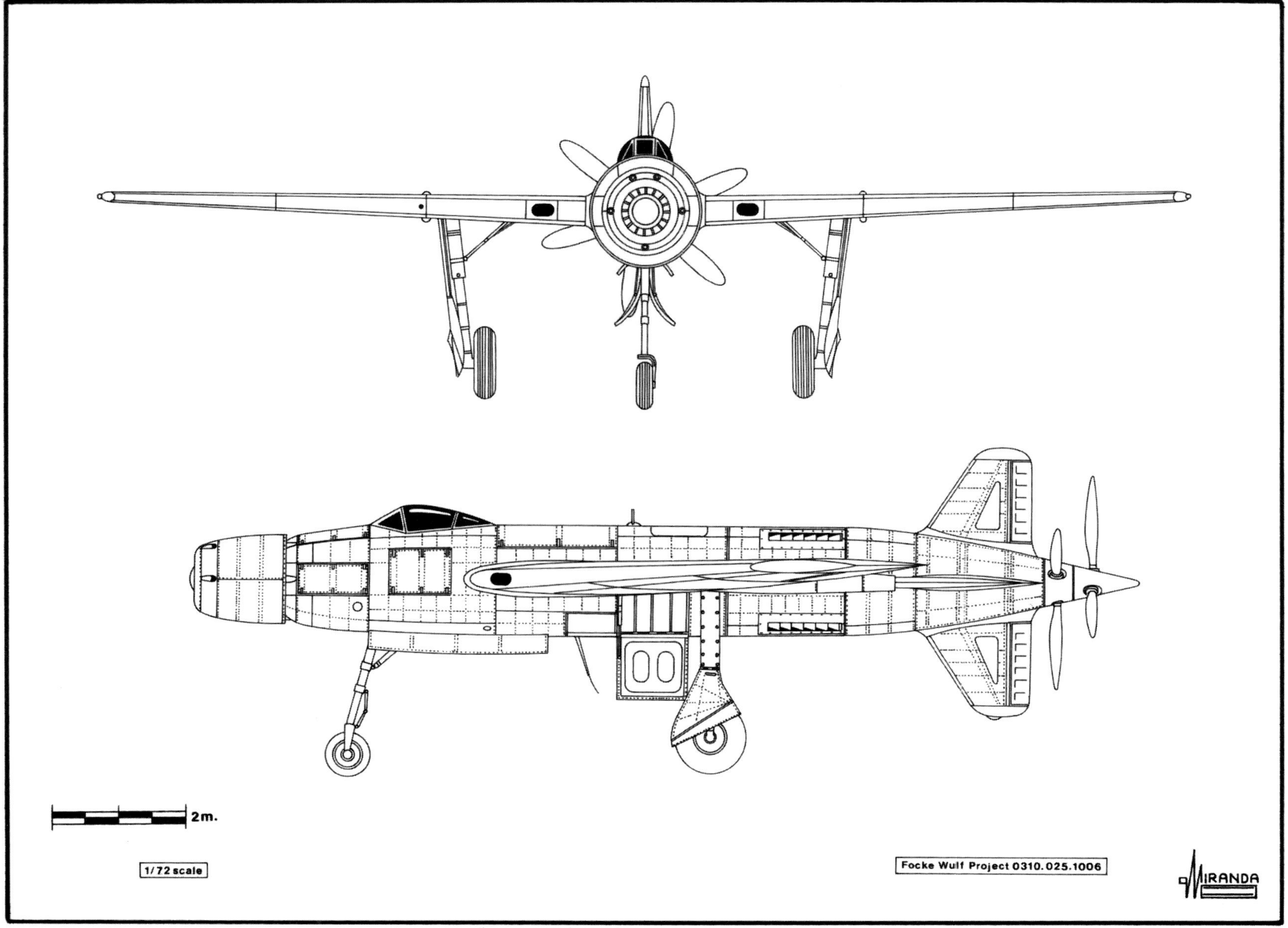
2m.
1/72 scale
Focke Wulf Project 0310.025.1006
MIRANDA

Focke-Wulf 2-TL *Nachtjäger Projekt I*

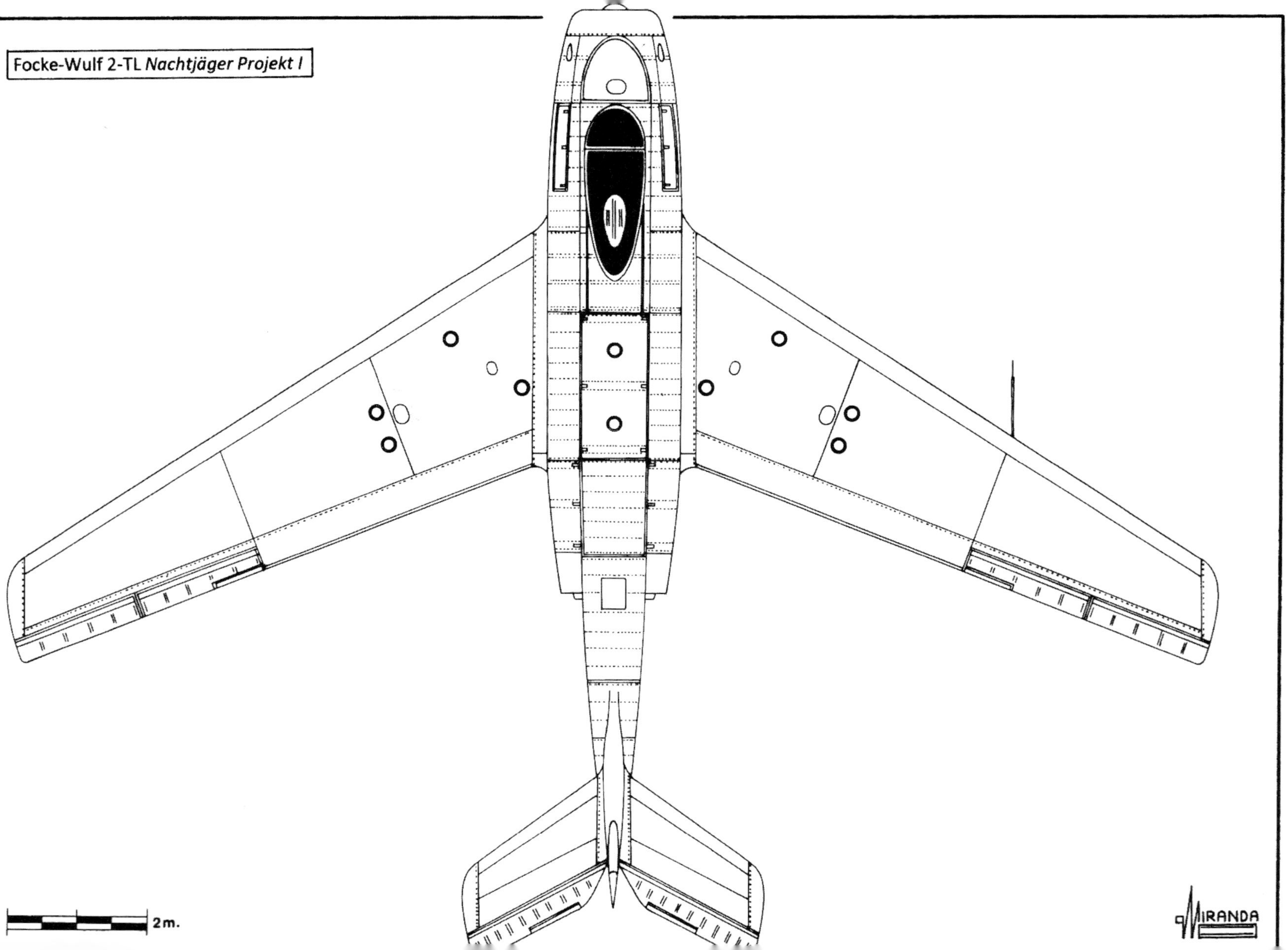

Focke-Wulf 2-TL *Nachtjäger Projekt I*

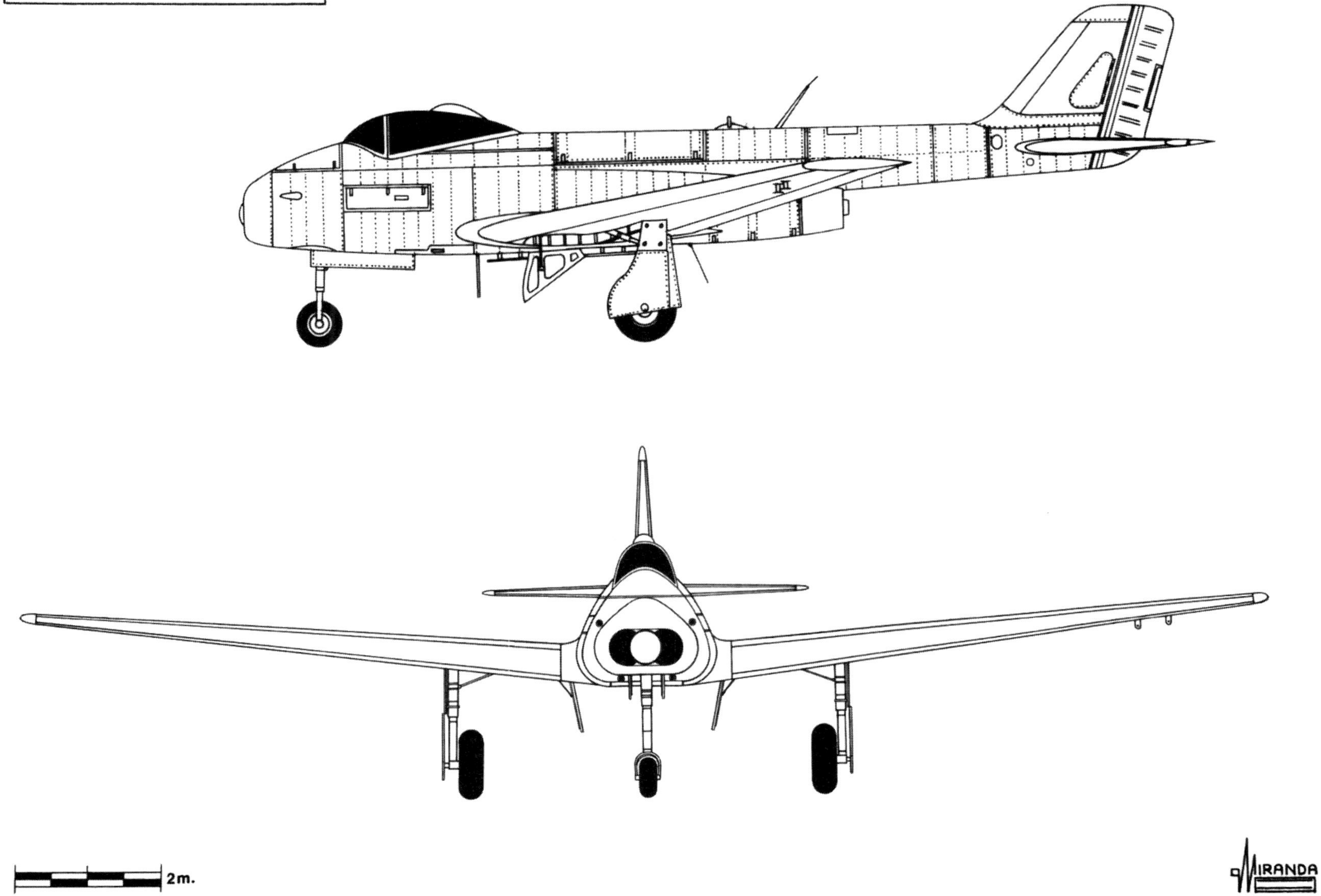

18

Focke-Wulf 2-TL *Nachtjäger Projekt II*

By the beginning of 1945, the Luftwaffe did not need an all-weather interceptor *Moskitojäger*, but a heavy night fighter with extended range and a great amount of electronic equipment.

On 27 February, the *Technisches Amt* published the *Hochleistung Nachtjäger* specification for a high-performance night fighter. It called for an advanced airplane, powered by two HeS 011 A turbojets, using the new search radar Telefunken FuG 244 Bremen 0, which had a parabolic mirror of 70-cm diameter and additional *Schräge Musik* weapons.

Several others were presented to the contest. The Me 262 B-2 (12 February 1945) was a variant of the Me 262 HG III high speed project. The Dornier P.256 was a jet version of the Do 435, a modified variant of the Focke-Wulf *Nachtjäger Projekt I*, with five flying wings. The Arado Ar I was the two-seat version of the Ar E.583. The Blohm und Voss P.215-02 was a scaled-up version of the P.212 project fighter. The Gotha P.60 C was also considered. The Horten Ho 229 B-1 was the combat version of the Ho 229 V6 trainer. The Junkers EF 128/N with the nose radome was modified for the Bremen 0 antenna.

On 2 March 1945, the OKL requested the inclusion of a third crew member and the addition of a tail warning radar device Siemens/FFO FuG 218 *Neptun R3* with a Yagi aerial. This left the Junkers, Heinkel, and Horten designs out of the contest as they could not increase the crew area for structural reasons. Messerschmitt was forced to enlarge the fuselage and redesign the wings for the version of 17 March 1945. Gotha solved the problem with great difficulty by installing the navigator and the radar operator inside the wing roots.

The Dornier P.256 design was aerodynamically inefficient due to the large drag induced by tail surfaces and underwing nacelles having an endurance of one hour and forty-five minutes, which was considered insufficient. For the same reason, the designs of Arado Ar 234 Series P, Ar II, and Ar TEW 16/43-19 were also rejected, as well as the Dornier P.252 / I because of the shortage of 87-octane B3 fuel consumed by its two DB 603 LA piston engines.

Unfortunately for the Germans, the Horten brothers did not have the industrial capacity for the series-production of the 229. The OKL assigned this task to the

Gothaer Waggonfabrik firm in May 1945. There was a confrontation there between the philosophy of design of the Hortens and the available production techniques. Finally, the Gotha design team, under the direction of Dr.-Ing. Hunerjäger, reached the conclusion that the additional weight of the electronic equipment and extra crew member penalised the longitudinal stability of the Ho 229 B-1 in such a way that made the take-off impossible without a considerable ballast of about 500 kg at the rear of the airplane. This was the last pure-wing design of Horten. After the crash suffered by the Ho.IX 2 on 18 February 1945, the OKL banned the manufacturing of airplanes without a tailfin.

The Blohm und Voss P.215-02 had a very radical shape to be accepted by the Luftwaffe and was designed without any possibility to move the FuG 244 antenna. The Gotha, even in its heaviest version, was considerably faster than the Arado. However, the former was chosen when the Luftwaffe suggested a last modification on 20 March 1945, recommending the use of rear-firing armaments to defend against the Mosquito NF.30 night fighters with electronic equipment Monica, AI, and ASH, which were more advanced than those of the Germans. The Arado Ar.I could carry a rearwards gun turret due to the location of its engines and crew. Like in the Ar 234, only a pair of fixed guns, aimed by radar, could be installed in the Gotha.

On 26 February 1945, during a meeting with the *Technisches Amt* held in Bad Eilsen, the main criticism was the excessive length of the air ducts in the *Projekt I*. The Focke-Wulf team of designers tried to solve the issue of the loss of thrust by installing the engines under the cockpit floor, to reduce the length of the air ducts to just 2.7 m. To balance the weight displacement, the main landing gear and *Schräge Musik* were positioned in the rear section of the fuselage. New mid-wings were designed with a 5.18:1 aspect ratio and a 36-degree rear sweep. The drag reduction allowed an estimated maximum speed of 904 kph at 7,000 m, a ceiling of 12,800 m, and the maximum take-off weight of 12,700 kg. The construction system, the armament, and the tail surfaces were the same as those in *Projekt I*; the wingspan was of 16 m, the length of 15.3 m, the height of 5.12 m, and the wing area of 48.4 sq. m. With 5,400 litres of internal fuel, its endurance was two hours and forty-five minutes, having the capability to transport up to 1,200 litres of additional fuel in underwing detachable tanks.

All these modifications were part of the Baubeschreibung Nr. 251–251 dossier proposed to the OKL on 6 March 1945 as *Hochleistung Nachtjäger Projekt II*.

The electronic equipment was updated with the installation of a search radar Bremen 0 with 70-cm diameter parabolic mirror, a tail warning radar *Neptun R3*, and an IFF discriminator Lorenz FuG 226 *Neuling* with two *Breitbanddipolen* vertical blade-aerials on the upper surface of the wing.

In 1949, the Soviets built the MiG I-320, an all-weather interceptor of 12 tonnes propelled by two RD-45F turbojets, with a Torii radar, equipped with a parabolic antenna of 60-cm diameter and two crew seated side by side. Some authors believe that its design might have been inspired by that of the *Projekt II*.

Focke-Wulf Nachtjäger Projekt II

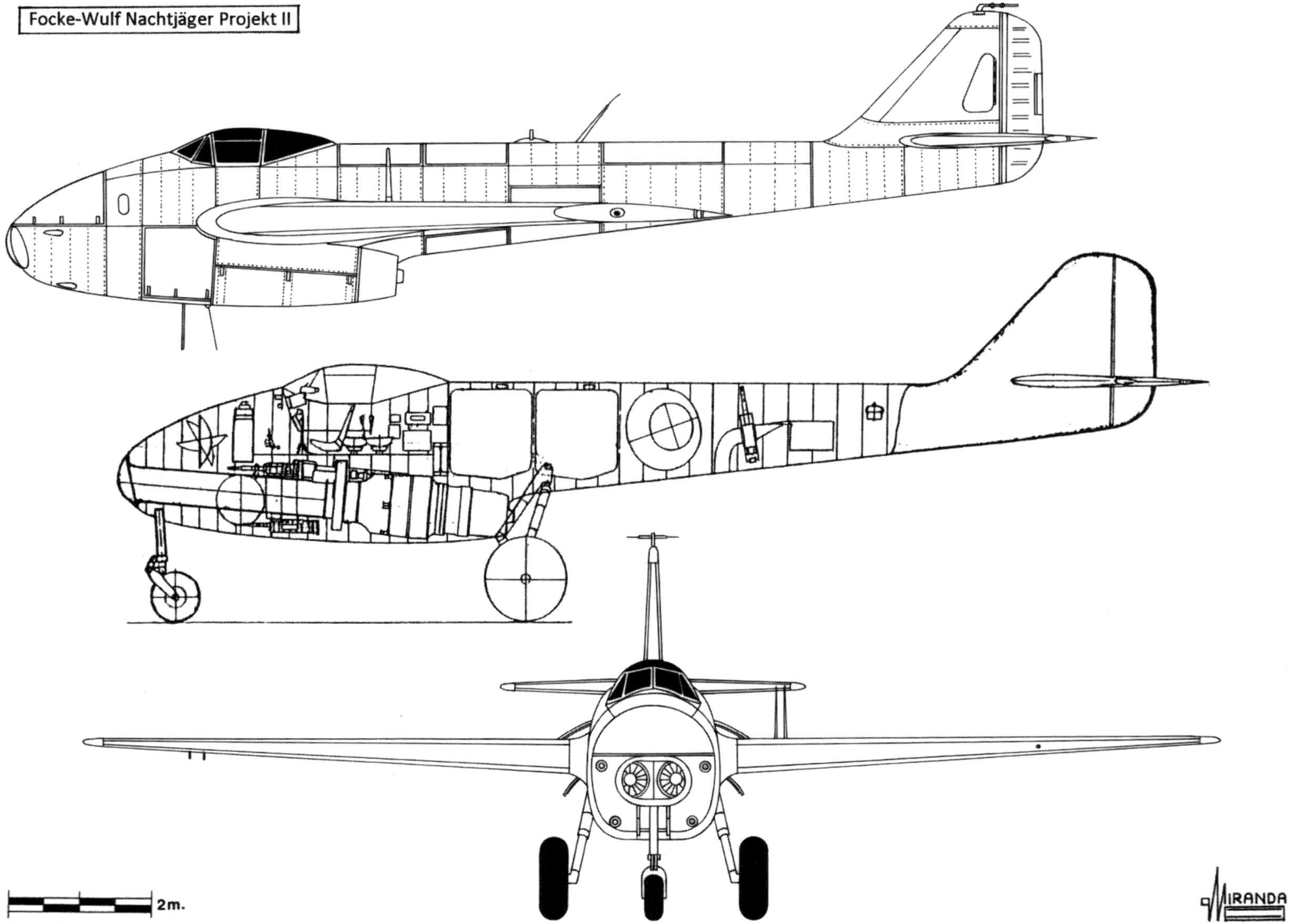

Focke-Wulf 2-TL *Nachtjäger Projekt II*

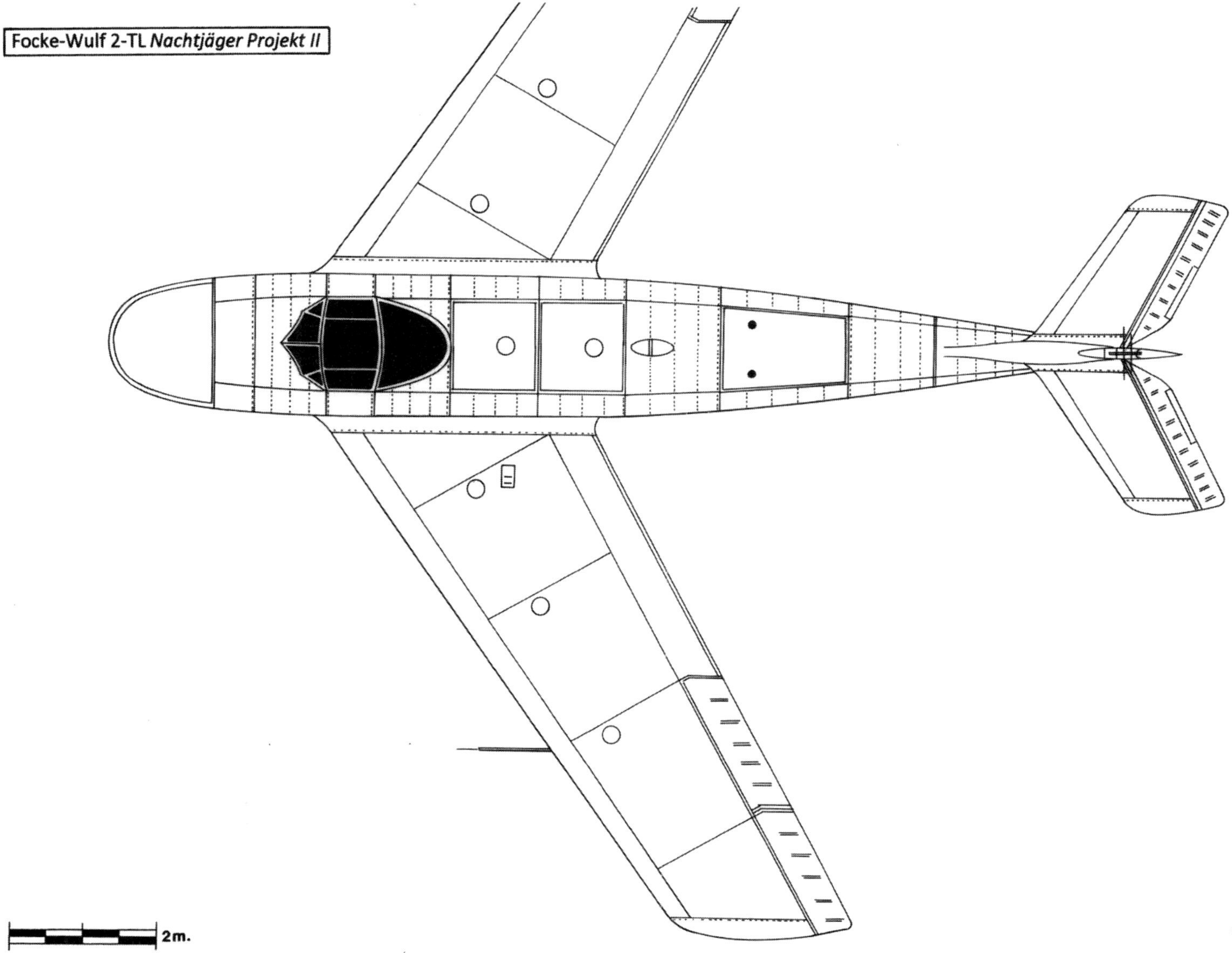

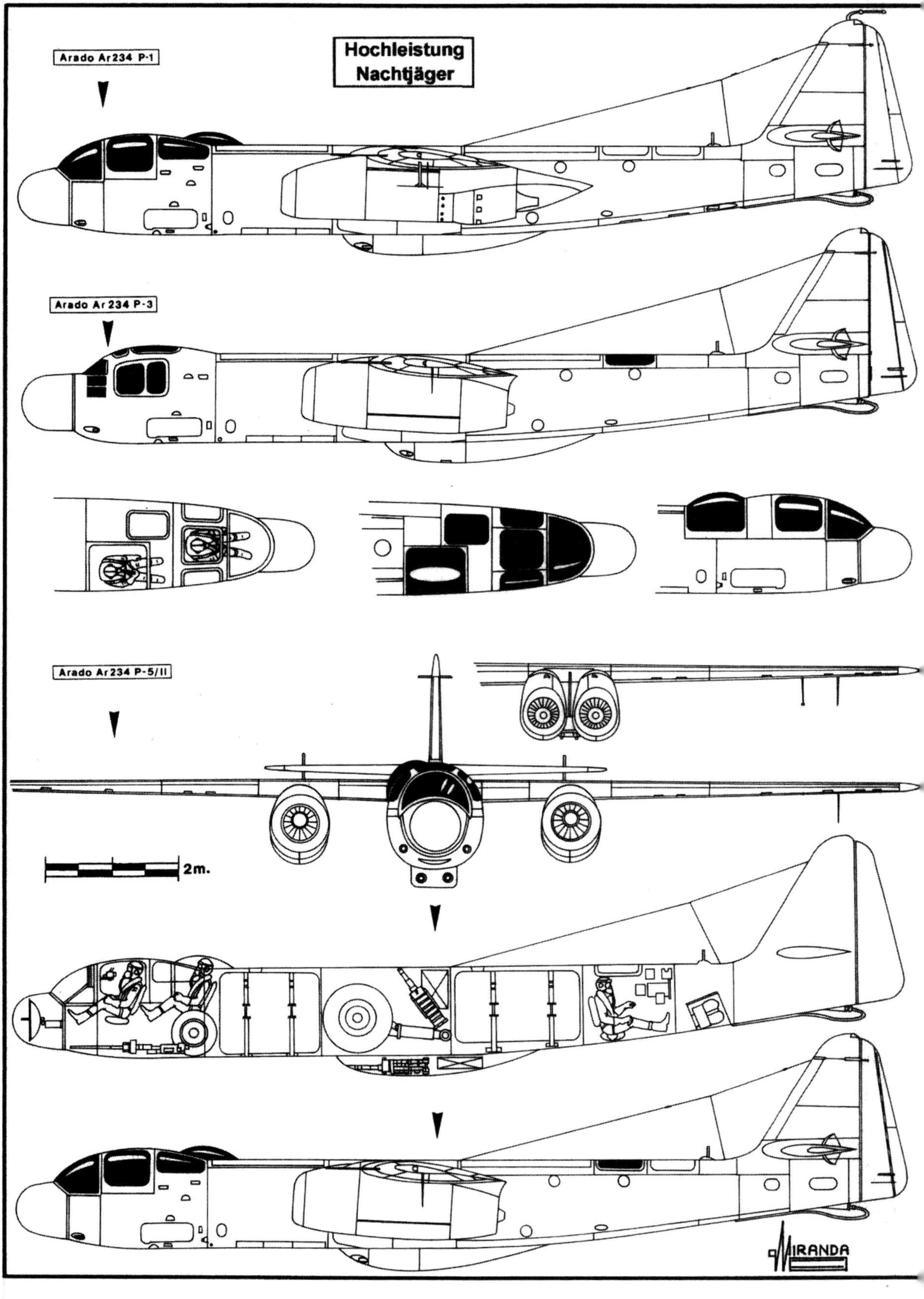

Hochleistung
Nachtjäger
Arado Ar234 P-1
Arado Ar 234 P-3
Arado Ar234 P-5/II
2m.
MIRANDA

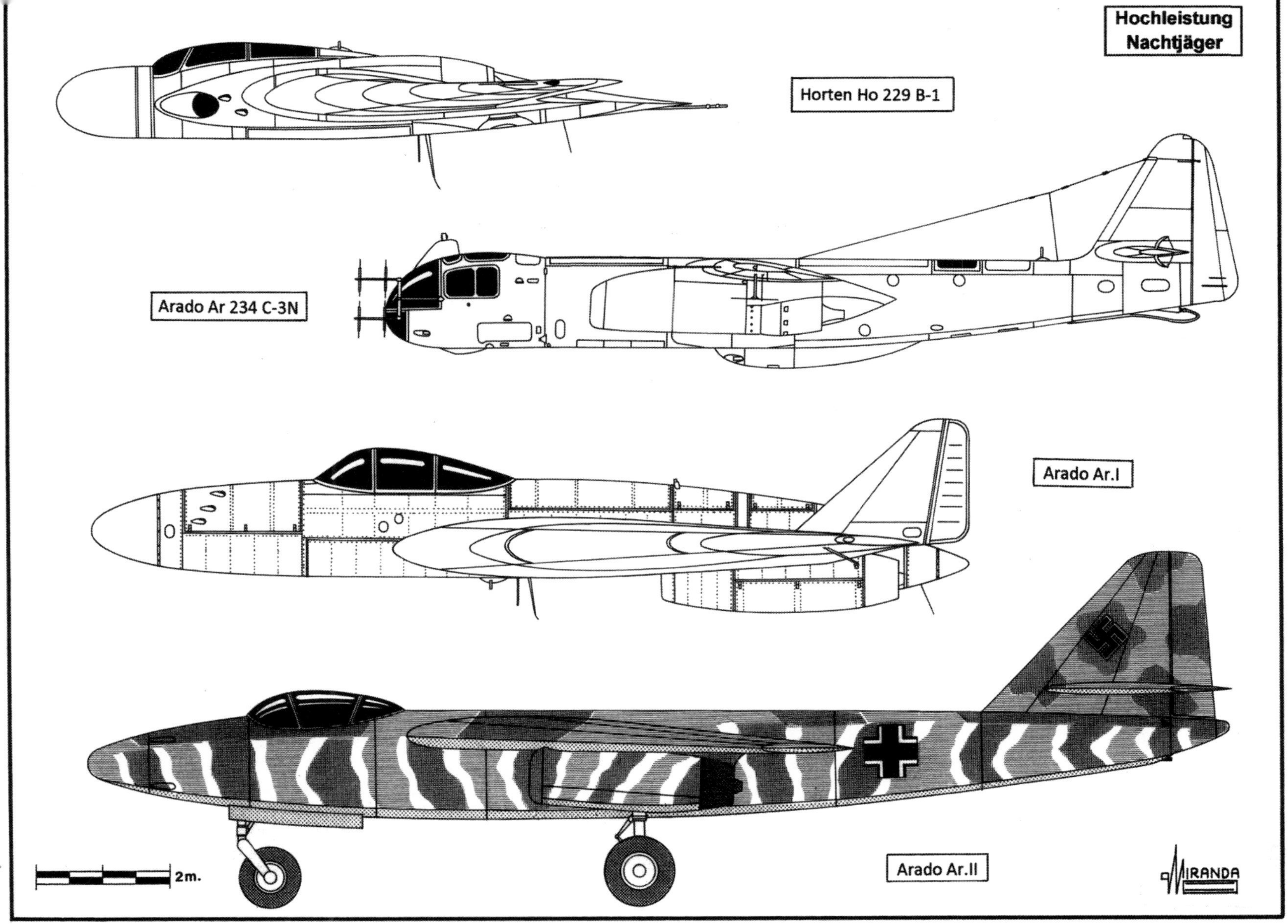
Hochleistung
Nachtjäger
Horten Ho 229 B-1
Arado Ar 234 C-3N
Arado Ar.I
Arado Ar.II
2m.
MIRANDA

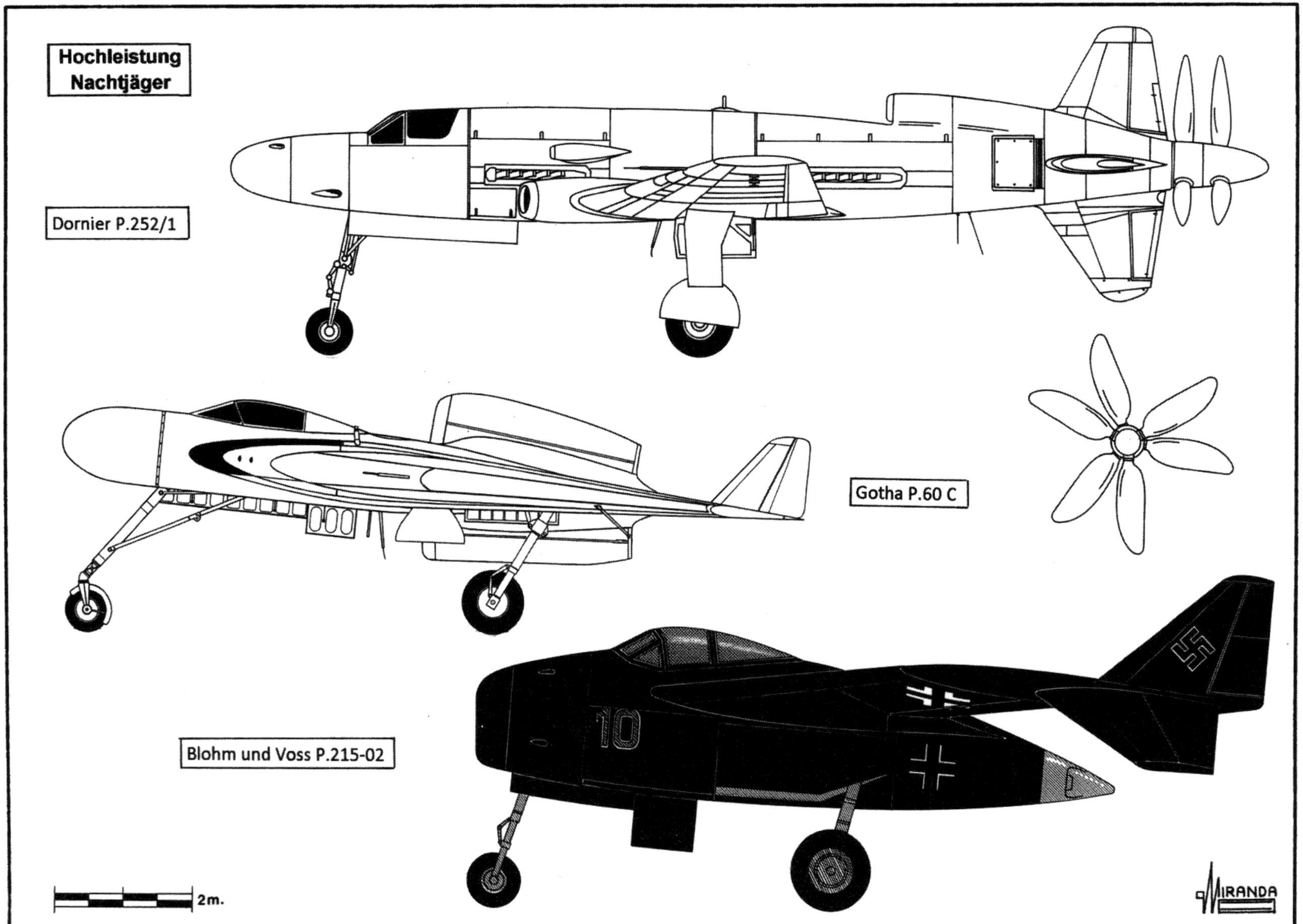
Hochleistung
Nachtjäger
Dornier P.252/1
Gotha P.60 C
Blohm und Voss P.215-02
10
2m.
MIRANDA

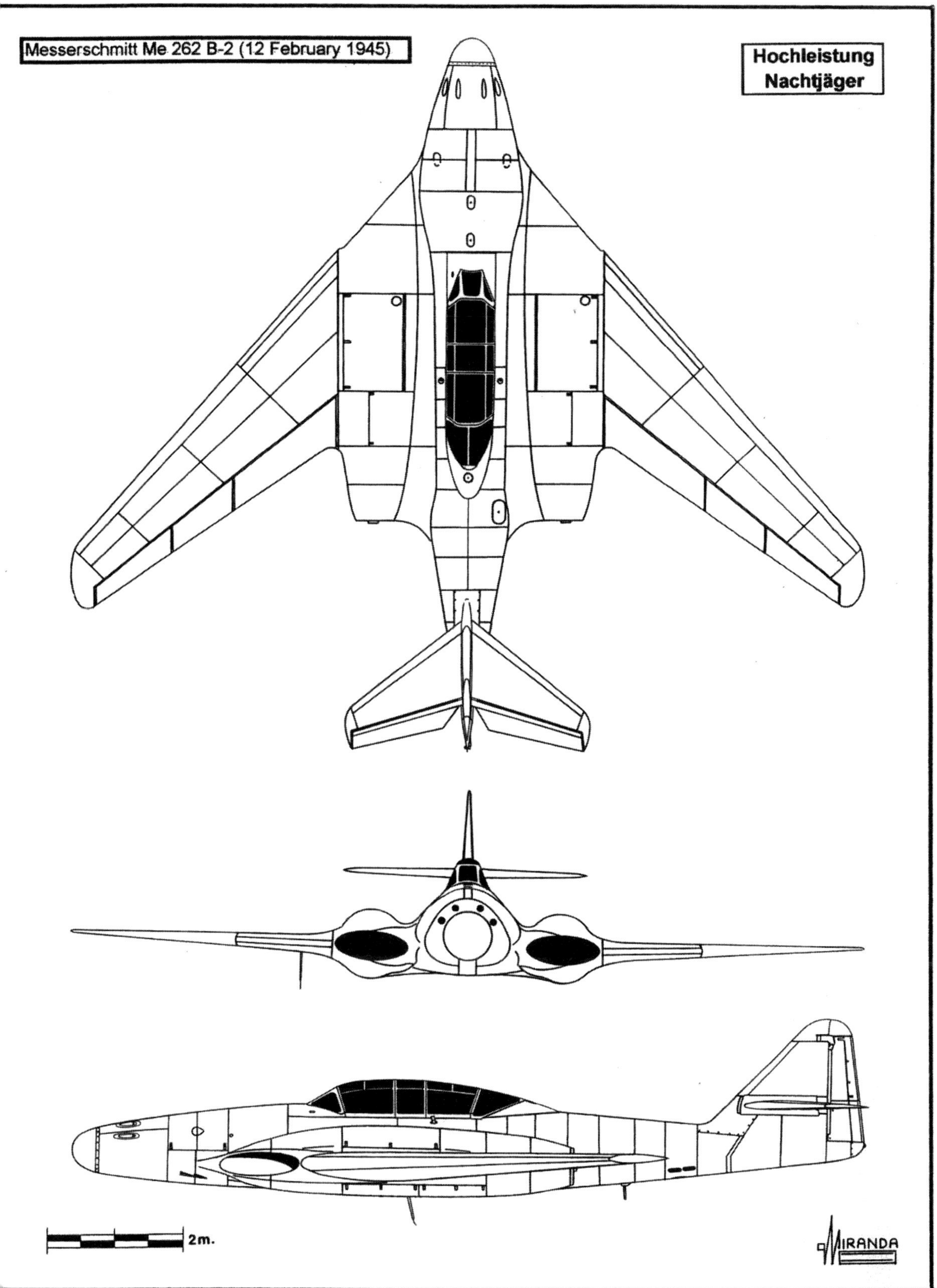
Messerschmitt Me 262 B-2 (12 February 1945)
Hochleistung
Nachtjäger
2m.
MIRANDA

19

Focke-Wulf 2-TL *Nachtjäger Projekt III*

On 2 April 1945, the OKL requested to increase the endurance to four hours so that the future night fighter would be better suited to the extended *Verfolgungsnachtjagd* operations that infiltrated the bomber stream. To increase its fuel capacity, Focke-Wulf proposed to save structural weight using duraluminium only and the same construction technique as with the Fw 190.

Projekt III was designed for this purpose. It was a light version of the previous one with an estimated take-off weight of only 10,500 kg, the wingspan reduced to 14.10 metres, a maximum speed of 945 kph, and a service ceiling of 13,300 metres.

The wing modification increased the landing speed, which was compensated by reducing the wing sweep angle to 31 degrees and increasing the tailplane surface. The length of the nose leg was also increased to facilitate take-off. The main differences with *Projekt II* consisted of a new air intake, which increased the overall length of the airplane to 13.45 metres and the reduction of the wing area to 40 sq. m.

Electronic equipment and armament remained unchanged, but ammunition for *Schräge Musik* increased to 160 rounds per gun. *Projekt III* was designated P.011-45 on 19 March 1945 for administrative purposes. With 4,500 litres of internal fuel, the endurance at full throttle was one hour forty minutes and three hours thirty minutes with one engine shut down.

However, it was not enough to meet the last requirement of the OKL. Only the Blohm und Voss of 14.7 tons and the TEW Arado of 16 tons could carry as much fuel, but with unsatisfactory take-off and climb capabilities. These aircraft required the use of RATO rockets and long take-off runways, which no longer existed in the Reich as a consequence of the bombings. At this point, the situation came to a standstill between the OKL and the aircraft manufacturers.

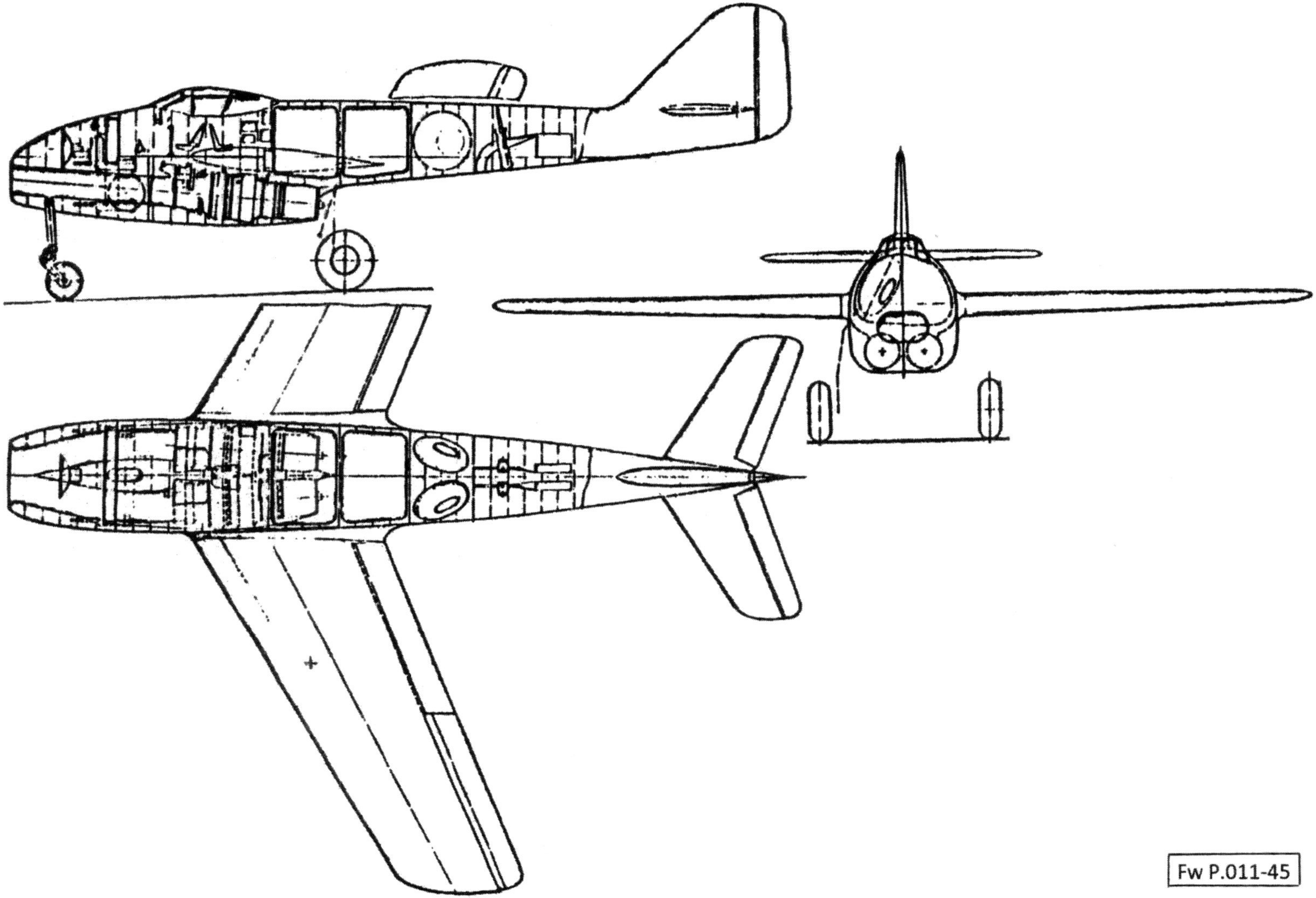

Fw P.011-45

20

Focke-Wulf 3-TL *Nachtjäger Projekt IV*

On 19 March 1945, Kurt Tank proposed to the OKL the construction of a 19.6-ton night fighter, capable of a take-off under overload conditions, with the 10,800 litres of fuel needed to fly during four hours. Described in the dossier Baubeschreibung Nr. 251–53 as *Nachtjäger Projekt IV*, the new aircraft would be propelled by three HeS 011 A turbojets using the same cockpit, landing gear, armament, and electronic equipment as the previous version.

To facilitate the rotation at take-off, one of the engines was installed under the cockpit floor angled down 5 degrees. The three turbojets would be used only for take-off, climb, and combat, with one remaining shut down for the rest of the flight to save fuel. The fuselage, built in light alloy, housed the armament, cockpit, electronic equipment, and landing gear, as well as a turbojet and three fuel tanks with a combined capacity of 8,400 litres.

The wings, with a 32-degree sweep-back angle and 5 to 1 aspect ratio, would be built in steel and wood, containing another 2,400 litres of fuel housed in two self-sealing tanks and two turbojets in underwing nacelles. The tail surfaces, built in wood and plywood, had the same design as *Projekt II* but were scaled-up by 20 per cent. The wingspan would be 19.4 metres, with an overall length was 19.04 m, height of 5.09 m, and the wing area of 75 sq. m. *Projekt IV* was designated P.011-47 for administrative purposes.

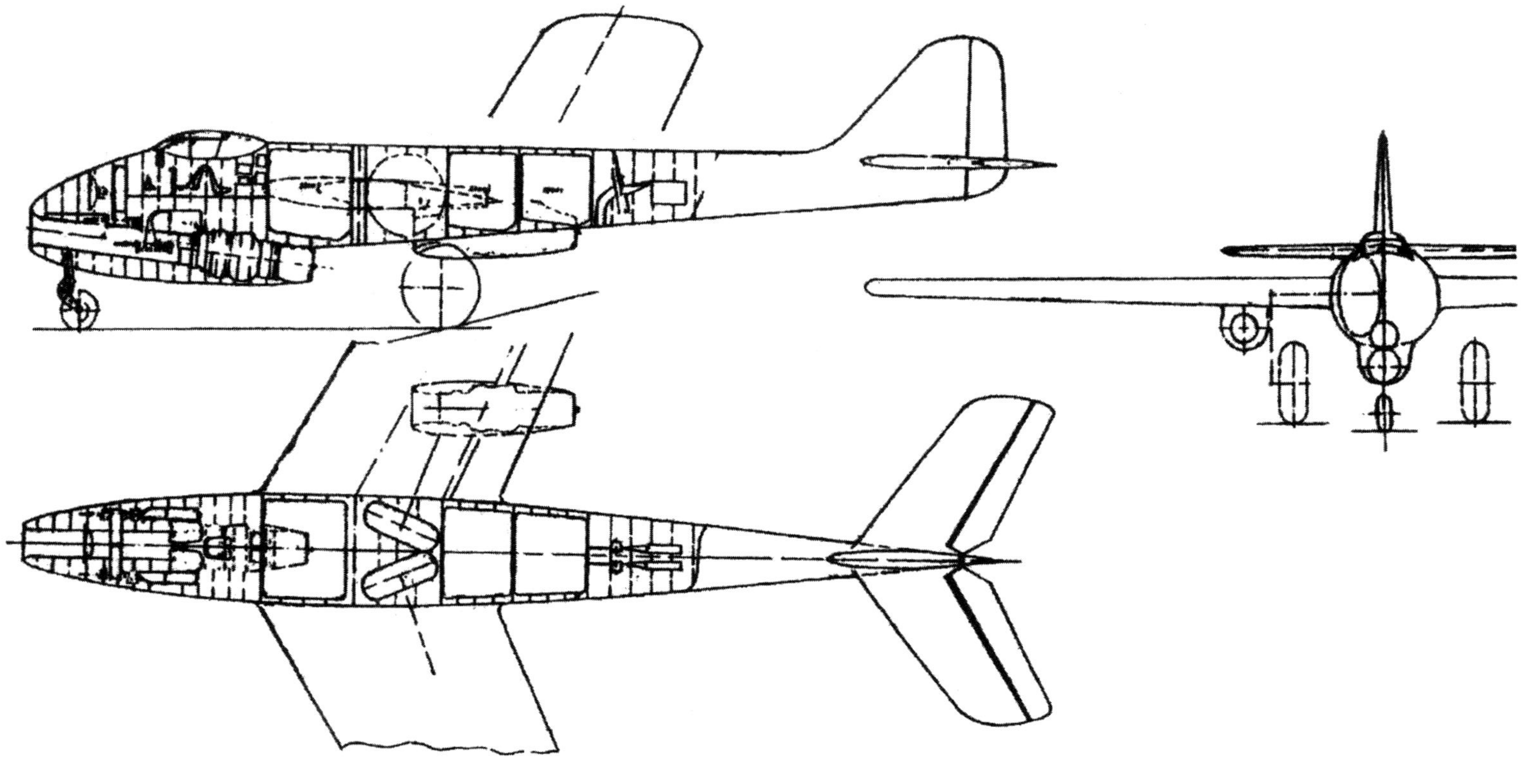
Fw P.011-47

21

Focke-Wulf 3-TL *Nachtjäger Projekt V*

This version of the previous project was designed to shorten the take-off run. The two turbojets, installed under the cockpit floor, helped raise the nose during rotation and climb, while the third, placed in the rear section of the fuselage, provided additional thrust. The take-off weight was reduced by 300 kg, the fuselage length shortened by 140 cm, the wing span by 10 cm, and the wing area by 0.5 sq. m. The tail surfaces were built in duraluminium. Armament, electronic equipment, and fuel capacity were not affected by the changes.

Removal of the drag generated by the underwing nacelles was compensated by an increase in the frontal area of the fuselage. To reduce the landing speed, a wing sweepback angle of 28 degrees was applied and the surface of the flaps increased. The installation of the rear turbojet, with two boundary layer suction air intakes, made it necessary to increase the surface of the tailplane.

Nachtjäger Projekt V, designated P.011-46 at the administrative level, was described in the Baubeschreibung Nr. 251–54 dossier and proposed to the OKL on the same day as *Projekt III* and *Projekt IV*.

In February 1947, the Americans designed the fast bomber Martin Model 234 using aerodynamic solutions from *Projekt V*. The prototype, named Martin XB-51, made its first flight on 28 October 1949, reaching a maximum speed of 1,070 kph.

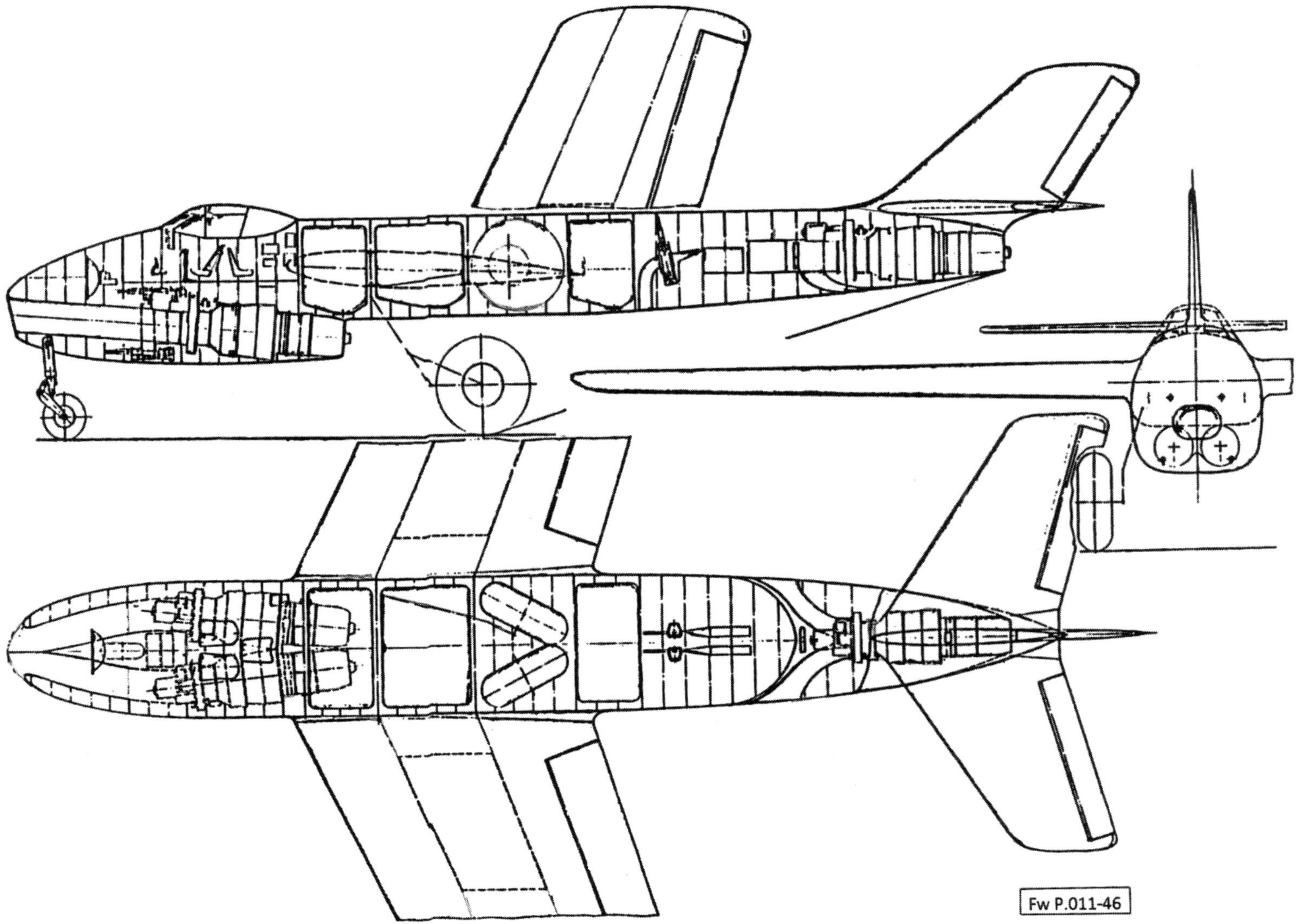
Fw P.011-46

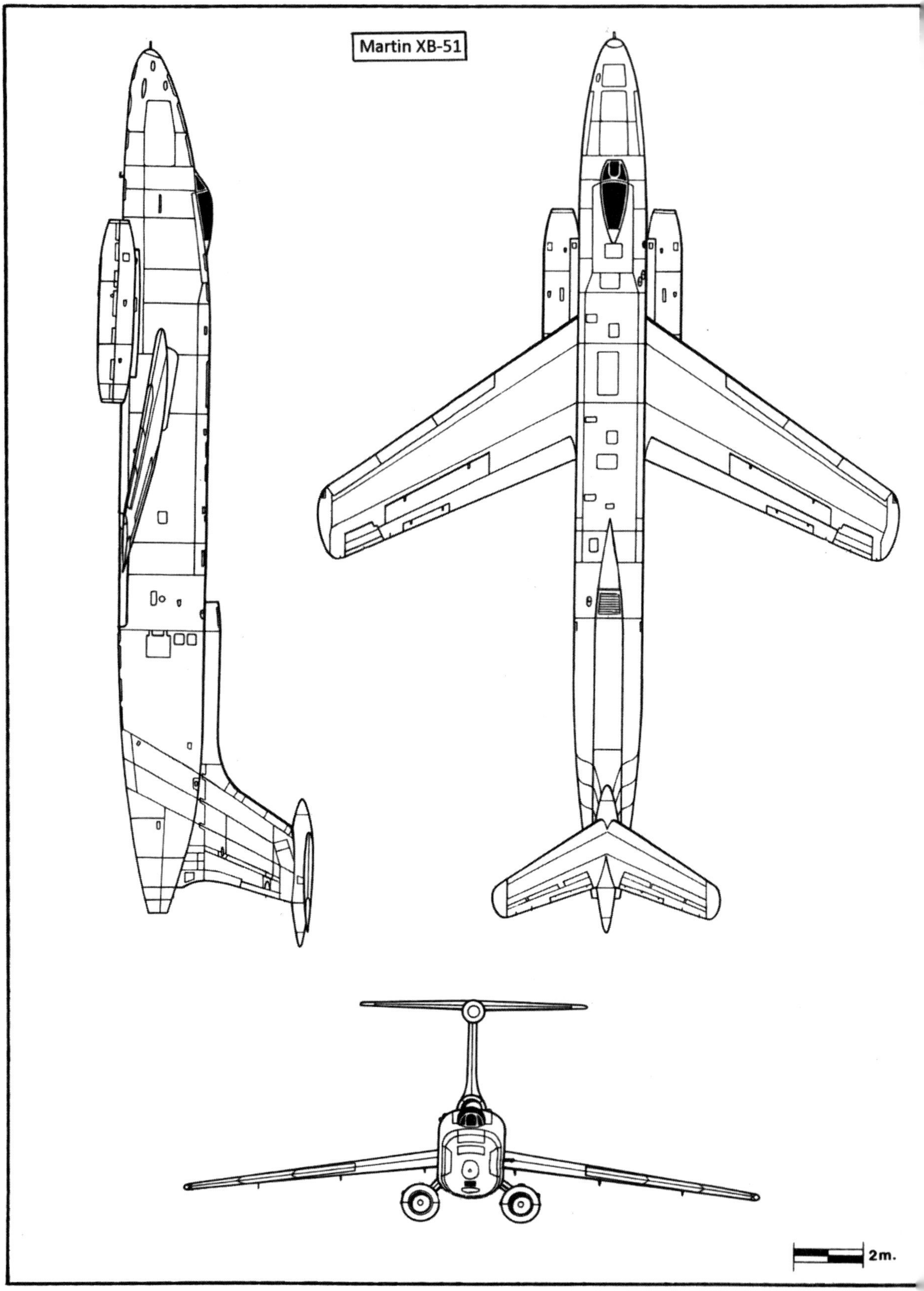
Martin XB-51
2m.

22

Focke-Wulf 2-TL *Nachtjäger mit* Jumo 222

As an alternative to the long-range night fighter projects powered by three turbojets, the design team of Kurt Tank proposed a series of heavy night fighters by the end of 1944, which, based on the aerodynamics of the Fw P.413.002, increased its size to 110 per cent and had a 28-degree swept wing. The RLM was to give it the Fw 272 designation, although in practice, this was never applied to the project.

They were large aircraft equipped with the FuG 244 Bremen 0 radar and a crew of three: pilot, navigator, and radar operator. The formula was like the one used in the Dornier P 247/252, but instead of two Otto engines in tandem, it had just one for extra-long-range patrol, complemented by two BMW 003 A-1 turbojets in underslung wing nacelles, for take-off and combat only. The reason for using the BMW turbojets was that they consumed the same 87-octane B4 fuel as the piston engines.

Given the usual uncertainty about the future availability of high performance piston engines, three different designs were made, each one adapted to the three most promising engines in development. The Fw 0310251-13 of 23 November 1944 would be driven by a Junkers Jumo 213 C/D (medium altitude version) with MW 50 power boost; the *Fw 0310251-22* (2 February 1944) was to be driven by a Daimler-Benz DB 603 N with MW 50 power boost and the high-altitude version Fw 0310251-23 (December 1944) would be driven by an Argus As 413 with GM-1 power boost.

The electronic equipment consisted of a FuG 244 Bremen 0 active search radar, a FuG 226 *Neuling* IFF discriminator, a FuG 139 *Barbarossa* command relay equipment, a FuG 130 autopilot, a FuG 101a radio altimeter, a FuG 24 SN R/T homing device, a Fu Bl 3F radio navigation equipment, and a Peil G6 *Ludwig* direction finder device.

The standard armament of four MK 108/30 could be complemented by another two guns of the same type in an 80-degree *Schräge Musik* configuration, positioned in the place usually allocating the triangular fuel tank, between the main wheels bays. It could also fire R100 rockets with the Oberon-Elfe system associated to the FuG 244.

The crew did not have ejector seats. Therefore, it may be assumed that an explosive device was used to detach the propeller blades in an emergency.

Fw 0310251-13 Technical Data

Type: Heavy all-weather fighter
Cockpit: Three seats, pressurised, control heating, armoured windscreen
Engine: A Jumo 222 C/D of twenty-four cylinders, liquid cooled, star, with six banks of four cylinders each and 3,000-hp driving a single 3.4 metres diameter, two three-blade contra-rotating propeller by means of an extension shaft and two BMW 003 A-1 turbojets with 800 kp thrust each
Armament: Four Mk 103/30 guns in the nose
Wingspan: 21 m
Length: 16.55 m
Wing area: 55 sq.m
Maximum weight: 14,000 kg
Max. speed: 880 kph
Service ceiling: 14,000 m
Endurance: Eight hours

Fw 0310251-22 Technical Data

Type: Heavy night fighter
Cockpit: Three seats, pressurised, control heating, armoured windscreen
Engine: One Daimler-Benz DB 603N of twelve cylinders, inverted 'V', liquid cooled, with 2,830 hp emergency power driving a single 3.4 metres diameter propeller of four blades by means of a 4.40 metres extension shaft and two BMW 003 A-1 turbojets with 800 kp thrust each
Armament: Four Mk 103/30 guns in the nose
Wingspan: 20.40 m
Length: 16.60 m
Height: 4.65 m
Wing area: 52 sq.m
Max. weight: 13,000 kg
Max. speed: 848 kph
Service ceiling: 13,400 m

Fw 0310251-123 Technical Data

Type: Heavy night fighter
Cockpit: Three seats, pressurised, control heating, armoured windscreen
Engine: One Argus As 413 of 24 cylinders, water cooled, with 4,000 hp, driving a single 3.10 metres diameter 2 x 3 blades, contraprops, by means of an extension shaft and two BMW 003 A-1 turbojets with 800 kp thrust each
Armament: Four Mk 103/30 guns in the nose

Wingspan: 22.80 m
Length: 16.75 m
Height: 5.10 m
Wing area: 65 sq. m
Max. weight: 19,000 kg
Max. speed: 850 kph
Service ceiling: 13,000 m

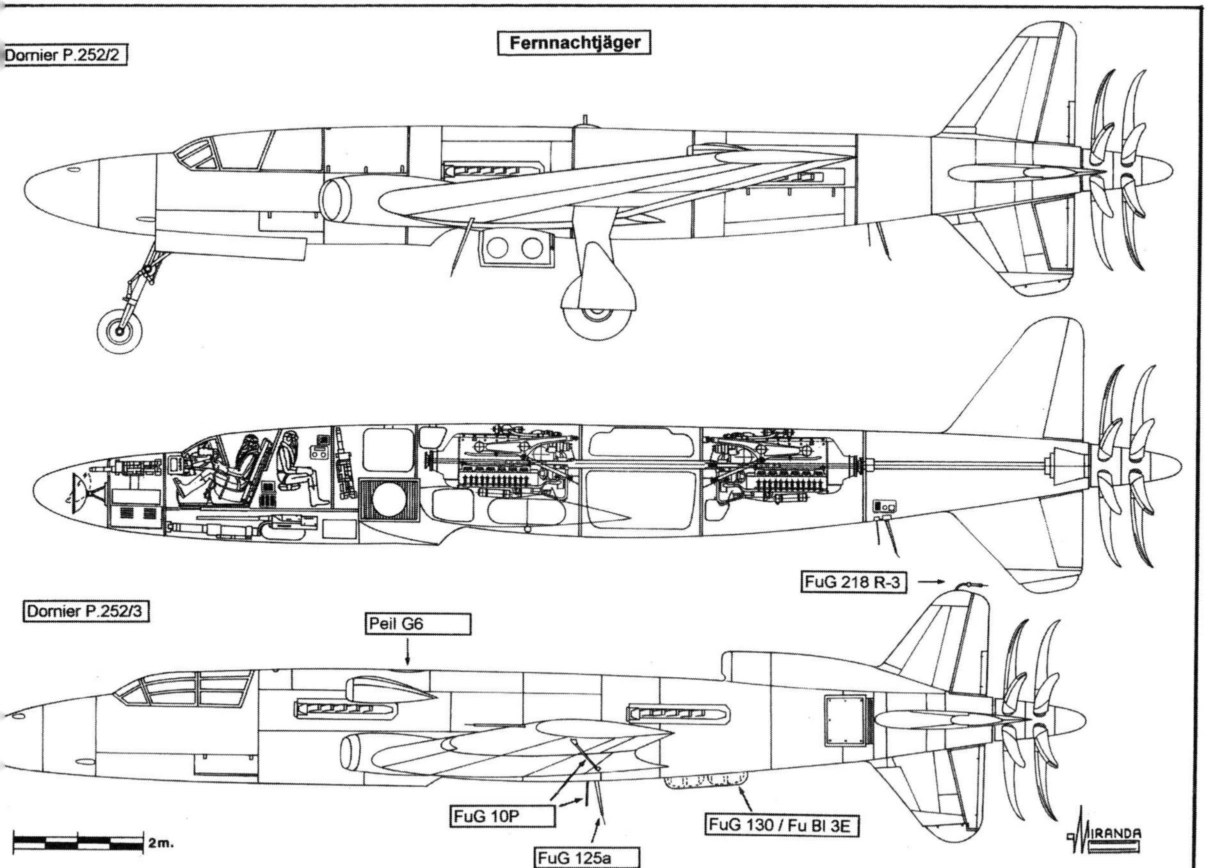

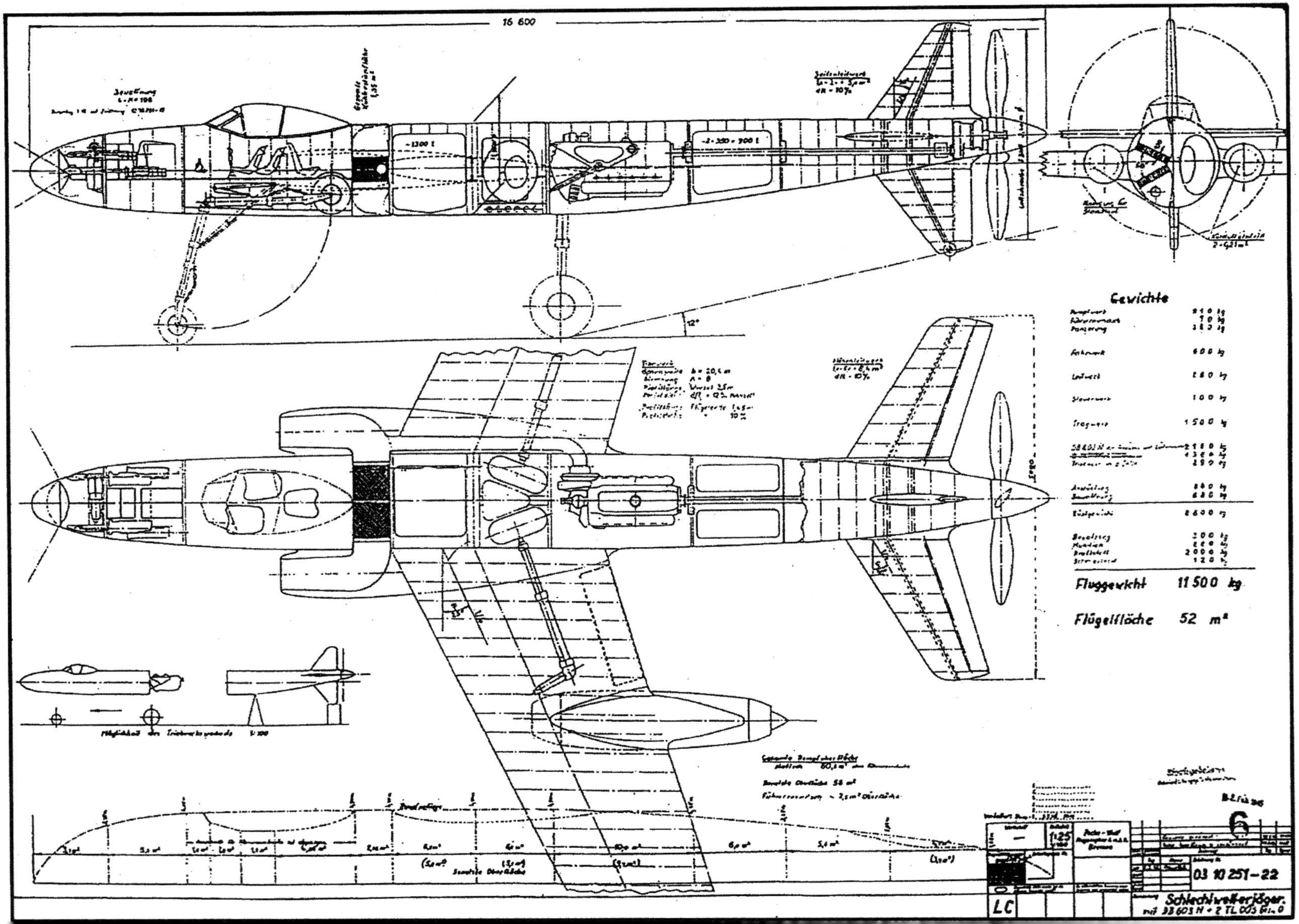

16 600
-1300 l
12°
Gewichte
Tragwerk 1500 kg
Fluggewicht 11 500 kg
Flügelfläche 52 m²
03 10 251–22
Schlechtwetterjäger
LC
6

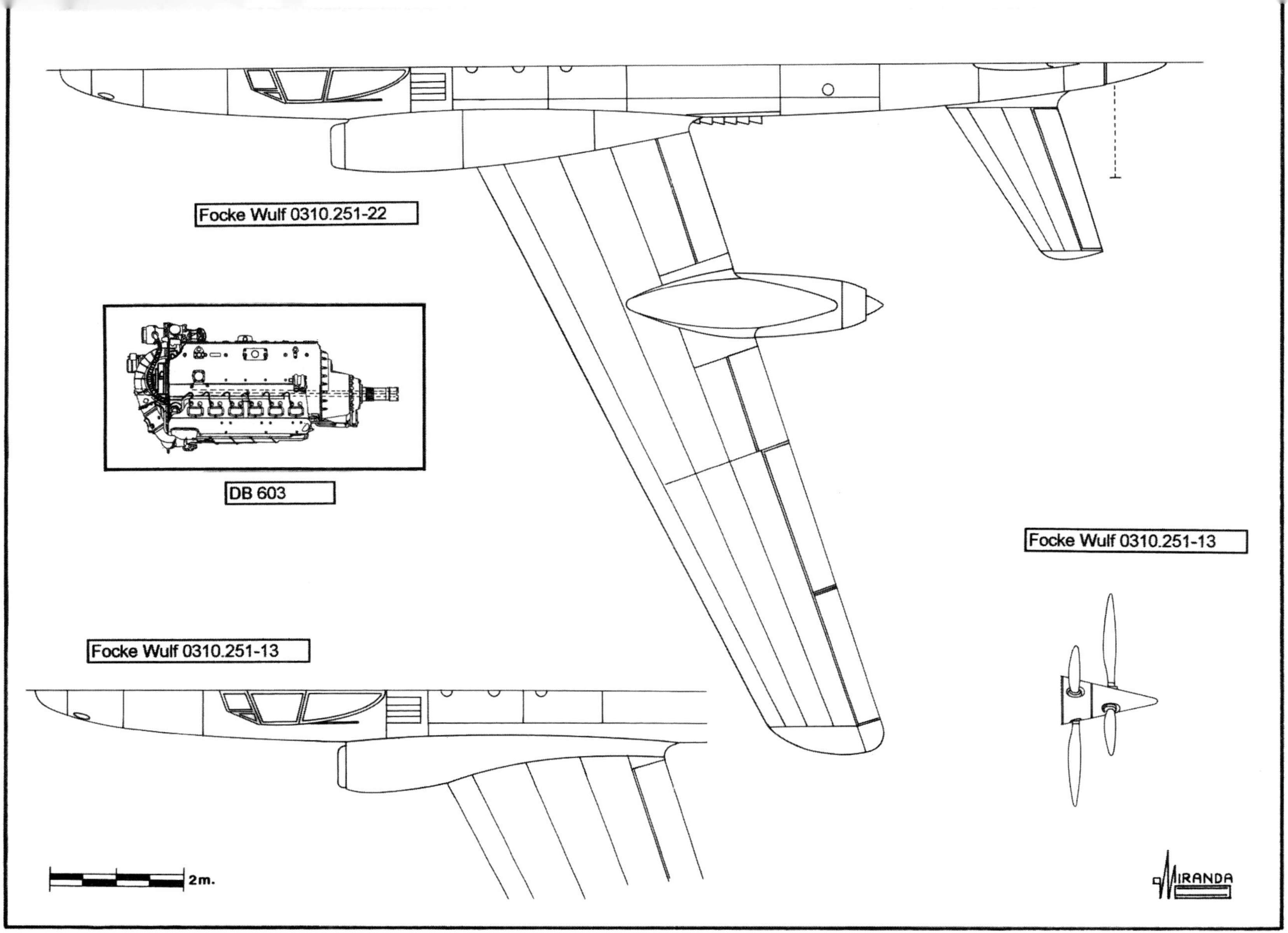
Focke Wulf 0310.251-22
DB 603
Focke Wulf 0310.251-13
Focke Wulf 0310.251-13
2m.
MIRANDA

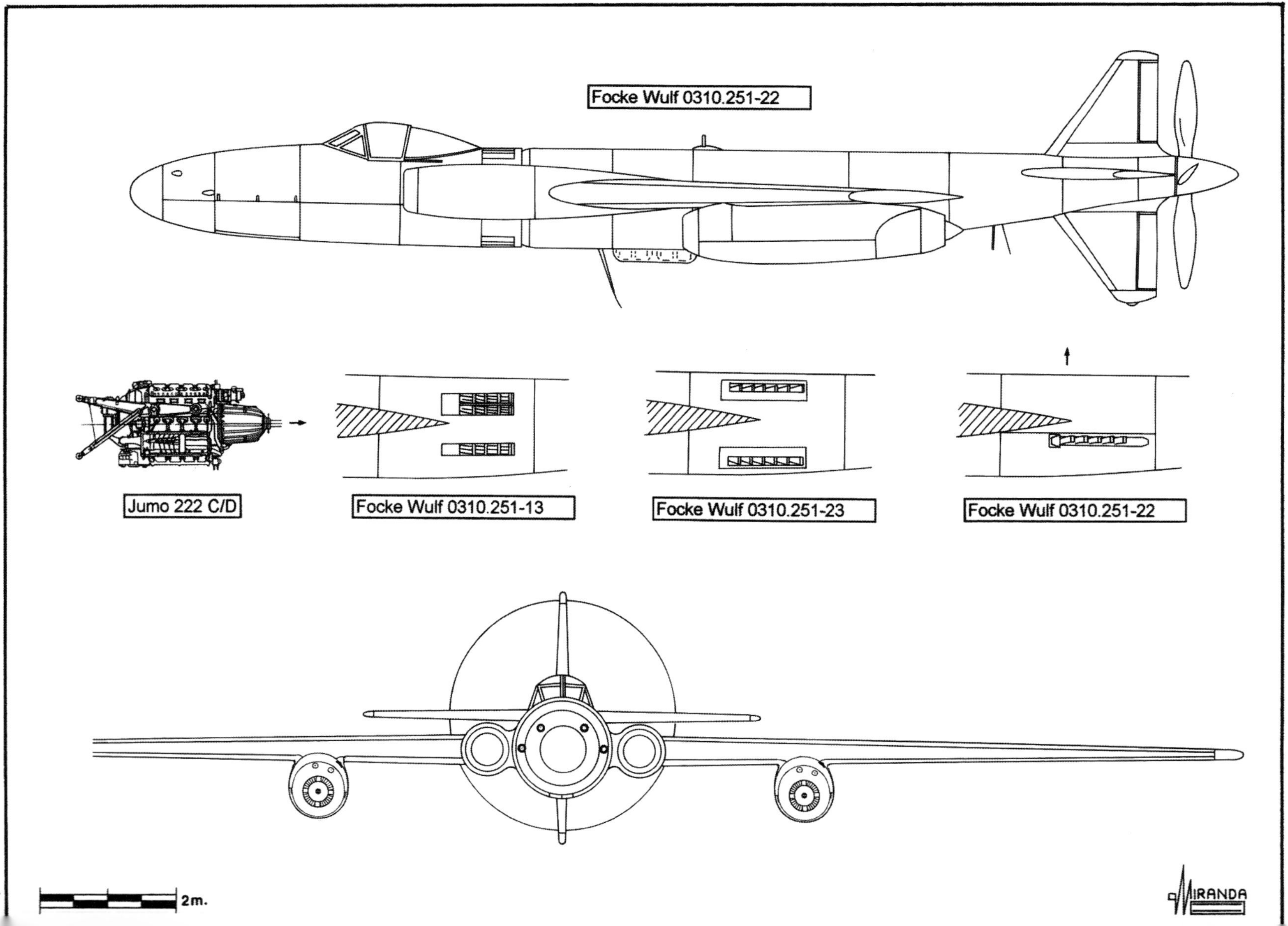
Focke Wulf 0310.251-22
Jumo 222 C/D
Focke Wulf 0310.251-13
Focke Wulf 0310.251-23
Focke Wulf 0310.251-22
2m.
MIRANDA

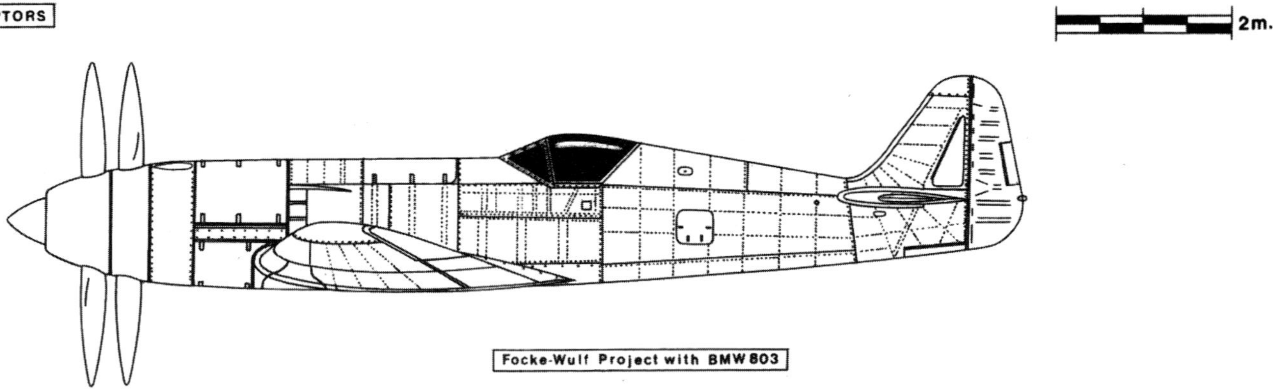

Focke-Wulf Project with BMW 803

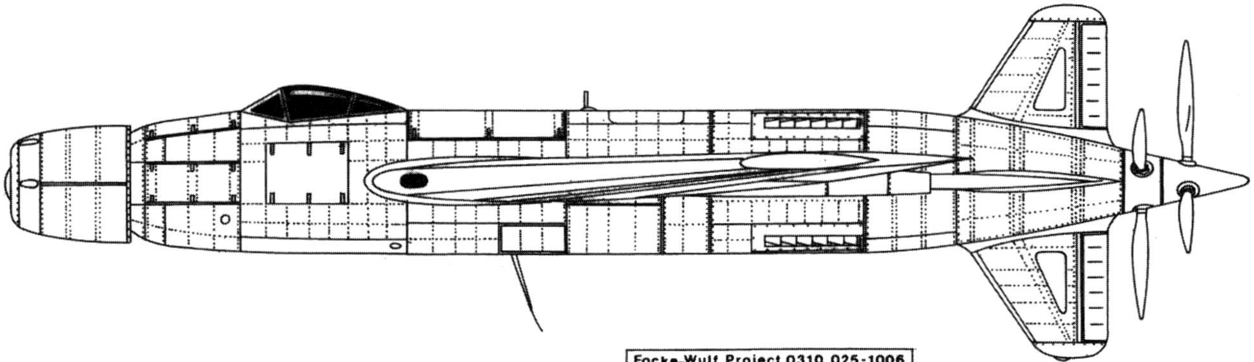

Focke-Wulf Project 0310.025-1006

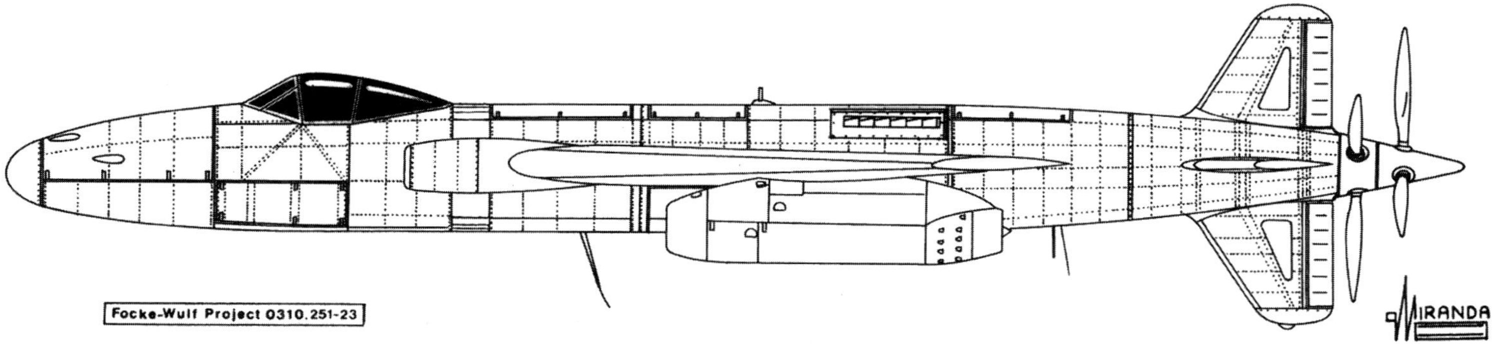

Focke-Wulf Project 0310.251-23

23

Focke-Wulf *Strahlrohrjäger*

Despite their appearances, the short range of the airplanes powered by rockets seriously hindered its military use. The logical alternative was to favour the development of the turbojet to achieve more reliable and powerful engines. Unfortunately, the German industry was not able to produce the required metallic alloys that were especially resistant to heat and stress. They lacked metals like chromium and molybdenum that were essential to harden the steel.

Chemists produced silicones to replace the rubber and synthetic oil of low quality from coal. However, the advanced materials for the compressor blades of the turbojets would not be ready on time and everyone was aware of it. The pulsejet of the V-1 did not have enough power and, although different variants of the He 162, Me 262, and Me 328 were designed (powered by two, four, and even six pulse jets), it was soon made evident that they were a dead end. The vibrations they generated were destructive to the airplane structure. The situation demanded a new type of engine capable of running on any fuel; it also had to be easy to build with cheap metals, so the German aircraft industry was forced to consider the use of ramjets.

The theory elaborated by René Lorin in 1913 established that this type of engine produced the maximum thrust at Mach 2, but the theoretical work carried out by Dr Eugen Sänger in 1940 showed that a ramjet built with a length to diameter ratio of 5 to 1 could work in the high subsonic speed range, with a lower specific fuel consumption than a rocket and higher thrust than a turbojet.

In the forward conical portion of the engine, the air flow was decelerated with simultaneous pressure increase to approximately one-sixth of the flight speed. In the cylindrical combustion chamber, the fuel is injected according to the throttling, and mixed with the flowing air. At a speed above 200 kph, the air inlet pressure is sufficient to start ignition using a ring of spark plugs, with the gases ejected from the jet pipe at a superior speed than that of flying. The first tests carried out in 1941 in the Völkenrode produced very long flames, which discouraged wind tunnel test with ramjets. Ground tests began in Autumn 1941 with a prototype mounted above the *Opel Blitz* truck.

In March 1942, a Sänger ramjet with 500-mm diameter was tested in flight, mounted above a Dornier Do 17 Z bomber provided by the Ainring Institut. In

December, a second test was carried out with a ramjet of 1,500 mm mounted above a Dornier Do 217 E-2. In the summer of 1944, the same airplane was used to test the final version of 1,000 mm. The ramjet worked correctly every time, although with low thrust due to the low speed of the bomber.

In theory, the Sänger 1000 had a nominal output of 17,400 hp, the Sänger 1500 of 22,000 hp, and the Sänger 2000 of 61,000 hp. However, this could only be demonstrated by installing them on an aircraft capable of flying at a speed of Mach 0.8 and an altitude of 15,000 m. In January 1945, the DFS Institut issued a report suggesting the mounting of two Sänger 1000 above the wings of an Me 262 A-1. It was expected to produce an increase of 200 kph in maximum speed, an increase of 4,000 m for the absolute ceiling, and the reduction of the climbing time to 10,000 m from twenty-six to six minutes. The plan was thereby frustrated by the shortage of J2 fuel available for flying tests.

On 30 November 1944, the RLM requested the design of a ramjet-propelled fighter. In December, the Oberammergau project bureau started working on a version of the Messerschmitt P.1101 powered by a Sänger 1000 in anticipation that the HeS 011 turbojet would not be ready on time. The modifications consisted in increasing the diameter of the fuselage, installing three fuel tanks of 1,500, 500, and 120 litres each, and designing a new landing gear with main wheels that would retract in tandem under the engine. The take-off was affected with the help of eight detachable RATO rockets of the Schmidding type 109-533, with 1,000 kp peak thrust each, which accelerated the aircraft to 120 m/sec. The new version was called Messerschmitt P.1101 L (Lorinantrieb).

In December 1944, Professor Sänger designed the *Überschall-Staustrahljäger* (supersonic ramjet fighter), a high-altitude interceptor of 7 tons propelled by a ramjet of 60,000 hp, but the DFS Institut lacked the facilities for its construction. In February 1945, the firm Škoda-Kauba Flugzeugbau, Cakowitz, who had carried out some discouraging experiments with foam coal ramjets, issued an order to the RLM for the design of an interceptor with ramjet propulsion based on the theoretical work of Sänger.

On 25 February 1945, the company produced the SK P.14-01 design, a Mach 0.815 fighter powered by a Sänger 1500 with 22,000 hp nominal thrust, 1,000 litres of fuel, pilot in prone position, one MK 103/30 heavy cannon, landing skid, and 10,000 m estimated absolute ceiling. The definitive design dated in April was the 7-ton SK P.12-02, powered by a Sänger 2500 with 60,000 hp nominal thrust, 1,400 litres of fuel, and 850 kph maximum speed. Take-off acceleration was provided by four Schmidding 109-533, mounted above a detachable tricycle trolley.

In March 1945, a Heinkel design team under the leadership of Dipl.-Ing. Siegfried Günter, designed a high-altitude tailless interceptor named He P.1080, with a 15,100 hp Sänger 900 in each wing root, an armament of two MK 108/30 cannon, and a maximum take-off weight of 3.325 kg. The P.1080 could fly for ninety minutes with 1,100 kg of fuel at an estimated maximum speed of 980 kph. The take-off was carried out from a detachable trolley propelled by four Schmidding 109-533. The P.1080 was the last project developed by the firm during the Second World War.

In October 1941, it was evident that the rocket engines planned for the Me 163 B would take months or even years to be ready and Alexander Lippisch started to consider the possibilities of the new Junkers T1 turbojets that had been successfully tested some days after the record had been achieved. However, they were too long for a Komet airframe. They should be installed in a larger airplane, a heavy fighter of six tons, equivalent to the Me 262 that, with the Me 163 aerodynamics, would have a better ceiling, climb rate, and maximum speed.

The new project, known as Lippisch P.11-92 13/09/42, was presented to the OKL as the answer to the specification published by the RLM's Technical Department on 20 October 1942. It required a bomber with 1,000 kg payload, 700 km/h maximum speed, and 1,046 km penetration depth. *Abteilung L* was disbanded within Messerschmitt in April and the Lippisch design team moved to Vienna to form the Aeronautical Research Institute (Luftfahrtforschungsanstalt Wien). The work on the P.11 continued there.

The original single tailfin was replaced by a double one in the *Zerstörer* version (named *Projekt Delta VI*) based on the P.11-121 formula. The whole production of turbojets was absorbed by the assembly lines of the Me 262 and Ar 234. The Jumo 004 and BMW 003 were unreliable and difficult to manufacture in great quantities given that the additives to harden the special steel of the blades, the spare parts, and the fuel were scarce. The new HeS 011 was just an unfinished prototype.

Lippisch turned his attention to the third type of jet engines, the Lorin Ramjets, to power his future designs. His first try, on 12 April 1944, projected the integration of a Delta VI airframe with a 20,000-hp Lorin Strahlrohr of oval section, with liquid fuel carbon disulphide self-igniting at the compression temperature of the air, at the end of the multiple Oswatitsch shock diffusers. The research continued with the P.12 and P.13, which already included ramjets designed by him.

The new design, named LP.12 *Entwurf I*, consisted of a triangular wing and tailfin fitted to the ramjet tube that acted as a fuselage. The pilot occupied the tailfin and the fuel tanks were in the wing. The ramjet needed to move at a minimum speed of 200 kph before being started. To achieve that, in August 1944, it was proposed to carry the PL12 up to 8,000 m over a Focke-Wulf Fw 58, in Mistel configuration, and launch it from there.

However, tests performed on the use of a ramjet for the project P.11 Delta VI in April the same year proved that they could generate more power by increasing the number of sprinklers in the grid of the fuel injection system and the volume of the combustion chamber. The new airframe *Entwurf II* was designed around a bigger ramjet, to adapt the new power plant to the LP 12. *Entwurf II* kept the circular intake. A dividing wall within this intake split the air in two D-shaped ducts on both sides of the pilot cockpit. The fuel mixed in those ducts after passing through the two sprinkling grids separated 25 cm from each other. Both ducts joined again in a hexagonal combustion chamber located behind the cockpit that stretched towards the exhaust nozzle. The wind tunnel tests proved that the model had too much drag.

Entwurf III added internal aerodynamic refinements, like the adoption of an elliptical section along the whole ramjet. As for the outer parts, the wing and tail surfaces were redesigned, and the landing gear consisted of a unique retractable wheel. Even so, the model still generated a great degree of drag due to the complex system of inner ducts and had no transonic capacity. *Entwurf IV* simplified the air intake by removing the bifurcation. To that purpose, the pilot should be in prone position, lying over the air intake, within an aerodynamic clear canopy. The air intake had an elliptical section, but with a flatter axis relation of 2.8 to 1, ending in an elliptical sprinkler grid that led to a hexagonal combustion chamber. The nozzle, equipped with four hydraulically operated flaps, had a variable geometry rectangular section.

During the last year of the war, the scarcity of oil suffered by Germany induced scientists and engineers to experiment with alternative fuels. The most refined types of gasoline were used for conventional piston engines. The BMW 003 turbojets worked with B.4 (87-octane petrol). The J2 and K1, burnt by the Jumo 004 and Heinkel He S 011 turbojets, were heavy kerosene. The Argus pulsejet of the V-1 worked with crude petrol. The Peenemünde engineers designed a V-2 that worked with diesel oil and S-Stoff—mixture of nitric acid (96 per cent) and ferrous chloride (4 per cent)—also called Salbei. Dr Pabst, from the Gas Dynamics section of the Focke-Wulf Company, suggested that the ramjets of the future Triebflügel fighter burned even less volatile fuels as pitch oil or lignite tar. To that purpose, they had to design a compact evaporating plant that could be installed onboard.

An airplane is certainly not a locomotive as it cannot carry the weight of a steam boiler. However, it is common knowledge among coal miners that air saturated with coal dust is a powerful explosive. Dr Zippermeyer, at the Speer Ministry research establishment near Lofer, built the vortex gun *Wirbelkanone* and the atmospheric whirlwind gun *Luftwirbelkannone*; both were based on this type of combustion. The prototype was satisfactory.

Dr K. Wahl, of the Kirchheim Technische Institut, made a Lorin ramjet that worked with coal dust fuel. The idea was adopted by Lippisch to power his P.13 project. They built a burner prototype of rectangular section to that effect, which burned a brown coal tablet in the middle of a strong wind flow. The tablet was made of suspended coal dust in pressurised inflammable oil foam and should be carried to the air stream in a wire mesh container set in the duct at a small angle of 6 degrees. It was 265 cm × 200 cm × 15 cm and weighed 670 kg.

The first configuration of the P.13 was named P.13a *Entwurf I*. The air came into the combustion chamber through two oblique air intakes fitted with deflector vanes. It was then guided by a hydraulically operated flap towards the upper part of the carbon tablet, already burning thanks to a gas burner. The air was forced to run through the whole surface of the tablet, spreading the combustion, thus increasing its volume and temperature and converting it into carbon dioxide. Afterwards, it went to an expansion chamber and was expelled through a rectangular nozzle fitted with hydraulically operated flaps. The burning speed (320 km/h) was achieved by means of a Walter rocket located at the base of the tailfin.

As it happened with the LP.12, the wind tunnel tests proved that the deflectors and the flap located within the air duct produced too much drag. This conclusion led to the LP 13a Enwurf II version, equipped with an air intake based on that of the

Entwurf I, rounded wingtips and tailfin tips and a cockpit with improved visibility. A reduced scale air model named LP 12/13 was also built to test the new ramjet in flight. It was discovered that the slope of the tablet generated too much drag and that the combustion geometry was not the right one. To obviate those defects, the LP 13a *Entwurf II* was equipped with a new type of burners, which would hopefully be the production version, and renamed LP 13a *Entwurf III*.

This modification consisted of changing the tablet to an oval axial section block of 800 kg, housed in a wire mesh circular basket of the same section, within the duct and positively rotated around its vertical axis at some 60 rpm by means of an electric engine. The combustion was initiated by a gas burner and could use liquid fuel to facilitate starting up. The coal now used took the shape of small granules and not irregular lumps as previously, since granules produced a more controlled and even burning. The system was tested in the LFW in Vienna before the end of the war and worked fine. It was expected that the new engine had a power superior to the 60,000 hp reached by the Sänger ramjets of liquid fuel and had a range of forty-five minutes powered flight. Although the power of the engine could be regulated by opening or closing the nozzle flaps, this could not be stopped at will by the pilot.

At the end of 1944, tests were carried out with several ramjet engines of the type called RL (Raketen Lorin) in the BMW wind tunnel at Oberwiesenfeld. They consisted of a 'cold' Walter rocket embedded into the air intake of a Lorin ramjet to induce the necessary airflow for operation while stationary. The rocket would be deactivated when ignition velocity was reached. Research with RL ramjets was sponsored by the Junkers company with the objective of increasing the range of the Me and Ju 263 fighter by adapting two RL of 84-cm diameter under the wing roots.

By mid-1944, Dipl.-Ing. Heinz Stöckel designed a ramjet bomber called Manuell Gesteuertes Raketenprojektil for the Blohm und Voss firm. It was 11 m long and 1.8 m in diameter and could carry a warhead of 4,500 kg at 300 km with an accuracy far superior to that of the V-2 rockets because it was a piloted missile. The bomber was guided from a parasite ramjet airplane docked on its back in Mistelschlepp configuration. Its pilot could change the trajectory of the whole set by operating the airbrakes located on the sides of the bomber.

During the terminal dive, at 800 m/second, the guidance plane detached, performing a high-*g* manoeuvre and using the speed to ignite its own ramjet engine, which would allow it to return to base landing like a glider. To better support the separation manoeuvre, the pilot adopted a prone position. In August, the Blohm und Voss firm proposed a reduced version called P.214, which could be used either as anti-ship or *Pulkzerstörer*. The lower element of 8 m long and 1 m in diameter could carry a warhead of 2,300 kg over 1,000 km. It would be powered by a ramjet, which should activate after its launch from a Dornier Do 217 Mistelschlepp.

In late August, Heinz Stöckel proposed the construction of a rammer based on the guidance airplane of the P.124, with an armoured nosecone of 150 kg, provided with eight radial blades, and a pilot seated conventionally. The engine, which was called Rammrakete and was based on the Walter RL, consisted of a monopropellant 'cold' rocket with 1,500 kp of thrust. With this power, the rammer could be launched vertically from a ramp of three rails, like a Natter. By increasing the height and speed, the air coming through the annular air intake mixed with the hot gases of the engine in a post-combustion chamber, acting as the oxidiser component of a bi-fuel rocket. The ramjet ignition speed was set at 720 kph with a thrust augmentation of 10,000 kp. The project was presented to the RLM as Rammschussjäger Entwurf I, a dispensable VTO rammer.

The RLM considered the vertical launch too radical as this type of engine did not allow to adjust the thrust and it was feared that a full power take-off could cause unconsciousness to the pilot, as it happened during the flying test of the Bachem BP 20 M23 in March 1945. Stöckel modified the project as Rammschüssjäger Entwurf II, a *Pulkzerstörer*/Rammer carried under the belly of a Dornier Do 217. In losing its VTO status, the airplane could be bigger and transport 1,500 kg of T-Stoff extending its range to 600 km. The rocket was activated after launch to take the plane up to an altitude of 10,000 m, where the ramjet was ignited, raising the speed to 1,000 kph.

The Entwurf III version was presented at the same time. Slightly larger and powered by a more powerful engine, it was based on the principle of the Walter Einstoff but used two types of propellants and one catalyst. In this model, the combustion chamber had been replaced by four smaller ones located inside the air annular duct. In these cameras, the T-Stoff reacted with the Z-Stoff catalyst, producing steam at 550 C, which then mixed with air from the outside in a ratio of 1 to 7. The steam increased its speed and temperature after crossing an annular Venturi. It then went through a ring of sprinkling injectors where it was mixed with M-Stoff (methyl alcohol) that had been superheated to 700 C in a pressurised coil. The ignition was spontaneous and the thrust superior to that of the Entwurf II.

Based on data published at the end of 1943 on the tests carried out at the *Deutsches Forschungsinstitut für Segelflug* (DFS) with the Sänger ramjets, Kurt Tank decided to construct a *Strahlrohr* of his own design. The programme was led by the Dr.-Ing. Otto E. Pabst in the Focke-Wulf gas dynamic department at Kirkhorsten. The first designs of the new engine, dated in spring 1944, represented a type of ramjet much shorter than the Sänger, with a length to diameter ratio of 2 to 1. The first prototype, described in Report No. 09045 in mid-August, was 237 mm in diameter and had fifty-nine injectors of the Fang-Diffuseur type. It was tested in the *Luftfahrtforschungsanstalt* (LFA) Brunswick, using hydrogen as fuel.

Starting September, hydrogen was replaced by propane in some tests, but the bombardment of the Leuna works factories advised to replace the propane with vaporised petrol in the operational versions. For this, it was necessary to design a compact heat exchanger to vaporise and superheat the fuel. The thrust produced by this type of ramjets depended on an absolute aerodynamic perfection of both the external surface and the internal air duct; Dr.-Ing. Theodor Zobel of the LFA Völkenrode and Dr.-Ing. Küchemann of the Aerodynamische Versuchs Anstalt (AVA) Göttingen intervened in the design.

The construction of the first two prototypes of 960 mm turned out to be more difficult than expected due to the high internal pressures and the deformation of the outer surface caused by the heat. At the end of the war in Europe, no units had yet been finished. Flight tests were expected to be performed using a Fw 190 A-10 (the 23 April 1944 project) with a BMW 801 F-1 piston engine and two Pabst ramjets (with fifty injectors, 960-mm diameter, 1,920-mm length, and 1,150-kp estimated thrust) installed on the wingtips.

The combat version, described in dossier Baubeschreibung Nr. 283, was presented to the OKL on 4 August 1944. Commonly referred to in the literature as Focke-Wulf Ta 283, it was a Mach 1.05 high-altitude interceptor faster and better armed than the projects proposed by Messerschmitt, Heinkel, and Skoda. It could take off and land using an internal bipropellant rocket engine and reach combat altitude in under three minutes. It also had good ground mobility after landing, thanks to its retractable undercarriage.

The long fuselage of triangular section, built in light alloy, housed the landing gear, the two fuel tanks (with 1,400 and 406 litres of K1 heavy kerosene), one rocket propellant tank with 960 litres of T-Stoff (sufficient for 420 seconds of autonomy, which would allow it to fly another circuit after a missed landing approach), one rocket propellant tank with 163 litres of C-Stoff, the pressurised cockpit with ejector seat, the integral tailfin, and one Walter rocket engine. The wings, set low on the fuselage with a sharp 50-degree sweep-back angle, were made of wood, plywood, and steel using the same technology as those in the Ta 183. They housed six fuel tanks with 1,000 litres of K1 kerosene, as well as the ailerons and flaps.

The tail planes, with a 60-degree swept-back angle, were entirely constructed in steel to withstand the vibrations and temperatures of 1,000 degrees Celsius generated by the ramjets, which were mounted at the tips to avoid detrimental disturbance of the airflow. The nose leg, with a wheel of 479 × 173 mm retracted backwards and the narrow track main undercarriage wheels of 740 × 210 mm, retracted vertically with rocking levers. The armour consisted of three steel plates of 20 mm to protect the cockpit and main fuel tank, another of 10 mm to protect the instrument panel, and an armoured glass wind screen of 50 mm.

The armament proposed initially consisted of two Mk 103/30 heavy cannon, with ZFR 4a telescopic gunsights. Later, considering the short duration of the attack, density of fire was preferred and two other possible configurations were proposed to the OKL with four MK 108/30 heavy cannon or four MG 213/20 rapid-fire cannon, with EZ 42 (Adler) gyroscopic gunsight. Take-off acceleration was provided for thirty-three seconds by the Walter HWK 109-509 A-1 rocket motor, with 1,700 kp peak thrust. This was sufficient to reach 240 kph, the ignition velocity of the Pabst ramjets of 135 cm in diameter and 270 cm in length, each providing 10,850 kp thrust at sea level and 2,270 kp at 11,000 m. Limited controllability of their engines was caused by the difficulty in synchronizing the throttling using the two electric driven pumps. A wooden mock-up may have been finished, but the project was cancelled by the OKL in the autumn of 1944 due to an excessive landing speed.

Technical Data

Estimated maximum speed: 1,125 kph at 10,000 m.
Take-off weight: 5,388 kg.
Estimated ceiling: 11,000 m.
Initial climb rate: 160 m/sec.
Take-off run: 500 m.
Range: 690 km.
Endurance: 43 minutes.
Wingspan: 8 m; length: 11.88 m; height: 2.9 m; wing area: 19 sq. m

Focke-Wulf *Jäger mit* 2 Lorin-Triebwerken *und* 1 TL

To solve the problem of the excessive landing speed of the Ta 283, the project team (led by Dipl.-Ing. von Halem) sent the dossier Baubeschreibung Nr. 246 to the OKL; it described a short-span STOL variant of the Super TL with an auxiliary turbojet providing vertical lift, one bipropellant rocket, and two ramjets. This project has been commonly described in the literature as Focke-Wulf Super Lorin.

Built in light alloy, the fuselage housed the pressurised cockpit with ejector seat, two MK 108/30 heavy cannon, the landing gear, one 270 litre tank containing the B.4 petrol for the turbojet, two K1 heavy kerosene fuel tanks of 650 and 845 litres for the ramjets, one C-Stoff rocket propellant tank of 345 litres, one T-Stoff rocket propellant of 575 litres, one HeS 8 turbojet with 720 kp static thrust, and one bi-propellant rocket Walter 109-509 A-1 rocket with 1,700 kp peak thrust. The wings, spanning 7.6 m and with a 15 sq. m area, were built in wood, plywood, and steel, and housed six K1 fuel tanks with 150 litres each.

The tail planes were built of steel and served as support for two Pabst ramjets of 10,850 kp thrust each. The landing gear was of the same type as that developed for the Super TL. The exhaust nozzle of the turbojet was located on the fuselage belly to the purpose of generating lift thrust during take-off and landing. High-altitude performances could also be improved, although a shorter wing span might make the airplane very fast at lower altitude, where the ramjets could produce the maximum thrust.

Focke Wulf Ta 283

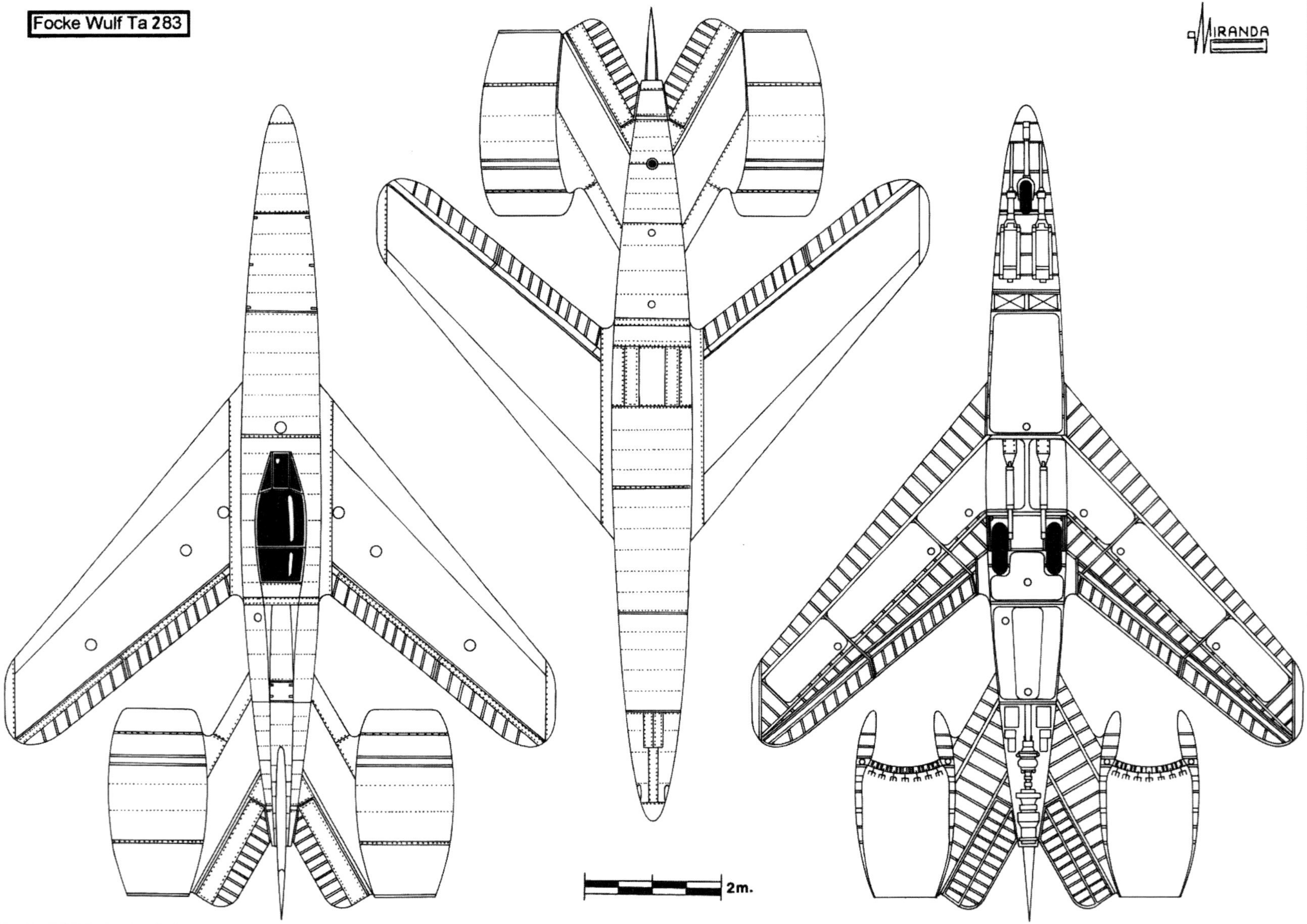

Focke Wulf Ta 283

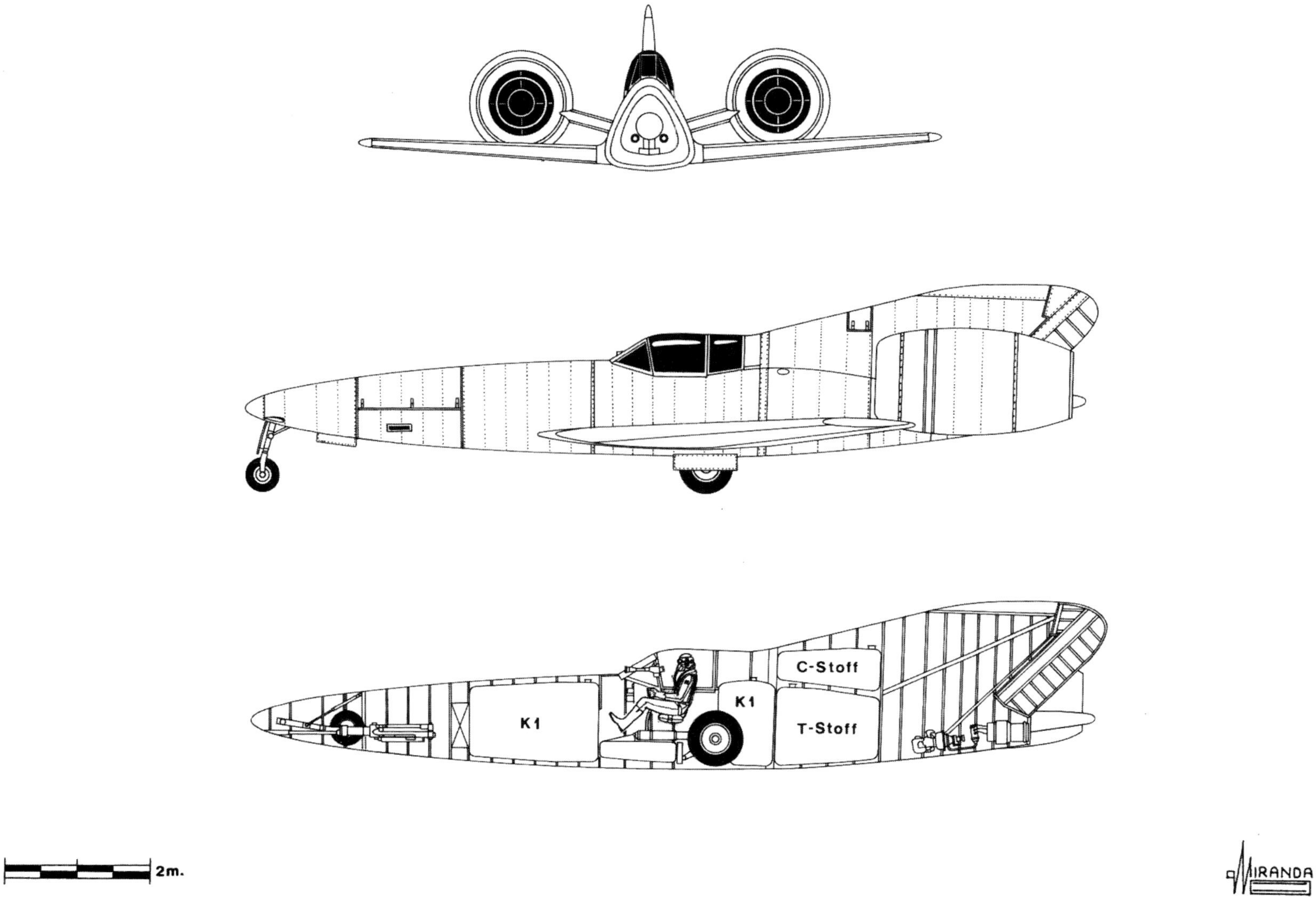

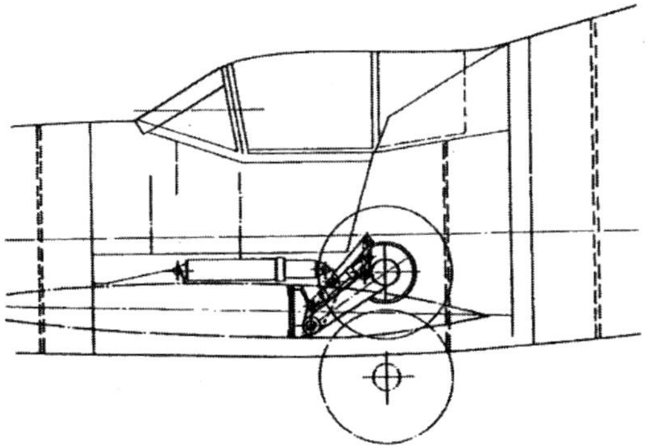

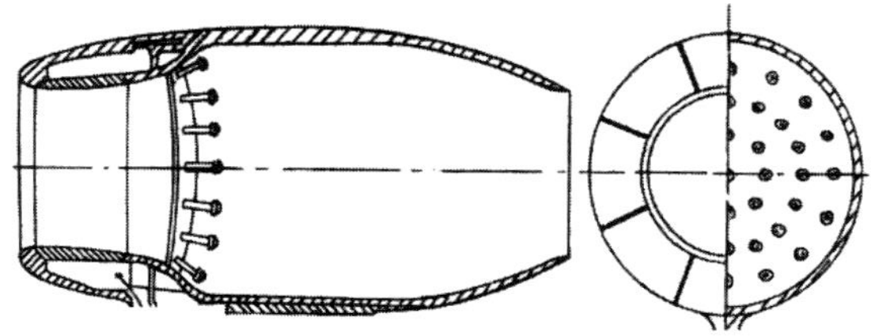

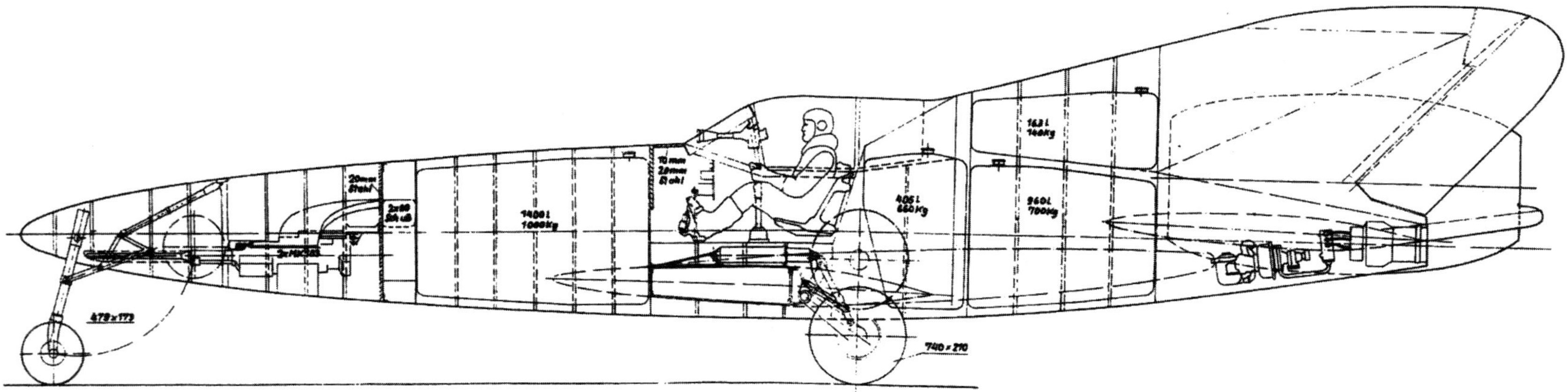
478 x 173
740 x 270

Focke-Wulf *Super Lorin*

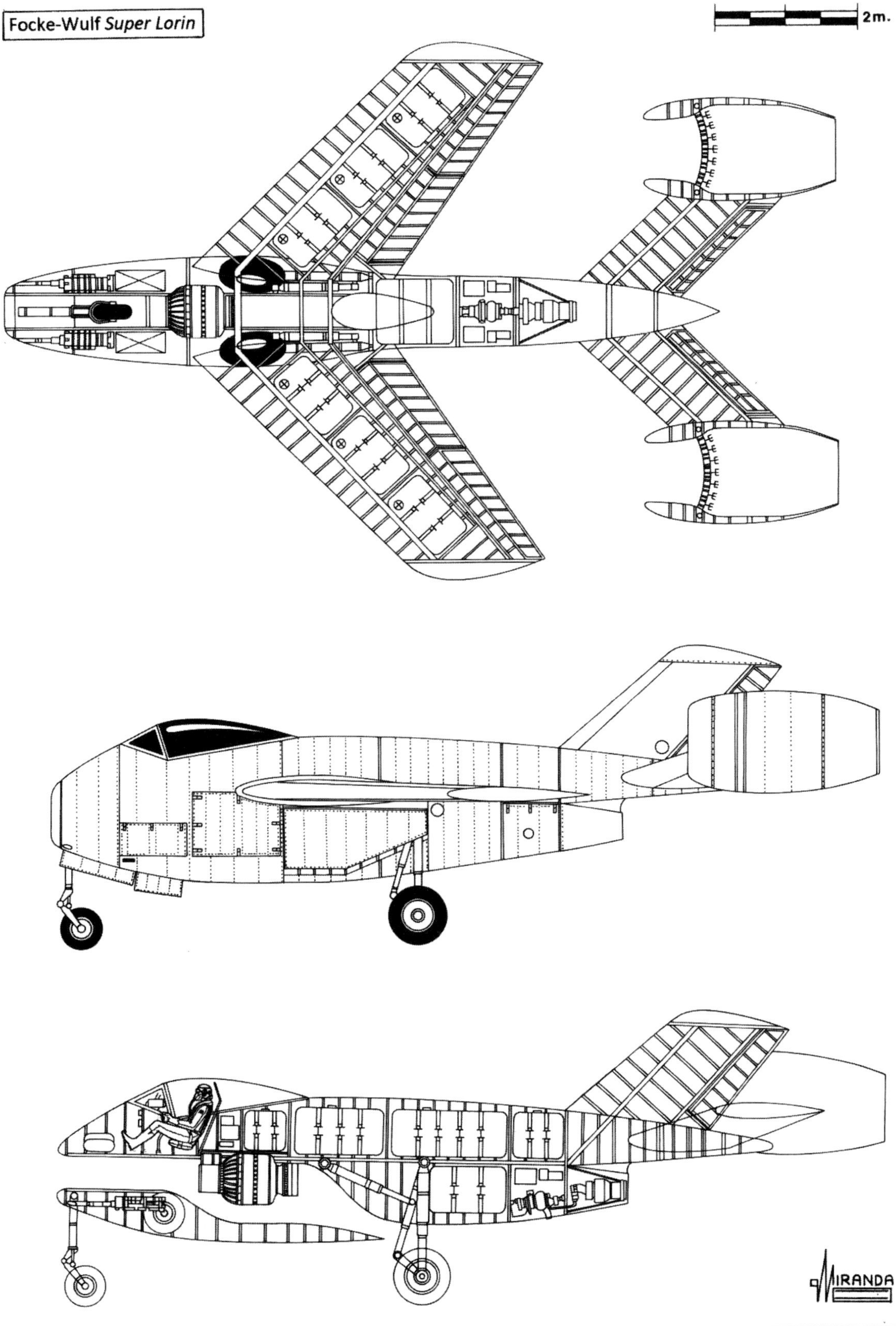

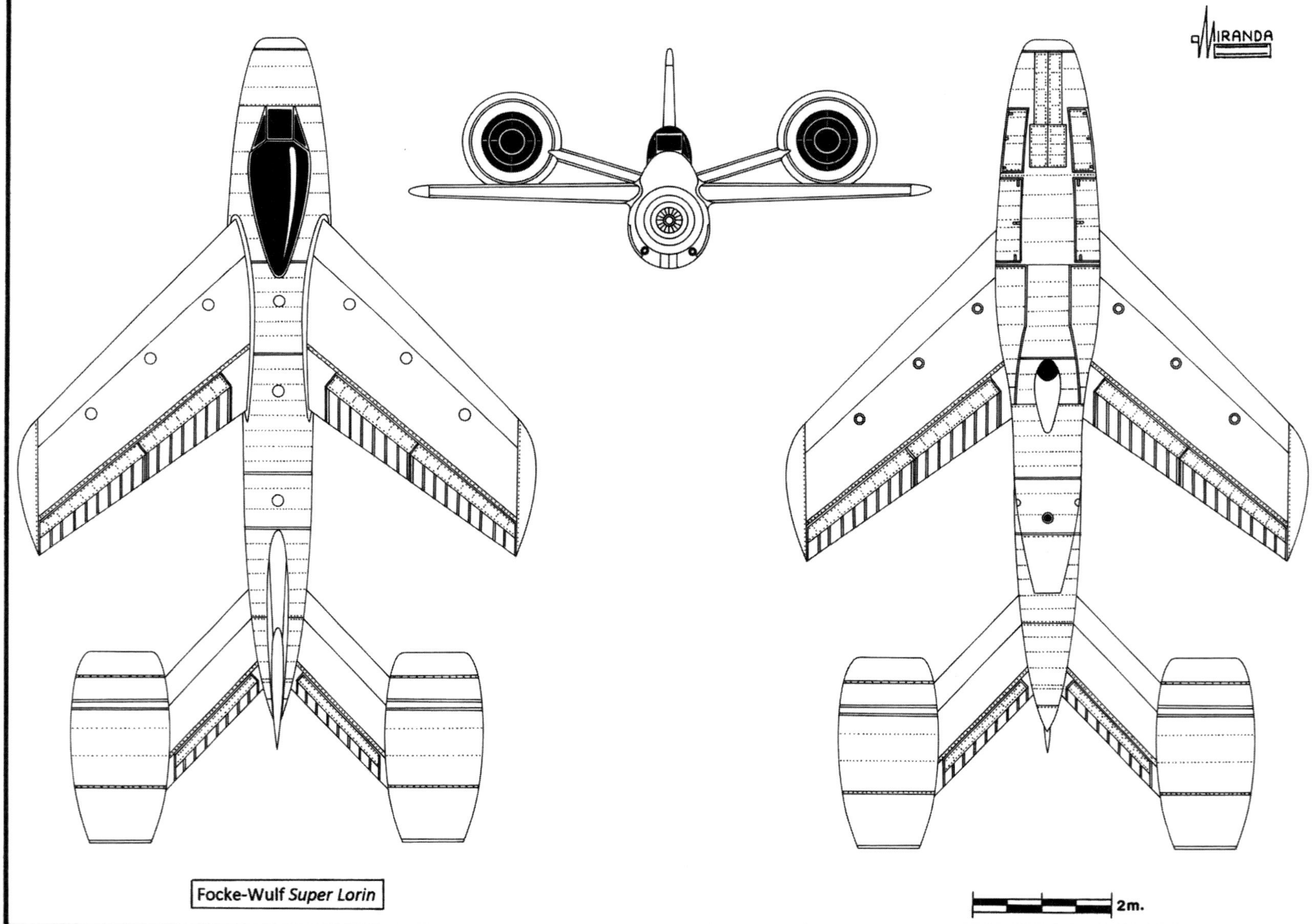

Focke-Wulf *Super Lorin*

GERMAN RAMJETS

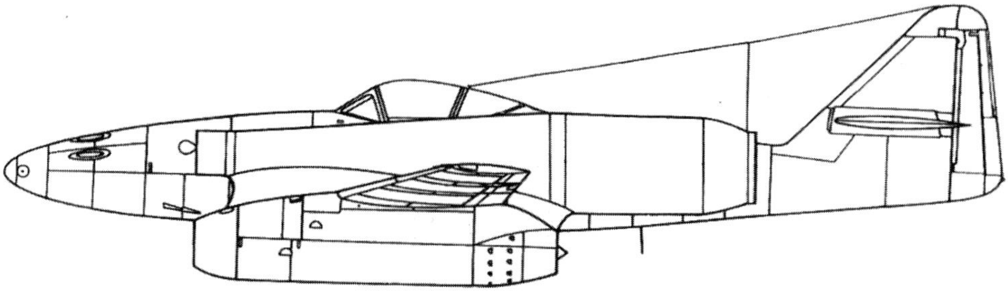

Me 262 A-1a with two *Sänger 1000* ramjets

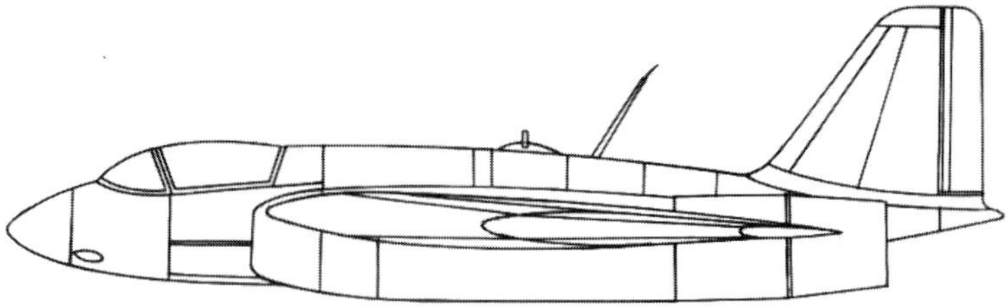

Heinkel P.1080-01 with two *Sänger 900* ramjets

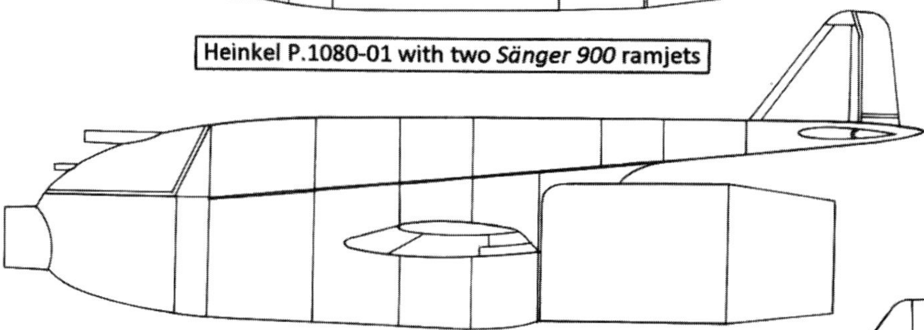

Skoda-Kauba P.14-01 with one *Sänger 1500* ramjet

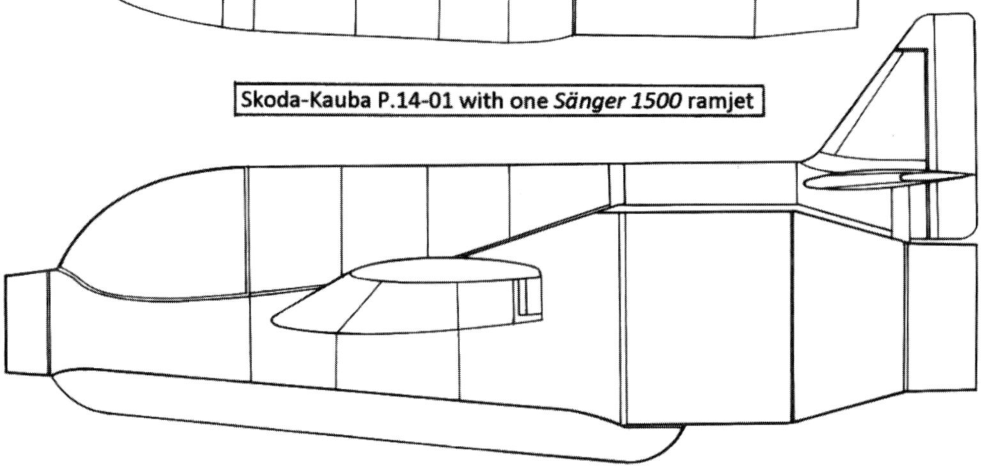

Skoda-Kauba P.14-02 with one *Sänger 2000* ramjet

2m.

Messerschmitt P.1101 L

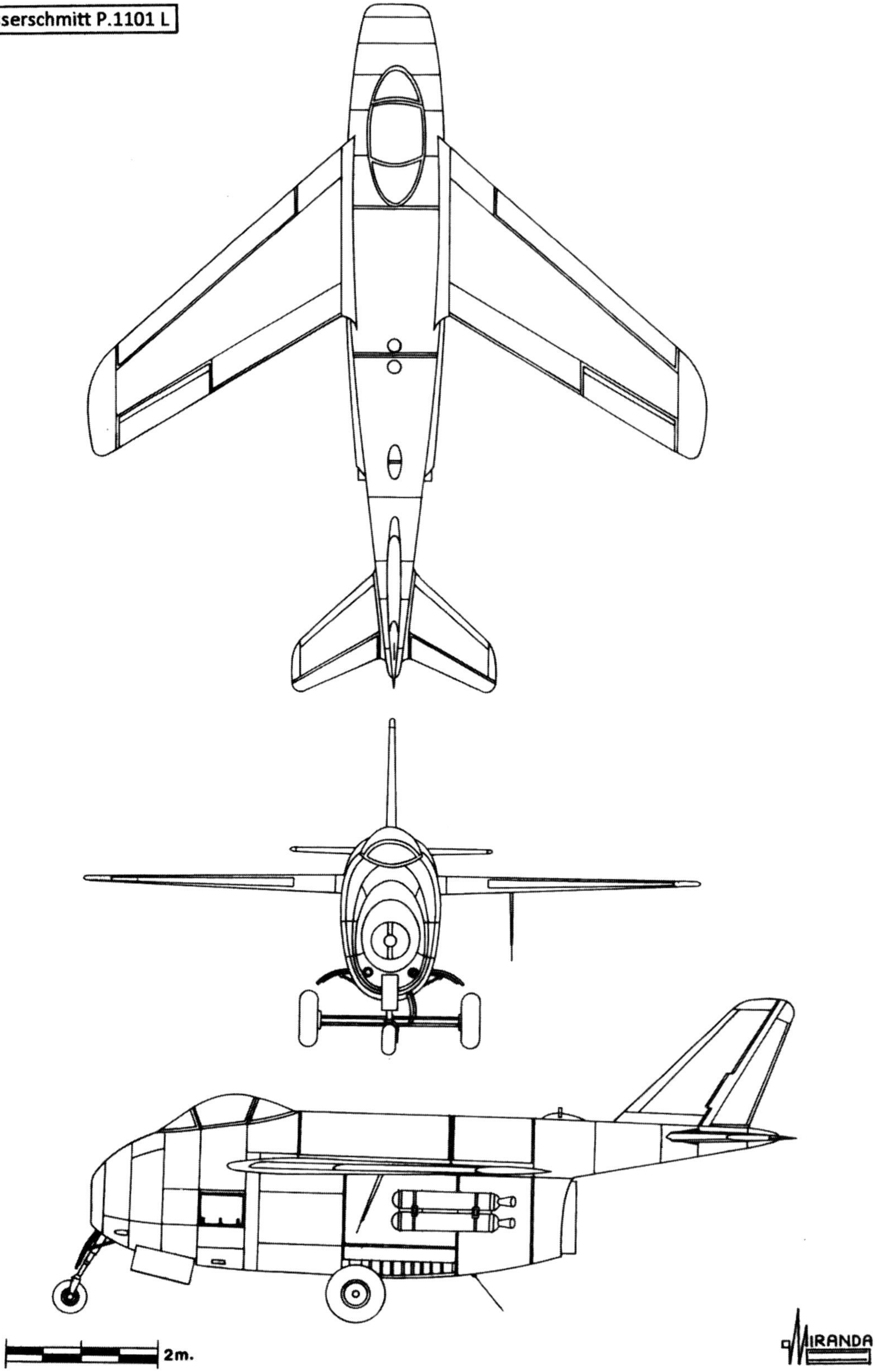

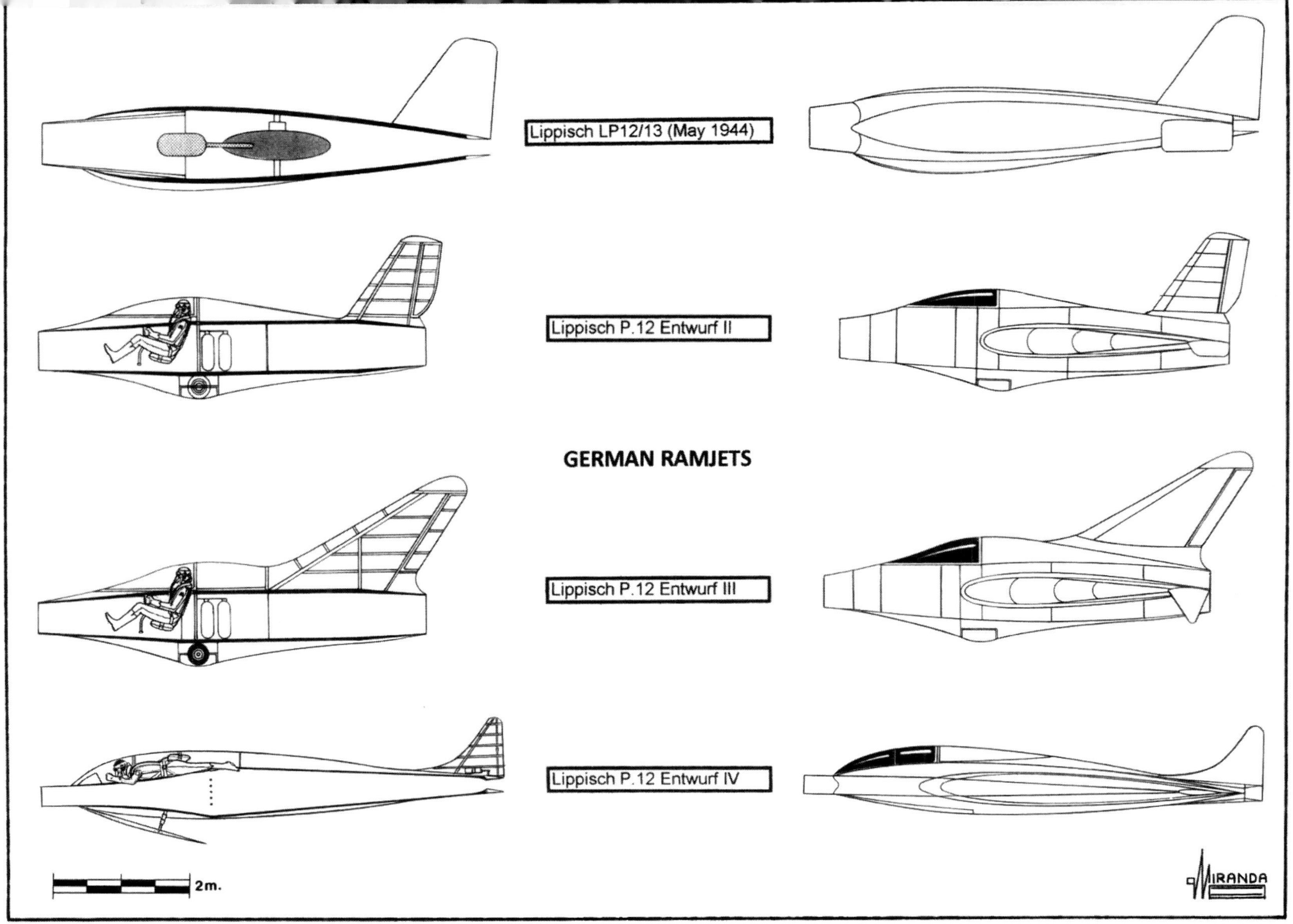
Lippisch LP12/13 (May 1944)
Lippisch P.12 Entwurf II
GERMAN RAMJETS
Lippisch P.12 Entwurf III
Lippisch P.12 Entwurf IV
2m.
MIRANDA

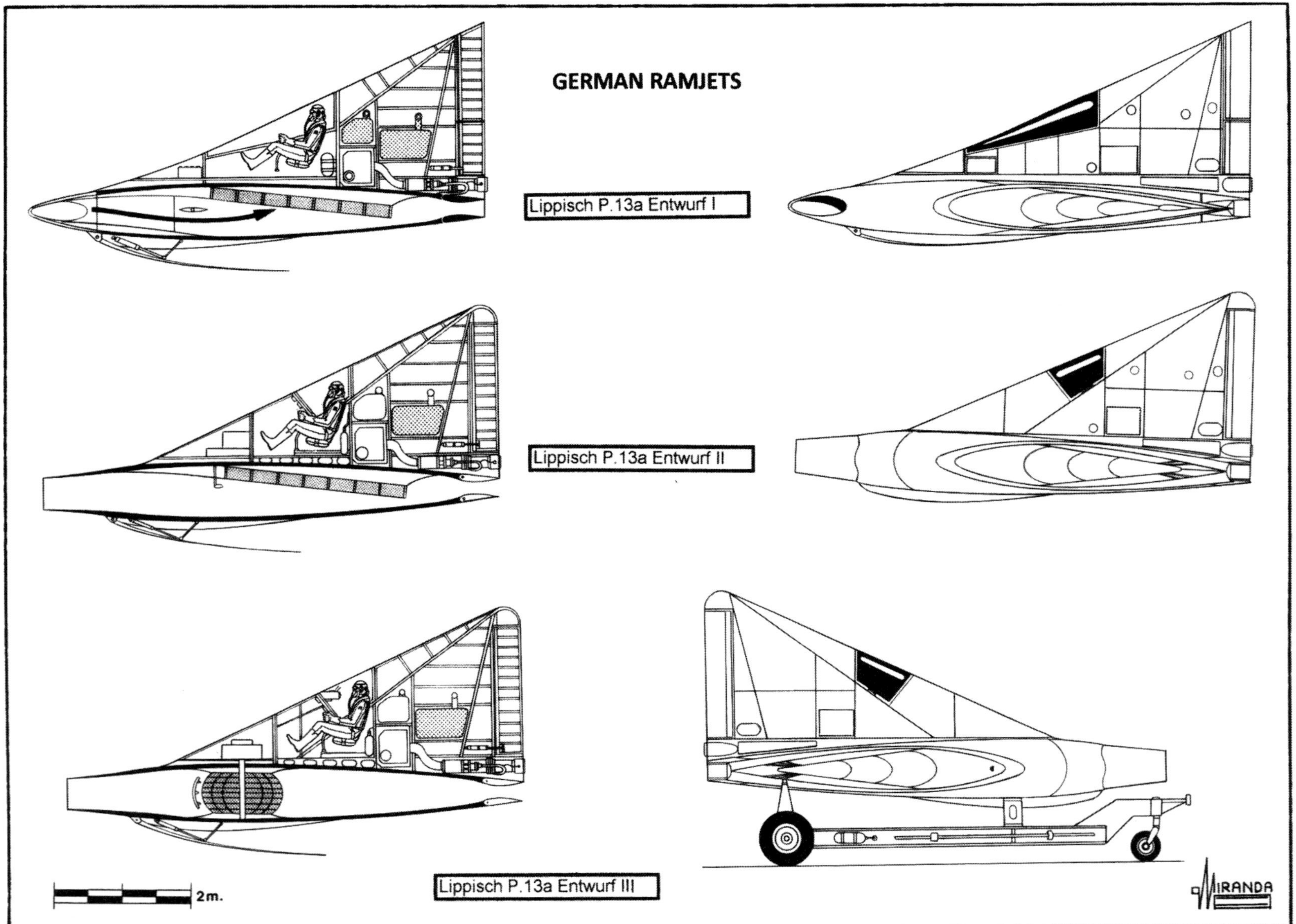
GERMAN RAMJETS
Lippisch P.13a Entwurf I
Lippisch P.13a Entwurf II
Lippisch P.13a Entwurf III
2m.
MIRANDA

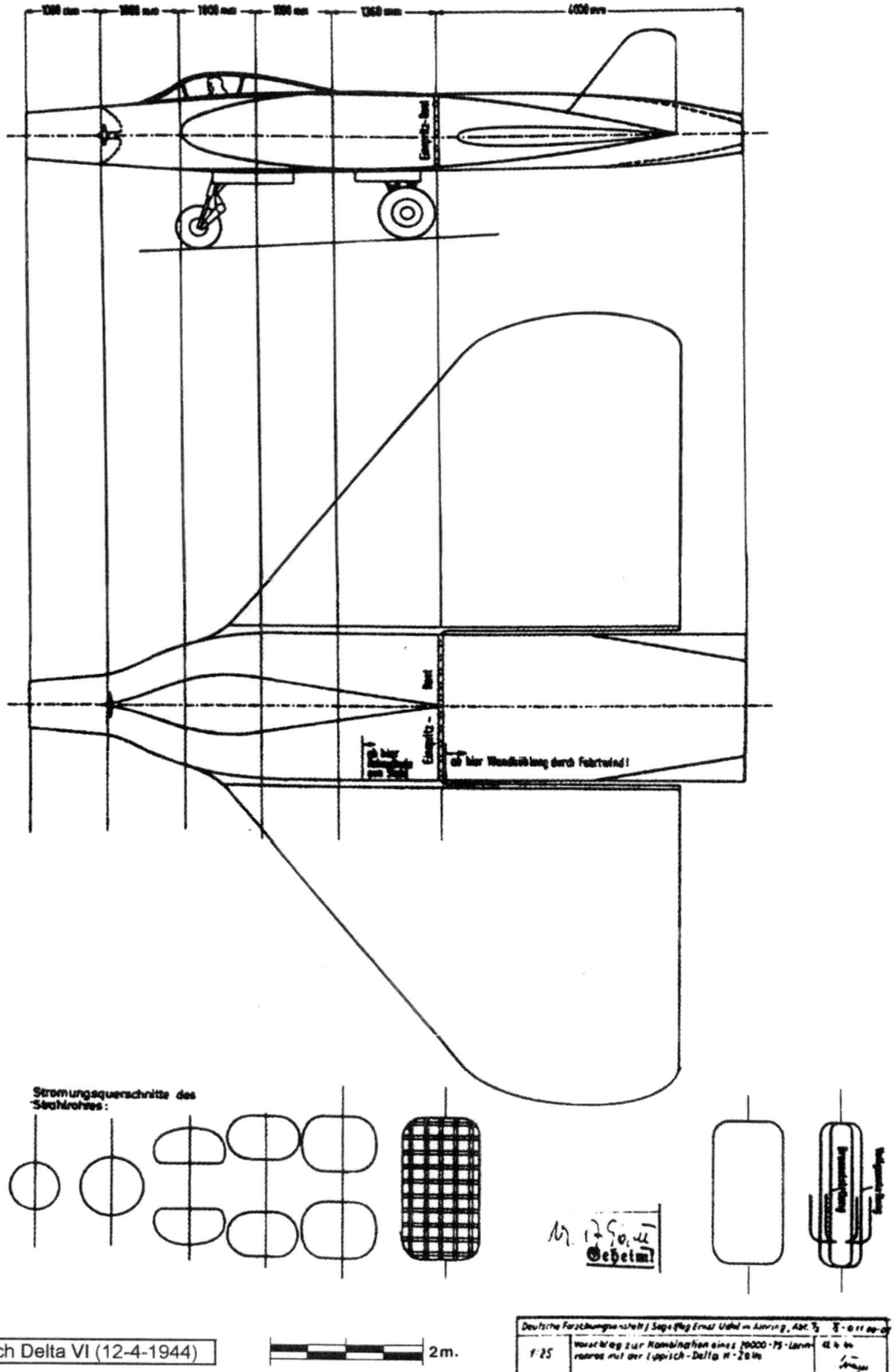

Lippisch Delta VI (12-4-1944)

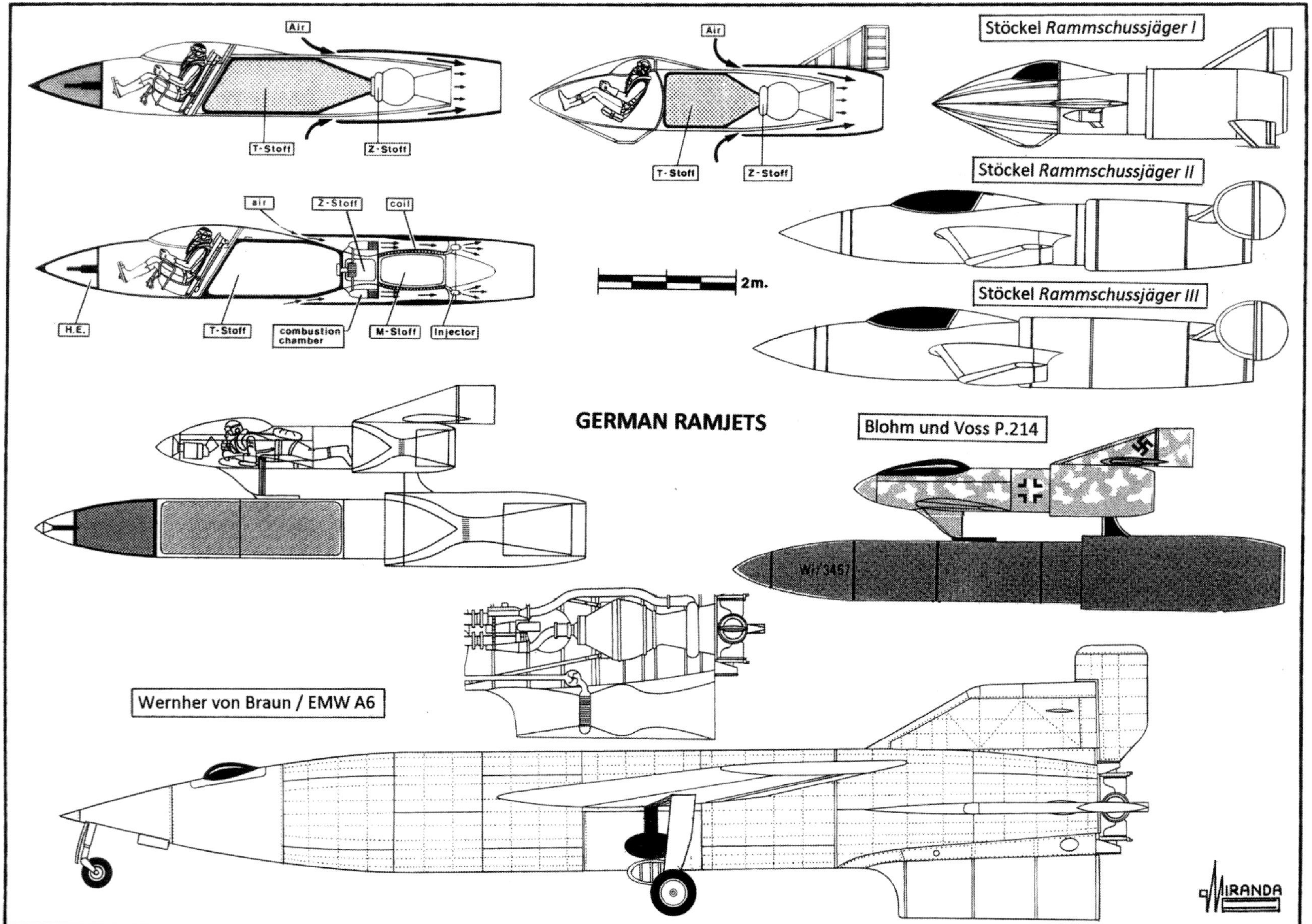

GERMAN RAMJETS
Air
T-Stoff
Z-Stoff
Air
T-Stoff
Z-Stoff
Stöckel *Rammschussjäger I*
Stöckel *Rammschussjäger II*
Stöckel *Rammschussjäger III*
air
Z-Stoff
coil
H.E.
T-Stoff
combustion chamber
M-Stoff
Injector
2m.
Blohm und Voss P.214
Wernher von Braun / EMW A6
MIRANDA

24

Focke-Wulf *Triebflügeljäger*

During the second half of 1943, the arrival of Mustangs to the British bases quadrupled the number of fighters of the Eighth Air Force, altering the course of the war over the *Reich* in favour of the Allies. In a few weeks, the *Jagdwaffe* began to experience increasing losses: 21 per cent of its fighters in November and 23 per cent in December. By early April, the Mustang and Thunderbolt pilots were ordered to pursue the German interceptors to their bases with groups of more than fifty aircraft and attack them while refuelling.

In May, they were joined by the British Tempest of the 2nd Tactical Force and before D-Day, the Luftwaffe had already lost about 9,000 aircraft along with air superiority over their own airspace. In June, the *Jagdwaffe* lost 50 per cent of its fighters and 25 per cent of its pilots; in November, it lost 348 pilots in only four days. All of the Reich air bases were within reach of the Mustangs and were regularly bombed to keep the runways unusable. Very few of the 39,807 German aircraft manufactured in 1944 had the opportunity to fight. Paralysed on land for lack of fuel, they were destroyed by air strikes. In 1945, the few survivors were forced to operate from the *Autobahnen*.

Between May and September 1944, the Eighth Air Force made eleven attacks on Leuna-Merseburg, the main production plant for petrol *Ersatz* (synthetic hydrocarbons), stopping its activity. In November, the Allies launched a bombing offensive against the hydrogenation plants of Gelsenkirchen, Wesserling, Scholven, Homberg, Wanne-Eickel, Sternkrade, Kamen, Bottrop, Dortmund, Hannover, Hamburg, Misburg, Böhlen, Zeitz, and Lützendorf. The RAF Bomber Command launched 13,000 tons of bombs, the Eighth Air Force 14,000 tons. The Fifteenth Air Force based in Italy attacked the plants located south of the Reich in Floridsdorf, Moosbierbaum, Blechhammer South, Korneuberg, Vienna, and Linz.

By December, German fuel production fell to 151,000 tons of first grade gasoline (Grade C3, 96-octane), aviation base gasoline (Grade B4, 87-octane), middle oil (B4 motor oil), and J2 heavy kerosene for turbojets. The production that was most affected was that of the C3 and B4 (used in piston engines of the fighters), with only 25,000 tons produced, compared to the anticipated 107,000 tons. Many small plants, also dedicated to the production of Benzol, were destroyed during the bombing attacks by zone, randomly made by the Bomber Command over industrial areas. During the last year of war in

Europe, the RAF attacked forty-two hydrogenation plants with 63,000 tons of bombs and the Eighth with 45,000 tons, finally achieving the collapse of the production system.

The piston-engine fighters were most affected by the lack of fuel. After Operation *Bodenplatte*, only 1,300 airplanes continued fighting. They were airplanes propelled by turbojets of the types Arado Ar 234, Messerschmitt Me 262, and Heinkel He 162, as well as 100 Me 163 rocket fighters that used *sonderkraftstoff* (experimental propellants). As German fuel reserves declined, the OKL cancelled a large number of aircraft projects: first the heavy bombers, then the piston fighters, and finally the turbojet powered aircraft that required long runways. Also eliminated were the rocket fighters with landing skids when the experience gained with the Me 163 proved that their low mobility on the ground made them extremely vulnerable to strafing attacks by enemy fighters. Finally, the VTOL was the only option left.

The *Forschungsfürung* (Fo Fü) was an OKL department for leading all research carried out by the aeronautical research institutes DVL, FGZ, LFA, LFM, AVA, TAL, DFS, FKFS, and FFO, which formed the most powerful scientific organization in the world. It consisted of four senior scientific leaders: Prandtl, Georgii, Seewald, and Bäumker. By early 1944, Professor Walter Georgii and Oberst Siegfried Knemeyer, director of the Research and Development Institute of the Luftwaffe, initiated contact with several aeronautical companies looking for ideas for the construction of a *Senkrechtstarter Jagdflugzeug* (tailsitter VTOL fighter) that could operate independently of the runways.

In the late 1930s, Dipl.-Ing. Otto Muck, of Siemens, patented a tailsitter aircraft with contraprop airscrews. In 1940, a team of engineers from AVA, Göttingen calculated that a VTOL aircraft of 5 tons would require 4,000 hp to lift-off, an engine that did not exist at the time. On January 1944, Daimler-Benz built a twenty-four-cylinder engine with 3,800 hp called DB 613; it was formed by two DB 603 G engines coupled together to drive a single-shaft power with contra-rotating airscrews. However, the set weighed two tons and was not useful to propel a VTOL aircraft. At the end of 1944, Dr.-Ing. Gerhard Schulz and designer Karl Reiniger of Heinkel in Vienna designed a tailsitter fighter with an annular wing, called Lerche, based on the aerodynamic theories of Dipl.-Ing. von Zborowski. It was propelled by two DB 605 DC piston engines, with 2,000 hp each, and installed nose-to-nose so propellers would rotate in opposite directions without using heavy and complex reduction gears. Its estimated lift-off weight was 5,600 kg.

In May 1944, Daimler-Benz received an order from RLM to concentrate on the development of a turboprop version of the Heinkel 109-011 turbojet, dubbed DB 109-021, with 2,400 hp of shaft power, 585 kp of residual jet thrust, and a weight of 1,266 kg. overall weight. It was selected by Heinkel to power a tailsitter fighter project, with Zborowski annular wing, called Wespe, with an estimated lift-off weight of only 2,140 kg. The turboprop operated two counter-rotating, variable pitch, three-bladed airscrews through reduction gearing with 1,800 rpm constant speed. The annular wing increased the propeller efficiency and generated lift during the horizontal flight. *Lerche* and *Wespe* were proposed to OKL on 2 February 1945.

In 1940, Professor Erich von Holst discovered the aerodynamic principle of the radial lift force, by which wings rotating around the longitudinal axis of the aircraft provided lift and thrust. In May 1944, he designed a *senkrechtstarter jagdflugzeug* for the firm Focke-Wulf. It was a helicopter with contraprop rotors in the nose, probably equipped with a propulsion system like that of Focke-Wulf Peterle. Unlike the tailsitters designed in 1938 by Otto Muck and by the American Arthur M. Young in 1941, the von Holst helicopter lacked fixed wings, flying in horizontal position with the tail depressed to transform part of the thrust into lift.

In helicopters, a complicated gear system connects the rotor to the engine, which in turn is firmly attached to the airframe that tends to rotate in the opposite direction of the rotor. To compensate for the torque effect, an auxiliary tail propeller or a rotor system that rotates in the opposite direction is used. The torque compensation equipment accounts for 20 per cent of the weight of the helicopter and requires frequent maintenance. The rotor of a gyrocopter rotates freely, generating lift when moving forward thanks to an aerodynamic phenomenon like the one used in the nautical parachuting. This design avoids the need for a tail rotor. The first gyrocopters manufactured during the 1930s were very light machines powered by motors of low power.

In 1942, the Austrian engineer Friedrich von Dobhloff, of Wiener Neustädter Flugzeugwerke, started the development of the jet-propelled gyrocopter WNF 342 with a two-blade tip-driven rotor. The propulsion elements were two combustion chambers made of a chromium-nickel-steel alloy, where they burned B4 fuel mixed with compressed-air at 2,000 °C, at a stoichiometric fuel to air ratio of 1 to 20. For horizontal flight propulsion, the WNF 342 used a conventional piston engine that also powered an Argus As 411 supercharger, sending 0.7 kg of compressed air to the combustion chambers every second. Vertical control was achieved by varying the rotor speed, but the system had problems of ground resonance vibration caused by the even number of rotor blades.

During the flight tests carried out in 1943, it was found that the compressed air system limited the thrust and by early 1945, it was decided to replace the combustion chambers with rotor-mounted ramjets.

After being examined by engineers of General Electric Corp in September of 1946, the basic design of the WNF 342 was used in several models of North American gyrocopters during the 1950s. The new propulsion system exhibited powerful lifting capacity. In 1953, the Bensen 'Midget' could lift four times its weight and the Hughes XH-17 flew with a gross weight of 23 tons. This quality would have been very useful for the air defence of the Reich during the last year of war in Europe.

American bombers flew in self-defensive formations, running the risk that one of the bombers would destroy all the planes in the 'box', which happened rarely when the bomb bay was hit by one of the millions of shells fired by the Flak. The Germans called this situation *Pulkzerstörer*, but lacked a weapon strong enough to achieve this effect regularly. None of the 55,000 anti-aircraft guns used by the *Flakartillerie* could launch the 2,000 kg of high explosive needed for the destruction of a 'box'. The 88-mm Flak 41 fired shells of only 9.4 kg, the 105-mm Flak 39 shells of 15.1 kg, and the 128-mm Flak 40 shells of 26 kg, out of which only 10 per cent were HE. The warhead of a *Wasserfall* ground-to-air missile weighed only 235 kg and that of an *Enzian* weighed 300 kg.

At the end of 1944, the suicide bombers Focke-Wulf Ta 154 A-0/U2, Gotha P.55, and Messerschmitt Me 328 SO were designed. They could carry out *Pulkzerstörer* missions loaded with 2,000 kg of amatol. In the April–May 1975 issue, the German magazine *Luftfahrt International* published the drawing of an unknown gyrocopter, named *Flakmine V7*, with a circular body and an eight-blade rotor propelled by four ramjets, which looked like a machine designed to lift-off a great charge of explosives.

It is possible that this propulsion system would have inspired Focke-Wulf designers during the planning of their second *senkrechtstarter jagdflugzeug* project. In the summer of 1944, Dipl.-Ing. Flugbaumeister Heinz von Halem and designer Ludwig Mittelhüber designed a gyrocopter with a two-bladed rotor spinning freely, which was propelled by tip-ramjets, a system called the *Triebflügel* (thrust-wing).

On ground, the aircraft was kept upright over four tailfins and the rotor was rotated in neutral pitch by means of a small ground engine, until the wingtips reached the necessary speed for the ignition of the ramjets. For lift-off, the pilot varied the incidence angle of the blades by 3 degrees. It was expected that after lift-off, the blades rotated 87 degrees, acting as un-tapered wings with a conventional aerofoil. Also, it was considered to use small turbojets, but the idea was dismissed because the acceleration of Coriolis negatively affected its operation. On the contrary, the ramjet, with no moving parts, compressed the air and added fuel by means of its shape and movement through the air without being affected by the changes in the angular velocity. The narrow landing gear track and rotor above the centre of gravity affected the stability of the aircraft floor. The use of a twin-bladed rotor produced the ground resonance effect and the fuselage could only contain enough fuel for a few minutes of flight.

In August 1944, the original design was modified by increasing the diameter of the fuselage and the capacity of the fuel tanks, and by using a new three-bladed rotor. The project was renamed *Triebflügeljäger*. Its considerable weight gain was offset by redesigning the landing gear by adding a central wheel with a powerful shock absorber. The outer wheels were installed at the end of the extensible supports, which increased the runway, improving stability during landing.

Hans Multhopp joined the design team and with his usual disdain for the safety of the pilots, proposed to install the rotor behind the cockpit at a 37 per cent fuselage length. The mechanical device that actuated the rotary collar was replaced by three *Aniass-Raketen* (Walter 109-509 B-0 bipropellants rockets) of 350-kp thrust each, installed in the air intake of each ramjet in *1. Einbauvorschlag* configuration. When the correct rotation speed of 220 rpm was reached, the ramjet would start and the rockets were shut down. The blades were designed with variable incidence so that they continued to generate lift during horizontal flight even with 90 degrees pitch at the root.

In September, some safety mechanisms were added. In case of emergency, the blades could be disengaged by explosive bolts, before the pilot operated the ejection seat. The ramjets were very vulnerable to the defensive fire of the Allied bombers and a single impact of 12.7 mm could alter the aerodynamic properties of the outer coating creating flameout and destructive vibrations in the rotor. It was estimated that the rockets would ensure emergency power but the drag generated by the ramjets would prevent safe landings by autorotation with an unacceptably high sink rate. The solution consisted of using explosive devices to detach the ramjets, changing the *Aniass-Raketen* location to the trailing edge of the blades, onboard the ramjet, in *2. Einbauvorschlag* configuration.

The forward section of the fuselage, 320 cm in length, would be made of light alloy and would house the pressurised cockpit, with an ejector seat, EZ 42 gyroscopic gunsight, and ZFR 4a telescopic gunsight. The electronic equipment was housed under the cockpit floor: FuG 24 SE, FuG 25a, FuG 101a, FuG 120K, FuG 125a, Patin PKS, and RF2C rear periscope. The armament (angled down 6 degrees) was on both sides of the cockpit and consisted of two Mauser MG 151/20 cannon with 250 rounds per gun, and two Rheinmetall-Borsig MK 103/30 cannon with 100 rounds per gun. The ammunition tanks were located behind the cockpit. The protection for the pilot consisted of a 15-mm thick armoured nosecone, containing one MG BSK sixteen-gun camera, one 50-mm thick armoured glass windshield, and two 12-mm steel plates behind the back and head.

The rotary collar, made of steel, would have had a diameter of 160 cm and length of 82 cm. It housed the rotor roller bearings, the hydraulic actuators of the collective pitch system, the electric generator, the fuel and propellants pumps, one rocket-propellant tank with 380 litres of T-Stoff, another tank with 70 litres of C-Stoff, and the evaporation plant. The rear fuselage section, 533 cm long, would have been made of steel and light alloy, and housed two tanks with 1,800 and 1,400 litres of ramjet fuel, the central steel tube, the main wheel shock absorber, and some electronic equipment.

The cruciform tailfins, with a 32-degree sweepback angle and four rudders, housed the hydraulic retraction systems of the auxiliary wheels with 5.4 m of (extended) track. The landing gear was made of a central wheel 780 × 260 mm, one main shock absorber with 50 cm maximum extension, and four auxiliary wheels of 300 × 150 mm. All wheels were steerable, with swivel mounts to facilitate ground towing. They were enclosed by streamlined tulip-shaped pods during flight. In-flight configuration, the overall length was of 9.35 m.

The rotor blades, 436-cm long and with 114-cm parallel chord, would be constructed entirely in steel with a tubular main spar containing the rocket propellant ducts, ramjet propellant, and electric cables for explosive bolts located at both ends of each blade. Those located in the root were used to detach the rotor and those installed in the tips served to detach the ramjets in autorotation emergency landing.

The rotor had a maximum diameter of 11.76 m and a disc surface of 108.56 sq. m. It was designed to rotate freely and no torque was transmitted to the fuselage. In level flight, the pitch at the root varied automatically to maintain a constant rotation speed of 120 rpm. During lift-off and landing, the (subsonic) rotation speed would be 220 rpm.

The *Triebflügeljäger* used three Pabst ramjets, 70 cm in diameter and 140 cm long, entirely built of steel. Each had thirty-five injectors and a thrust of 840 kp, with the operating speed between 300 kph and Mach 0.9, and an 18,000-m estimated ceiling. The specific fuel consumption rate varied with the speed of rotation and the type of fuel used. With hydrogen, it was 1.47 at Mach 0.8 and 900 °C; with crude oil (superheated and vaporised to achieve rapid mixing with the incoming air), it was increased by about 3 per cent.

Ramjets would run on any combustible medium that could be vaporised, passing through the heat exchanger designed by Otto Pabst. It consisted of a tiny ramjet that worked with non-refined petrol Br-Stoff, consuming only 2 per cent of that of the main engine, and could process substances that were as not very volatile, such as lignite tar and pitch oil. The high fuel consumption, compared to piston or turbojets engines, was caused by the subsonic speed at the rotor tips. The low compression ratio of the air intakes generated inefficient combustion, high noise, poor range, high night-time visibility, and induced current effects.

The circular movement of the ramjet left a low-pressure zone behind. To prevent the formation of vortex and destructive vibrations on the external face of the nozzle, an aerodynamic fence of 56 cm in length was installed to the area. The three rockets could be run for 200 seconds using a mixture of T-Stoff (highly concentrated solution of hydrogen peroxide) and C-Stoff (57 per cent methyl alcohol, 30 per cent hydrazine hydrate, and 13 per cent watery solution of potassium cuprocyanide). T-Stoff and C-Stoff were unstable and dangerous hypergolic substances, which reacted explosively on contact, so an ignition device was not necessary.

During the rocket's ignition, the rotor tips had a neutral pitch and their roots a 30-degree negative pitch. The generated negative lift avoided a premature take-off before all the ramjets operated at full power. When the rotor reached the 220 rpm, the pilot disconnected the electric-driven pumps from the rockets and gradually increased the collective pitch angle to perform the take-off. The transition at forward flight was made at 300 m altitude and 120 rpm, increasing the rotor pitch up to 90 degrees at the roots and 120 degrees at the tips. The higher thrust to lift ratio was obtained by flying with the tail depressed by 6 degrees, so the armament and gunsight were also installed 6 degrees downwards with respect to the longitudinal fuselage axis. With a range of only 500 km, the *Triebflügeljäger* was considered a point defence interceptor that would only start the flight when detecting a bomber stream near its base.

Once the service ceiling had been reached, it would be directed towards the target following the instructions of the *Reichsjägerwelle* communications network via the FuG 120k device. The MK 103/30 heavy cannon were powerful enough to destroy a four-engine bomber with only five hits of 30 × 184B *Minengeschoß* ammunition and could be fired from a safe distance of 1,500 m, using the ZFR 4a telescopic gunsight. The MG 151/20 rapid-fire cannon and the Adler gyroscopic gunsight were more useful in dogfights against escort fighters.

An experienced pilot could perform some conventional fighter manoeuvres with the *Triebflügeljäger*: using the collective pitch, he could stop its advance by easily changing direction and even flying backwards, and he could also avoid combat because of its superior rate of climb. Hovering under the bomber stream, he could shoot the belly of the planes from a safe distance, out of the reach of their ventral turrets. Guided by the FuG 125a radio-beacon receiver, the pilot could return to his base to hide the aircraft. A base that might be a section of autobahn surrounded by forests and signalled with ground radar-reflectors as a reference for the FuG 101a radio-altimeter.

The small diameter of the auxiliary wheels suggests that the gyrocopter would be towed from the landing site to the maintenance area through a network of tarmac path. There, the ground crews would attach stairs to both sides of the fuselage to replenish oxygen, ammunition, fuel pumps, B4 petrol from the evaporation plant, heavy kerosene from ramjets, and rocket propellants. Afterwards, the fighter would be towed to one of the take-off sites covered by nets stretched between the trees.

Data on the semi-automatic landing procedure planned for the *Triebflügeljäger* was not kept. It might be expected that it could have used part of the 'blind bomb' and 'level bomb' electronic equipment developed for the Arado Ar 234 and adopted by the firm Focke Wulf for its project 1000×1000×1000 bomber. After transitioning to the vertical flight on the landing area, the pilot would connect the three-axis Patin PKS autopilot and the Lofte tachometric bomb-sight rear periscope. Both devices acted together, driving the airplane according to the pilot's movements over the bombsight.

The rate of descent to 120 rpm would be regulated by varying the rotor pitch until reaching the landing point predicted by the computer. To get a view of the ground from the cockpit, it would have been necessary to modify the RF2C rear-periscope by installing the PV1B sighting head at the end of a retractable tube, which would be long enough to save the visual obstacle of the rotating collar. The FuG 101a radio-altimeter, designed for horizontal flight, used two inverted 'T' dipoles, which were normally installed under the wings of the big airplanes, but the *Triebflügeljäger* would require that they were installed in the tailfins for its use during vertical landing.

The indications of the FuG 101a were only reliable for altitudes above 200 m due to the phenomenon of interference between the transmitter dipole 'S' and the receiver 'E', suggesting that the final descent step would be carried out manually by the pilot following indications from the ground crews. The conclusion is that the *Triebflügeljäger* had to operate in well-provided bases of fuel, towing vehicles, reflectors, communications equipment, and ground crews. This dependence made it less effective than the *Natter*, which only needed a truck, six men, and a launching ramp hidden among the trees. The probable electronic equipment for a Luftwaffe fighter in 1945 would have been as follows:

EZ 42 (Adler) gyroscopic gunsight Zielgerät developed by Askania and Zeiss, which automatically computed the deflection angle required to hit a target when both aircraft were manoeuvring.

FuG 24 SE VHF *Funksprechgerät* R/T device developed by Lorenz for single-seat fighters and operation frequencies between 37.8 and 47.75 Mhz. It was used in combination with the ZVG *Zielflugrorsatzgerät* direction finder device. It had a power of 5 Kw, VHF wave, whip antenna, and a weight of 18 kg.

FuG 25a Erstling IFF device *Kenngerät* manufactured by GEMA and *Brinkler* Emission frequency of 160 MHz, reception frequency of 125 Mhz. Its range was of 100 km, had a power of 600 W, a 10-degree rear swept rod antenna under the fuselage (300 mm long), and responded to *Freya*, *Würzburg*, and *Gemse* ground control radars. It could be used to calculate the distance of an airplane from the ground radar. The need to operate in several frequencies between 0.53 and 2.40 m considerably delayed its entering into service with the Luftwaffe. It was used in combination with the EGON (Erstling Gemse Offensive Navigation) for radio navigation of bombers in combination with the FuMG 401A *Freya LZ* radar, as an alternative to the *Y-Gerät*. Its weight was of 12 kg.

FuG 101a *Feinhöhermesser* of 1.5 Kw, radio-altimeter developed by Siemens/LG Operation, operating on frequencies between 337 and 400 MHz in continuous wave and frequency modulation (CW-FM with a 2-m error). It had a power of 1.5 W, a weight of 16 kg, and a range between 150 and 1,500 m. It used two *Sender* S101 and *Empfänger* E 101 dipoles to transmit and receive.

FuG 120a *Bernhardine* radio beacon teleprinter developed by Siemens to receive the emissions from the rotating beacon FuS An 724/725 Bernhard (30–33.3 MHz). The data was presented over a band of printed paper to diminish the efficiency of the enemy interference systems. The FuG 120k was a simplified version for single-seat fighters. The FuG 120 could be used in combination with the FuG 10 K2 and FuG 16 radio transmission system and with the EBL3 receiver of the *Funklandegerät* FuBl2 blind landing system. It had a range between 5 and 400 km.

FuG 125a *Hermine* radio-beacon receiver was developed by Lorenz. It operated in frequencies between 30 and 33.3 Mhz with a precision of 5 degrees. Its weight was of 10 kg and its range between 200 and 250 km. It operated in combination with the FuG 16 ZY *Zypresse* direction finder and the FuG 16 R/T device, using the antenna and the D/F loop and *Morane* mast from these devices. It received the emissions from the FuS An 726 Hermes and could be used in combination with the FuG 120 K *Bernhardine* to receive emissions from the FuS An 724/725 *Bernhard*. Combined with the EBl 3F system, it acted as radio landing device. The presentation of data was in audio via earphones.

The movement of the ramjets and the high temperature of the exhaust gases in this type of gyrocopter used to ionise the air, causing corona discharges and inducing current effects. The electromagnetic phenomenon called evanescent field could affect the operation of electronic equipment, so it is assumed that most antennas would be installed in the front section of the fuselage. The radio-altimeters in the tailfins should be retractable or located inside the tulip-shaped landing gear pods to avoid interference. The *Triebflügeljäger* should use static electricity dischargers wicks in the wing trailing-edges and rudders and ground contact whips.

Technical data

Estimated maximum speed of 1,000 kph at sea level, 900 kph at 7,000 m, and 840 kph at 11,000 m.
Initial climb rate: 125 m/second.
Service ceiling: 14,000 m.
Empty weight: 2,800 kg.
Maximum lift-off weight: 5,175 kg.
Range: 500 km at 675 kph and 14,000 m.
Endurance of forty-two minutes at sea level.

Dipl.-Ing. Otto Muck patents

Zu der Patentschrift 728 256
Kl. 62 b Gr. 29 01

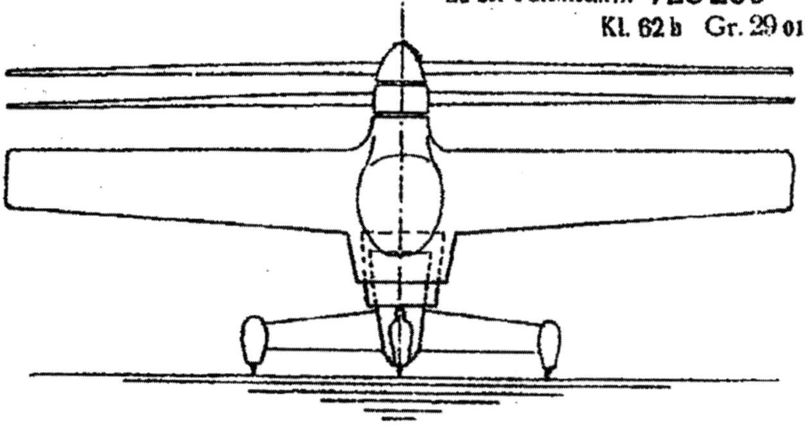

September 10, 1938

Zu der Patentschrift 714 001
Kl. 62 b Gr. 29 01

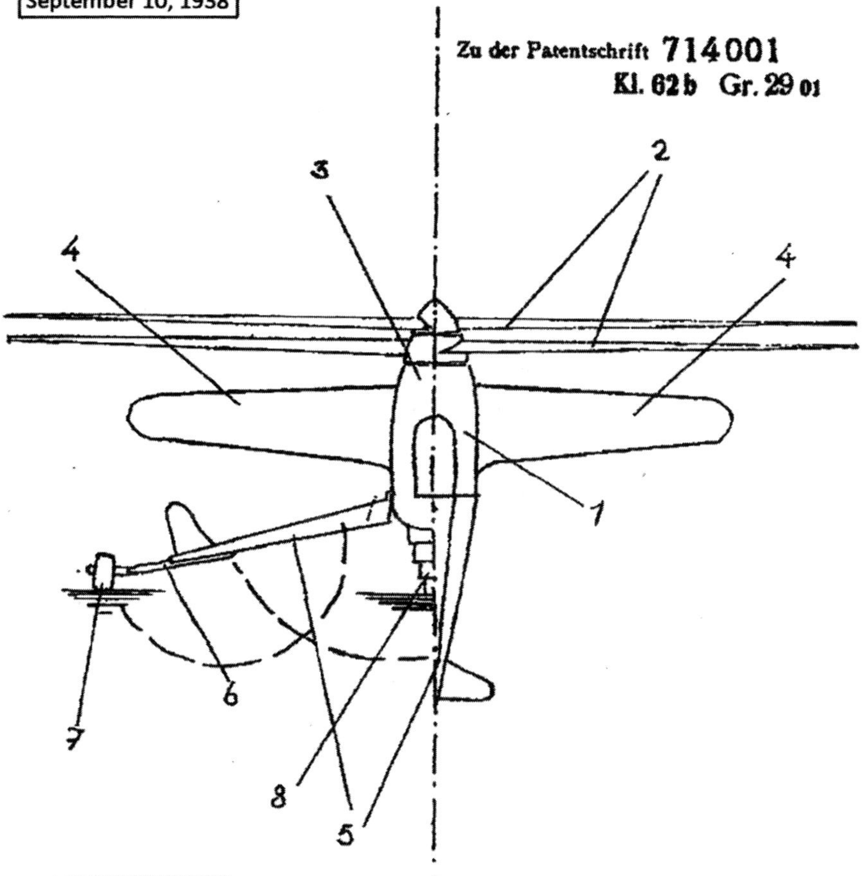

November 1, 1938

Aug. 14, 1945. A. M. YOUNG 2,382,460

AIRCRAFT

Filed Jan. 8, 1941 6 Sheets-Sheet 1

Fig. 1.

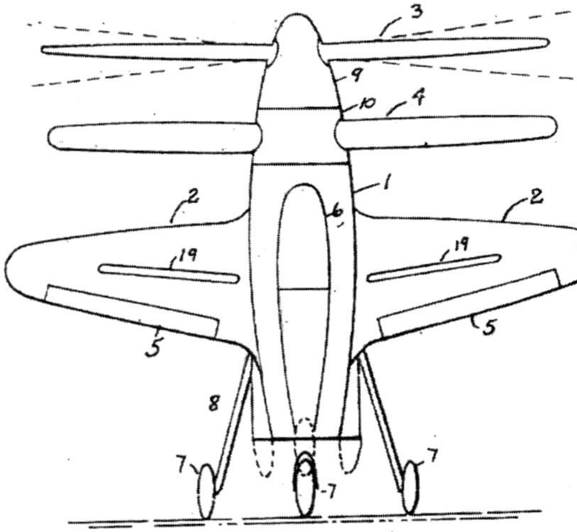

Fig. 2.

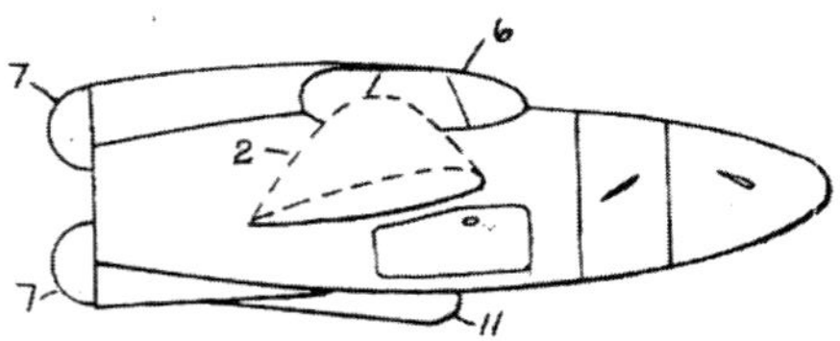

Fig. 3.

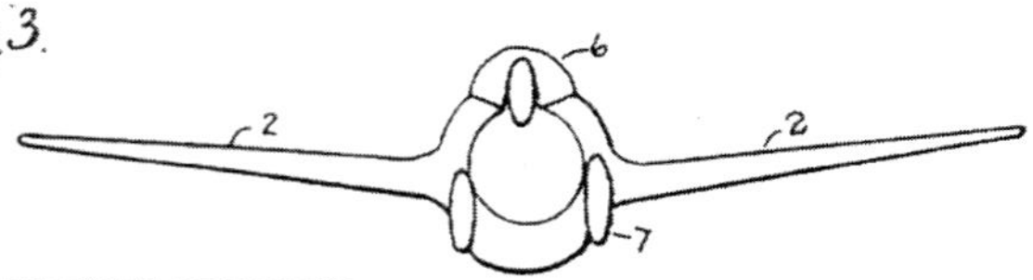

Arthur M. Young patent

Aug. 14, 1945. A. M. YOUNG 2,382,460

AIRCRAFT

Filed Jan. 8, 1941 6 Sheets-Sheet 2

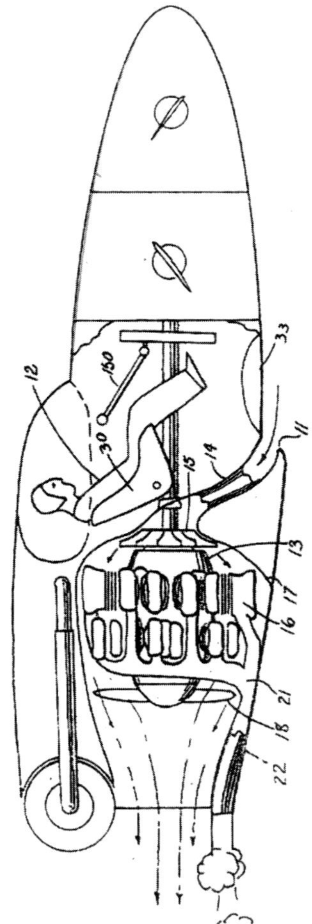

Fig. 4.

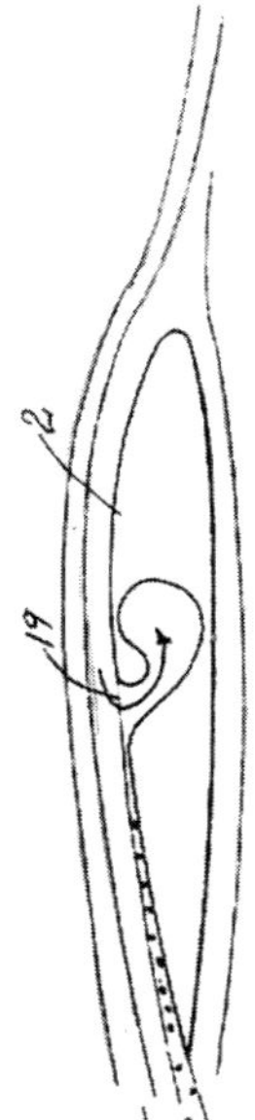

Fig. 4a.

INVENTOR

Arthur M. Young

Professor von Holst´s ornithopter

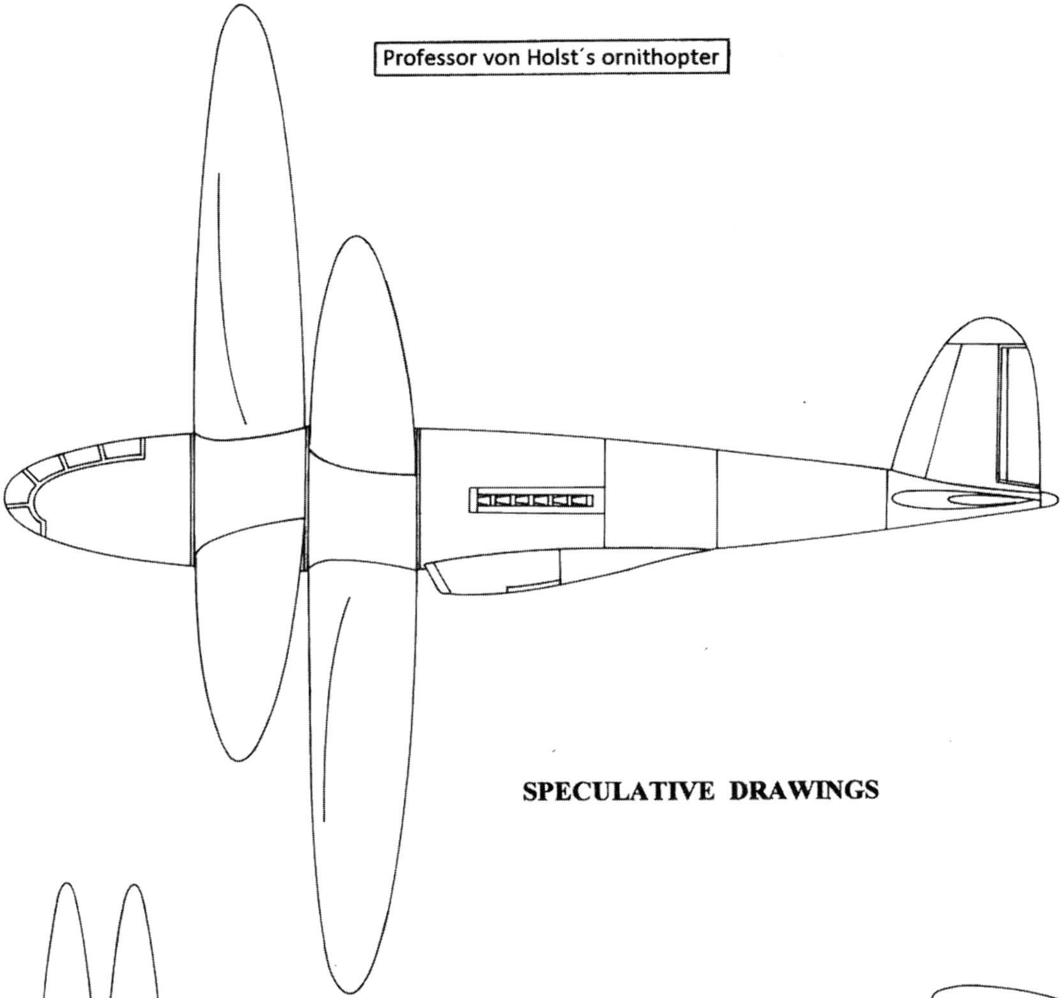

SPECULATIVE DRAWINGS

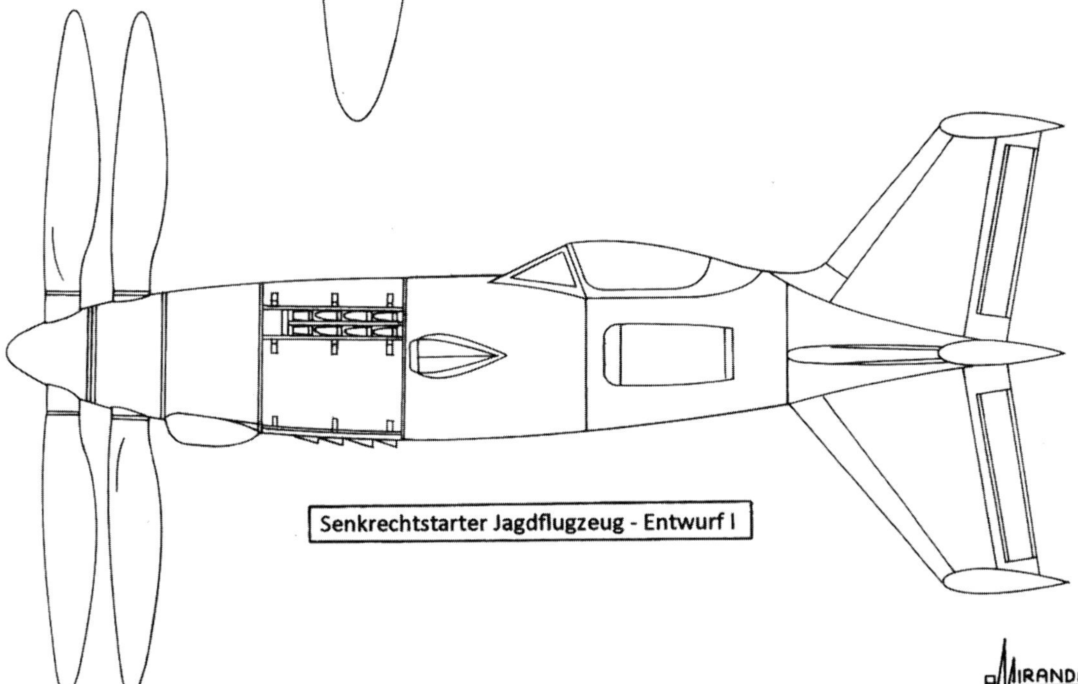

Senkrechtstarter Jagdflugzeug - Entwurf I

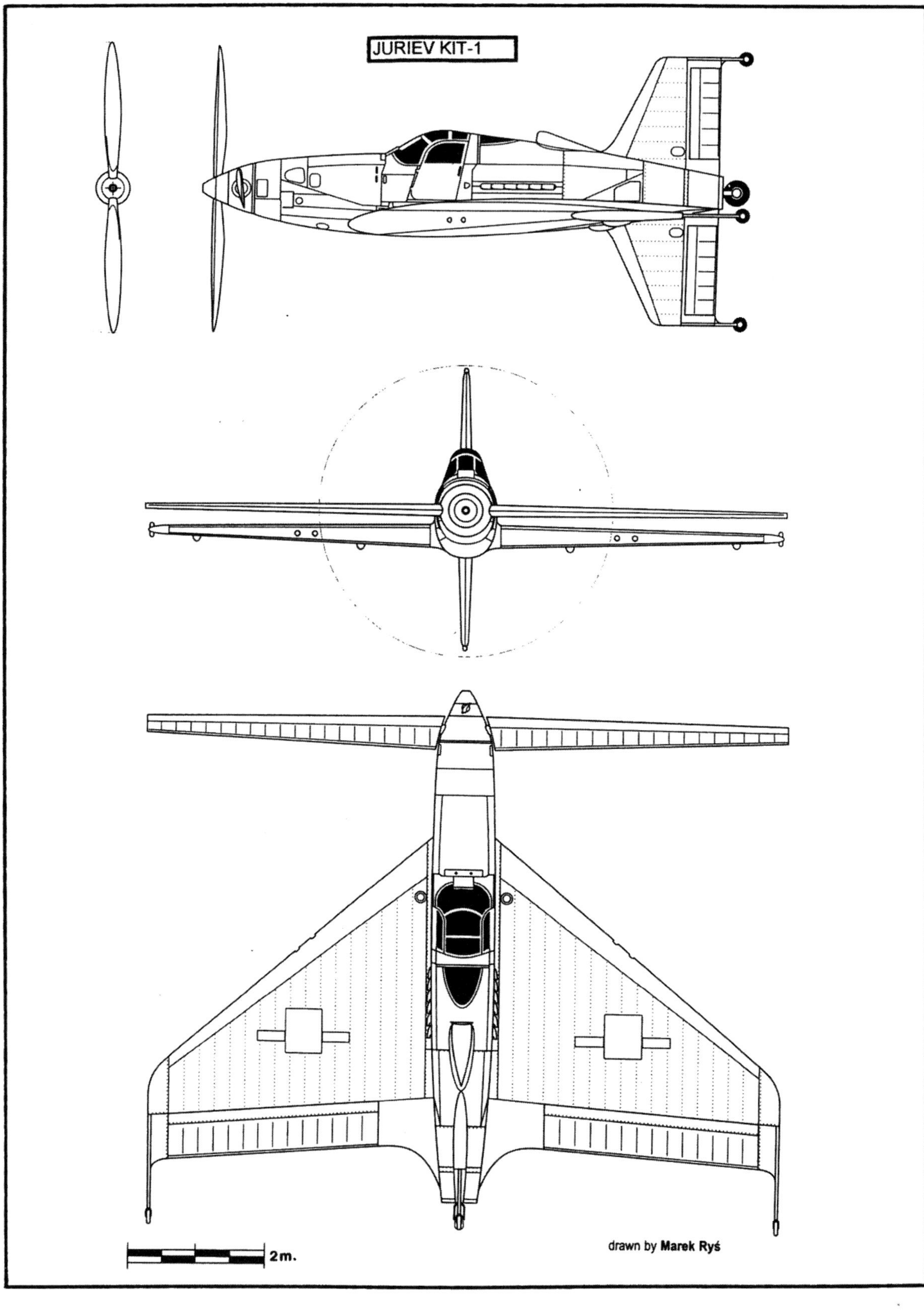
JURIEV KIT-1
2 m.
drawn by Marek Ryś

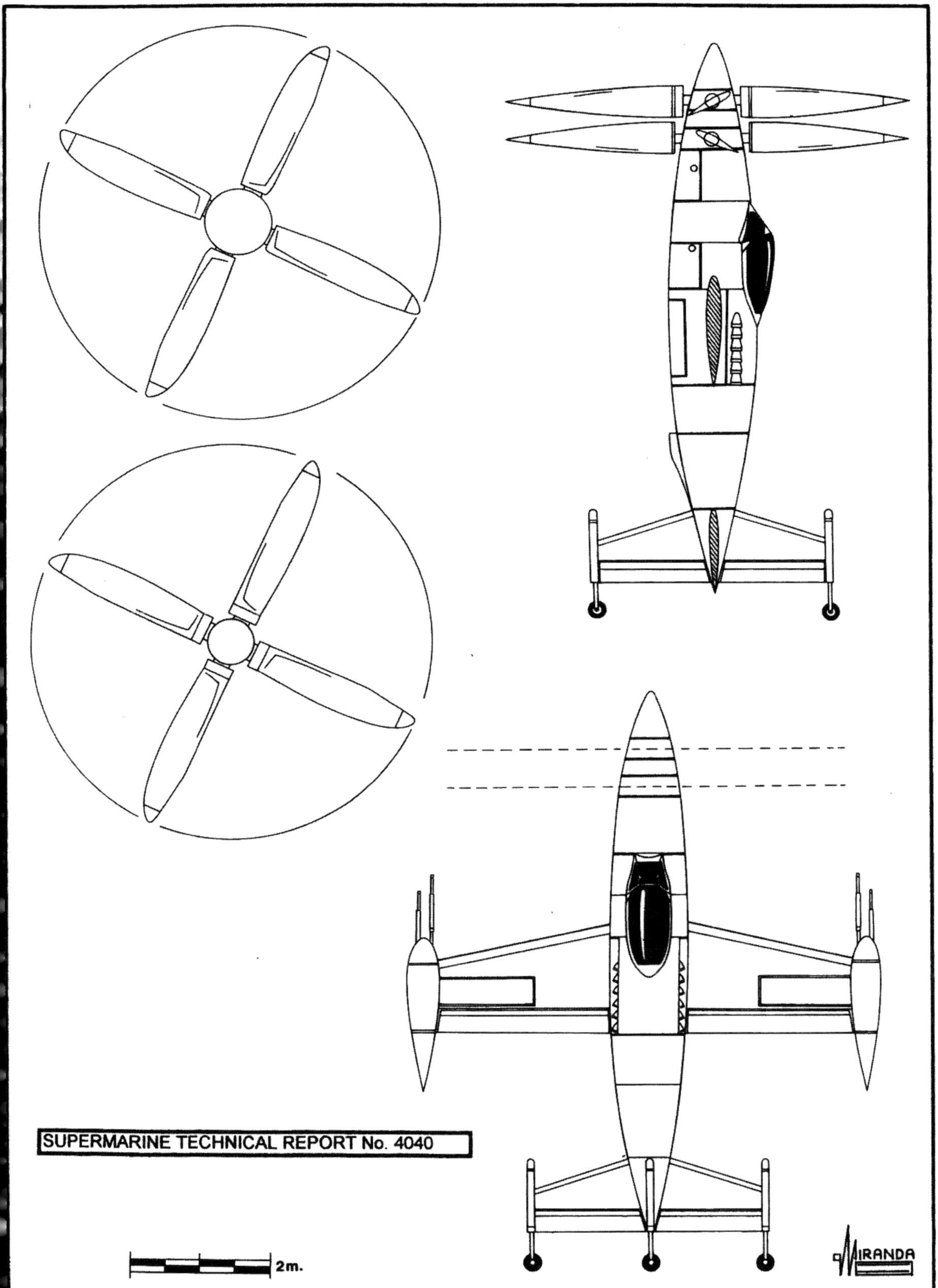
SUPERMARINE TECHNICAL REPORT No. 4040
2m.
MIRANDA

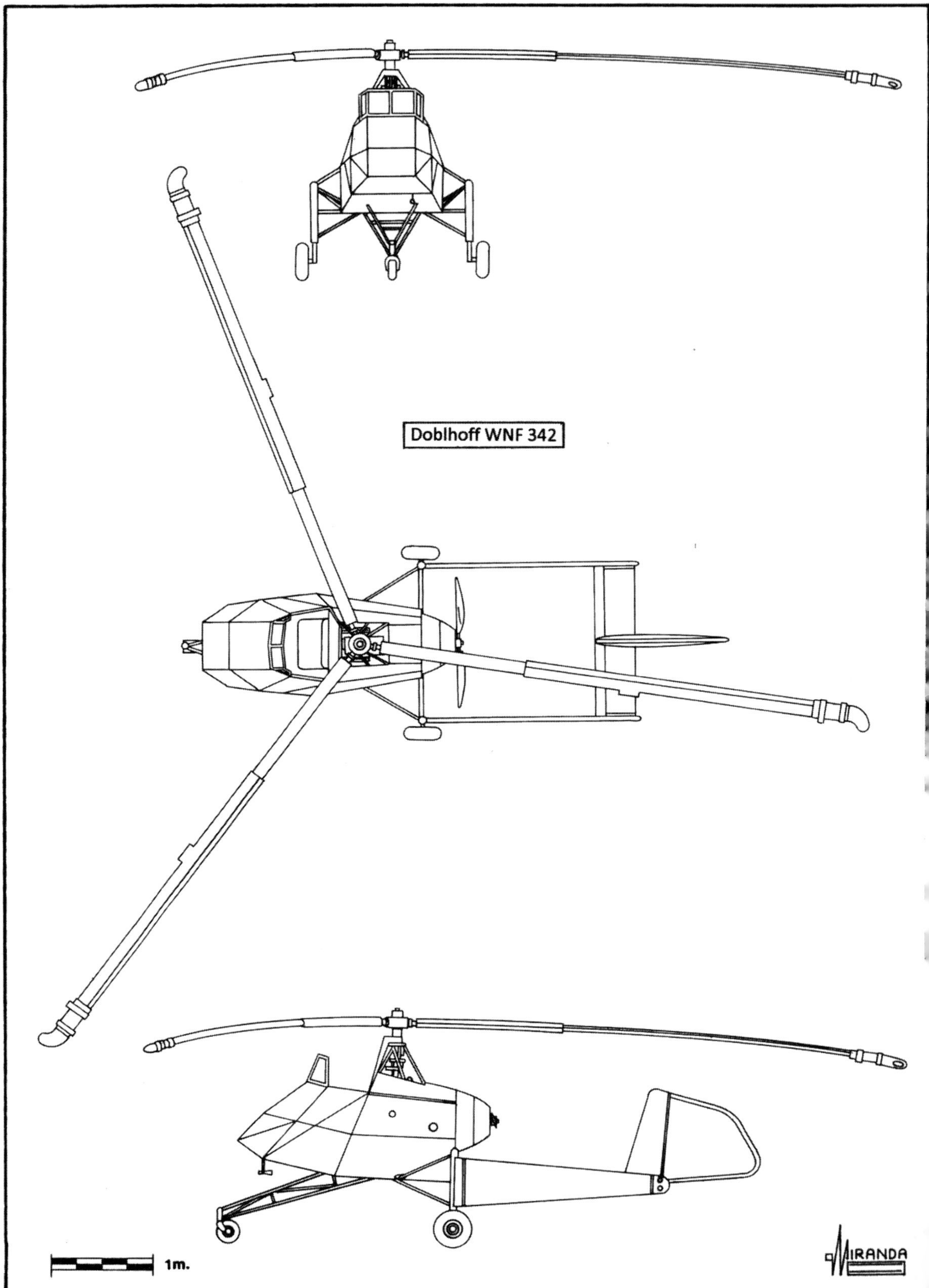
Doblhoff WNF 342
1m.
MIRANDA

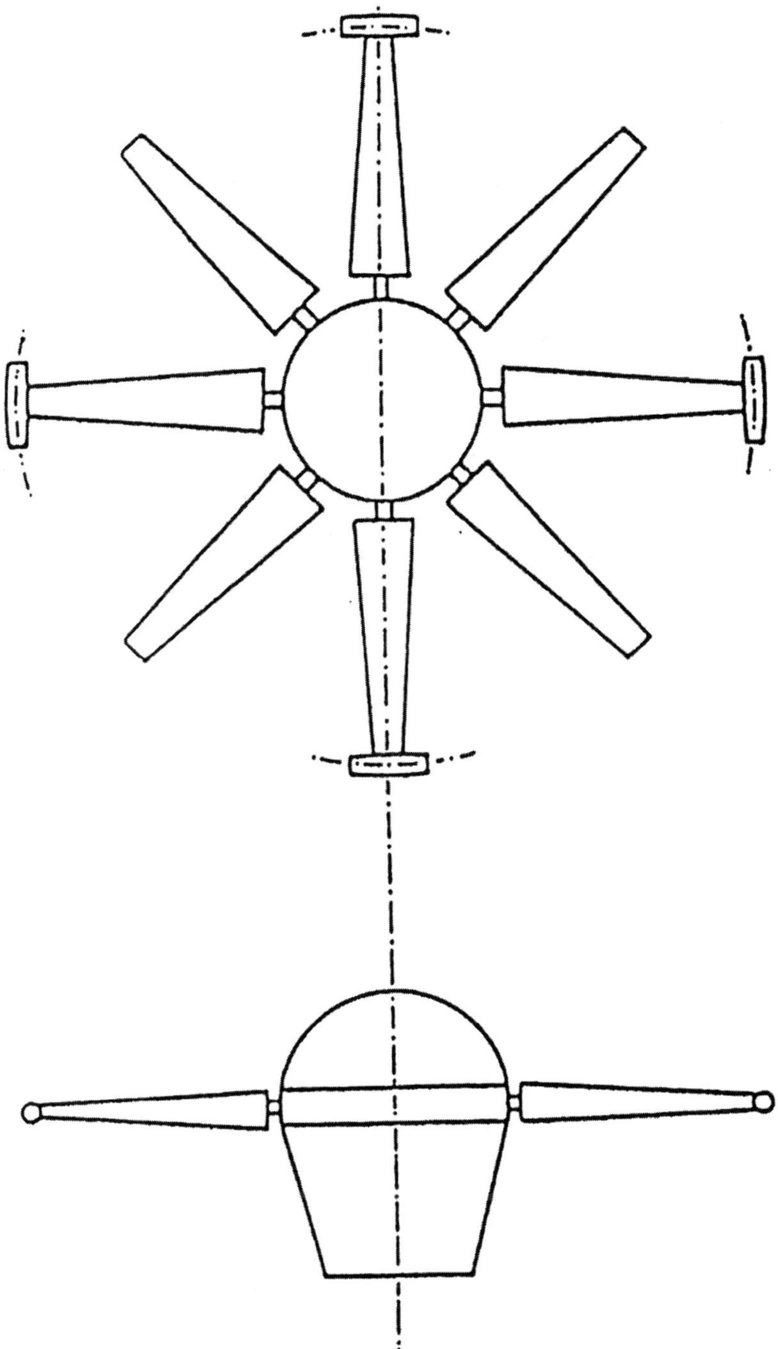

Abb. 5: So soll die Flakmine V 7 angeblich ausgesehen haben.

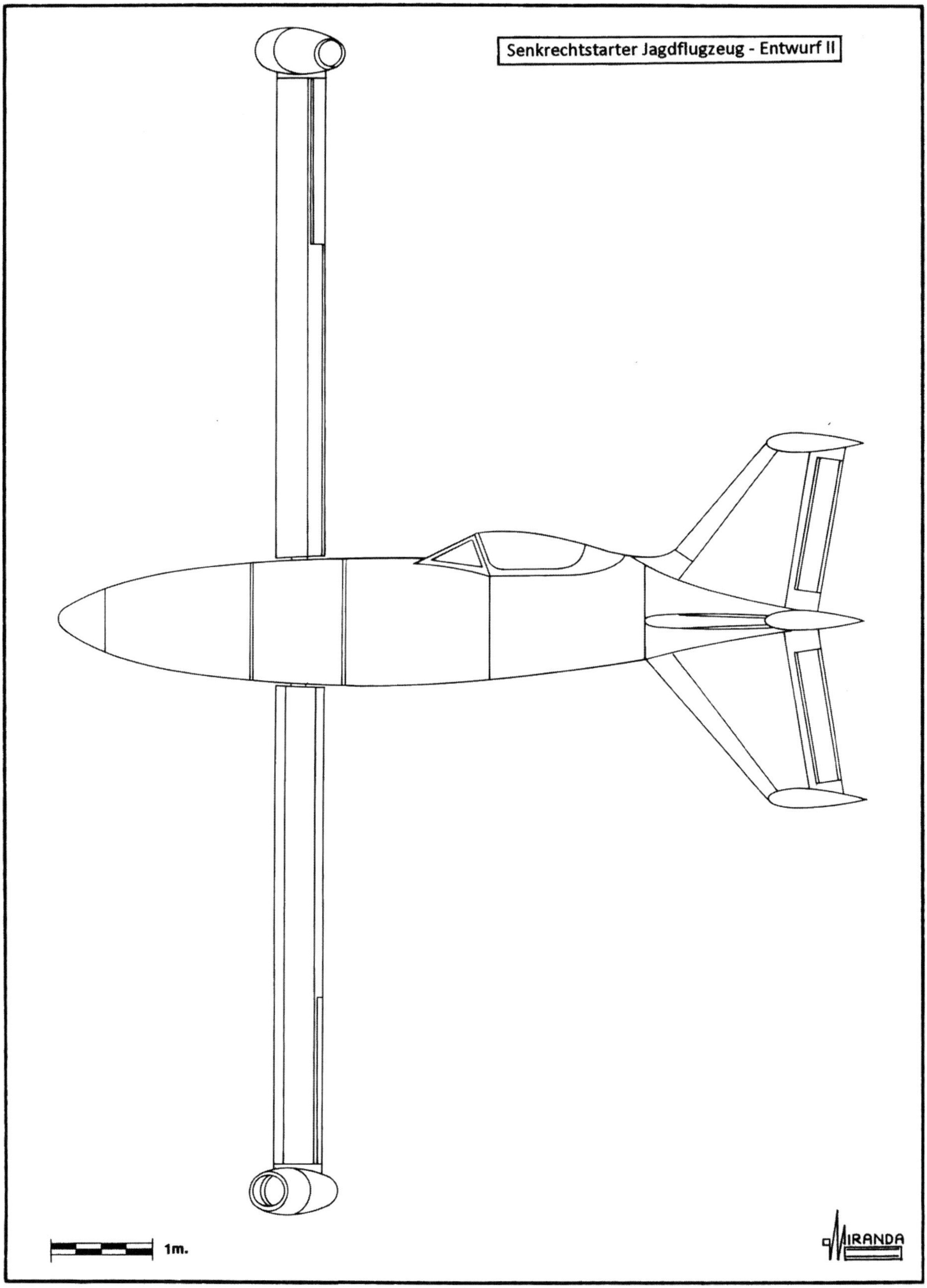
Senkrechtstarter Jagdflugzeug - Entwurf II
1m.
MIRANDA

Senkrechtstarter Jagdflugzeug - Entwurf II

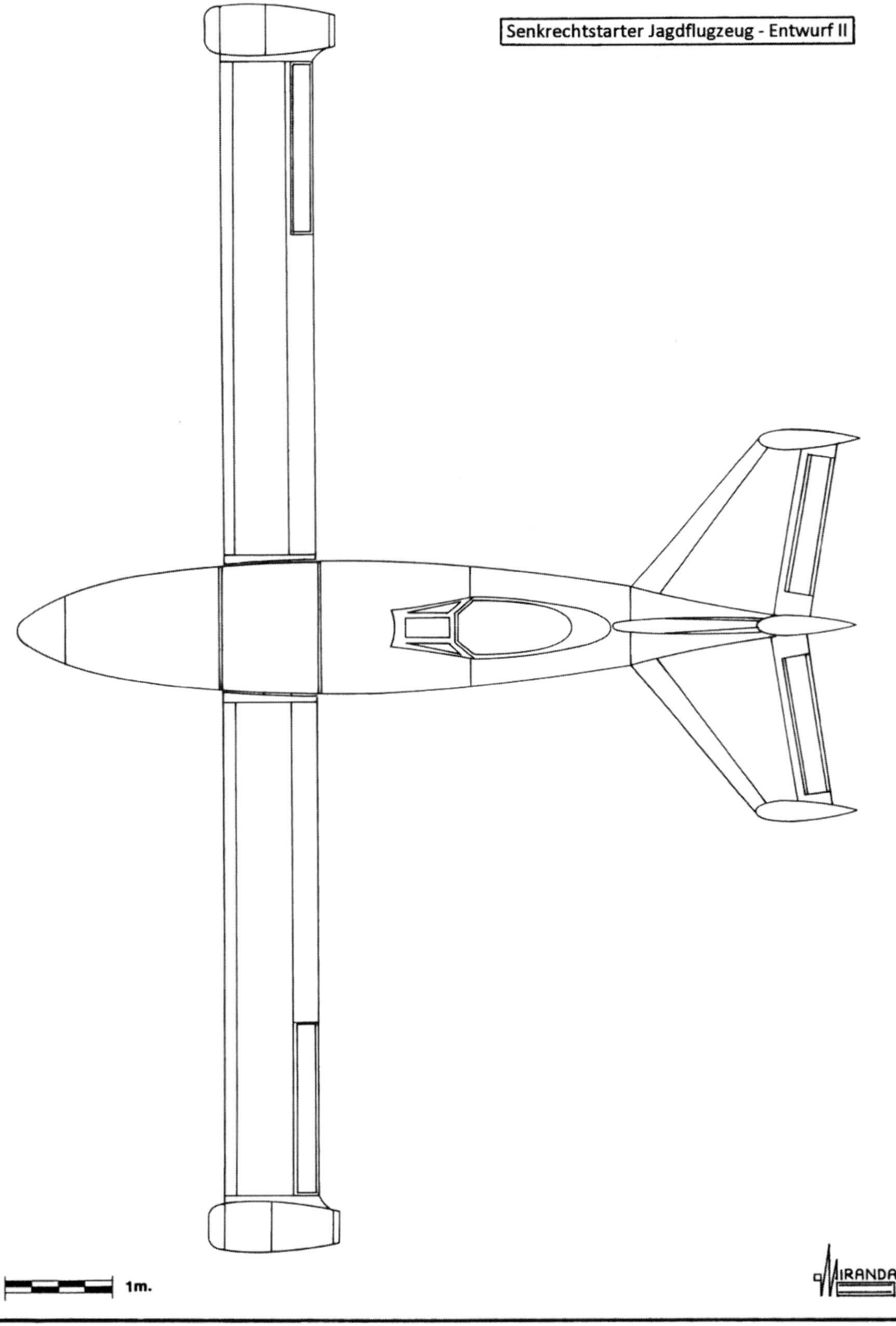

Focke-Wulf *Triebflügeljäger*

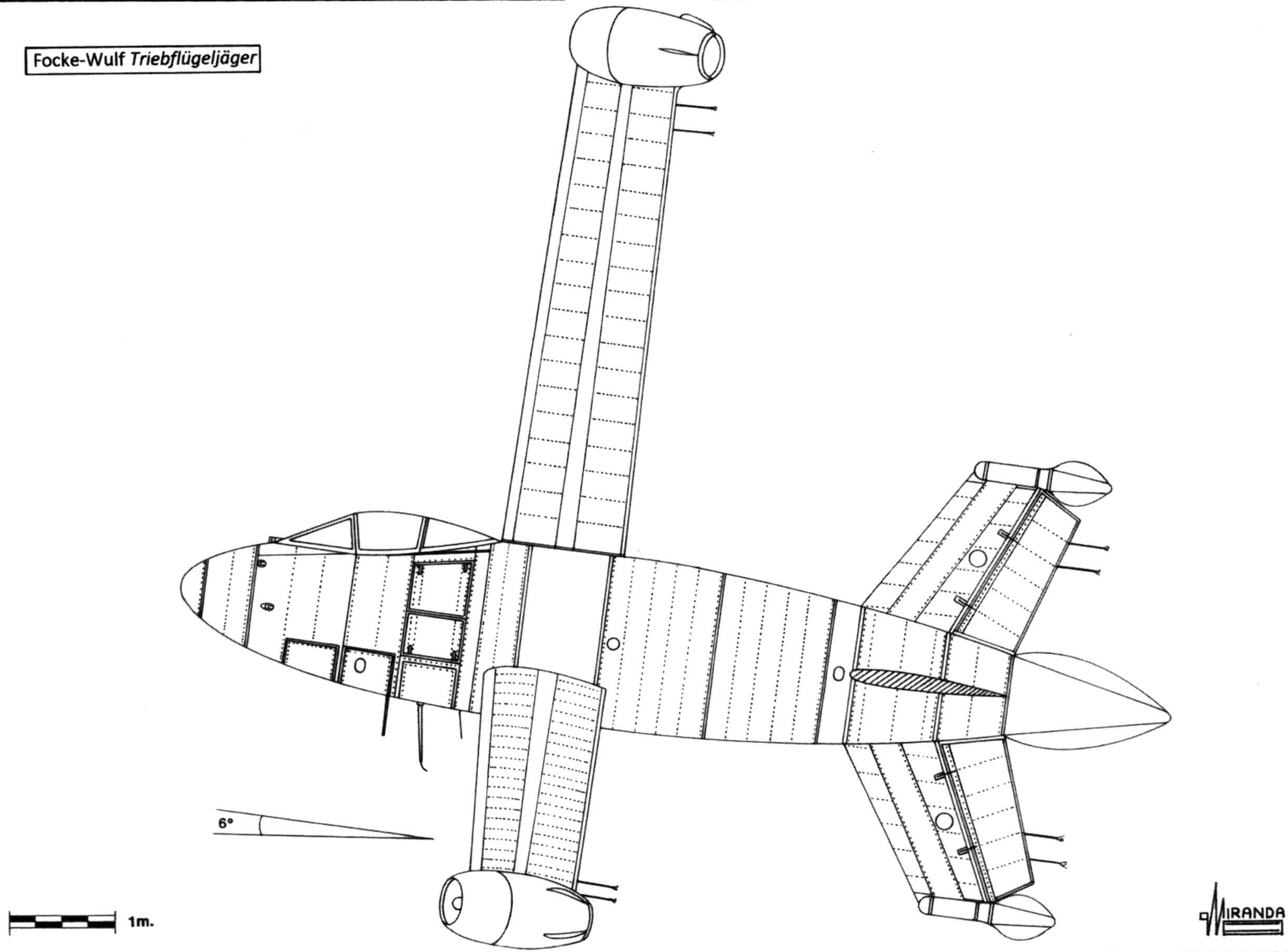

Focke-Wulf *Triebflügeljäger*

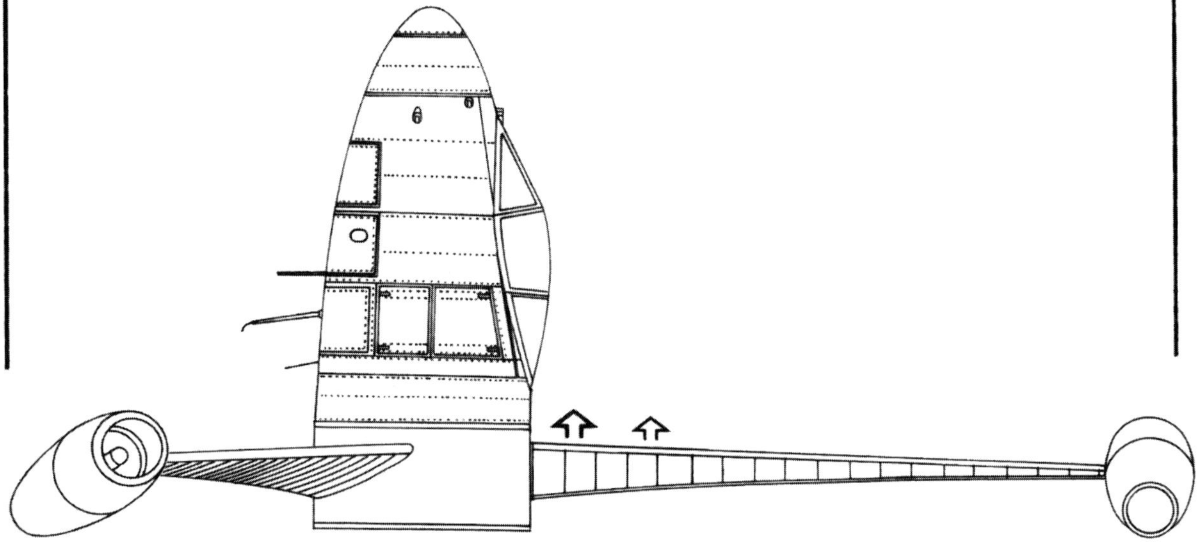

Take off

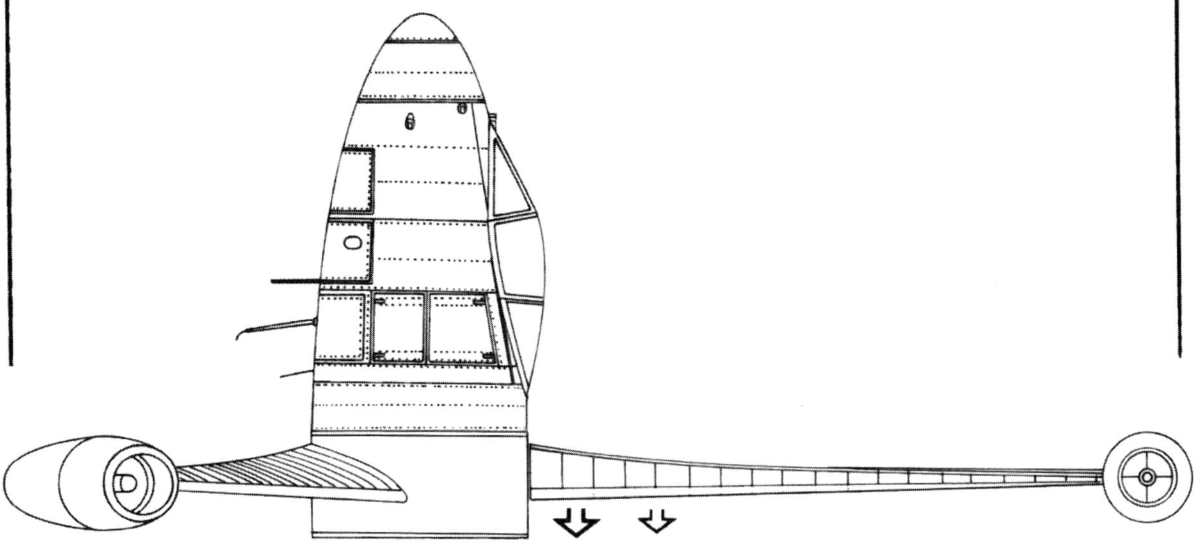

Ignition

1m.

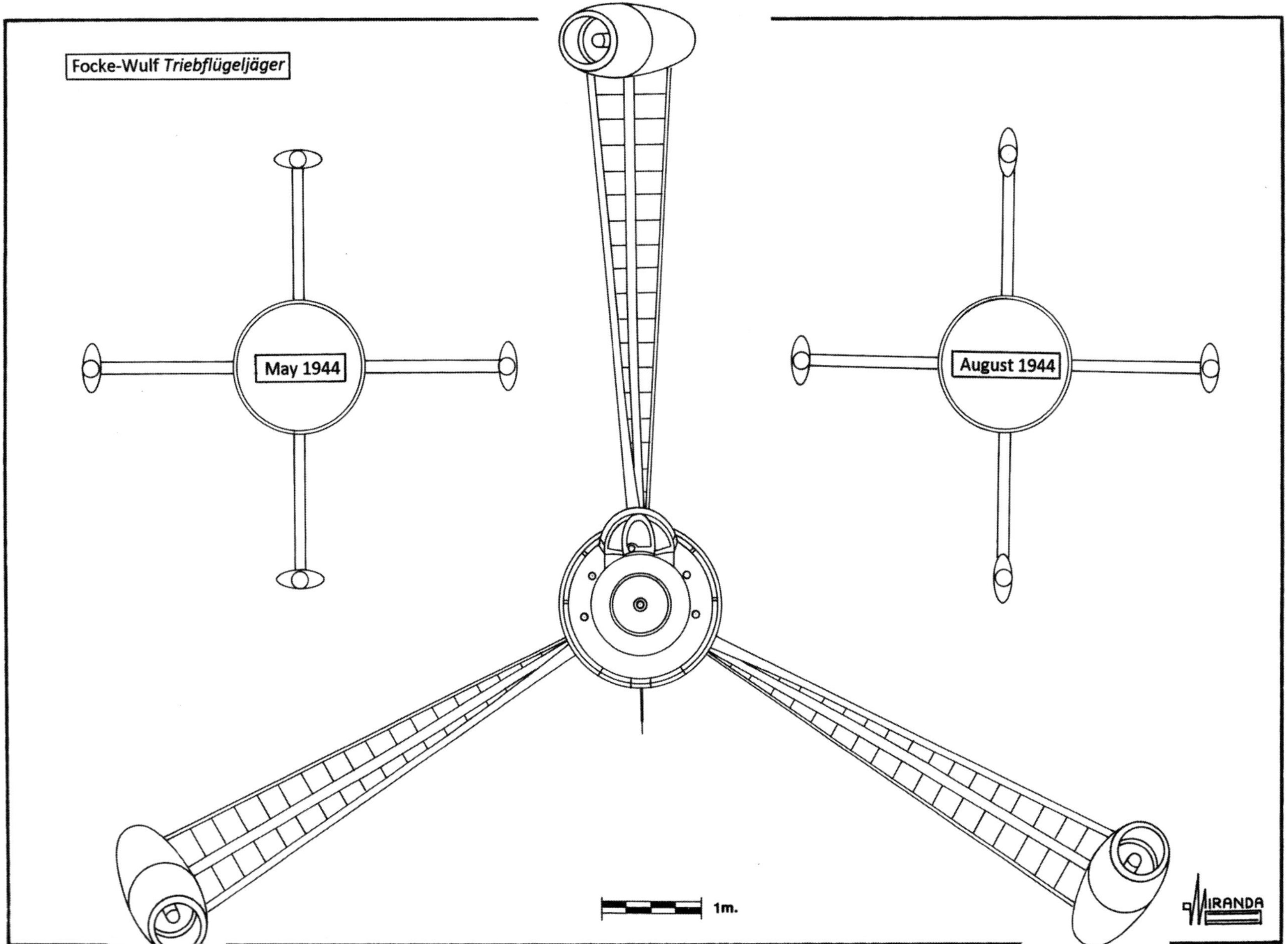
Focke-Wulf *Triebflügeljäger*
May 1944
August 1944
1m.
MIRANDA

Focke-Wulf *Triebflügeljäger*

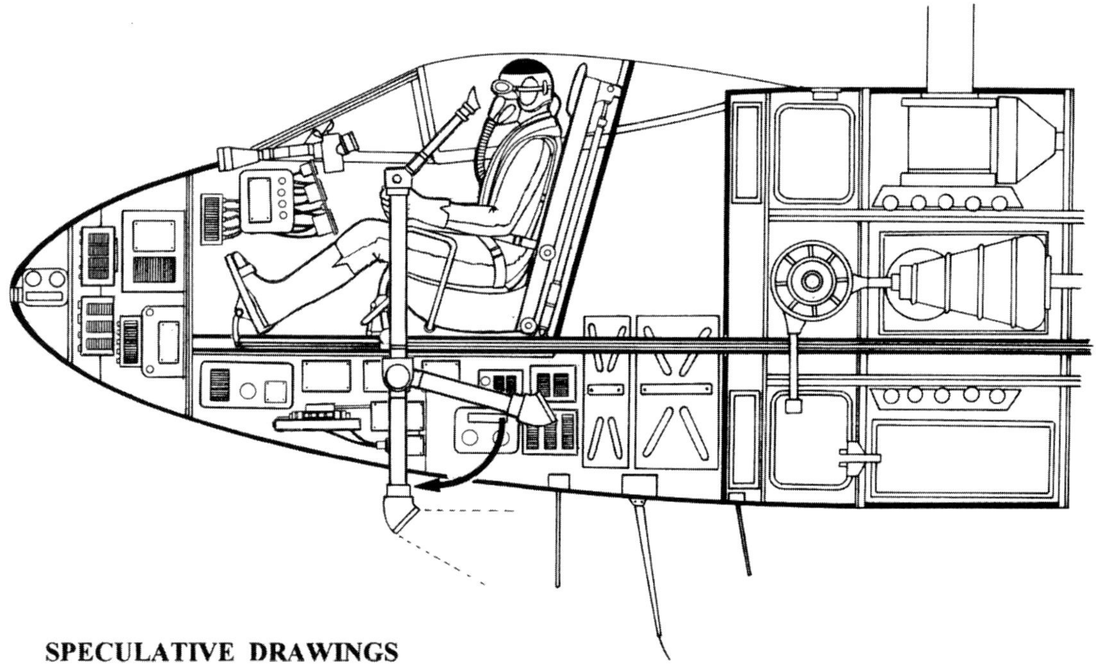

SPECULATIVE DRAWINGS

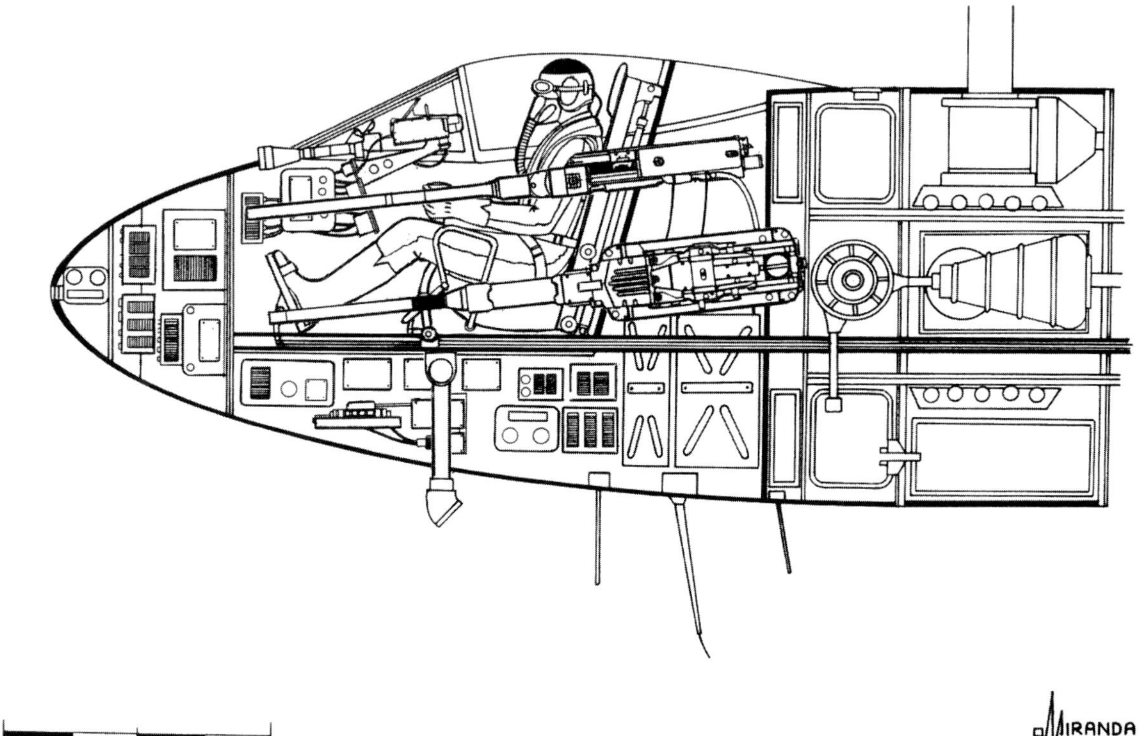

Focke-Wulf *Triebflügeljäger*

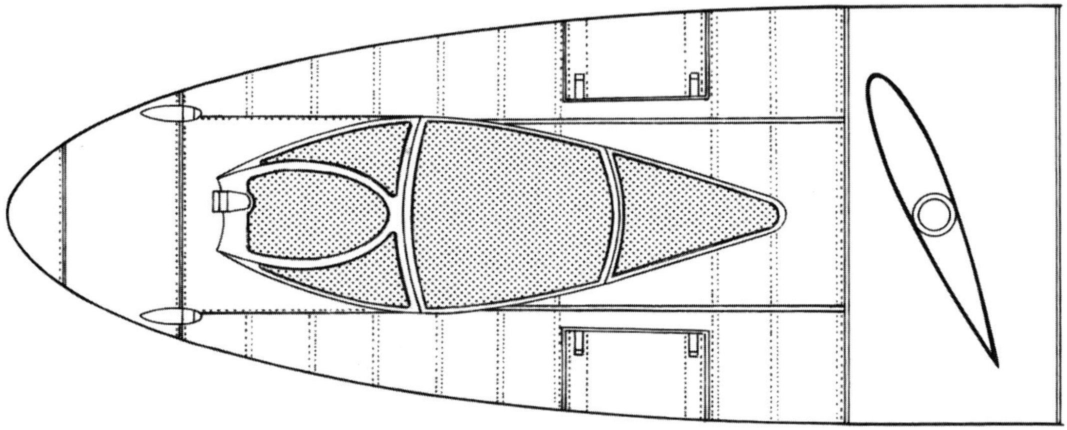

SPECULATIVE DRAWINGS

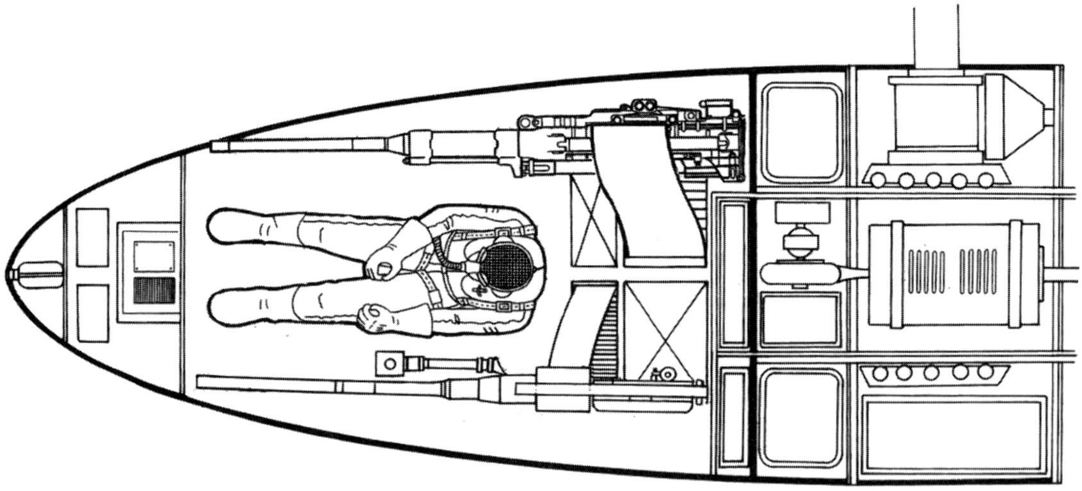

Focke-Wulf *Triebflügeljäger*

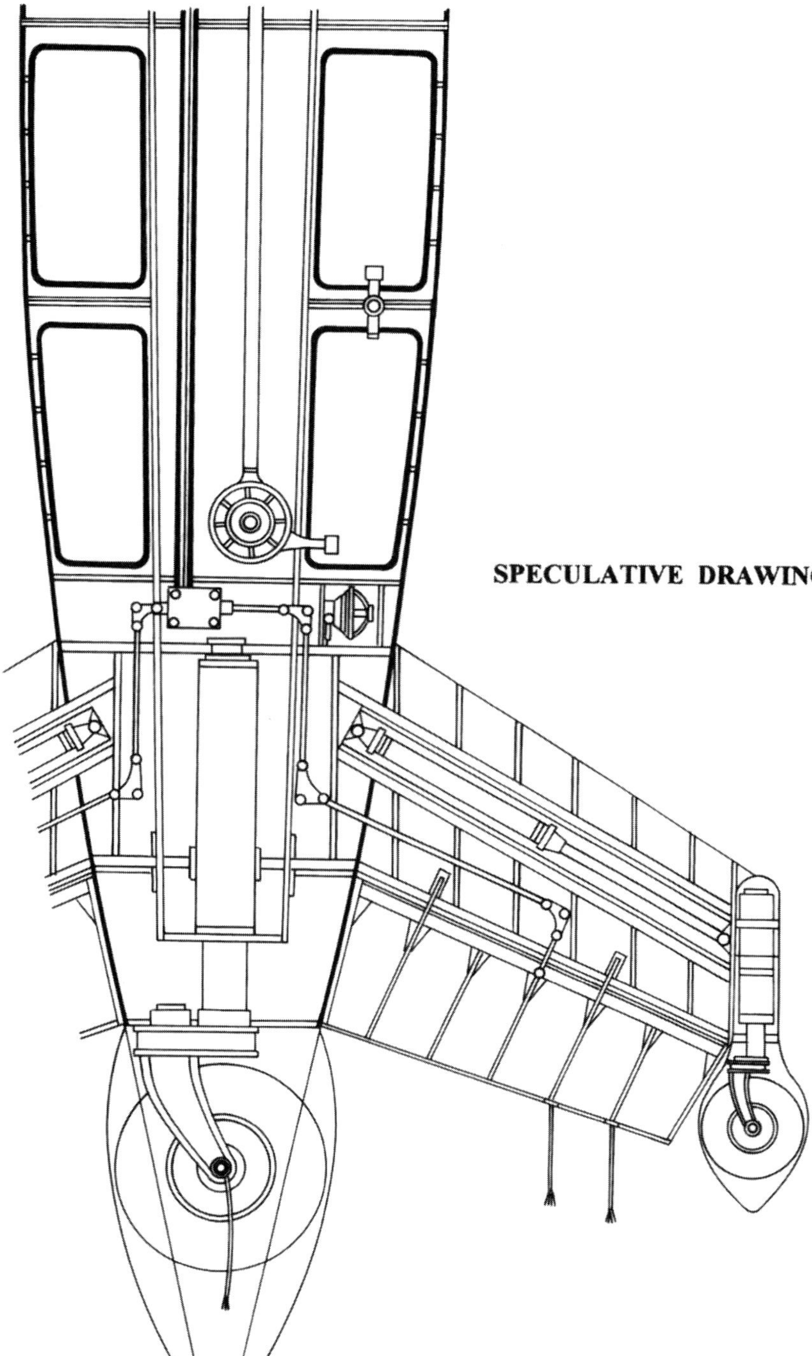

SPECULATIVE DRAWINGS

1m.

MIRANDA

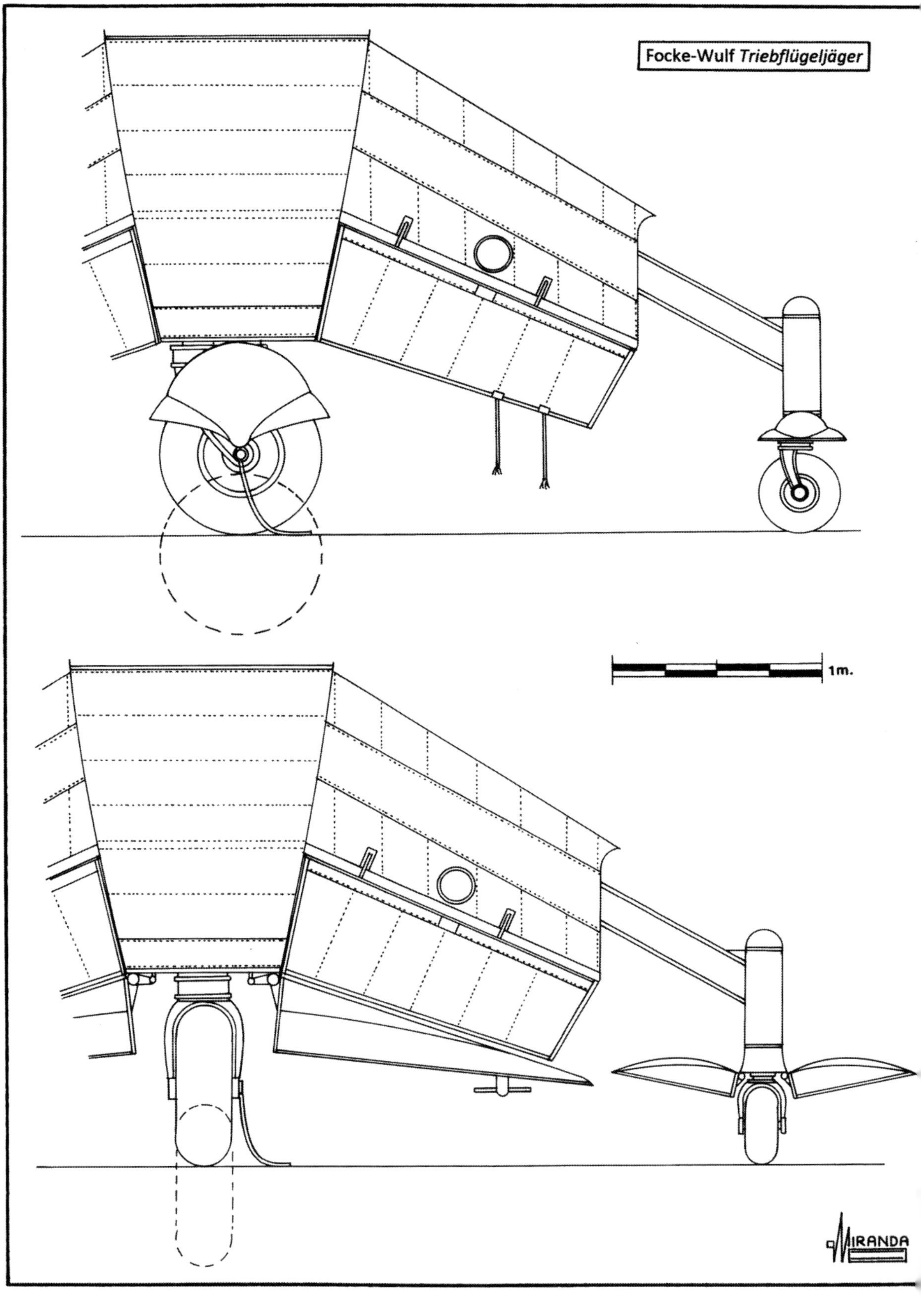
Focke-Wulf *Triebflügeljäger*
1m.
MIRANDA

Focke-Wulf *Triebflügeljäger*

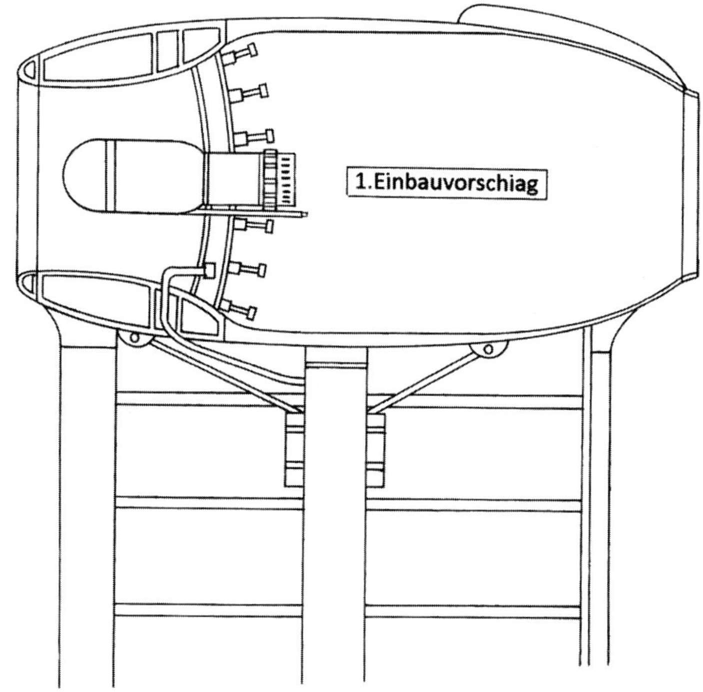

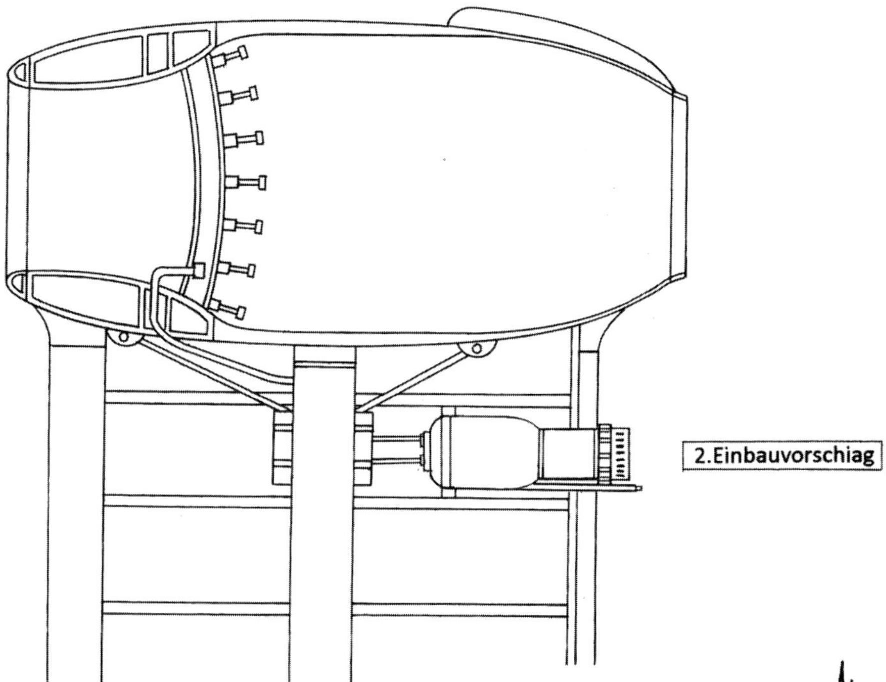

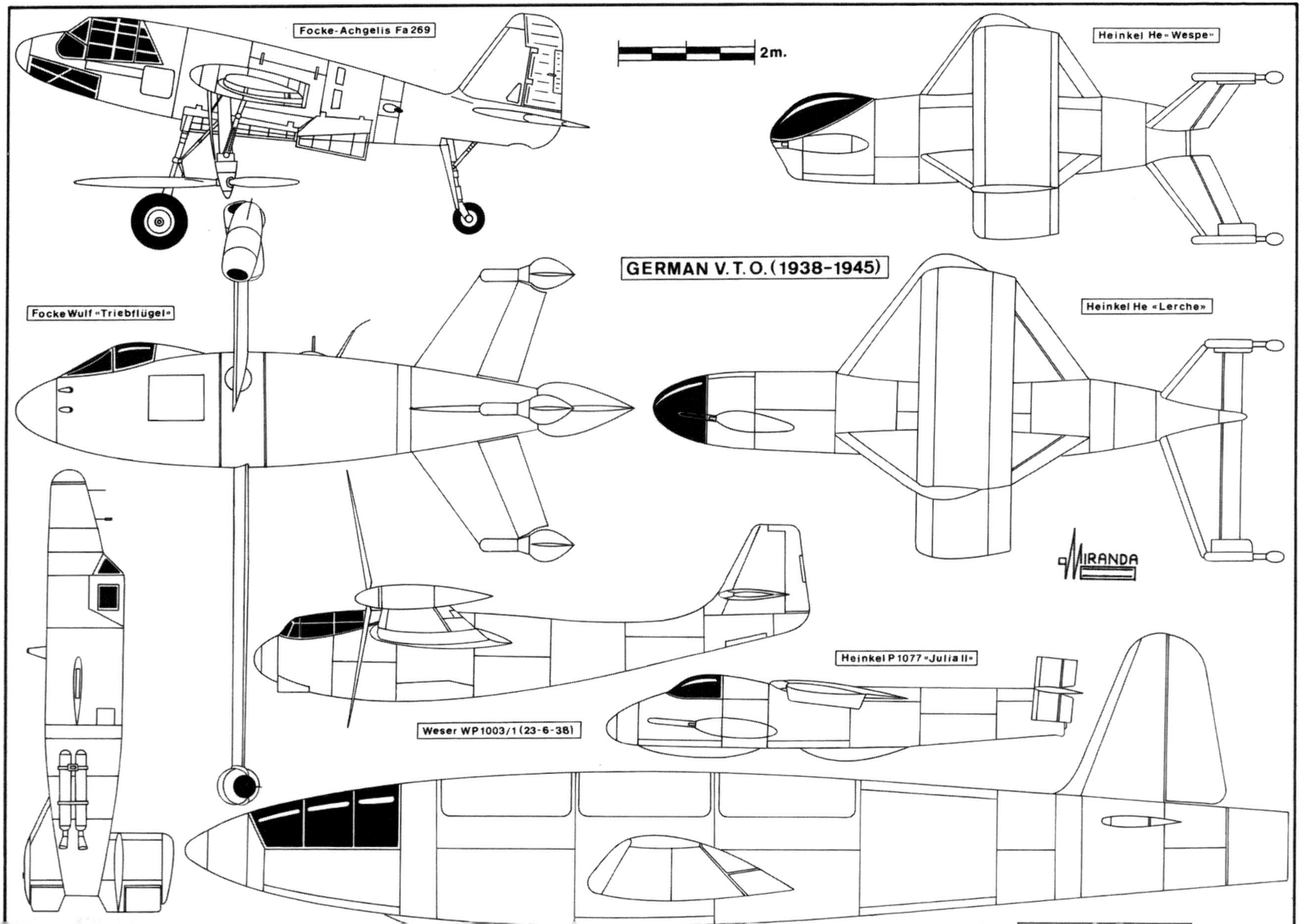
Focke-Achgelis Fa 269
2m.
Heinkel He «Wespe»
GERMAN V.T.O. (1938-1945)
Focke Wulf «Triebflügel»
Heinkel He «Lerche»
MIRANDA
Heinkel P 1077 «Julia II»
Weser WP 1003/1 (23-6-38)

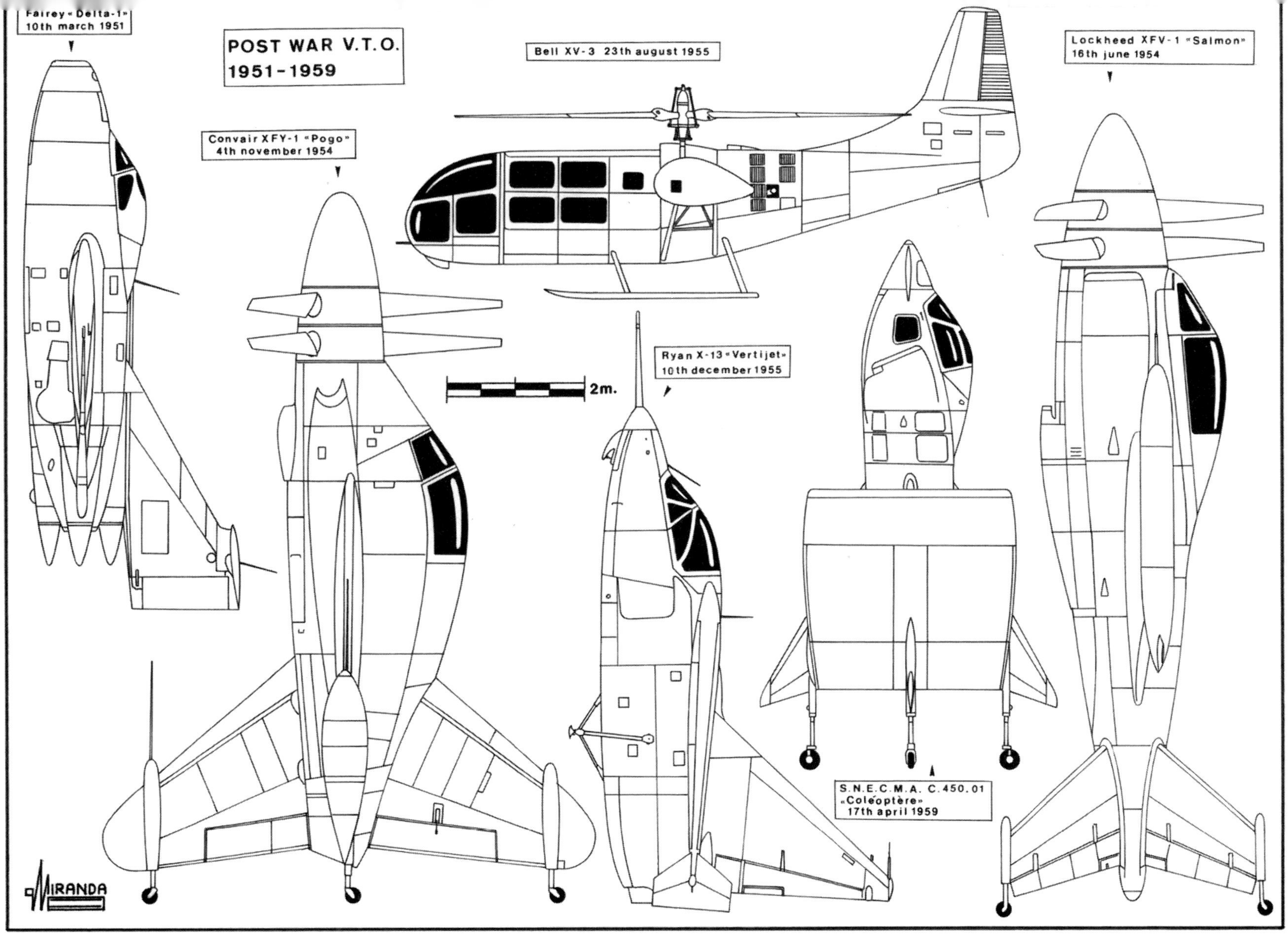

POST WAR V.T.O.
1951-1959
Fairey «Delta-1»
10th march 1951
Convair XFY-1 «Pogo»
4th november 1954
Bell XV-3 23th august 1955
Ryan X-13 «Vertijet»
10th december 1955
2m.
S.N.E.C.M.A. C.450.01
«Coléoptère»
17th april 1959
Lockheed XFV-1 «Salmon»
16th june 1954
MIRANDA

25

RAE Transonic Project

During the Second World War, the Allies could not solve the problems presented by the local transonic flux at high altitude diving in their second-generation fighters Lockheed P-38, Republic P-47, Hawker Typhoon, and Westland Welkin. The odd phenomenon was called compressibility. Different types of airplanes suffered it at different speed and manifested itself in different ways that were usually defined under the term 'compressibility buffeting'.

Many airplanes and pilots were lost due to unexplained structural failures. The cause of all this was a strange physical phenomenon known by the aerodynamicists as 'Coanda effect'. It explained that any fluid running above a curved surface tends to adhere to it and increases its speed proportionally to its curvature. It is an accepted fact nowadays that the Allied designers never understood the true causes behind the compressibility phenomena due to their scarce means for aerodynamic testing.

At the end of the war, when they had access to the research made by the Germans on the areas of the swept wings, transonic flux, Mach critical numbers, and air-flow separation of the boundary layer, the cultural shock they suffered led them to cancel the construction of some of their best projects in favour of the new German ideas. One of the most regrettable cases was the Miles M.52, an excellent Mach 1.5 design that would have been the first British supersonic airplane, had the Ministry of Supply not cancelled the project in February 1946.

In 1947, German aerodynamicists Hans Multhopp and Martin Winter received the request to design an experimental airplane able to fly at Mach 1.24. The project was developed at the Royal Aircraft Establishment (RAE), Farnborough, using all the aerodynamic research done for the Focke-Wulf Ta 183 as a basis. It was too advanced for its time, with a 60-degree rear swept wing and the pilot in prone position to best reduce the size of the frontal area of the fuselage, with a diameter of just 1.20 m.

A jettisonable trolley would help it with taking-off and a retractable skid system was included for landing, although their small fuel capacity and the high consumption rate of the turbojet advised its launching from a bomber in the same fashion as the American Bell X-1, the DFS 346 tested in the URSS, or the unmanned prototypes of the Miles M.52. The project was not cancelled but evolved and converted itself into the Hawker P.1067, a predecessor of the Hawker Hunter, based in Spec F3/48.

The British used the T-tail formula in the experimental airplanes and projects Avro 724; Armstrong Whitworth AW.58 and AW.169; BAC VC10; Blackburn B-89; Bristol 177, 178, 183, and 188; de Havilland DH.116; Fairey Delta 1; Gloster P.250, P.259, P.272, P.285, P.356, and F.135D; Handley Page HP. 88 and Victor; Hawker P.1062, P.1064, P.1067, P.1068, P. 1071 and P.1097; Saunders-Roe P.121, P.177, P.148, P.149, P.163, and P.187; Short P.D.7; and Westland PJD.143 and W.37.

Technical Data

Type: Single-seat supersonic research airplane
Wings: with 60 degrees rear sweep at the leading edge, 42 degrees at the trailing edge, 6 per cent thickness to chord ratio at the root, and 10 per cent at the tip.
Tail surfaces: tailplane with 60 degrees rear swept at the leading edge, 46 degrees at the trailing edge, tailfin with 67 degrees rear swept containing the cooling system.
Fuselage: with circular section, prone pilot housed in a transparent container within the air duct with ventral hatch.
Landing gear: two hydraulically retractable skids.
Engine: one Rolls-Royce AJ.65 Avon turbojet with 2,722 kp static thrust.
Fuel tanks: in the wings, ahead of the main spar.
Wingspan: 7.62 m; Length: 10.29 m;
Height (folded skids): 2.4 m; Wing area: 17 sq. m.
Estimated maximum speed: Mach 1.24 at 10,975 m.
Initial climb rate: 71 m/sec
Service ceiling: 18,290 m
Powered endurance: thirty minutes
Touchdown speed: 275 kph

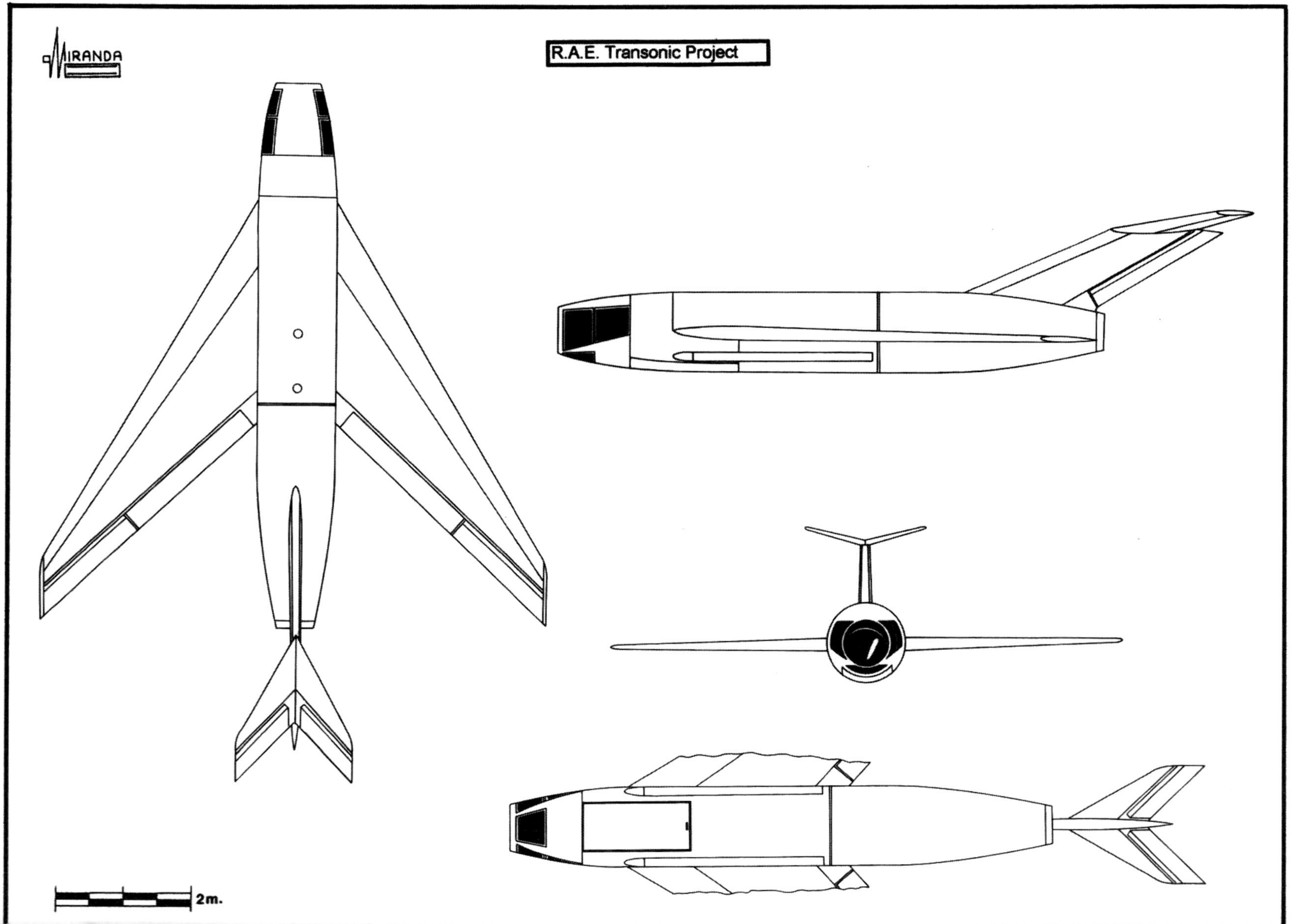
R.A.E. Transonic Project
MIRANDA
2m.

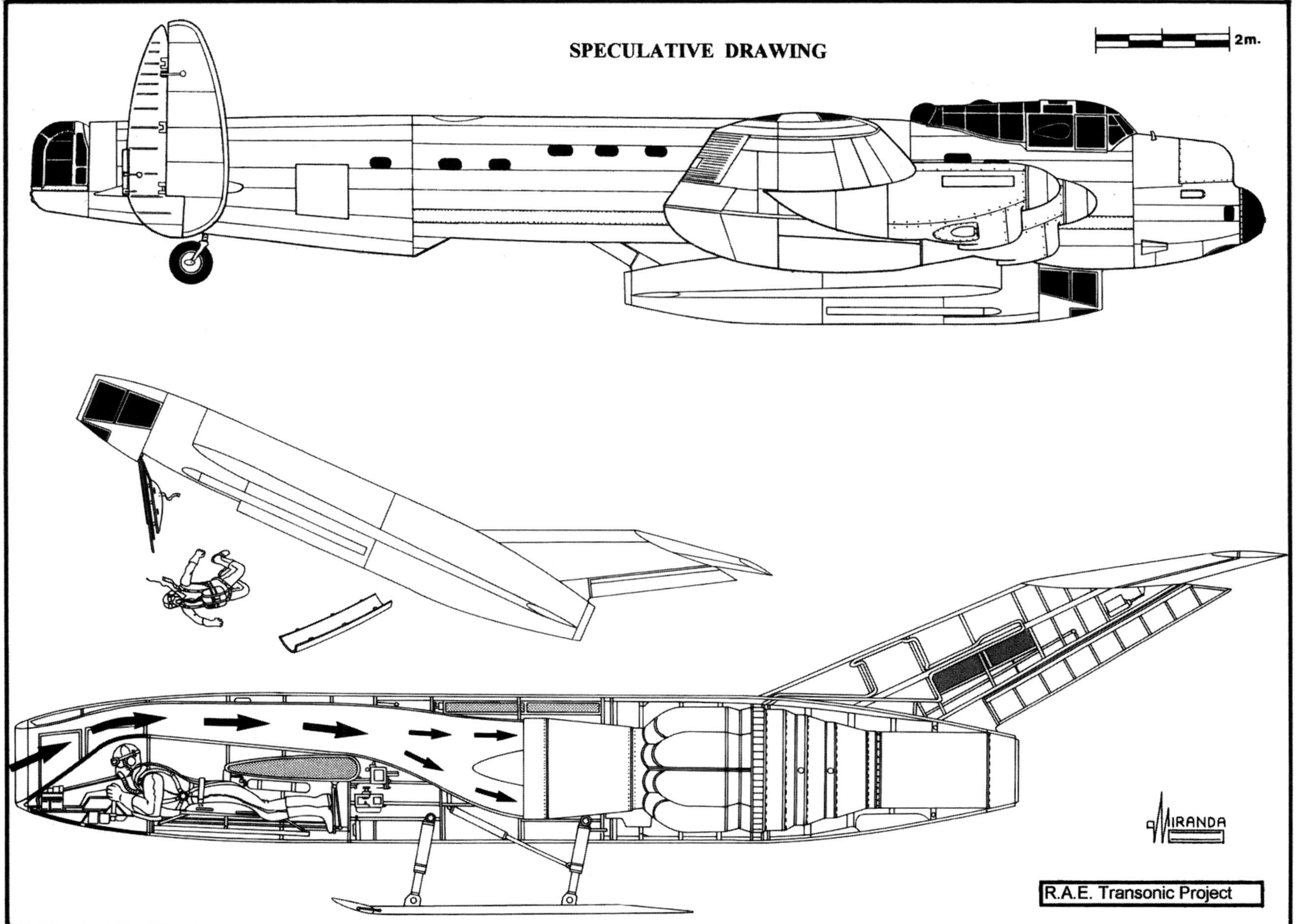
SPECULATIVE DRAWING
2m.
MIRANDA
R.A.E. Transonic Project

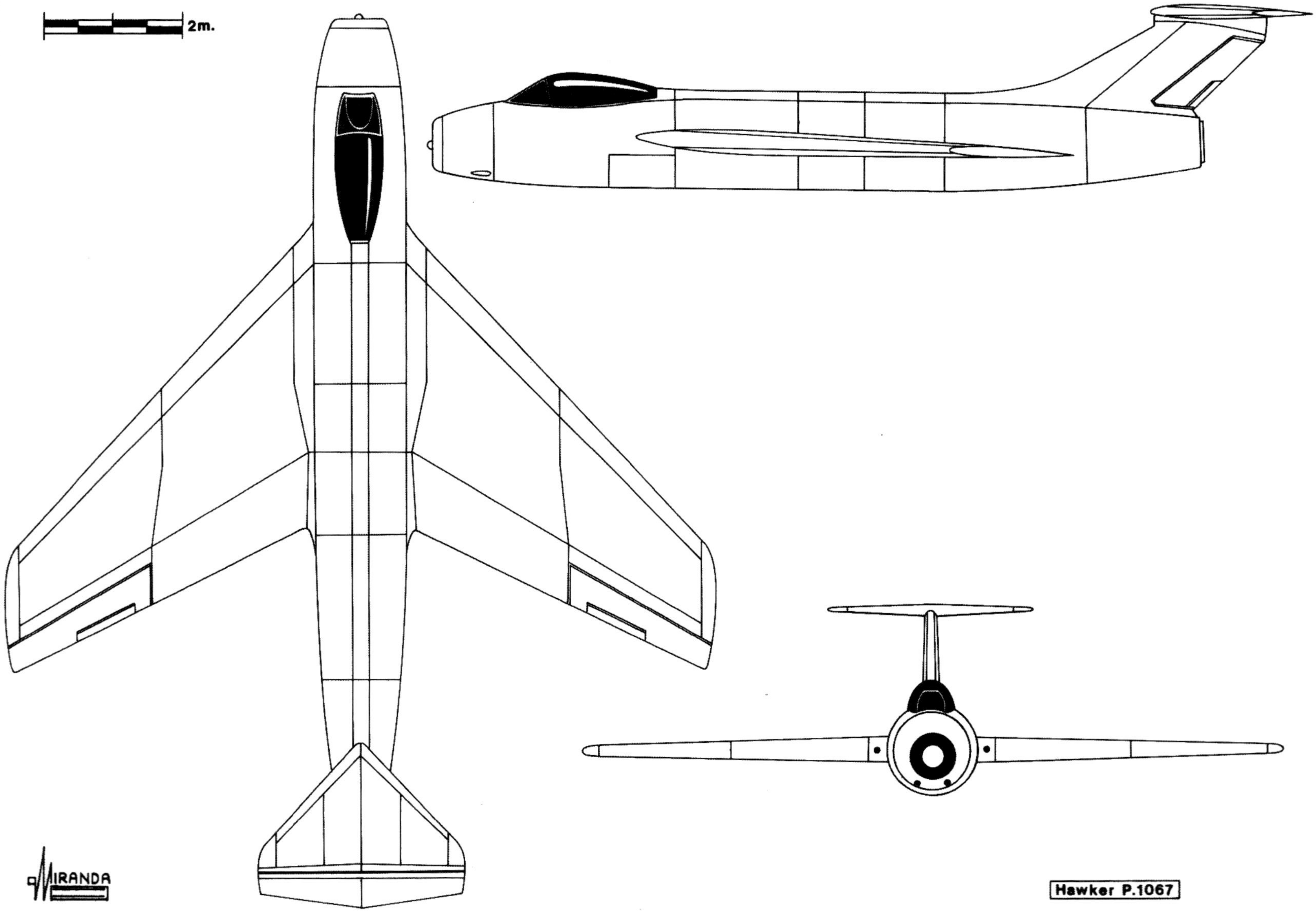

Hawker P.1067

26

Tank IAe 33

Developed by Kurt Tank in Argentina between 1947 and 1955, the IAe 33 was a transonic interceptor derived from the Focke-Wulf Ta 183. Two test gliders and five prototypes were built of this aircraft. The scheduled production of 100 operational units was cancelled for political reasons in 1957.

The first glider was built with the collaboration of Reimar Horten in early 1948, to study the aerodynamic behaviour of the design at low speeds. It flew for the first time on 20 October, towed by a Glenn Martin W-139 bomber, proving that the 55-degree swept tailfin did not offer sufficient lateral stability. The second glider was built with a 35-degree swept tailfin, with a surface that had been increased by 30 per cent.

The construction of two prototypes started in 1949. The IAe 33-01 was used for structural testing and the IAe 33-02 was fitted with a Rolls-Royce Nene II centrifugal turbojet with 2,270 kp static thrust. The first flight was made on 16 June 1950, showing lateral instability at speeds above 700 kph and loss of lift at low speeds. It was modified with the installation of a wider rudder and wing leading extensions, a pressurizing system and a cockpit hood reinforced with metallic strips. A deflector was added over the nozzle to protect the rudder from the heat of the exhaust gases.

On 23 October, during the second test flight, the IAe 33-02 climbed to 8,000 m in 6 minutes reaching a speed of 1,040 kph. During the third flight, it reached an absolute ceiling of 13,000 m, landing at 170 kph without loss of lift. It was destroyed due to wing structural fail on 31 May 1951.

The IAe 33-03 was the pre-production version. It had an increased fuel capacity and better lateral stability, resulting from the installation of a new flight control system. Its flight testing began at the end of 1951, getting destroyed due to an engine stoppage on 9 October 1952.

The IAe 33-04, built in 1953, was equipped with four hydraulically operated airbrakes on the rear section of the fuselage and fences on the upper side of the wings, to delay the migration of the centre of pressure at transonic speeds. It had an improved pressurised system and was armed with four 20-mm Hispano-Suiza Mk 5 cannon installed under the air duct. During the flight tests performed in 1954, the IAe 33-04 reached an absolute ceiling of 15,000 m and 1,080 kph maximum speed.

The IAe 33-05 was started in 1957, without fences but with four anti-spin fins in the rear section of the fuselage, flying for the first time on 18 September 1955 and the last in 1960. The IAe 33 airframe was built entirely of light alloy. The wings, spanning 10.6 m with a 40–45-degrees rear sweep angle and 8 per cent thickness, housed two fuel tanks with 150 litres of capacity each, two with 154 litres, two with 170 litres, and two with 160 litres, as well as the ailerons and the hydraulically operated flaps.

The fuselage housed the pressurised cockpit with armoured windshield; the Mk IIc gyro gunsight from a Gloster Meteor F.4; a Martin-Baker Mk 1 ejector seat; the armament; the landing gear; the air intake with bifurcated air duct; three fuel tanks with 656, 485, and 156 litres of capacity; the engine pressure compensation chamber; the turbojet; the tailpipe; four airbrakes; and the 35-degree rear-swept tailfin.

The tailplane, with a 45-degree rear sweep, was fitted with an electric motor to vary its incidence. Both the Dutch and Egyptian governments were interested in the acquisition of the IAe 33. An all-weather version with radar, two Sidewinder missiles, and a Rolls-Royce AJ.65 Avon turbojet was also planned. It would have been a good competitor to the Sabre K. The coup of 16 September 1955 ended production plans. Instead, the new government acquired twenty-eight units of the North American F-86 F-30/40 Sabre.

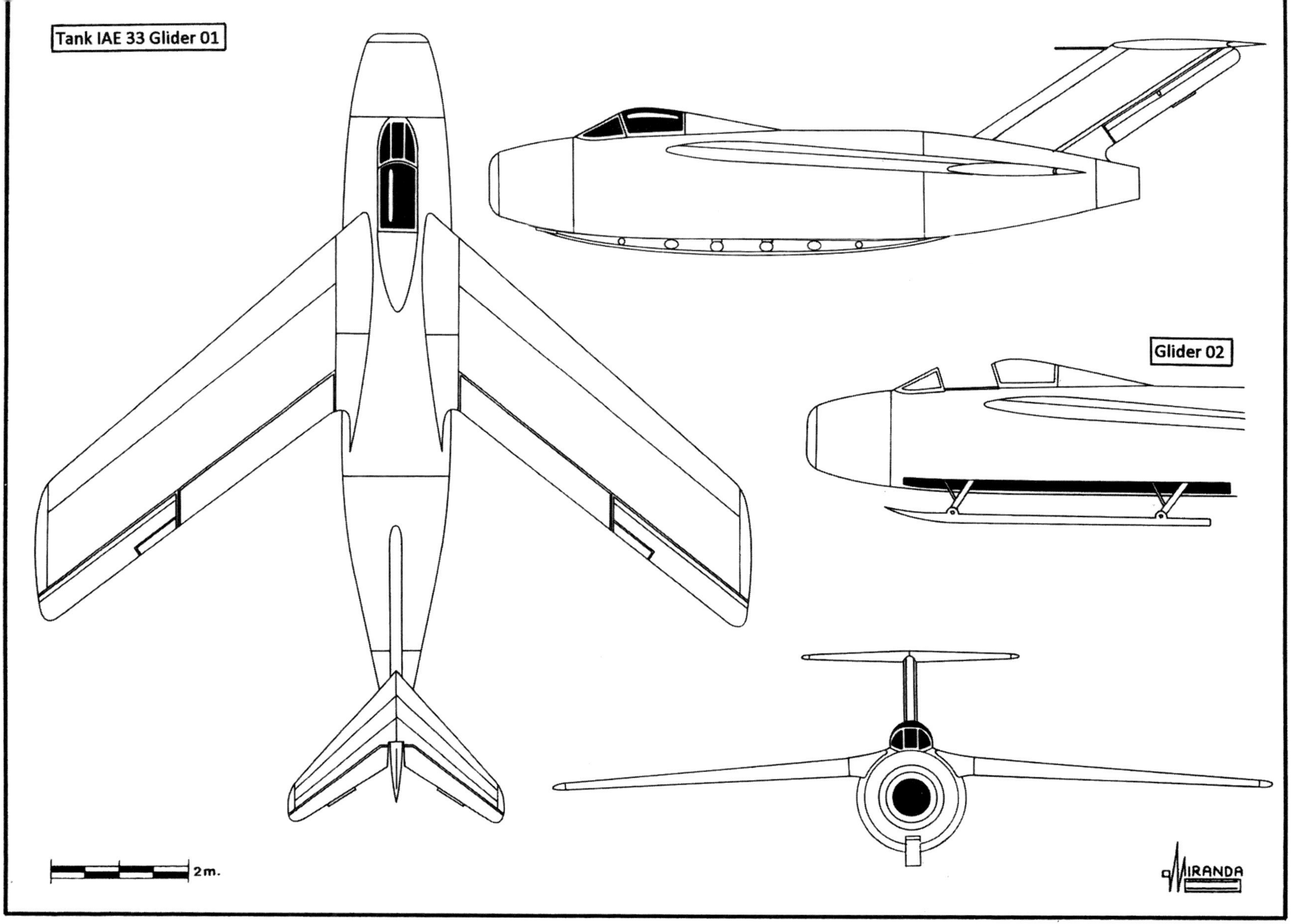
Tank IAE 33 Glider 01
Glider 02
2m.
MIRANDA

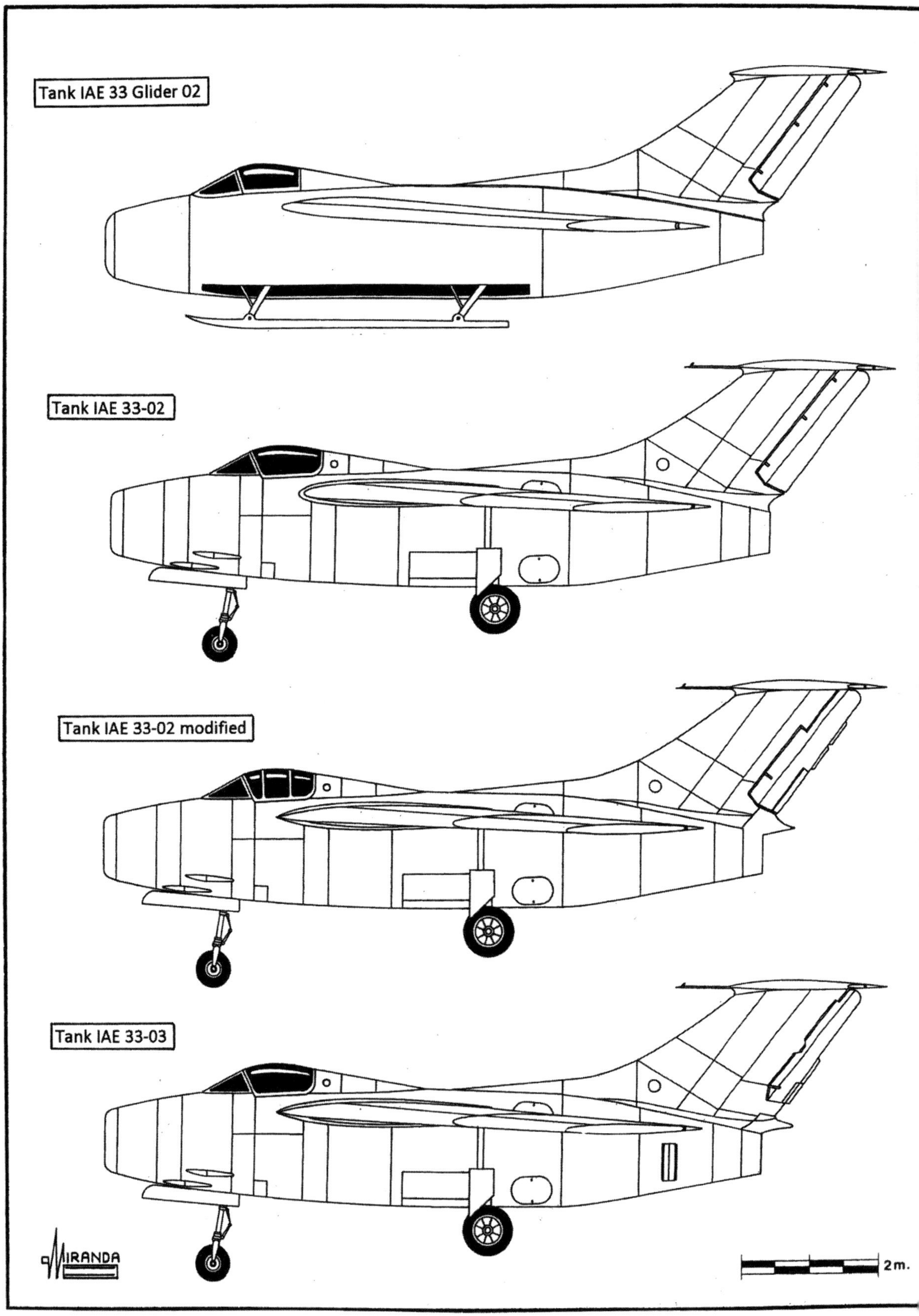
Tank IAE 33 Glider 02
Tank IAE 33-02
Tank IAE 33-02 modified
Tank IAE 33-03
MIRANDA
2m.

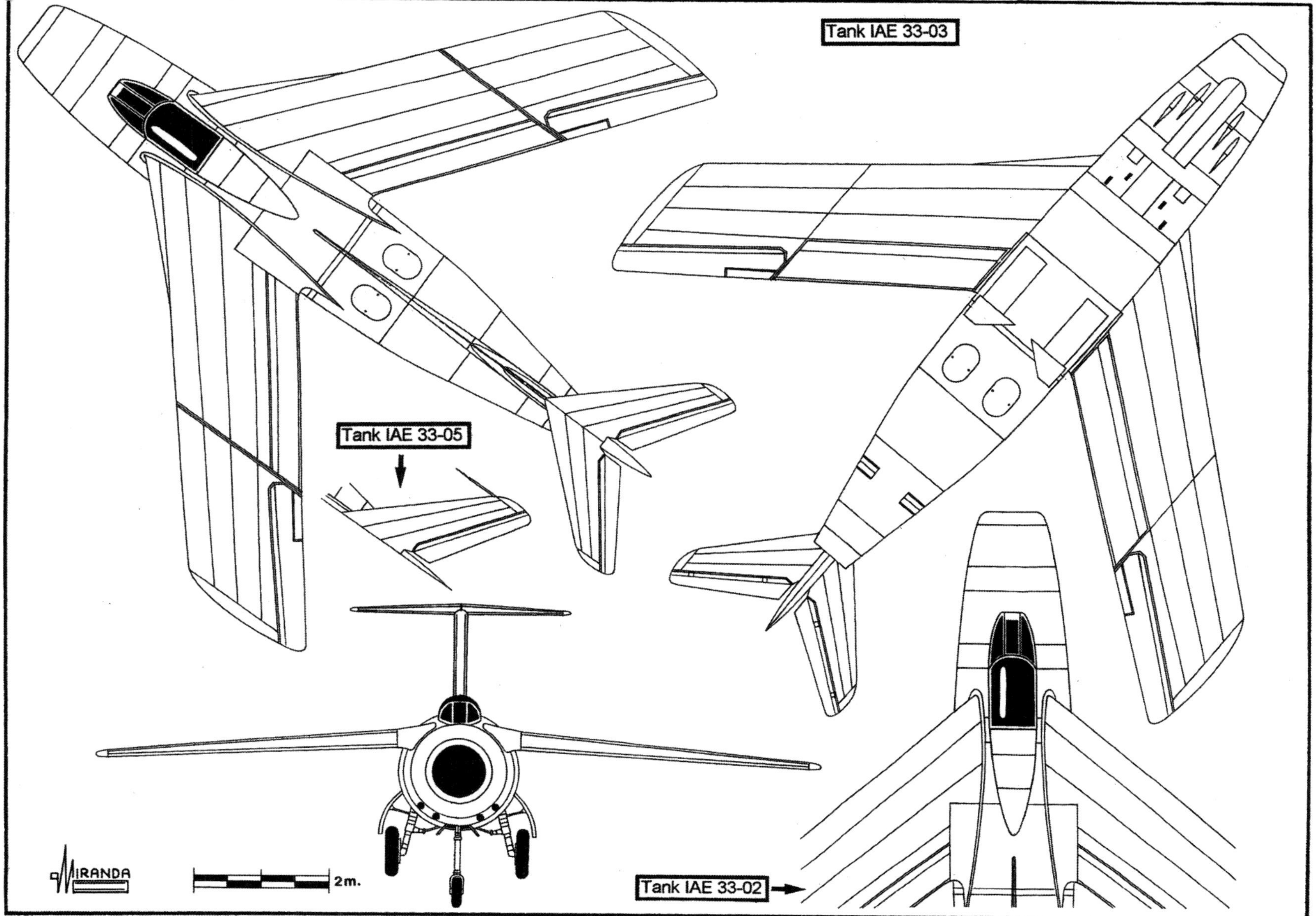

Tank IAE 33-03
Tank IAE 33-05
Tank IAE 33-02
2m.
MIRANDA

Tank IAE 33-03

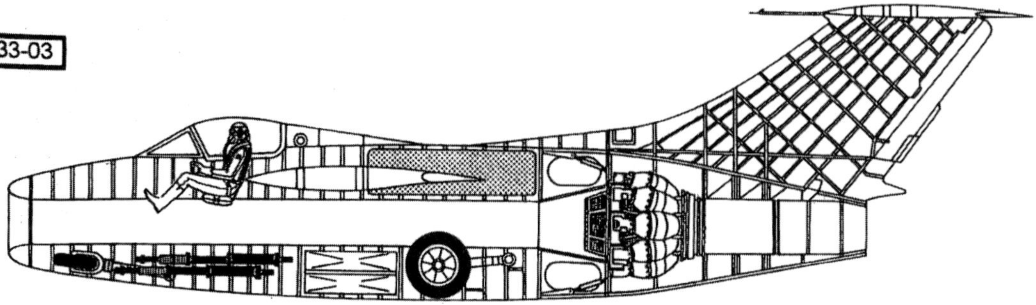

Tank IAE 33-04

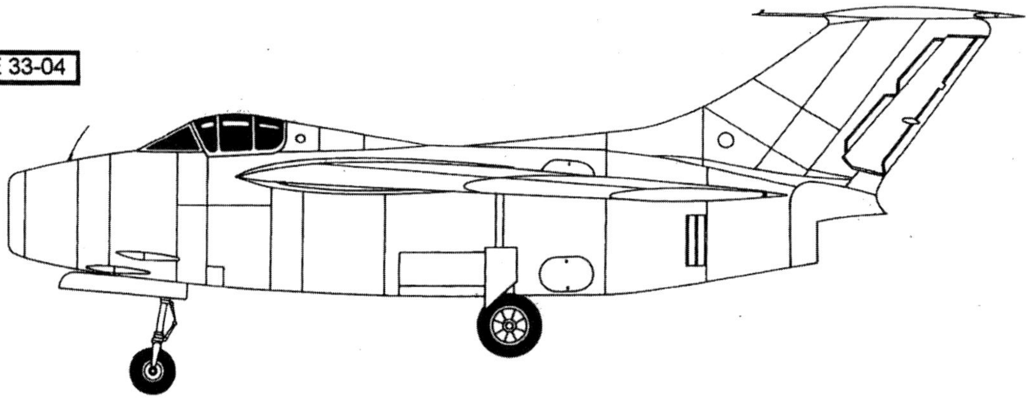

Tank IAE 33-05

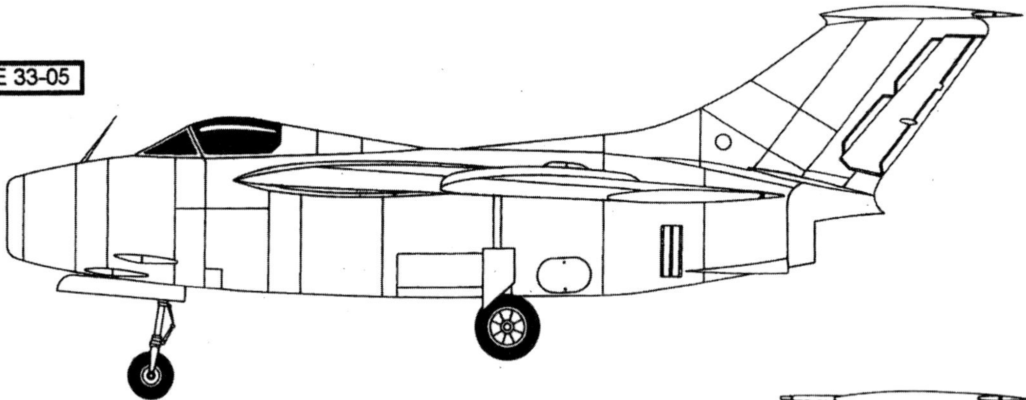

Tank IAE 33-05/R

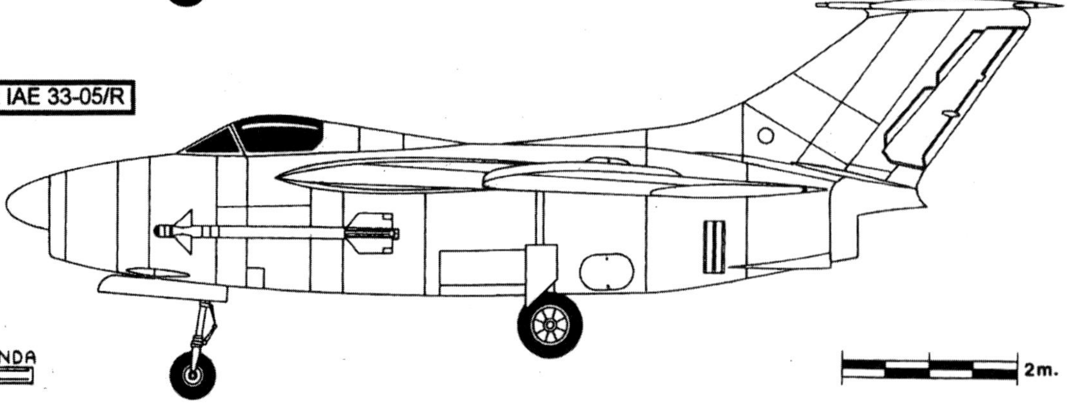

MIRANDA

2m.

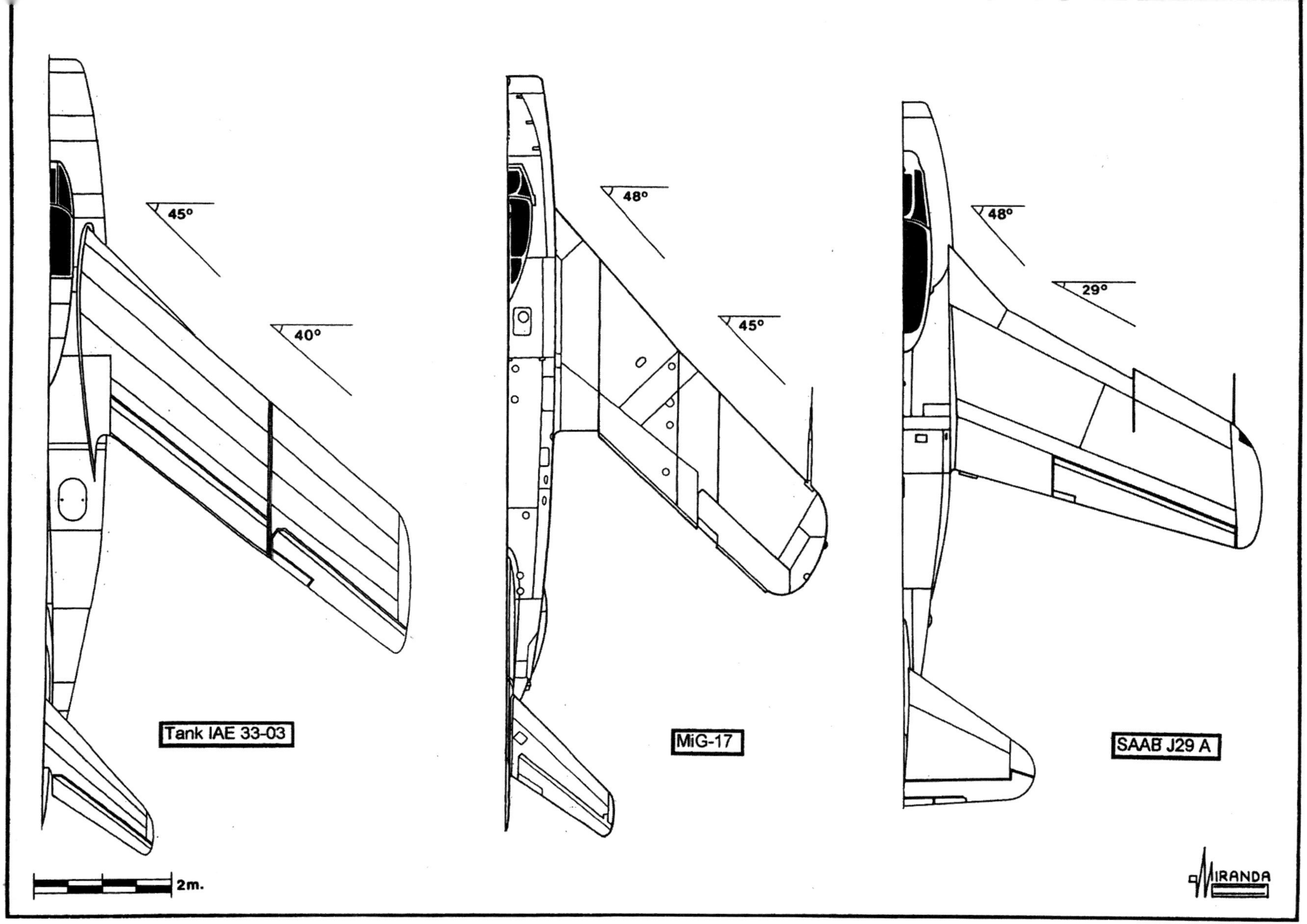
45°
40°
Tank IAE 33-03
48°
45°
MiG-17
48°
29°
SAAB J29 A
2m.
MIRANDA

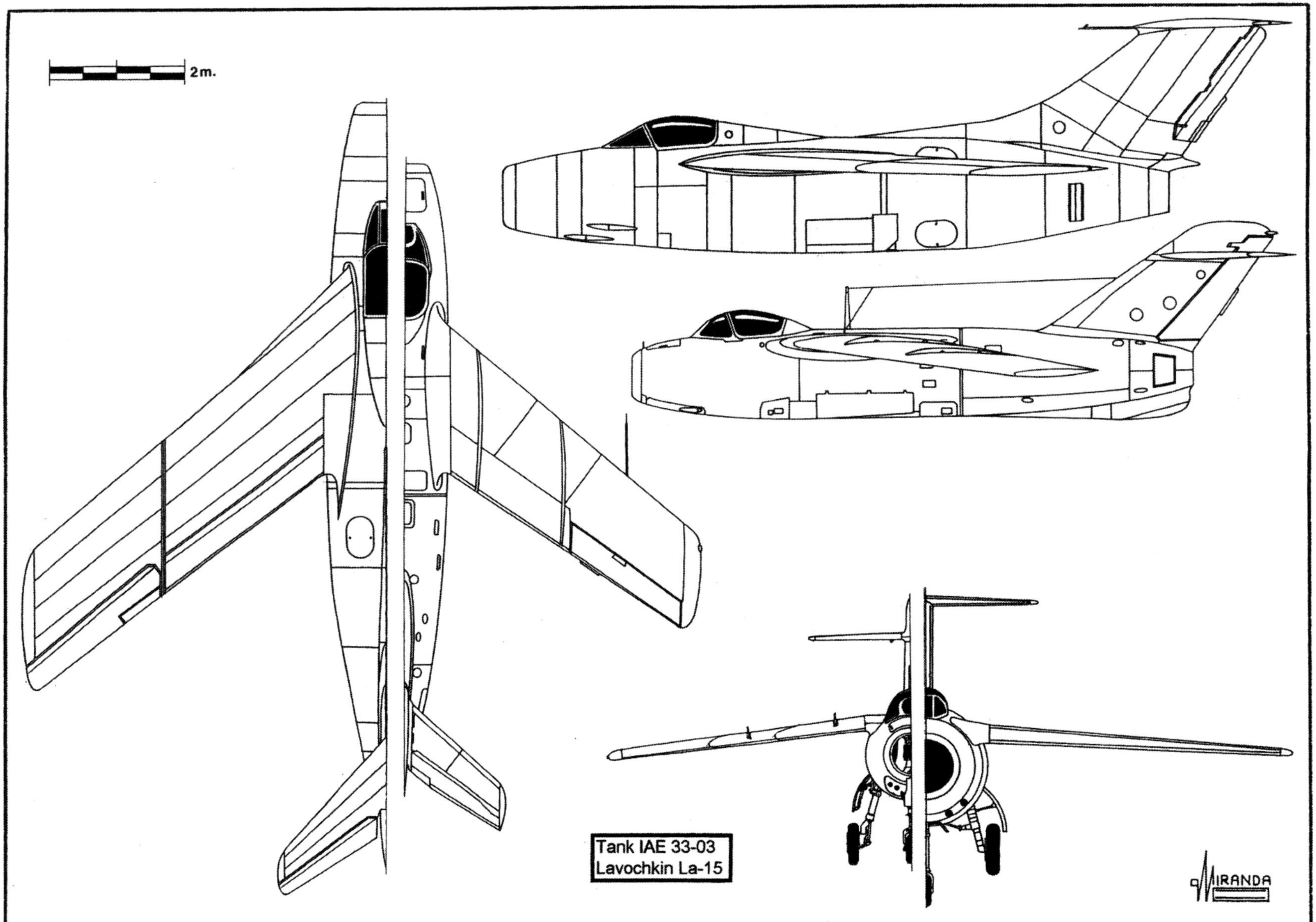
2m.
Tank IAE 33-03
Lavochkin La-15

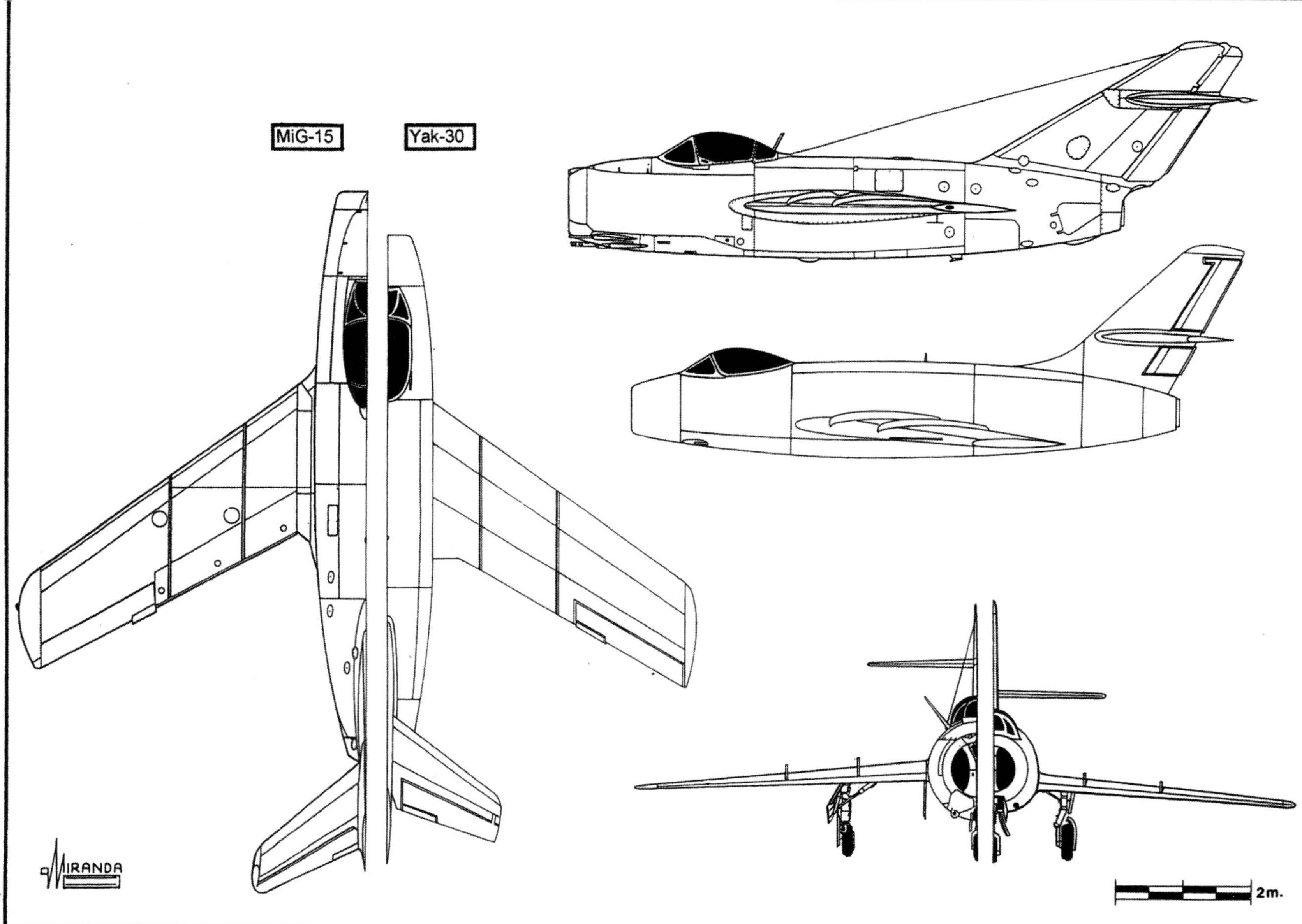
MiG-15
Yak-30
MIRANDA
2m.

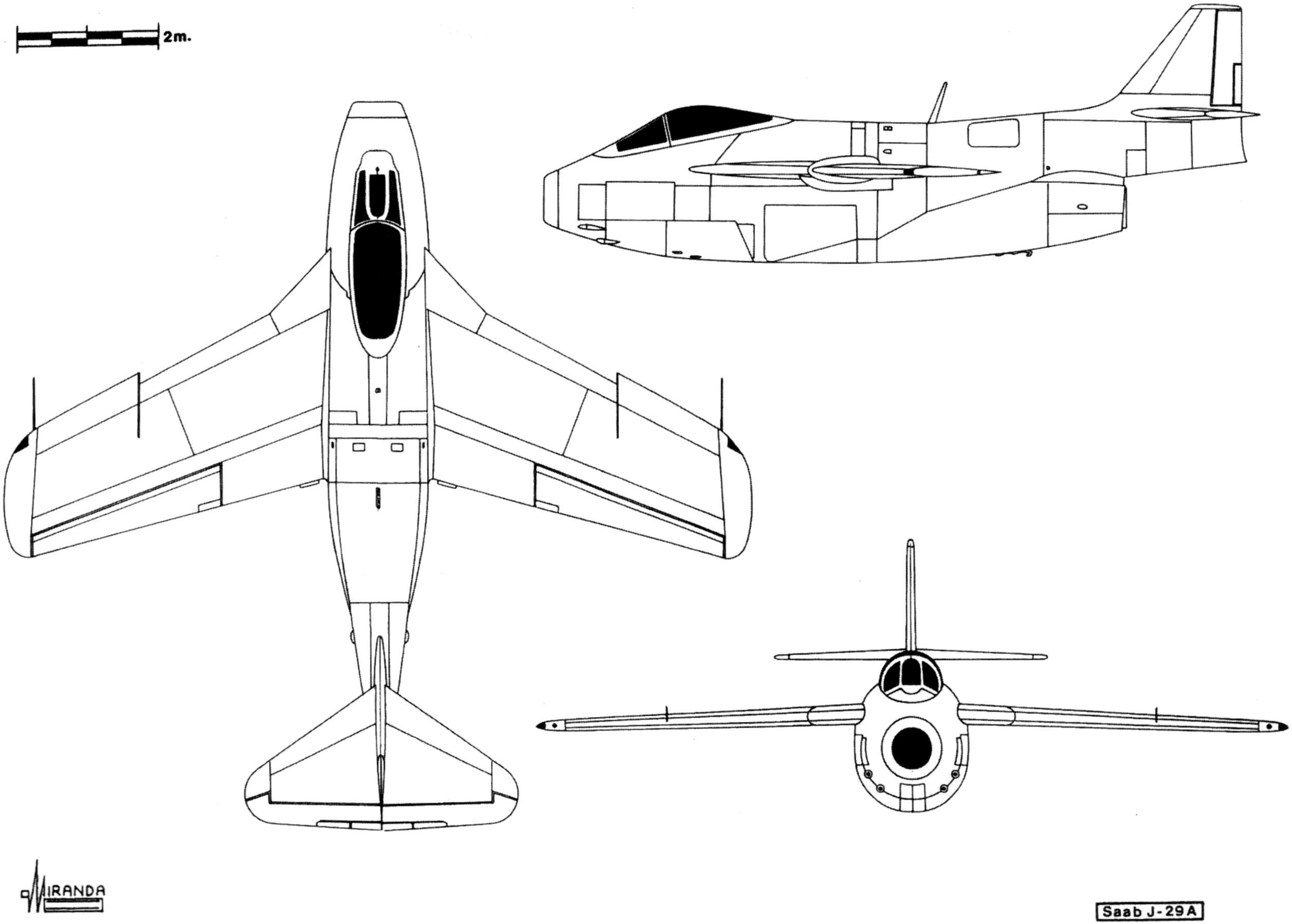

Saab J-29A

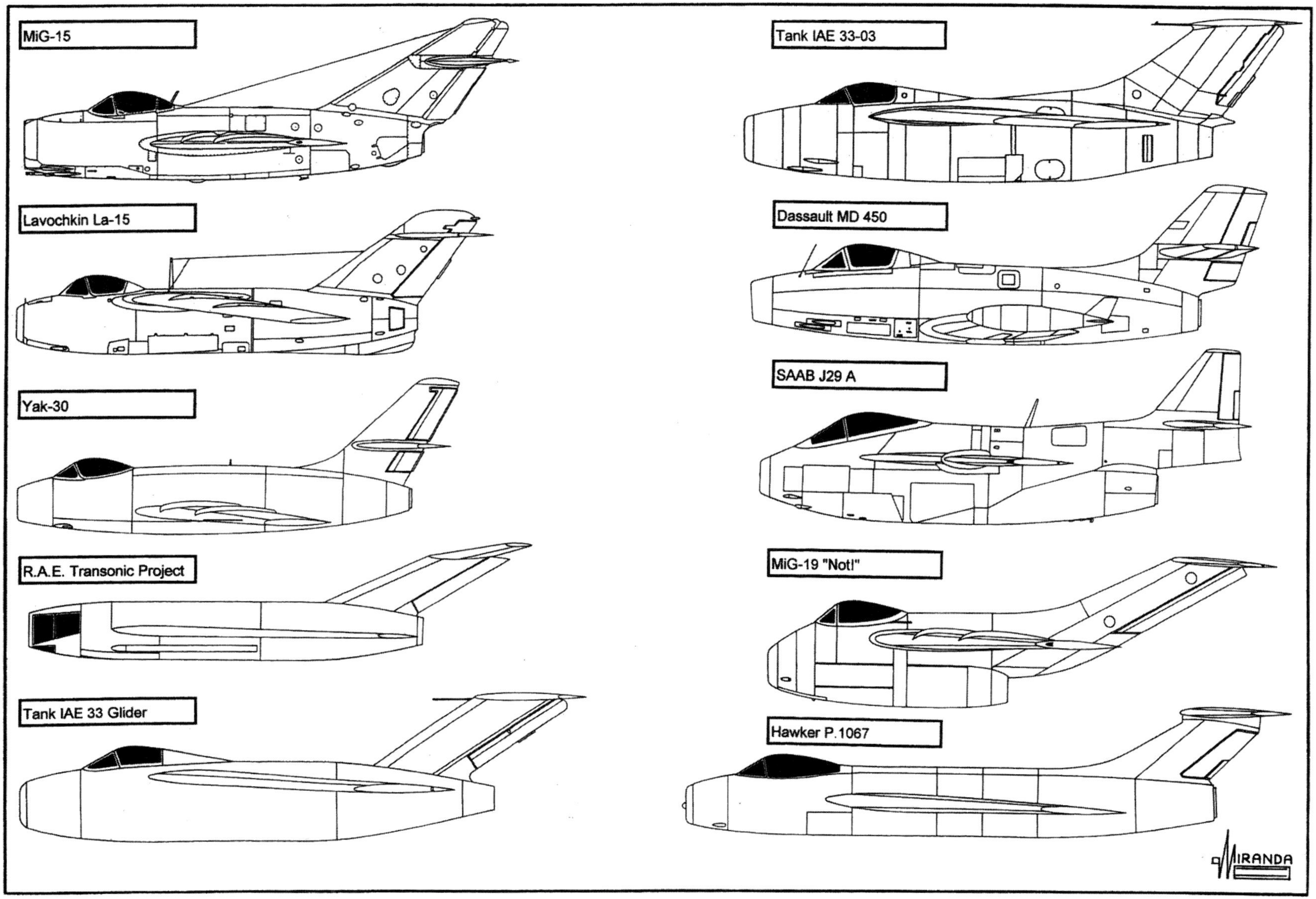
MiG-15
Lavochkin La-15
Yak-30
R.A.E. Transonic Project
Tank IAE 33 Glider
Tank IAE 33-03
Dassault MD 450
SAAB J29 A
MiG-19 "Not!"
Hawker P.1067
MIRANDA

27

Tank IAE 43

When the firm Bristol Siddeley published the features of its new turbojet Orpheus in early 1954, a team of German designers integrated by Kurt Tank, Wilhelm Basemir, and Ludwig Mittelhuber began to work in the project of an all-weather supersonic fighter, called IAE 43, in Argentina.

The fuselage would be built of light alloy, housing the radar parabolic mirror, four Hispano-Suiza Mk 5 20-mm cannon, the nose undercarriage leg, and the cockpit (pressurised at 0.25 kg/sq. cm). It had a Martin-Baker ejector seat and armoured glass windshield, a space designed to house a second crew member or a fuel tank, two airbrakes, two fuel tanks, the main undercarriage wheels, two semicircular air intakes, two air ducts, two Bristol Siddeley Orpheus BOr.1 with 14.61 kN static thrust each, the tailfin and the tailplanes rear swept by 50 degrees, and low set to minimise any tendency to pitch-up.

The wings, spanning 9 m, with a 50-degree rear sweep, 6 per cent thickness to chord ratio and 25 sq. m area, would be built of steel and Dural. Each wing panel housed one fuel tank, hydraulically operated flaps, and a landing gear retraction system. The development of the IAE 43 in Argentina was interrupted in September 1955 for political reasons, being continued in India as HAL HF-24 Marut.

Tank IAE-43

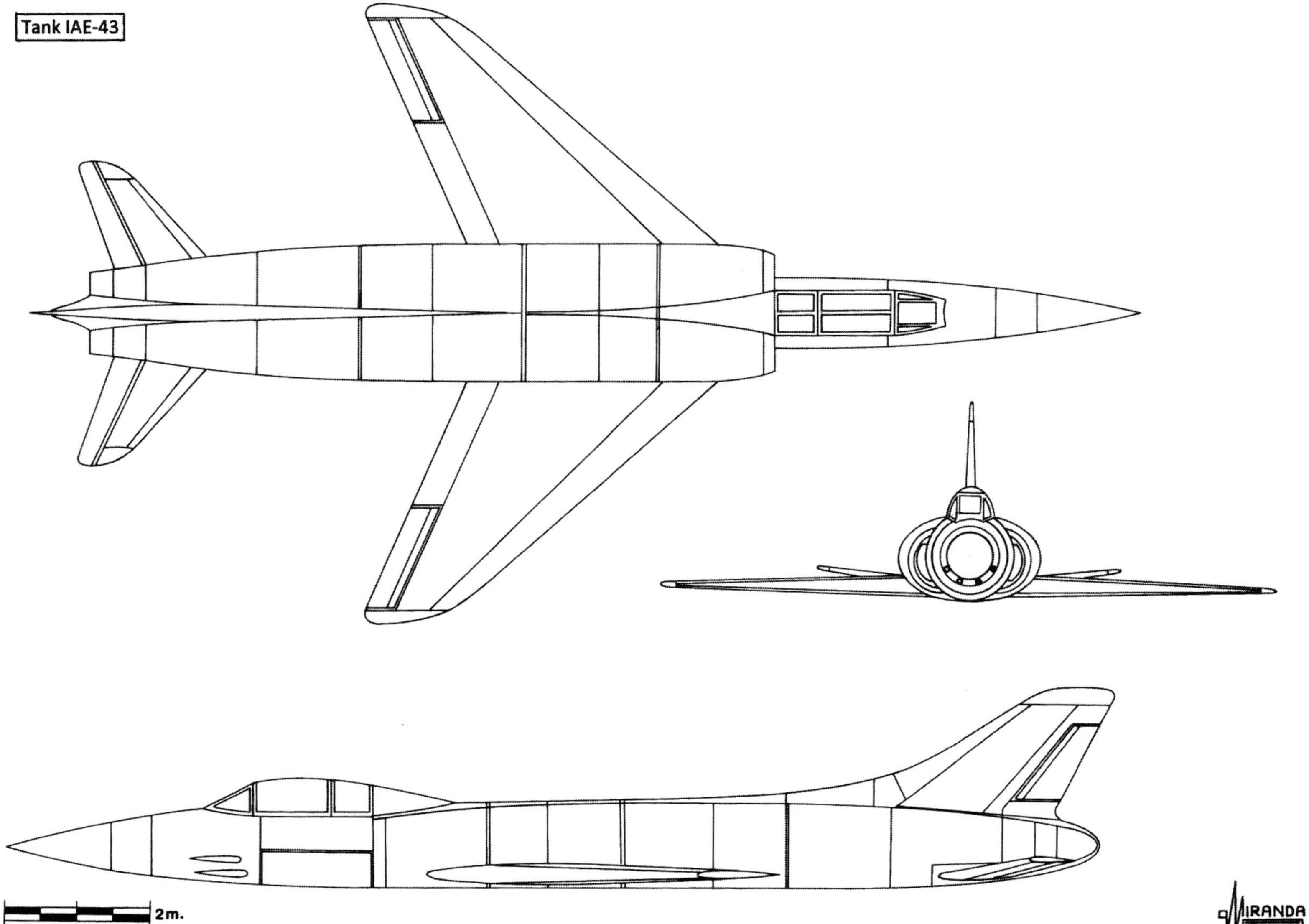

28

Hindustan HF-24 Marut

In the years following the Second World War, many countries were forced to modernise their Air Force by acquiring the new technology of the turbojet to the winning powers. Those who chose to use the export versions of the Gloster Meteor regretted their decision when the performances of the new Soviet fighters were known. Dutch and Egyptians, interested in the work carried out by Kurt Tank's team in Argentina, began negotiations for the acquisition of the IAE 43.

In 1955, the pursuit of self-reliance in aviation by the Indian Government led the Air Staff to issue a requirement calling for a homemade multirole aircraft suitable for both high-altitude Mach 2 interception with a ceiling of 60,000 feet and low-level ground attack with a combat radius of 800 km. Furthermore, the specification demanded that the basic design be suitable for an advanced trainer, an all-weather interceptor, and shipboard versions.

The Air Staff overestimated the complexity of the task. The local aircraft builder Hindustan Aircraft Ltd (HAL) had been building Vampire FB. 52 and T-55 under licence but its only autochthonous design experience was the HT-2 primary trainer.

The Indian Government decided to solve the problem by hiring thirty-one German specialists from Argentina. In response to the Indian invitation, Kurt Tank and his assistant, Dipl.-Ing. Ludwig Mittelhuber, arrived in Bangalore in August 1956 with the purpose of continuing the development of the IAE 43.

The HAL X-241 prototype was built early in 1959. It was a full scale wooden mock-up with 50-degree rear swept wings, spanning 9 m, with a 6 per cent thickness to chord ratio and 25 sq. m area. Between April 1959 and March 1960, it was used as a flyable air-launched two-seat glider, towed by a Douglas C-47 for low speed stability and oscillation trials. The X-241 lacked ejector seats and, during its first flight, revealed a worrying rate of descent of 3,800 feet per minute and the stall warning was found to be too low. To visualise airflow effects, the left-wing panel had wool tufting and a fin-mounted camera.

To improve the stall warning margin, the wing surface was increased up to 28 sq. m, with the fitting of the saw tooth on the leading edge extending the chord wing at the root by 10 per cent to improve handling. Other modifications consisted of the installation of an anti-spin parachute, a variable incidence tailplane, a boundary layer separator in the air intakes, and the extension of the nose leg oleo to facilitate take-off. The undercarriage retraction system, wheel-brakes, flaps, and air brakes (with holes drilled into them) were operated with a pneumatic air bottle.

The improvements made by the extensive test program in the original design were used for the construction of the HF-24 Marut, an aerodynamically stable aircraft with excellent handling characteristics and with fine control responses for aerobatics, which was pleasant to fly. The aircraft was capable of supersonic flight to 1.5 Mach with manual controls in the event of hydraulic failure. The design of Marut had been based on the availability of the 3,705-kp thrust Bristol Orpheus B.Or. 12 reheat turbojet.

Unfortunately, the British Government cancelled its financial support for the development of this engine and the Marut had to be fitted with a pair of non-afterburning Orpheus 703 engines (which HAL was currently building under licence for the Folland Gnat Mk I lightweight fighter) with 44 per cent less thrust than the B.Or 12. As a result, the Marut offered only marginal improvement on the Hawker Hunter's performance. On 17 June 1961, the prototype HF-001 coded BR 462 made its first flight powered by two Bristol Orpheus 703s, with 2,595 kp static thrust.

It differed externally from the glider in the new design of the air intakes, with shock half-cones and upper lip extended to ensure smooth flow at high incidence, and in the adoption of wing slats.

The all-metal area-ruled semi-monocoque fuselage, with 15.87 m length, and the wet wing with tapering steel frame were very difficult to construct with the available means in HAL, but the great structural strength of the airframe compensated the effort. The aircraft required no artificial augmentation or auto-stabilisation. It had Fairey hydraulic-powered controls, with artificial feel and manual reversion in emergency, which were effective over the entire speed range. The pressurised cockpit included a Martin-Baker S.4C ejector seat. The landing gear retraction system was a Dowty Rotol, with Dunlop wheels, Maxaret anti-braking device, and steerable nosewheel. The structural test airframe was completed in November 1961 and the second prototype BR-463 flew eleven months later.

Between 1962 and 1967, both aircraft performed 1,800 test flights to iron teething troubles. During the armament trials carried out in 1964, it was verified that the vibrations caused while firing the four 30-mm Aden Mk 2 cannon produced structural damage.

The very low production rate and the extensive programme of tests delayed the entry of the Marut Mk 1 fighter-bomber into service until April 1967. The IAF removed the two upper cannon, operating only with the lower two, with 120 rounds per gun, in squadron service. The lack of appropriate power plant meant that the HF-24 could not fulfil its role as an interceptor and never came to install the radar provided in the original design.

Out of the 145 Maruts produced, 130 entered squadron service. No aircraft was lost in air combat during the December 1971 hostilities and with the destruction of about 100 enemy tanks and one Canadair Sabre VI in dogfight, the HF-24 proved to be a stable weapon platform. Throughout the sixties, HAL directed a great search for more powerful engines, from various foreign sources to exploit the latent potential of the Marut airframe, evaluated by U.S. experts for a Mach 2 flight. However, the turbojets under consideration either could not provide a sufficient thrust, required too great structural redesign or became unavailable due to political reasons.

In 1961, the Russians were approached with the centrifugal-flow Klimov VK-7 turbojet, a very reliable engine with 3,525 kp thrust but with an excessive diameter that could not be fitted to the existing HF-24 without major design changes. The Tumansky RD-9F was also considered; it was a small-diameter axial-flow turbojet with 3,750 kp (afterburning) used in the MiG-19 SF Mach 1.5 interceptor. Six engines were imported and bench-tested at Bangalore, while its installation in the HF-24 was found to be called for a little airframe modification. But the negotiations initiated in Moscow in July 1962 failed at the Soviet refusal to grant the manufacturing under licence in India.

At the same time, the Egyptian government started the development of the Bradner E-300, an axial turbojet to power the Messerschmitt/Helwan HA-300 supersonic fighter. The new engine was tested in 1963, installed on an Antonov An-12, producing 4,800 kp dry and 6,700 kp with reheat. On 2 November 1964, the Indian Government proposed a collaboration agreement to develop the EL-300 version, with a smaller afterburner and 4,355 kp thrust for the Marut.

In July 1966, the pre-production aircraft HF-020 was modified as HF-24 Mk 1 BX, with a rear fuselage capable of accepting either Orpheus 703 or the EL-300. On 29 March 1967, the prototype started the test flights at Helwan, Egypt, revealing that the estimated performances of the EL-300 had been overestimated. In 106 hours of flight testing, the aircraft was unable to exceed Mach 1.1. After the June 1967 Arab-Israeli conflict, the EL-300 programme was cancelled.

In 1964, the British firm Bristol Siddeley proposed to fit the Pegasus inner spool to the Orpheus 703 to create a hybrid engine with similar performances to those of the Orpheus B.Or.12, but the Indian Government preferred to develop its own version of the 703, with afterburning. Called Orpheus 703R, the new turbojet initially had an 18 per cent greater boost than the standard model and was installed in the pre-production aircraft HF-005, later called Marut Mk 1A. The test flights began in 1965 and by the end of the decade, the engine already produced a 27 per cent greater thrust, being installed in two prototypes of the Marut Mk 1B that flew until 1973. The 703R had development potential, but the limited power increment was considered insufficient to result in a production order.

Meanwhile, HAL decided to focus its efforts on the production of the Marut Mk 1 fighter-bomber (with internal fuel capacity of 2,962 litres, take-off weight of 10,900 kg, and top speed limited to Mach 1.02 at 40,000 feet) definitively discarding the Ferranti AIRPASS radar. The attack version had four underwing pylons, rated at 454 kg each, and one retractable launcher for fifty French SNEB 68-mm rockets in internal pad behind the pilot.

The experience gained during the War served to introduce several modifications: the chord wing was extended by 10 per cent to improve handling and was fitted with a stable weapons platform. Combat flaps and JATO (jet-assisted take-off) rockets were also installed. The rudder was provided with a booster and the Babaud gunsight and the radio compass AD722 were replaced by a Ferranti ISIS 124 and a Bendix DFA-73. The total production of the Marut was 145 aircraft: two prototypes, eighteen pre-production, sixty-two Mk 1 of the first production series, and forty-five of the second, including eighteen two-seat aircraft of the Mk 1T training version.

In 1967, Kurt Tank returned to Germany, but he continued collaborating in the future developments of the Marut. In 1970, HAL considered the possibility of using two Rolls-Royce RB.172/T.260 Adour or two RB153 turbofans to propel the new Marut Mk II version, but its installation required a major redesign of the rear section of the fuselage and the resultant drag penalties made the project impracticable. In 1971, HAL designed the HF-24 Mk III, a deep penetration strike aircraft with twice the weapons load than the HF-24, propelled by two Turbo-Union RB199-34R turbofans with convergent nozzles. The Mk III retained the wings and tailfins of the Mk II but with new ram intakes for air conditioning in the Panavia Tornado. A new dorsal structure was also placed behind the cockpit to contain additional fuel.

By mid-1972, Kurt Tank, by now with Messerschmitt-Bölkow-Blohm (MBB), made a formal proposal to cooperate with HAL in the development of the new aircraft. The following year, the project was named HSS-73 (Hindustan Supersonic Strike). It externally differed from the Mk III in the removal of the dorsal fuel tank, to improve the pilot's later visibility, in the installation of a heat-exchanger in the base of the tailfin and in the replacement of the tail planes by others with a double-swept leading edge.

In 1974, the design had undergone considerable modifications, being renamed HF-73 with the installation of a second crew member, delta wing, twin tailfins, Jaguar-style air intakes, two 27-mm Mauser cannon, HUD, INAS, and a laser ranging device. Performance parameters included Mach 2 at altitude, low-low-low range of 500 in strike configuration, with secondary task of air defence and tactical reconnaissance.

The HF-73 was cancelled the following year due to the low availability of the RB-199 that was dedicated primarily to the production of the Tornado. In 1975, the French were willing to provide the SNECMA M.53 (Atar) turbofan to propel a single-engine version of the Marut, called HF-25. The rear fuselage was redesigned and the air intakes modified for the higher air mass flow. Also, it was proposed to install a new nose section, with a glazing for a laser-ranging device, and multiple underwing weapons stations, but the project was not completed due to its excessive cost.

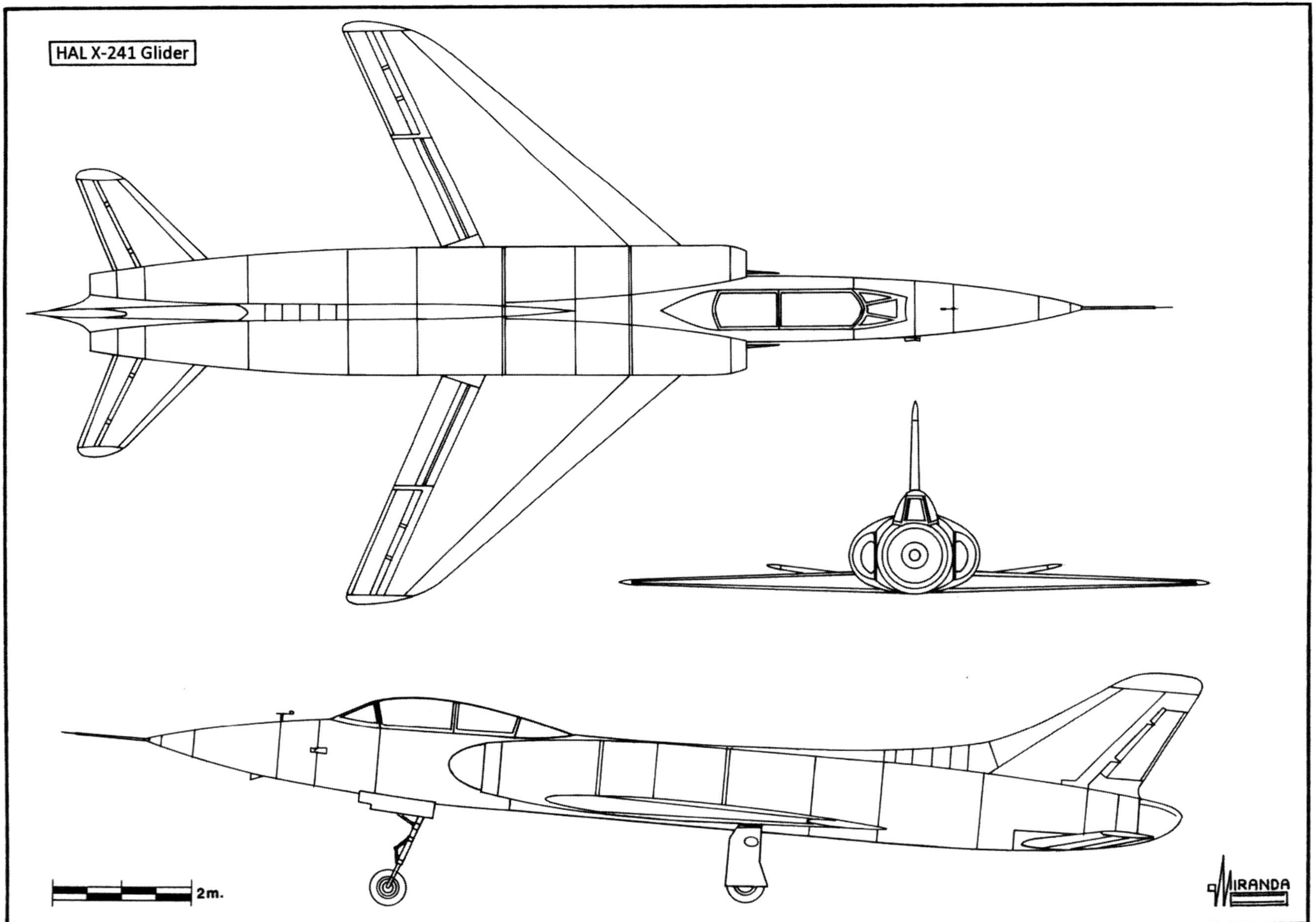
HAL X-241 Glider
2m.
MIRANDA

Hindustan HF-24 Mk.1 *Marut*

HF-24 Mk.1T

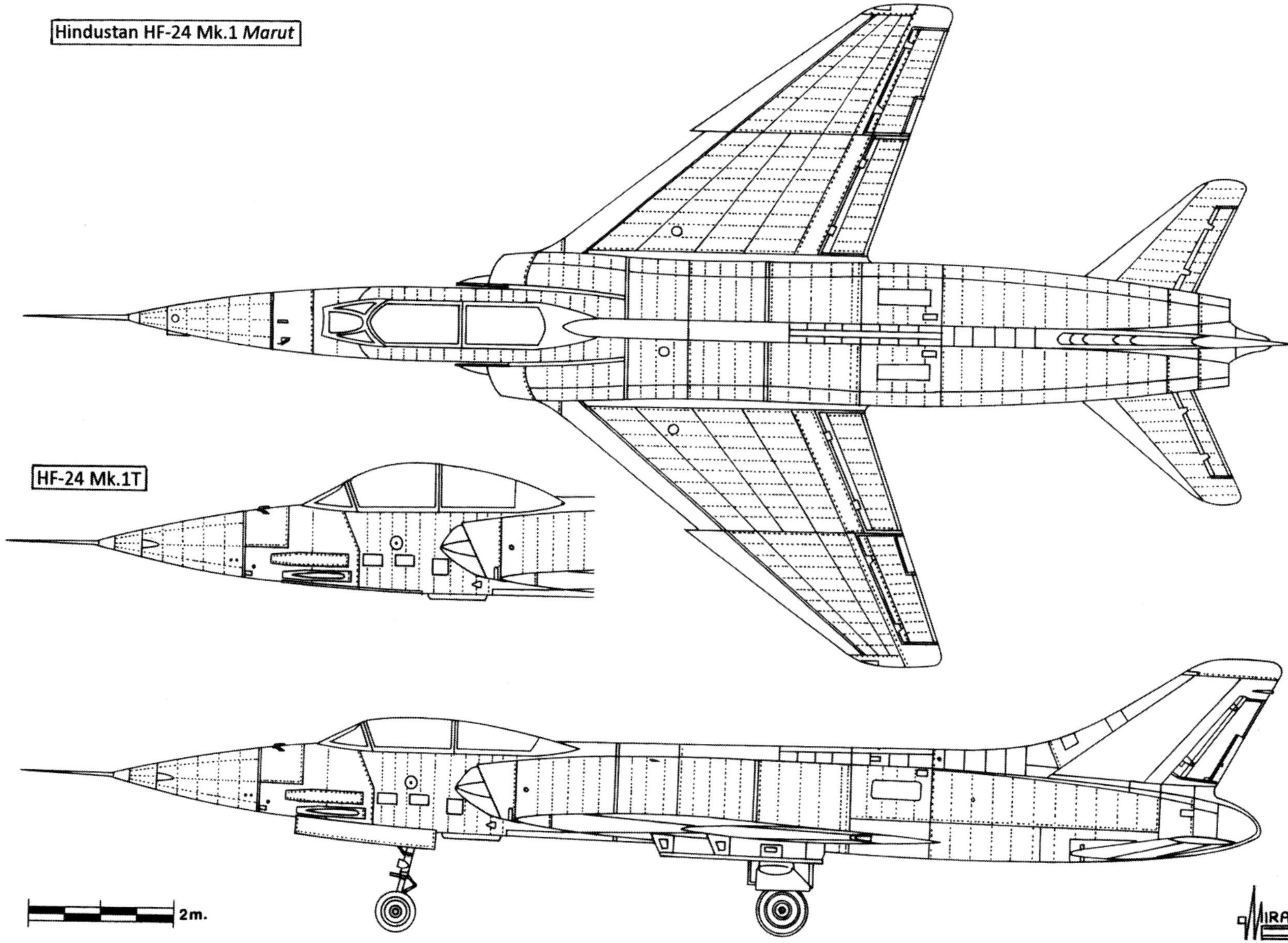

Hindustan HF-24 Mk.1 *Marut*

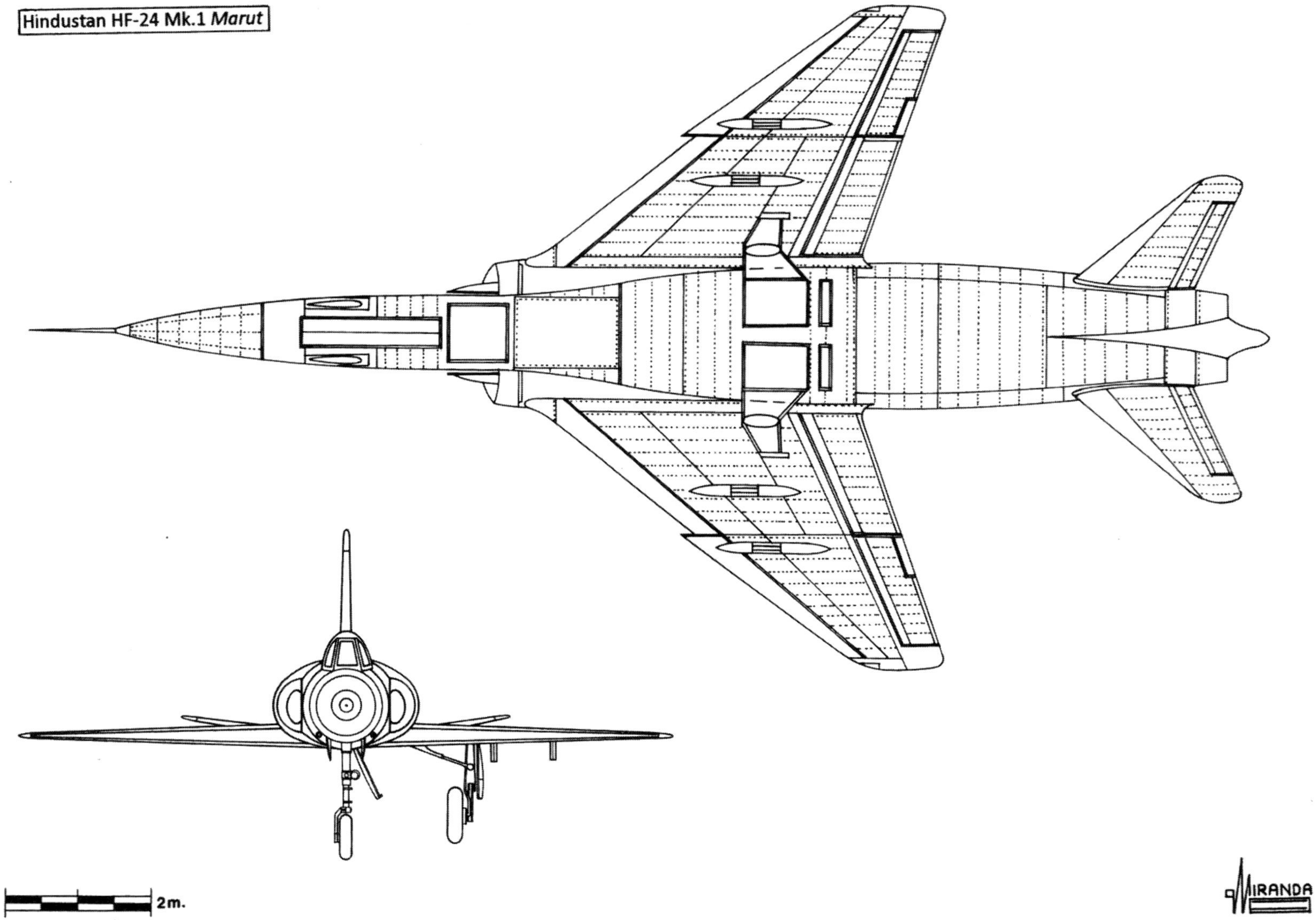

Hindustan HSS-73

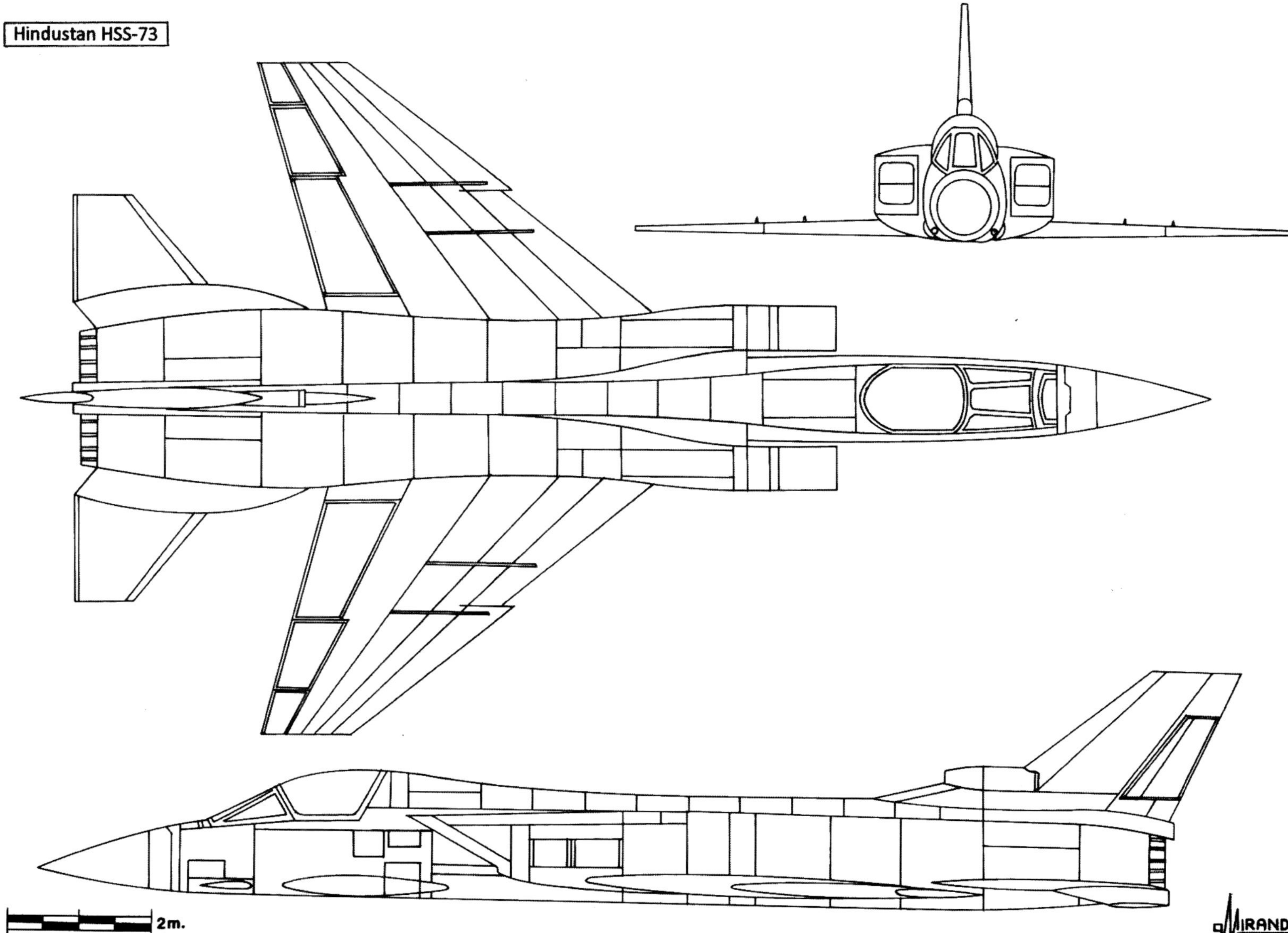

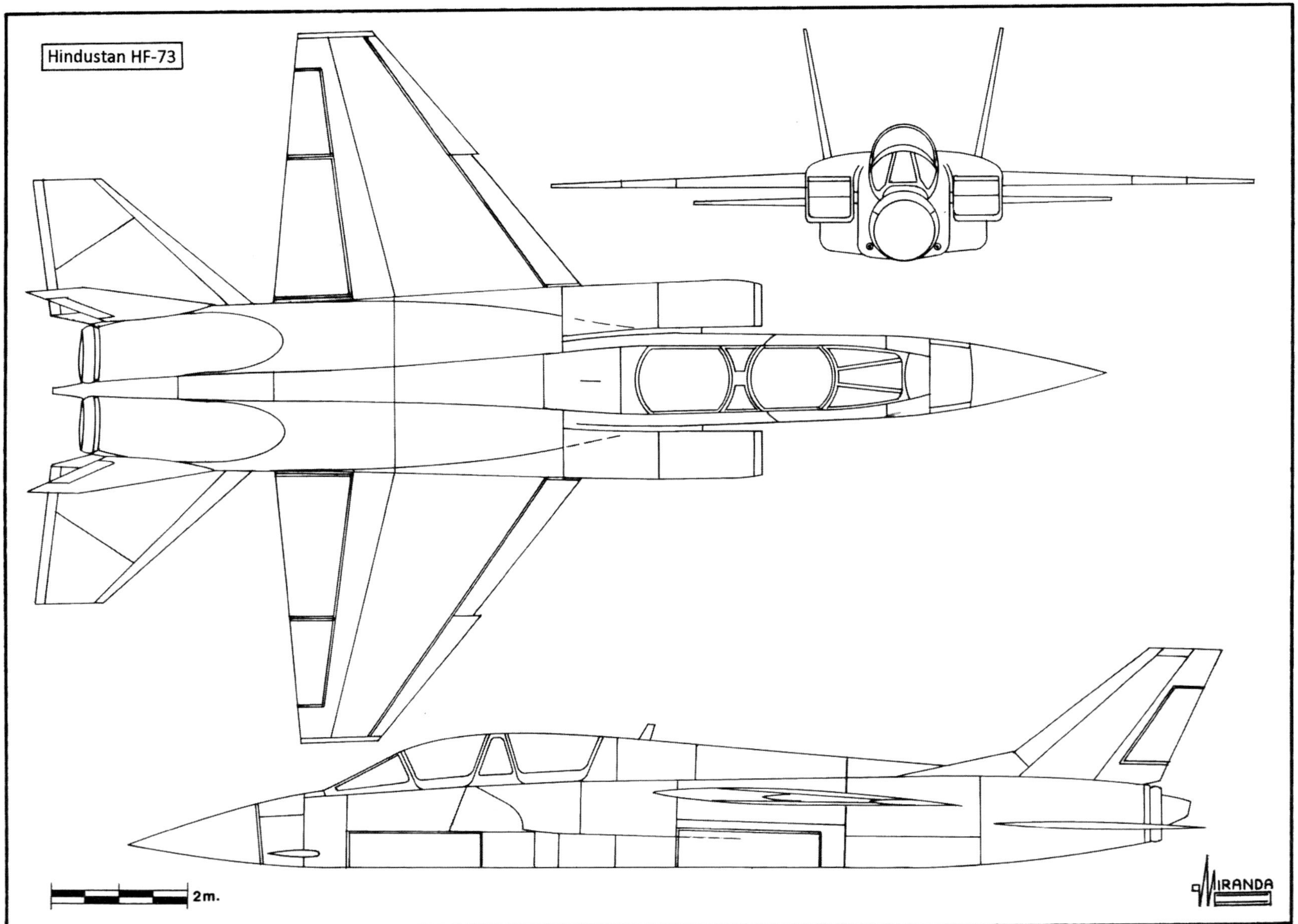
Hindustan HF-73
2m.
MIRANDA

29

Russian Fakes

The Soviet industry proved to be unable to build and efficient turbo-supercharger during the Second World War and all the programmes for the construction of high-altitude interceptors (MiG-7 and MiG-11; Polikarpov VP, K; Sukhoi Su-1 and Su-3; and Yak-9 PD) were affected by that. The turbojets of Soviet design did not have much success either and the rocket-propelled interceptors were not practical.

To achieve high speed fighters, they resorted to desperate measures, fitting the aircrafts with a conventional piston engine that would be complemented by an unsophisticated Campini-type afterburner located in the rear fuselage (MiG I-250 *Samolet N*, Sukhoi Su-5). By the end of the war, the Western powers had centrifugal turbojets with a thrust of 1,500 kp whereas the Soviets just had some Junkers Jumo 004B-1s with 900 kp static thrust and BMW 003 A-1s with 800 kp that had been captured from the Germans. Both proved to be insufficient for the needs of the time given that, even using the Jumo 004 C (RD 10F) with afterburner, they only reached 1,100 kp.

With the help of German scientists and prisoners of war, the Soviets tried to develop the Jumo 004 H of 1800 kp, but the technological step required several years of testing. Therefore, they found themselves forced to design very light fighters, with the shortest possible air-intake ducts and tailpipes, to best profit of the scarce power available. The first generation of Soviet jet fighters Lavochkin La-150, La-152, La-156, and La-174; MiG-9; Sukhoi Su-9; and Yakovlev Yak-15, Yak-17, and Yak-19 were straight-wing designs propelled by the axial flow turbojet, Jumo 004 B-1.

The only way to increase their performances consisted on using rear swept wings and tailfins developed by the German aerodynamicists of the TsAGI research centre. A swept-winged fighter was ordered to the Lavochkin and MiG design teams under the codename 'Project S'. The engine should be a Jumo 004 C. Lavochkin just built a version of the La-174 TK with a 35-degree rear swept wing; it was named La-160.

During the Cold War, the Soviets adopted a policy of maximum secrecy to hide their technical inferiority. Within this concept, in which the mystery and the lack of information about what happened at the other side of the Iron Curtain favoured the curiosity of the western public, several journalists working in aircraft publications had the temptation to speculate what could be the next Soviet fighter.

The Soviets revealed the existence of six new types of jet fighters, including the Lavochkin La-160, in the Summer Aviation Day display at Thusino Airfield on 3 August 1947. The variety of unknown models caused some confusion among the journalists attending the event and it was the origin of a lucrative traffic of tricky photographs coming from East Germany, which remained active until the early sixties.

The introduction of the MiG-15 in North Korea in August 1950 was, without any doubt, a bad surprise for the Western world. Aviation specialists were waiting, with a certain apprehension, for its successor.

In 1951, *Aviation Age* published an eye-catching picture of a Soviet fighter like the Focke-Wulf Ta 183, with a large tailfin of the same length as the fuselage and two fences in each wing panel, with the caption: 'The latest product of Russia's aircraft designers, a very fast interceptor-fighter designated MiG-19'. The dark painting, the red stars bordered with white, the number '125' painted in the nose section, and the radical aerodynamic design were a very credible set for the public, but it did not deceive the experts who ruled that an airplane with these characteristics would be useless as a weapons platform due to excessive snaking.

Despite this, the U.S. *Flight* magazine published the same photograph in 1957, including some 'technical data': supersonic speed, 45,000-foot ceiling, 34-foot wingspan, 12-foot height, and over 14,000-lb maximum weight. On 16 February 1953, *American Aviation Magazine* published a trick photo of a Ta 183 model with wing fences, overall aluminium paint and the number '72' in the nose.

The Aurora Company marketed a plastic model kit called 'Yak-25' in June, which was based on the photo of *Aviation Age* but with a nose radome inspired by the real prototype MiG-15bis (SP-1). In the 1954 edition, the name was changed to 'MiG-19' in the box art. In 1955, the Italian magazine *Edizioni Cielo* published an article by E. Bignozzi that included a three view and one artist profile of the *Aviation Age* MiG-19, which had a maximum speed estimated at 1,200 kph. In 1957, the photo of '72' was published again in the French magazine *L'Aviation Nouvelle*. The Soviet Ta 183 myth continued until April 1961 with the publication of a trick photo in the German magazine *Flugwelt*.

Certain information on the MiG I-320, an all-weather interceptor of 1949 that never exceeded the prototype phase, was filtered to the western press in 1953. It had two superposed turbojets and one nose radome for the parabolic mirror of the Toriy radar. Based on a photo that did not allow to see the location of the turbojets, the intelligent illustrator De Lancey drew a three-view scale drawing and a detailed cutaway with side-by-side turbojets; these were published in June 1953 in the U.S. Magazine *Air Trails* to illustrate an article by James I. Pech entitled 'Inside Story of the MiG-19'.

De Lancey possibly believed that the I-320 was an advanced version of the MiG-9 (a real airplane well-known in the West that was equipped with straight wings and tail surfaces) and used the information available on the MiG-9 as the basis for his work. The article was widely circulated among aircraft enthusiast and modellers, prompting Paul Lindberg to commercialise the plastic kit called 'Russian Jet Fighter' in 1954, based on De Lancey's drawings. In the 1955 edition, the denomination in the box art changed to 'Russian MiG-19'.

At the end of the Second World War, the Soviets continued the research on rocket-fighters using the material captured from the Germans. In December 1946, the MiG I-270 made its first flight. It was a Soviet version of the Me 263, equipped with tailplane and straight wings. The confusing information available on this model was interpreted by Western analysts as a version of the Focke-Wulf *Volksjäger*, which was given the arbitrary name of Yak-21. On 13 April 1953, a cutaway was published in *Life*. The illustration depicted a *Volksjäger* propelled by a Walter 509 rocket. In March 1955, the drawer of *Air Trails* presented it like a version of the Me 163 with tailplane.

In 1973, Lockheed and the US Air Force began to work on a radar-evading strike aircraft under the codename Have Blue. In the early 1980s, some information about this secret project was leaked to the aviation press. In 1986, in the techno-thriller novel *Red Storm Rising*, Tom Clancy called it 'F-19', describing it as an airplane that employed a shape that deflected radar waves.

The hypothetical airframe had rounded-off wingtips and fin tips. This design idea was the result of deliberate disinformation by Loral, Northrop, and Lockheed in several published artworks to draw attention away from the real F-117 shape. In 1986, Testors commercialised a plastic kit based on the description of Clancy, called 'Lockheed F-19 Stealth Fighter', the best-selling model kit of all time. In 1987, the competitor Monogram commercialised its own version of the F-19, a hypothetical single-engine variant of the Lockheed SR-71 (a real airplane).

By that time, although specifics were vague, it was known that the secret plane employed technology of faceted surfaces developed by the mathematician Denys Overholser. Based on this new concept, Testors model designer John Andrews created the Soviet version, marketed in 1988 as 'MiG-37B Ferret-E Stealth Fighter'. However, the myth vanished that same year when the real Lockheed F-117 was revealed to the public.

INSTRUCTIONS FOR ASSEMBLING RUSSIAN MIG-19
ALL PLASTIC 1/4 INCH SCALE MODEL

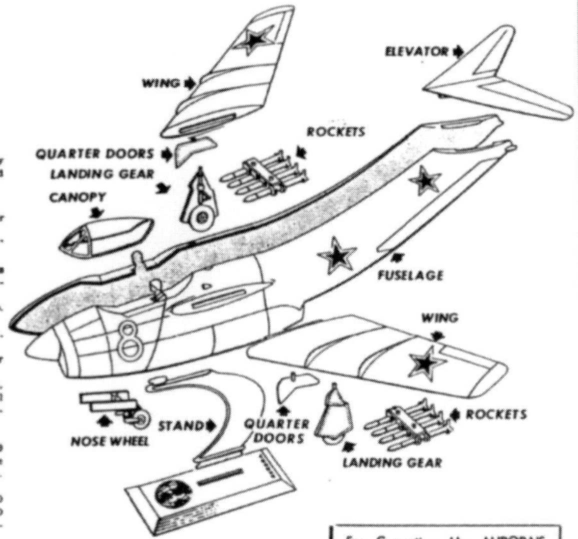

The Russian MIG-19 was originally labeled the Yak-25 and was adapted from an early German design.

SPECIFICATIONS
Type-Single Seat - Interceptor Fighter
Wings - High, Swept-Back Type.
Tail Unit - Cantilever, Radical "T" Design.
Power Plant - Russian-built Junkers Jumo centrifugal flow turbo-jet engine.
Armament - Rockets, or 2 - 1000 - lb. bombs carried under the wings.
Dimensions (approximate) - Span, 33'. Length, 36½'.
Weigth, and Performance - Speed over 600 MPH. No other data available.
Engineer's Conclusion - This model, even though based on scanty factual data, is considered about 90% accurate.

Before assembling Russian MIG-19 carefully study above sketch and place all parts on work table as indicated.

IMPORTANT — APPLY CEMENT TO INSIDE SURFACES ONLY — AVOID GETTING CEMENT ON OUTER SURFACES OF PLANE SECTIONS.

In order to obtain maximum strength and neatness it is suggested that all cemented sub-assemblies be given ample time to dry before further handling.

1. Cement both parts of stand together and allow to dry.
2. Cement right and left wing to fuselage by inserting wing tab into slot in fuselage section and apply cement on the inside. NOTE: — Be sure that tongue and slot match so that wings are on correct side. Set aside to dry.
3. Cement fuselage and wing sub-assemblies together by applying cement to edges of fuselage halves. Join halves together and allow to dry.
4. Cement elevator to fuselage by applying cement to tongue on underside of elevator and place into corresponding slot in fuselage assembly.
5. Apply cement to edges of cockpit canopy and press firmly over cockpit.
6. Cement rockets to underside of left and right wings by applying a small drop of cement to pegs on rocket assemblies and inserting same into corresponding holes in wings.
7. Cement left and right landing gear quarter doors to underside of left and right wings by applying cement to small pegs and top edge of quarter doors and inserting each into its corresponding hole (hole closest to fuselage) in left and right wings as indicated in above sketch.
8. Cement landing gear to underside of left and right wings by applying a small drop of cement to small pegs on landing gear and inserting same into corresponding holes in wings. NOTE: Place plane in upside down position and hold or prop landing gear in proper position until cement has enough time to set or dry.
9. Cement nose wheel and door halves together by applying cement to inside surfaces of halves.
10. Cement nose wheel and door assembly to fuselage assembly by applying cement to top edges of doors and placing same on outlined area on underside of fuselage nose section, in proper position, as indicated in above sketch.
11. Apply cement to tab on arm of base and place into slot on underside of fuselage and hold or prop into position until dry.
12. Cut out sections of decals to correspond with markings on plane. Read directions on back of decals before applying.

For Cementing, Use AURORA'S POLYSTYRENE CEMENT for plastic model airplanes.

CAUTION

Apply the cement only to those places which are to stick together.

THIS CEMENT MAY BE PURCHASED FROM YOUR DEALER!

LOOK FOR OTHER ALL-PLASTIC MODELS BY AURORA

F9F Panther Jet, F-90 Locheed, P-40 Flying Tiger, ME-109 Messerschmitt, F86D Sabre Jet, Jap Zero, P-38 Lightning, Spitfire, SS Nautilus Atomic Submarine and U.S.S. Halford Destroyer.

A HOBBY AURORA FOR EVERYBODY

AURORA PLASTICS CO. U.K. LTD. · CROYDON · ENGLAND

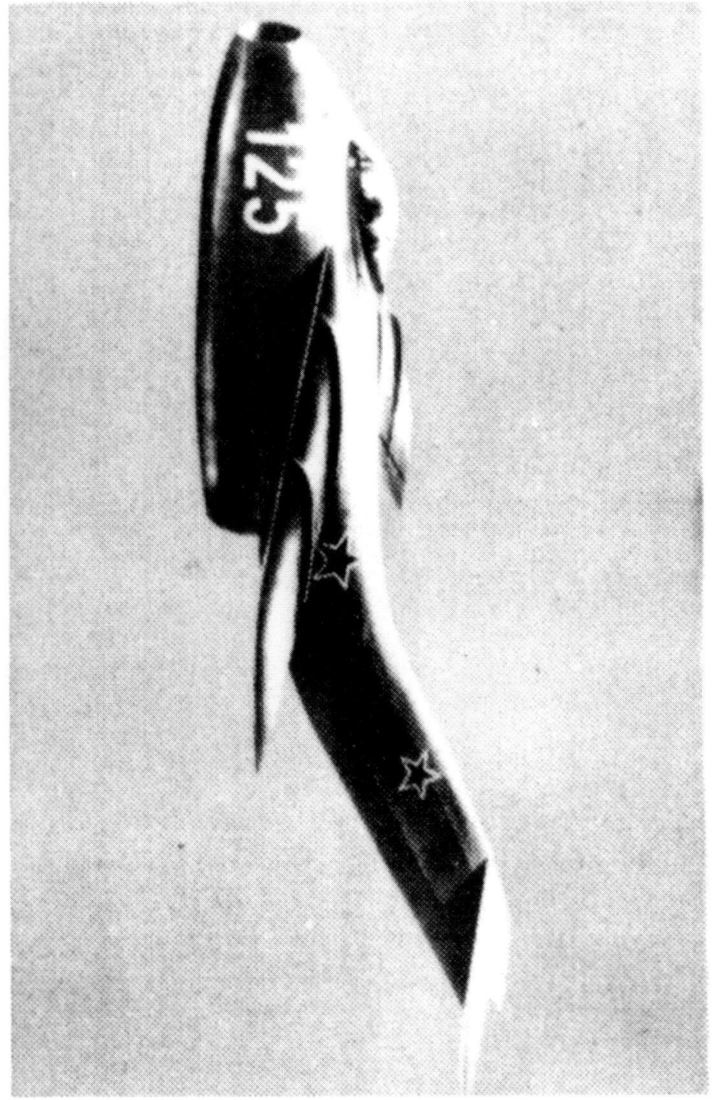

AVIATION AGE

SPECULATIVE DRAWINGS

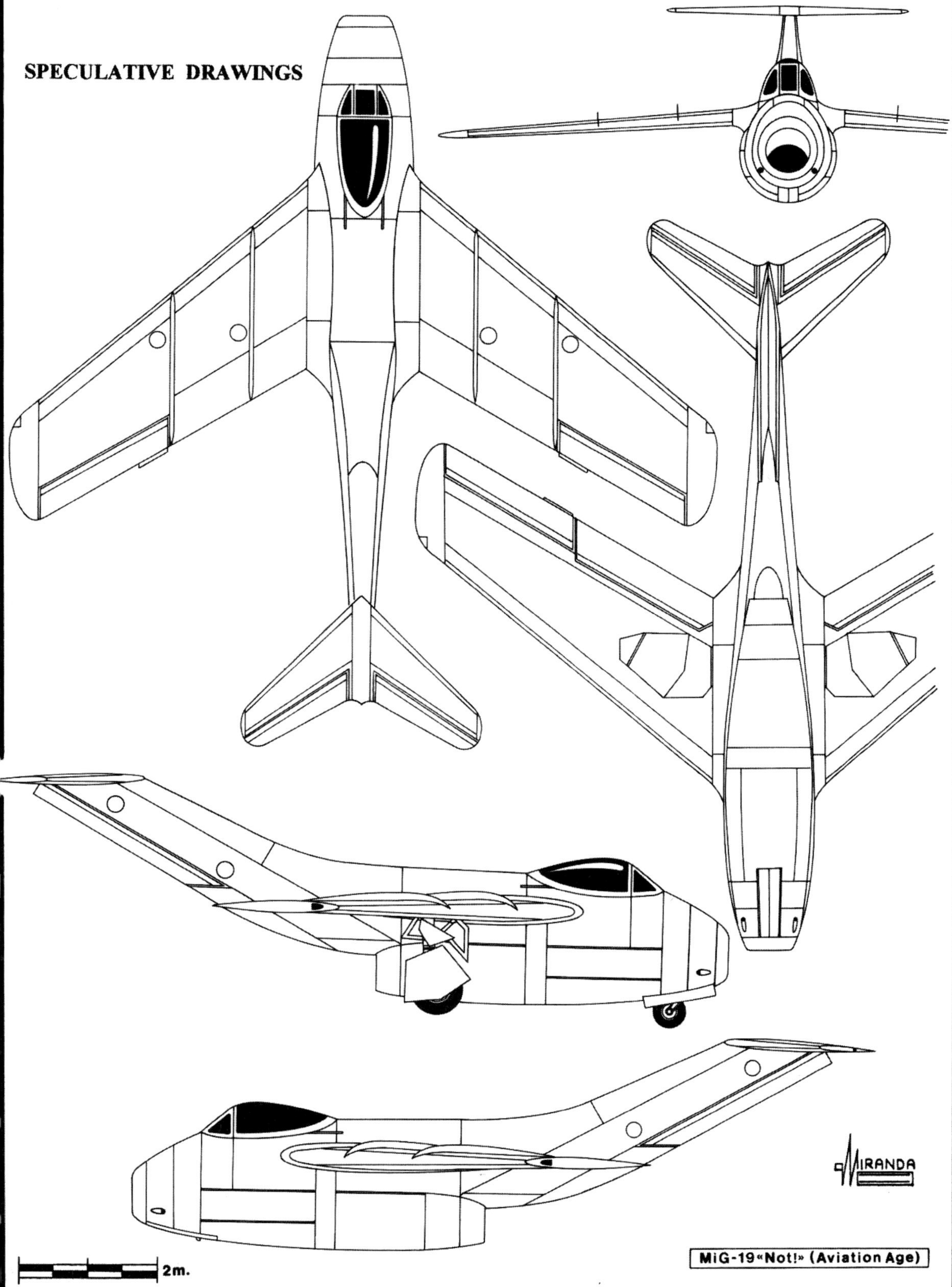

MiG-19 «Not!» (Aviation Age)

SPECULATIVE DRAWINGS

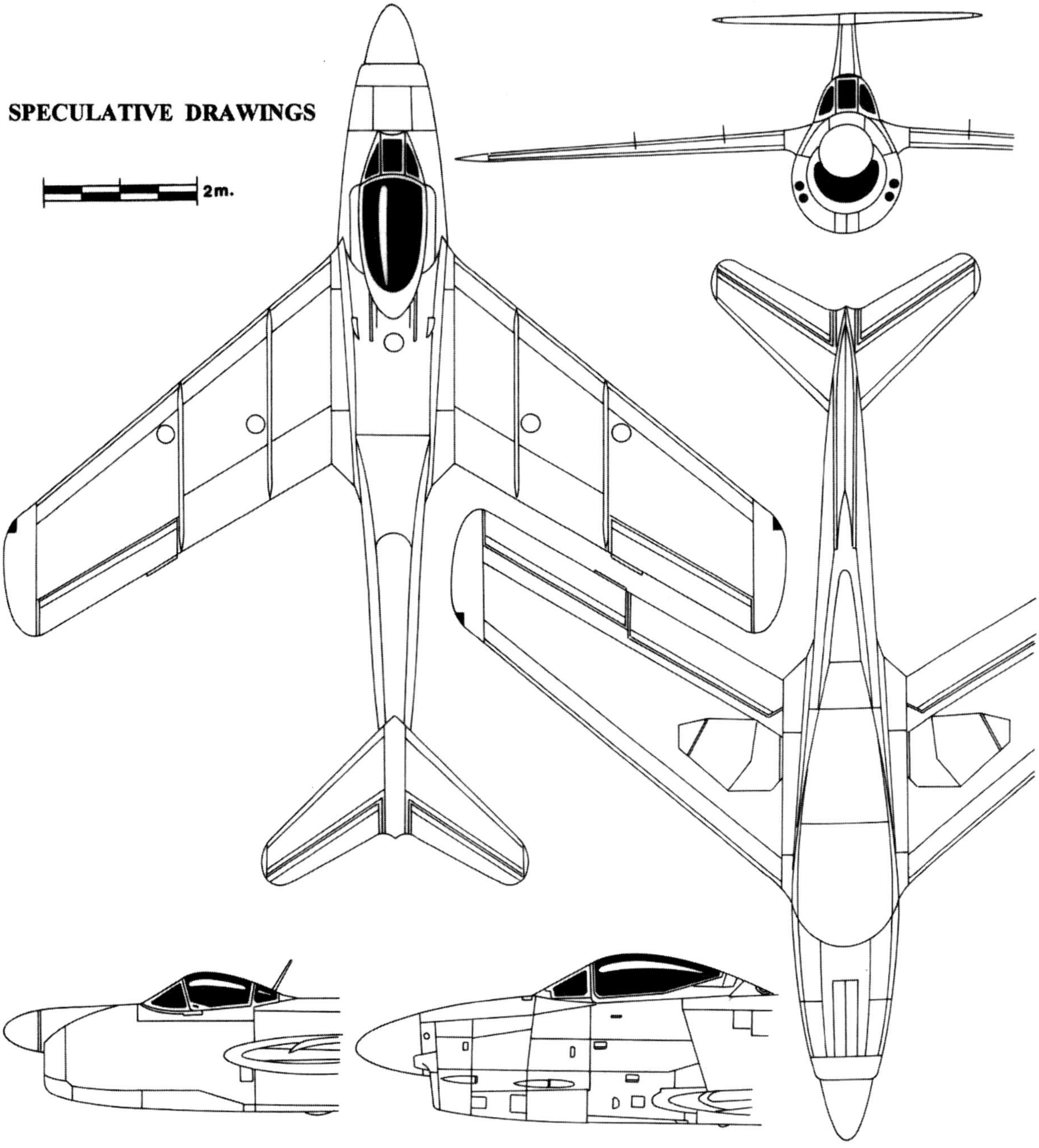

MiG-15 SP-1

North American F-86K

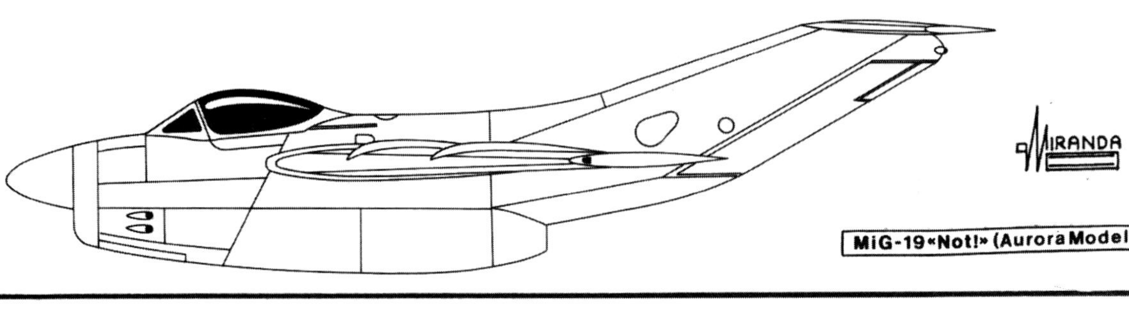

MiG-19 «Not!» (Aurora Model)

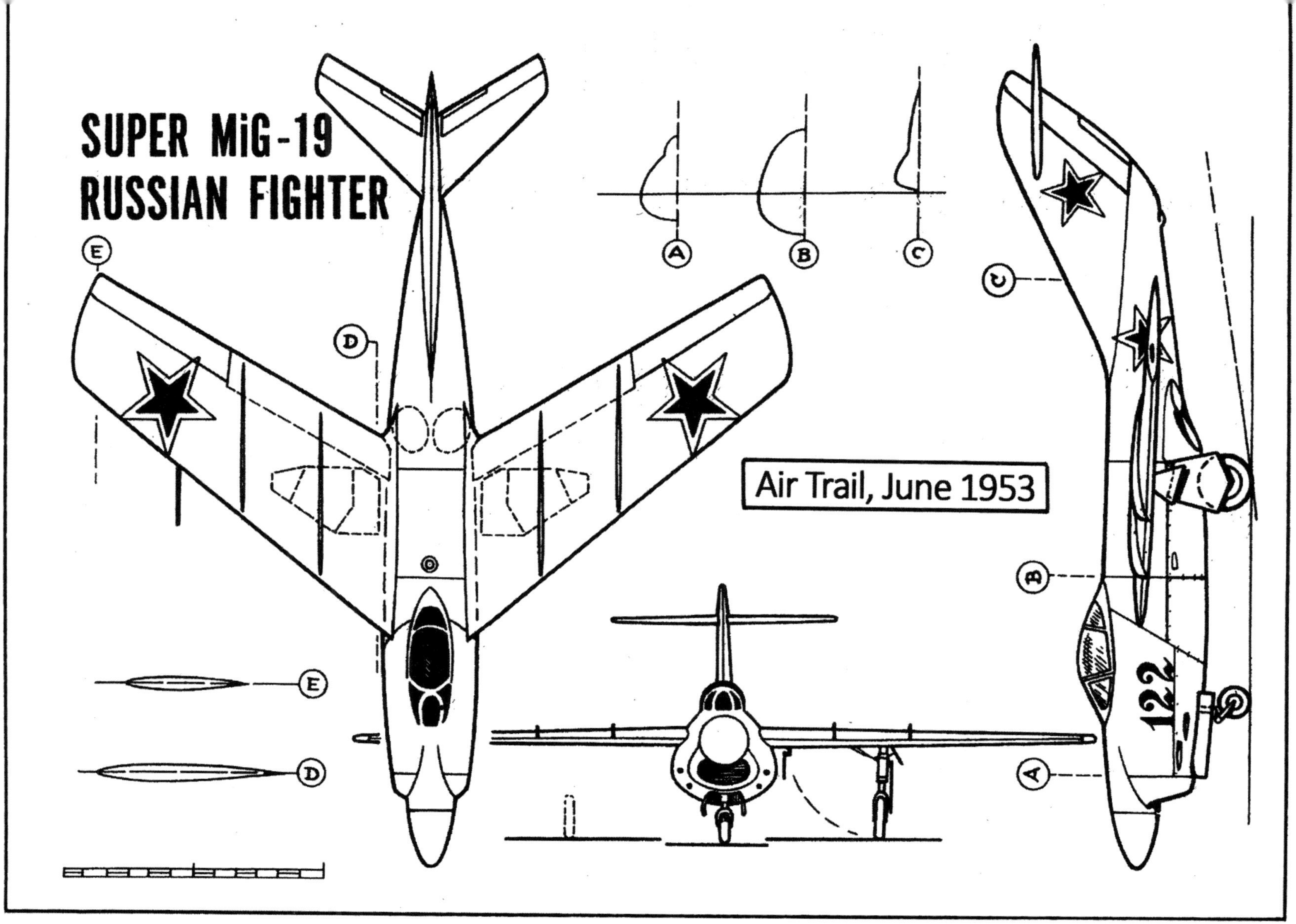
SUPER MiG-19
RUSSIAN FIGHTER
Air Trail, June 1953
A
B
C
D
E
122

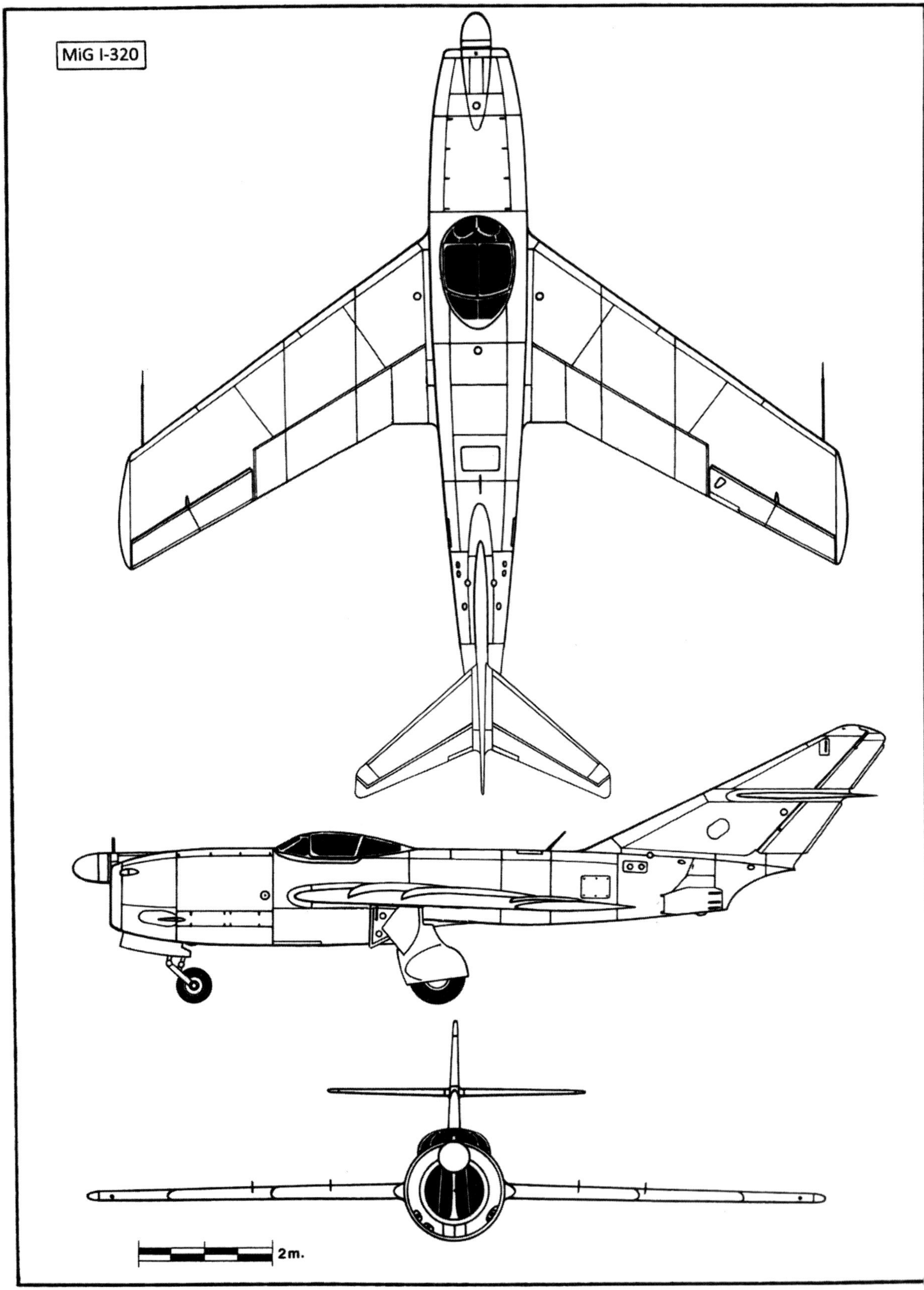
MiG I-320
2m.

Bibliography

Books

Burzaco, R., *Las Alas de Peron II*, (Banfield, Ediciones Eugenio B 2007)

Burzaco, R., *Las Alas de Peron*, (Argentina, Editorial Da Vinci 1995)

Dressel, J., and Griehl, M., *Die Deutschen Raketenflugzeuge 1935-1945*, (Stuttgart; Motorbuch Verlag 1989.

German Explosive Ordnance TM9-1985-2 (Departments of the Army and the Air Force, March 1953)

Griehl, M., *Jet Planes of the Third Reich, the Secret projects, Volume One*, (Sturbridge, Massachusetts; Monogram Aviation Publications 1998)

Griehl, M., *Jet Planes of the Third Reich, the Secret projects, Volume Two*, (Sturbridge, Massachusetts; Monogram Aviation Publications 2004)

Herwig, D. and Rode, H., *Luftwaffe Secret Projects, Ground Attack and Special Purpose Aircraft*, (Hinckley; Midland Publishing 2003)

Herwig, D., and Rode, H., *Geheimprojekte der Luftwaffe-Band III*, (Stuttgart; Motorbuch Verlag 2002)

Kay, A., *German Jet Engine and Gas Turbine Development 1930-1945*, (Shrewsbury; Airlife Publishing Limited 2002)

King, H., German Aircraft New and Projected Types, A.I.2(G) Report N° 2383, (January 1946)

Masters, D., *German Jet Genesis*, (London; Jane's 1982)

Meyer, I., *Die Luftwaffe Projekte der Deutschen Luftrüstung*, Band 1, (Kissing; 2004)

Myhra, D., *Dragonfly, The Luftwaffe Experimental Triebflügeljäger Project* (Atglen, PA; Schiffer 2003)

Nowarra, H., *Aircraft & Legend Focke-Wulf Fw 190 & Ta 152,* (Somerset; Haynes 1988)

Nowarra, H., *Die Deutsche Luftrüstung 1933–1945, Band 1 to 4,* (Koblenz; Bernard & Graefe Verlag 1993)

Paper Planes of the Third Reich, Based on British Air Intelligence Reports, (London; Toros Publications, ISO PUBLICATIONS)

Radinger, W., and Schick, W., *Secret Messerschmitt Projects* (Atlen, PA; Schiffer 1996)

Sengfelder, G., *Flugzeugfahrwerke*, (Stuttgart; Motorbuch Verlag 1979)

Sharp, D., *Luftwaffe Secret Jets of the Third Reich*, (Lincolnshire; Mortons Media Group Ltd. 2015)

Smith, J., and Creek, J., *Jet Planes of the Third Reich*, (Boylston, Massachusetts; Monogram Aviation Publications 1982)

Magazines

Air International, July 1978
Air International/September 1976.
Air Trails, June 1953.
Air Trails, Mach 1955.
American Aviation Magazine, (February 1953)
Aviation Age, (1951)
Aviation History, May 2002.
Avion Revue, 6/1982.
Bentley, A., 'FockeWulf Fighter' *Scale Models,* June 1987, (United Kingdom; Model & Allied Publications Ltd 1987)
Flieger Welt Deutscher Aero-Digest, (Heft 1/1951)
Flugwelt, April 1961.
Flugzeug, 1/2000.
Flugzeug, 2/94.
Jets, Winter 2001.
LIFE, April 1953.
Luftfahrt International 10 (1975)
Luftfahrt International 17 (1980)
Luftfhart International 9 (1975)
Malmassari, P., 'Découverte de Quelques Projects Autour de V-1', *Le Fana de l'Aviation* (Paris; September 2000)
SAFO N° 53, January 1990.

Correspondence with Johnson, D.
Correspondence with Berthold, T.